The Cold War In Europe

THE COLD WAR
IN EUROPE

Edited by
CHARLES S. MAIER

Harvard University

M
W Markus Wiener Publishing, Inc.
New York

First Markus Wiener Publishing, Inc. edition 1991.

For information write to:

Markus Wiener Publishing, Inc.
225 Lafayette Street
New York, NY 10012

Library of Congress Cataloging-in-Publication Data

The Cold war in Europe : Era of a Divided Continent
  edited with introduction and commentary by Charles S. Maier.
    Includes bibliographical references and index.
    ISBN 1-55876-029-6 (cloth) : —ISBN 1-55876-034-2 (paper)
    1. Cold War.   2. World politics—1945–   3. Europe—Politics
and government—1945–   4. Economic assistance, American.
I. Maier, Charles S.   II. The cold war in Europe.
D843.C57732   1991
327'.09'044—dc20   90-13075
                                                        CIP

Book design by Cheryl Mirkin

Printed in the United States of America on acid-free paper

Contents

III THE POLITICAL ECONOMY OF THE COLD WAR ERA

Acknowledgments

The author gratefully acknowledges the following authors and publishers:

Johns Hopkins University Press for permission to reprint Chapter III and pp. 43–71 of AMERICA'S HALF CENTURY by Thomas J. McCormick, copyright © 1989, Johns Hopkins University Press; Elie Abel and Random House for permission to reprint chapter XIV, pp. 315–334 of SPECIAL ENVOY TO CHURCHILL AND STALIN, by W. Averell Harriman and Elie Abel, copyright © 1975, Random House; Radomír Luža and Princeton University Press for permission to reprint pp. 387–415, "Czechoslovakia Between Democracy and Communism", from A HISTORY OF THE CZECHOSLOVAK REPUBLIC, 1914–1948, edited by Radomír Luža and Victor S. Amatey, copyright © 1973, Princeton University Press; John Lewis Gaddis and Oxford University Press, Inc., for permission to reprint Chapter III, pp. 48–71, "Spheres of Influence: the United States and Europe, 1945–1949" from THE LONG PEACE: INQUIRIES INTO THE HISTORY OF THE COLD WAR, copyright © 1987, Oxford University Press; Geir Lundestad and *The Journal of Peace Research* for permission to reprint pp. 263–277: "Empire by Invitation? The United States and Western Europe, 1945–1952", from THE JOURNAL OF PEACE RESEARCH, XXIII (19868), copyright © 1986, Geir Lundestad; University of Wisconsin Press and Cambridge University Press for permission to reprint Part I, Chapter III, pp. 121–152, "The Politics of Productivity", from IN SEARCH OF STABILITY: EXPLORATION IN HISTORICAL POLITICAL ECONOMY, by Charles S. Maier, Cambridge University Press, 1987, copyright © 1977. University of Wisconsin Press, which published this essay in INTERNATIONAL ORGANIZATIONS 31 (Autumn, 1977) pp. 607–633; Michael Hogan and Cambridge University Press for permission to reprint Chapter II, pp. 54–87 of THE MARSHALL PLAN, by Michael Hogan, copyright © 1987 Cambridge University Press; Alan S. Milward and the University of California Press for permission to reprint pp. 90–113, 123–125 of THE RECONSTRUCTION OF WESTERN EUROPE, 1945–51, by Alan S. Milward, copyright © 1984 University of California Press; Lutz Niethammer and the Bund Verlag of Cologne, Germany, for permission to reprint the major portion (pp. 313–354) of the essay, STRUCTURAL REFORM AND A COMPACT FOR GROWTH: CONDI-

TIONS FOR A UNITED LABOR UNION MOVEMENT IN WESTERN EUROPE AFTER THE COLLAPSE OF FASCISM, being the translation of STRUKTURREFORM UND WACHSTUM-SPAKT in: Vom Sozialistengesetz zur Mitbestimmung, copyright © 1975, Bund Verlag; and to Anthony Carew and Manchester University Press for permission to reprint pp. 111–130, 240–250 of LABOUR AND THE MARSHALL PLAN: THE POLITICS OF PRODUC-TIVITY AND THE MARKETING OF MANAGEMENT SCI-ENCE, by Anthony Carew, copyright © 1987, Manchester University Press.

I

CONTEXTS OF INTERPRETATION

1

Charles S. Maier

After the Cold War: Introduction to the 1991 Edition

"If there's no Cold War, what's the point of being an American?" asks John Updike's aging Rabbit Angstrom in the author's most recent novel. The question is relevant for the historian as well. If there's no Cold War, what's the point of Cold War history? Phrased less bleakly, how will Cold War historiography be altered by the end of the perpetual struggle, which for so long gave the issues at stake their immediate relevance? I have asked myself this question in publishing a new collection of chapters and essays on the Cold War and its impact on contemporary Europe. When the original collection was issued in 1978, the Soviet-American antagonism still set the overriding agenda for world politics. It does so no longer.

Of course, historians do not depend on the fact that the conflicts whose origins they describe still continue. The causes of the American Revolution, the First World War and the Second remain fertile terrain for historical debate. The Habsburg Empire has long since disappeared, but the political calculations of its ruling elite in 1914 remain a fascinating issue. We can learn to live with Cold War history as just history—not a more refined version of the conflict itself. But it will take detachment and study. It will require asking anew one very big ques-

What was it was about (handwritten margin note)

tion: what was the Cold War about? An ideological conflict? A struggle for hegemony between two superpowers equipped with weapons of mass destruction? A rivalry to organize the political economy of Europe, or even the world, in terms of markets and private capital accumulation on the one side, by means of state compulsion and planning on the other? Now—perhaps only now—as enmity fades, will we be able to return to this fundamental issue and take it up again, more clearsightedly.

Despite the contending theses that separated them, some of the most interesting historical treatments of the Cold War—William McNeill's early balanced survey, Herbert Feis's self-assured studies of wartime and immediate postwar diplomacy, Gabriel and Joyce Kolko's "revisionist" works—never lost sight of this question.[1] But for a generation or more the question of what the Cold War was about was often overshadowed by, or at least could not be separated from, a different issue: who was responsible? The issue of significance could not be divorced from the issue of blame. After all the struggle was still under way. There was a special urgency in understanding who had forced it upon the world. If Soviet ambitions had been responsible, then American Cold War responses were appropriate; if the United States had somehow triggered the confrontations, long-standing American policies should be changed. Which power, which actors, if any, were to bear the guilt for a confrontation that occasionally brought humanity to the brink of nuclear catastrophe? And by extension, what were the reasons behind policy? Why had policy makers taken the decisions they had?

Who was resp. (handwritten margin note)

Responsibility and Causation

During the past forty years, Cold War historians proposed several successive answers to these questions. They continued to revise the assessment of responsibility. At the same time, they suggested different views of how history works. Some focused on individual policy makers; others felt that "structural" or collective determinants of behavior were crucial. The early historians of the Cold War were convinced that United States leaders had reacted rationally to Soviet expansion in Eastern Europe. Most accounts from the 1950s presupposed that the Cold War and the division of Europe arose because Joseph Stalin, Soviet leader from the late 1920s until his death in early 1953, was bent on putting as much of Europe as possible under the dictatorial control of Communist parties that followed Soviet orders uncritically.[2] There had been some dissent in public life from those who felt that heavy-handed American policies precluded cooperation with Moscow, but most advocates of such views had been consigned to the political wilderness between 1946 and 1950. The British physicist P. M. S. Blackett argued that America had used the atomic bomb against Japan in a crude effort to cow the Russians—a charge elaborated by Gar Alperowitz in 1964.[3] Denna Fleming's two volumes, written in the late 1950s and based on the press and secondary sources, presented the first major alternative interpretation and assigned major responsibility for the Cold War to Washington.[4] By the 1960s this "revisionism" became a major movement, drawing political urgency from the opposition to U.S. policy in Vietnam. William Appleman Williams, Lloyd Gardner, and Gabriel and Joyce Kolko argued that American policy had its own expansionist thrust that in some cases (so Kolko especially implied) had forced the Soviets to defend the socialist bloc.[5] The resulting debates reached a bitterness rarely encountered in academic life.[6] For some non-revisionists the worthy intentions of the United States—and the lifetime commitments of a generation of academics who had come to prominence during the post-1945 era—seemed impugned and under attack.

Since that confrontation more recent historians have often merged different elements of both historical scenarios. John Gaddis has given the term "post-revisionism" to a modulated synthesis which insists that Washington's diplomacy was non-aggressive but recognizes that reciprocal escalation of conflict was almost inevitable.[7] We have all, so Gaddis intimates, accepted some of the revisionist criticisms, although hardly the essential one of American guilt. Post-revisionism seems willing to concede that in the bipolar distribution of world power, America was "imperial," but not "imperialist." (Searching for an appropriate term to describe our uneasiness about admitting to American power, I once referred to it "as the empire that dared not speak its name.") Accusations of imperialism strike us as slightly vulgar. Chastened cold warriors, we understand that the Soviets might have really felt threatened by American power.[8]

Thus we have three major narrative scenarios, each based on a different assessment of moral responsibility, each largely oriented around the issue of culpability, each relying on a different explanatory model. (There is finally an even more recent interpretation, what might be called the catalytic theory of British responsibility. It suggests that the British, most concerned of all about Soviet expansionism from 1944 to 1946, prodded Washington to interpret world politics from London's point of view.[9] Too weak to stand up to Moscow on their own, Winston Churchill, Ernest Bevin, and the Foreign Office at least tutored the Americans in the realities of power and instigated the Cold War. The argument is exaggerated, but comes naturally to researchers who immerse themselves in the massive, well-organized, and self-assured British documents. Historians can become captured by their archives.)

Each of the three major scenarios implies a different causal mechanism. The early "orthodox" narratives tended to share the notion that

Western political leaders, at least, were rational actors, responding as they saw fit to challenges from abroad. Moscow was expansionist, and ultimately Soviet policy emanated from Stalin's paranoid and ambitious agenda. But the Free World under Washington's leadership consulted its best interests, offered the Marshall Plan, saved half of Germany, organized NATO, managed to quarantine the subversive communist parties within France, Italy, and other western states, and fought in Korea to establish a security frontier in Asia as well—challenge and response. The model was classic: an ultimately "non-rational" drive for hegemony on one side, a primal urge to dominate and rational coalition building for defense on the other.

But even as the moral certainties faded, so too did the simple notion of how history worked. Most early challengers to cold war orthodoxy still looked at personality and character. They felt that Harry Truman's supposed truculence, after Roosevelt's continuing search for coopera-tion with the Soviet Union, played a major role in catalyzing Stalin's suspicion of the West. But building on earlier critiques of American interventionism and assimilating economic theories of imperialism, revisionist critics soon proposed a fundamental indictment of United States policy.

In judgments of both contemporary politics and the origins of the Cold War, they sought the explanation for what they felt was destructive policy in the underlying social or economic system. Looking at Viet-nam, critical historians often came to argue that it was not, say, Lyndon Johnson's flawed decision-making that explained American involve-ment. It was rather the entire hegemonic thrust of American capitalism and racialism. Assessing the origins of the Cold War, critics suggested that the logic of American capitalism required pressing the socialist countries to open up to United States investment. The claims of cap-italism had to be universal, transforming the underdeveloped world, insisting on access for products and investment in the socialist world. Hence America's economic structure was inherently expansionist and naturally provoked a Soviet effort to preserve socialism where Russian influence might still be applied. The Cold War in this perspective became just the latest episode in the longer-term history of capitalist expansion.

The work of Williams, Gardner, and the Kolkos that was published in the 1960s all built on this neo-Marxian model, what Williams had termed "open door imperialism." For this volume, I have selected a chapter from Thomas McCormick's recent synthesis along these lines. "Throughout its five centuries, capitalism has been an inherently ex-pansionistic type of economy," McCormick argues.[10] The implicit cor-ollary—never really demonstrated, and certainly a debatable proposition—is that capitalism must therefore embroil national political units in political rivalry and conflict. Perhaps most useful about McCormick's ambitious neo-revisionist synthesis is that it places United States policy in a larger framework of world politics; America must be understood in a longer succession of claimants to international leadership.[11]

The strength of the most serious revisionist works has always been their effort to explain what the Cold War was about, that is, what significance it had for general historical development. Many positivist historians, concerned with evidence and focused questions, find this preoccupation baffling, or even perverse. "Significance," they would argue, is too subjective a finding to be tested by the normal evidential criteria of the discipline. (This objection, moreover, leaves aside problems with the evidence itself: simple error, willful citation of texts to buttress an argument, ignorance of countervailing data, etc.) And even for those of us who share the aspiration to contextualize the Cold War, or any specific episode, in a "larger" historical transition have to recognize that the more a historian addresses the so-called larger issues of meaning, the more flawed his or her answer may be. Historians who prize questions of significance often provide general explanations that are confuted by particular circumstances. Those who value correct answers (pinning down who did what, when, and why) often have contempt for big issues.

Because some of the most important recent scholarship on the postwar era has addressed issues of political economy, I have included several articles on this aspect. To show the connection between economic stabilization and foreign policy need not imply a one-way causal relationship. It does not require blaming the cold war on capitalism. It is notable that the Cold War as a dominant configuration of international relations in the forty years after World War II was contemporaneous with a restructuring of Western political and economic systems such that they became more responsive to working-class demands, efforts to sustain high employment, and institute welfare states. These developments at home paralleled the development of nuclear strategy and deterrence, which was arguably the other major factor behind the Cold War. The rise of mass politics and the perceived demand for economic growth and welfare in capitalist societies gave the Cold War its ideological outlines—ensured that it would not be conceived as a simple anti-Russian coalition. The advent of nuclear weaponry helped determine the wary but restrained pattern of stand-off that prevailed for over a generation.

From the perspective of the revisionist historians, systemic or structural explanations did not mitigate American responsibility. They shifted guilt for the Cold War from individual subjects (e.g. President Truman or hawkish advisers such as Secretary of Defense James Forrestal, or later Secretary of State Dean Acheson) to collective subjects: e.g., American capitalism. But the historians of the 1960s still had a moralizing thrust. They still believed that the institutions of American life were deeply at fault.

The logic of structural explanation, however, can obviously work the other way. It can diffuse rather than reassign guilt. It can dilute the issue of responsibility. For many analysts the recourse to collective factors adjourned the whole heated and vexing debate of who might be at fault. Political scientists, for example, came to distrust narratives which presupposed that policy makers acted upon rational, instrumental calculation. Some suggested that the Cold War arose because men in power tend to misperceive what their national adversaries intend.[12] Competence or incompetence may be at stake in such a view of international politics, but moral responsibility is largely irrelevant.

According to other explanations, decision makers followed scripts largely written by the organizations they spoke for. They acted on policies less in response to foreign danger than in an effort to preserve their agency's influence against domestic rivals for influence or budgetary resources. The Air Force fought the Navy, the Atomic Energy Commission, the Air Force; the State Department sniped at the Treasury; the CIA had contempt for the Defense Department; the Bureau of the Budget (today's OMB) was determined to rein in everyone: an endless war of all against all on the Potomac, and presumably within the Kremlin as well, although we have far less information available. Policy recommendations were allegedly tailored to prevail in that continuing struggle. This methodological approach, sometimes hallowed as "bureaucratic politics," also came of age in the 1960s and 1970s.[13] It proved useful to explain why one sort of cold-war response might be chosen over another—why, for instance, American authorities might react to a crisis with a show of force on one occasion and a more measured riposte on another. It accounted less well why there was a sense of overarching conflict with the Soviets to begin with.

There were related models of organizational behavior, which stressed not the rivalries among agencies, but the similar pressures exerted within any large-scale, hierarchical organization. Promotion within departments depends upon conformity to the group interpretation of how the world does and should operate. Dissent is discouraged. Those who rise to the top have often internalized so-called operational codes, which include traditional ways of interpreting national interest.[14] Large-scale organizations also reward certain types of decision-making procedures just for the sake of making action feasible. They encourage self-reinforcing or "cybernetic" approaches to decision making from participants, not exhaustive testing of all alternatives, or protracted experimentation.[15]

In effect, most historians of the Cold War who sought to leave behind the harsh exchanges on blame and guilt relied on some form of systemic explanation that diffused responsibility. Post-revisionism, it can be argued, by and large looked to the nature of the international system itself as a source of conflict. Sovereign states, those of this temperament tended to emphasize, live in an international jungle. Their leaders must be mistrustful because no common ruler constrains them. Conflict there will always be; the postwar era just assured that only two major blocs had the resources and ambitions to dominate. The insights of game theory—whose applications teach that opposing players may be led by rational strategic calculation to a level of confrontation higher than either would have sought at the outset—lend a certain appeal to the "post-revisionist" stance. What historians earlier criticized as outright belligerence (either on the part of the Soviets or Washington) tends to be reinterpreted as the unfortunate necessity to act prudently under conditions of uncertainty. Given the apparent risks of backing down on contested issues, it would have been difficult for two sovereign super-powers to avoid confrontation. Assigning blame seems beside the point. Disputes over guilt and responsibility can be transcended. Of course, post-revisionism has aroused controversy. Its somewhat weary deflecting of issues of guilt and innocence angered impenitent revisionists, who felt it incorporated a dimension of evasiveness.

But assuming that the Cold War has ended, how will the ongoing debates be affected? It does not require much prescience to understand that there will be less patience with revisionist critiques given the Soviets' critical examination of their own history. In the face of the Russians' harsh indictment of Stalin and one-party rule, for a Western historian still to insist on Washington's responsibility will involve a lonely stance. Will it not seem self-evident at last that the Cold War must be laid at the feet of communism, that it was the responsibility of Stalinist policies? Will Soviet responsibility not be confirmed by the fact that once Moscow renounced domination of Eastern Europe and East Germany, tensions eased, that in effect the Cold War ended?

This author was never a revisionist, but I do not think that historical understanding will be well served just by reasserting the old orthodox pieties. Simple answers are satisfying, but not always adequate. Soviet domination of Eastern Europe, in my opinion, was the underlying cause of the Cold War (somewhat the way slavery was the underlying cause of the Civil War). Americans ended World War II believing that they had fought for the emancipation of abused and conquered peoples, and they were rapidly disillusioned by the spread of a new form of domination. After a period of testing different responses, United States policy reacted with coordinated economic and military program which helped consolidate the division of Europe.

But underlying causes and complete explanations are not the same.

Citing slavery alone will not get the historian of the Civil War to Fort Sumter. To answer the question of why Stalin intervened so brutally throughout Eastern Europe requires a progressive reconstruction of events. Crack-down came progressively over a two-year period, and some buffer zones were left relatively uninfringed. The historian still has to probe the evolution of Soviet policy. Soviet totalitarianism had no commitment to democracy abroad, but it is not certain that the pattern of creating a Russian security zone had to be so repressive.

The West was not responsible for the repression. Conceivably we might have helped forestall some of the worst of it—perhaps by firmer resistance at the outset (as historians such as Adam Ulam and Vojtech Mastny have argued).[16] Might conversely a more conciliatory policy have helped, as revisionist historians have suggested? It is hard to know what we could have granted the Soviets that we withheld so as to induce them to live easily in a world of pluralist neighbors. The leverage afforded by postwar loans was relatively minimal, although had we been more forthcoming on the German reparation issue, some contentiousness might have been minimized. Would just the willingness to write off Eastern Europe to Soviet control have forestalled some of Moscow's later hostility to the West? This is what Henry Wallace urged, believing that it would win Russian good will. So to a degree did George Kennan, understanding that it would not. In effect, we refused to write off Eastern Europe, but neither could we preserve its liberty. It is doubtful, however, that in the immediate aftermath of the Second World War, Americans would have easily renounced democratic hopes for so large an area where our efforts had been so engaged.

One can thus envisage new debates on responsibility and blame that will follow from contemporary events. One view will be the "triumphalist" one, according to which the U.S. won the Cold War; it deserved to win; its tenacity in opposing the Soviets finally allowed the Hungarians, Czechs, Poles, and others to emerge from the shadow of Soviet domination. This view will stress resistance to the Soviets, not detente, as the major force for liberation. An opposed interpretation will argue that American resistance tended to prolong Moscow's control because it reinforced the position of the Soviet hardliners. This view will suggest that ultimately it was the willingness to talk across the Iron Curtain, not just to resist, that undermined the Soviet hold.

No matter how brutal, the nature of the Communist system cannot entirely explain the pattern of the Soviet-American confrontation. It is a cause—a far more plausible cause than the nature of American capitalism. The ebbing of international tension in tandem with the dismantling of Communist control does demonstrate how inextricably communism and the Cold War were connected. But historical explanation requires more than finding an underlying cause. The role of the historian is not exhausted in that search; she or he must reconstruct a process or progression of events from cause to result. In that reconstruction, I believe, the other systemic factors that historians have examined—the nature of political economies, the logic of international competition—deserve continued research. They structure the process of responses. They translate domestic impulses into international outcomes. They also require us to go beyond the issue of responsibility, to the logic of confrontation. The end of the Cold War should certainly have established that some ascriptions of blame were essentially sound, and others fanciful. But it should also allow us to probe beyond the issue of responsibility. The end of the Cold War does not make its history irrelevant. It should make it more wide-ranging.

Anticipations of Future Debates

New epochs create new questions. For forty years postwar history was interpreted as a great contest. But for the countries of Eastern Europe, just emerging from Soviet domination, it sometimes appeared as a joint conspiracy, allowing each superpower to dominate its half of Europe. The interpretation of Yalta is a revealing litmus. It has been taken as the high water mark of allied agreement (the interpretation in 1945, and again by the Left in the 1960s); as an American sell-out to the Soviets (the prevailing view of American conservatives in the 1950s); or as joint condominium over legitimate national aspirations. As György Konrád, a noted Hungarian dissident and author, wrote in 1984:

> To find the main reason for today's threat of war, we must go back to the year 1945, to Yalta. It was there that a helpless Europe was divided; it was there that agreements were reached for military zones of occupation that would become political spheres of interest as well. Yalta gave birth to a system of international relations based upon a state of rivalry and equilibrium between the Soviet Union and the United States. Whether the three old gentlemen who met there knew it or not, the idea of the Iron Curtain was born at Yalta, a symbol of great-power logic. Three old men—Roosevelt, Stalin, and Churchill—decided the fate of hundreds of millions for decades to come, the hundreds of millions having to respect their decision.[17]

Konrád's interpretation will become even more widespread as American and Soviet influence recedes in Central and Western Europe. It raises problems, however. Roosevelt hoped at Yalta that he was in fact defending Europe against a simple partition into spheres of influence. On his departure from the Crimean conference site, he certainly understood what weak leverage he had secured. He conceded Communist preponderance in the East European governments, hoping that the guarantees for minority pro-Western representation would keep liberal options open. Yalta also provided for free elections in liberated Eastern Europe, but they took place only as a travesty, or the results were trounced upon. Were these outcomes foreseeable? Had there been any practical alternative in view of the presence of the Soviet army? Certainly creation of the satellite regimes took place against the will of the Americans, not in accordance with their wishes. Nonetheless, no matter how the defender of FDR's policies may protest, historical interpretation will entail a re-evaluation of Yalta. The close of the Cold War, the end of the postwar era, and the possible abdication of the Soviet Union and the United States as superpowers will lead historians to focus on the Europeans who lived between them.

I do not share the view of Yalta as a condominium. Certainly it was not intended as such. Nonetheless, if we can get beyond a renewed fixation with guilt for the Cold War, Konrád's comments alert us to a new perspective. If Cold War Europe should be viewed less as an arena for conflict than as a pattern of settlement, how do we characterize that settlement? What characteristics allowed a sociopolitical equilibrium to emerge that preserved the communist-capitalist distinction, but likewise prevented it from becoming so disruptive a difference that it led to war? If Konrad has a point, the future historian has to account for coexistence, not Cold War.

The essays in Part II, "Dividing Europe," will provide material for judging Konrád's concept of Yalta. Averell Harriman served as Ambassador in the Soviet Union from mid-1943 to the end of 1945. His memoir suggests why Poland became the site of original conflict between the Soviets and Americans. It reveals how Washington sought to resist an early division of Europe at the expense of the small powers, but it also shows how complex the issues were and how crucial it seemed to retain Soviet cooperation in ending the war. Harriman offers the viewpoint of a disillusioned observer, who found himself caught in the middle of very thorny issues. On the other hand, John Gaddis looks at the longer-term evolution of events to explain how American policy makers finally came to terms with a *de facto* partition. In a sense Gaddis documents how the Yalta era, which Conrad laments, came to be instituted. But the vigor of the internal U.S. debates that he recapitulates suggests that the outcome Washington came to accept was not the result that was originally intended.

How influence was instituted on each side of the Iron Curtain can be better understood after reading the Lundestad and Luža essays, which conclude Part II. Geir Lundestad stresses how the United States was drawn into a hegemonic role in the West. He does not doubt the extent of American influence; he proposes, however, that it was solicited more than assertively sought. Radomír Luža, on the other hand, shows how the process of Communization took place in the last satellite to fall in Europe to Communist domination. But questions remain. Had the Soviets intended before 1947 to transform the country into so compliant (and brutal) a satellite, or might they have been content with a continuing coalition role for the Communist Party? In either case, once the Czechs showed enough independence to pursue Marshall Plan aid into the fall of 1947, Moscow apparently decided that total subjugation was necessary. Repeated miscalculation by the Czech democrats—from Eduard Beneš's early trust in Stalin to their resignation in the final crisis of February 1948—probably made the take-over easier than it might otherwise have been. Caught in the logic of the overarching Cold War, each country in Eastern Europe nonetheless has its own historical specificity.

Nor, despite Konrád's summary above, was the overall outcome the result of a simple process. The East-West division was neither side's apparent intention; as World War II ended, Washington and Moscow seemed to have compatible expectations for a postwar order. What Stalin ultimately intended—whether or not he even had a final objective, will remain uncertain.[18] Both sides appeared initially prepared to be content with a continuing governmental voice for their respective liberal or communist allies. The Soviets seemed to feel that pluralism was acceptable if Communist preponderance was assured in the bordering countries and some continuing coalition role was ensured in the West. This result would have meant that they faced no hostile coalition or revived German threat. Neither Washington nor Moscow was prepared to have its political friends or clients simply excluded from influence. On the other hand, local political leaders—Communists in Eastern Europe, Social Democrats or Christian Democrats in Western Europe—saw themselves locked in a struggle that required removing their rivals from influence. By 1947–48 the Soviets and the Americans each had to come to terms with mounting evidence that their supporters were in fact being removed from office, and, in Eastern Europe, arrested and tried. Each side finally accepted that the division of Europe into exclusive spheres on influence was the next best alternative. If partial influence could not be preserved throughout, then the other side's political foothold had to be eliminated where it could. If Yalta thus became a paradigm for spheres of influence, the outcome took some getting used to.

If as historians we want to explain how the division of Europe became so durable, how coexistence came into existence, then we have to look at two sorts of mechanisms. The most obvious is what came to be called the balance of terror, the role of atomic deterrence. Although some notable books and essays follow this development, I have not included a sample here.[19] The nature of deterrence and the slow learning of the rules of the game are worth study, but the reader will find ready treatments of this problem elsewhere. The question that remains is how robust deterrence really was. Had the Soviet-American antagonism persisted indefinitely, would nuclear stand-off have continued to provide stable reassurance against the other side's aggression? Most professional commentators on strategy who tackled the subject were convinced that each side had mastered the rules of the game sufficiently, such that neither would have taken dangerous risks. This was obviously not the opinion of the peace movements in Europe. They argued that someday deterrence was likely to fail. No matter how one evaluates that prediction, it would be hard to argue that nuclear deterrence made little difference to the stability of the Cold War while it lasted.

The other mechanism for stability lay in the fact that the Cold War division comprised an alignment of economic and political systems and not just a coalition of unrelated partners. The essays grouped below in Part III should reveal the ground rules of the Western system, how it came into being, and wherein its economic principles lay. I have included the essays on political economy for several reasons. First, because my own research interests lie in this direction, and this collection is designed as a personal statement of what themes retain importance. Similarly, I remain convinced that economic arrangements explain a good deal of European stability over forty years. Finally, the reader is less likely to find this literature sampled elsewhere.

The contribution of political economy to the stability of the East-West configuration is less intuitively obvious than the role of nuclear deterrence. In the remainder of this essay, I should like to make the case for its importance. Alongside its democratic convictions, what united the West was a new welfare capitalism based on sustained economic growth. Postwar Western societies effectively overcame prewar ideological and social divisions by the incorporation of major spokesmen for labor in an ongoing system of bargaining over the fruits of economic growth. Whereas prewar ideological divisions had helped undermine democracy in much of continental Europe, a new consensus on growth helped account for its postwar success. I need not detail the nature of the postwar social contract here, for I have included in Part III, below, an older essay that sets forth some of the premises which contributed to democratic stability.

More than any other single policy innovation, the Marshall Plan helped consolidate the premises of productivity and growth among the Western economies. Michael Hogan's chapters present the concepts behind the European Recovery Program, as it was formally called; his close examination develops some of the same American notions that my piece outlines more generally. Whereas the success of the Marshall Plan as an ideological rallying point is generally acknowledged, its actual economic working is subject to debate. I have included the major dissenting view of its efficacy, that of Alan Milward. Milward is skeptical about the economic necessity of the Plan, as it was usually defended. He also ascribes a far more limited result than most American writers. Nonetheless, he too, has admitted that it played an important role—if less than the one its American admirers claimed. Finally I have included some studies of European labor in the postwar period. Integration of the working class into a system of political bargaining was a critical component of Western stability. If a democratic anticommunist consensus was to be maintained after World War II, it was essential that the spokesmen for labor not all be pushed into the Communist camp. Indeed most of the Christian and social-democratic union leaders deeply distrusted communist aims from early in the postwar period, but the Resistance efforts had placed a premium on unity of working-class action against Nazis and Fascists. How the currents came to divide anew is explained by Lutz Niethammer, whose essay has been carried over from the older edition of this book, in part because it remains a comprehensive and knowledgeable short survey. Niethammer stresses the anticommunist thrust of American labor policy, which any perusal of the AFL and CIO documents can confirm. Nonetheless, the reasons for this behavior are perhaps less manipulative and arise out of better-founded democratic convictions than the perspective of the late 1960s suggested. Finally, Anthony Carew provides a good case study of how the American ideas found a fertile ground within the British managerial and trade-union circles. Although I have not included them here, similar accounts exist for the German and Italian experiences.[20]

Such a heavy dose of political economy should suggest that the history of the Cold War repays study as a key to understanding the internal development of the United States and European societies in the virtual half century after World War II. That is why the question of what the Cold War was about—and not merely who was responsible—shall have to be addressed anew. It was not merely about Russian-American rivalry, or the confrontation of communism and capitalism. The Cold War structured historical development on many levels at once: as a strategic or geopolitical contest after the collapse of German power in Europe; as a momentous claim of two sources of ideological legitimacy; as an umbrella under which new representational forms could be finally stabilized for the classes created earlier by industrial society but still locked in conflict before 1945.

The period of the Cold War, after all, resolved issues that had lacerated Western societies in the first half of the twentieth century. The question of Germany's bid for imperial hegemony had been a major factor in unleashing World War I and even more directly World War II.

It was finally settled by the very partition that the Cold War preserved for forty years. Japan's imperial venture was also overcome, and while the country was not divided it was safely tucked into the American security sphere. The question of what political role should be granted to the urban working classes created by industrial development had also proved an agonizing issue and had engendered such extreme ideological answers as Communism and Fascism. The fascist answer of repressing autonomous labor movements within a nationalist authoritarian system was discredited by the policies and then the defeat of Germany and Italy. The Communist project of legitimizing a dictatorial party authority on the supposed basis of the working class had never attracted more than a minority of West European workers and intellectuals before World War II. But it could emerge as a plausible principle for an international coalition after the Soviet Union played so key a role in defeating Nazi Germany. Only the Western counter-project of the democratic welfare state based on growth and corporate bargaining was a plausible contender. With the Right discredited, in effect the Cold War represented a contest between those latter two alternatives.

Both alternatives ran into serious difficulties after a generation. Western welfare capitalism had to limp through the crisis of the 1970s. This demoralizing decade brought long-term inflation and renewed high unemployment, the over-capacity of basic industries, and intense policy disagreement in place of earlier consensus on macroeconomic objectives. The crisis of the 1970s shook the political systems of Western Europe and by the end of the decade resulted in the electoral defeat of those parties who had sought unsuccessfully to master the adverse economic trends. But the crisis that afflicted the Eastern bloc by the late 1980s proved even more disabling and led to the decomposition of communism.

In retrospect the Cold War can be seen to have rested on two transitional institutional equilibria. One was the exceptional bipolar international alignment that was the legacy of World War II, but which became increasingly artificial as Europeans and Asians gained economic influence. Certainly, the superpowers controlled nuclear arsenals of unparalleled destructive capacity, but insofar as deterrence was really successful, such weapons could hardly be invoked to maintain their hegemony.

So too, the ideological alternatives that the Cold War incorporated were the expression of an epoch in world economic history that was also vanishing. They expressed the centrality of an industrial working class—in the case of Soviet communism even more fundamentally than Western social democracy. But the technological and industrial basis of that class was being rapidly undermined by the 1970s and 1980s. The West accepted the consequences earlier than the East; it closed its mines and shut its steel mills and sacked its workers over two decades. The Soviets began the process of *perestroika* belatedly and half-heartedly. In both cases, however, the economic infrastructure of the Cold War—the mass-production factory, the grimy coal mine, the huge steel mill—was becoming obsolete. Historians happily are entitled to vaunt retrospective wisdom. We can understand that short of an inadvertent military collision (recall the effect of Afghanistan), the Cold War was destined to pass into history. Liberated from the burden of fighting it, we can start to understand it.

Endnotes

1. William H. McNeill, *America, Britain and Russia: Their Cooperation and Conflict, 1941–1946* (London, Oxford University Press, 1953); Herbert Feis, *Roosevelt, Churchill and Stalin: The War They Waged and the Peace They Sought* (Princeton, Princeton University Press, 1957); also Feis, *Between War and Peace: The Potsdam Conference* (Princeton, Princeton University Press, 1960); Gabriel Kolko, *The Politics of War: The World and United States Foreign Policy, 1943–1945* (New York, Random House, 1968); Joyce and Gabriel Kolko, *The Limits of Power: The World and United States Foreign Policy, 1945–54* (New York, Harper and Row, 1972)—the latter being works that I have criticized, but which still offer the most complete alternative assessment of American objectives.

2. Arthur Schlesinger, Jr. provided a useful summary of this position in 1967: "The Origins of the Cold War," *Foreign Affairs* 46 (1967): 22–52.

3. P. M. S. Blackett, *Fear, War, and the Bomb* (New York, 1949); Gar Alperowitz, *Atomic Diplomacy: Hiroshima and Potsdam* (New York, Vintage Books, 1965). Valuable summaries of the issues concerning use of the atomic bomb are available in various essays by Barton Bernstein; see especially "Roosevelt, Truman and the Atomic Bomb: A Reinterpretation," *Political Science Quarterly,* 90 (1974–76), pp. 23–69. Also Bernstein, "The Uneasy Alliance: Roosevelt, Churchill, and the Atomic Bomb, 1940–1945," *Western Political Quarterly* 29 (June 1976): 202–31. For a recent review of the literature see J. Samuel Walker, "The Decision to use the Bomb: A Historiographical Update," *Diplomatic History* 14, 1 (Winter, 1990): 97–114.

4. Denna F. Fleming, *The Cold War and its Origins, 1917–1960*, 2 vols. (Garden City, N.Y., 1961).

5. Williams, William Appleman, *The Tragedy of American Diplomacy* (New York, Dell, 1959, and rev. ed. 1962); Lloyd C. Gardner, *Economic Aspects of New Deal Diplomacy* (Madison, University of Wisconsin Press, 1964); also Gardner, *Architects of Illusion: Men and Ideas in American Foreign Policy* (Chicago, Quadrangle Books, 1970); G. Kolko, *The Politics of War;* J. and G. Kolko, *The Limits of Power.*

6. For guides to the controversies, with extensive citations of the relevant

literature, see Charles S. Maier, "Revisionism and the Interpretation of Cold War Origins," *Perspectives in American History,* IV (1970), pp. 313–347, which was reprinted in the first edition of this book (New York, 1978) with a further update of bibliography. I have not chosen to reprint the article anew since much of the literature reviewed was derivative and the details are of less importance two decades later. For another major survey see Robert W. Tucker, *The Radical Left and American Foreign Policy* (Baltimore, Johns Hopkins University Press, 1971); and for a recent update, which shows how old revisionists have become judicious moderates, Geir Lundestad, "Moralism, Presentism, Exceptionalism, Provincialism, and Other Extravagances in American Writings on the Early Cold War Years," *Diplomatic History* 13 (Fall 1989): 527–545.

7. John Lewis Gaddis, "The Emerging Post-Revisionist Synthesis on the Origins of the Cold War," *Diplomatic History* 7 (Summer 1983): 171–190. For Gaddis's own work, see also *The United States and the Origins of the Cold War, 1941–1947* (New York, Columbia University Press, 1972); *Strategies of Containment: A Critical Appraisal of Postwar American National Security Policy* (New York, Oxford University Press, 1982), and the essay reprinted below.

8. I use the pronoun "we," because in large measure the stance largely reflects my own views, even though the occasionally complacent tone of postrevisionism bothers me, as it has unabashedly unreconstructed revisionist critics.

9. Peter G. Boyle, "The British Foreign Office View of Soviet-American Relations, 1945–46," *Diplomatic History* 3 (Summer 1979): 307–320; Fraser J. Harbutt, *The Iron Curtain: Churchill, America, and the Origins of the Cold War* (New York, Oxford University Press, 1986).

10. Thomas J. McCormick, *America's Half-Century: United States Foreign Policy in the Cold War* (Baltimore, Johns Hopkins University Press, 1989), p. 2. There are internal difficulties with the model. McCormick argues (pp. 4–7) that the leading economic powers seek hegemony to impose an international capitalism which will reinforce their supremacy in the international division of labor. The lesser powers coalesce to resist this endeavor by setting up a balance of power to protect their national economic independence. France under Napoleon, Germany under Hitler also sought hegemony—but both championed versions of continental autarky, not capitalist internationalism. Along with other historians, I would argue further that Britain did not really achieve "hegemony" during the 1815–1870 period that McCormick singles out.

11. For the most ambitious recent effort to place American predominance in a broad historical framework see Paul Kennedy, *The Rise and Fall of the Great Powers: Economic Change and Military Conflict from 1500 to 2000* (New York, Random House, 1987). Kennedy does not ascribe the clash of empires to capitalist expansion, but finds a recurrent trend for military needs to outrun economic capacity.

12. See above all, Robert Jervis, *Perception and Misperception in International Politics* (Princeton, Princeton University Press, 1976).

13. The classic statement is Graham Allison's *Essence of Decision: Explaining the Cuban Missile Crisis* (Boston, Little, Brown, 1971).

14. For examples of these and related approaches see the essays by Alexander George, Ole Holsti, et al., in Paul Gordon Lauren, ed., *Diplomacy: New Approaches in History, Theory, and Policy* (New York, Free Press, 1979); also

Alexander L. George and Richard Smoke, *Deterrence in American Foreign Policy: Theory and Practice* (New York, Columbia University Press, 1974).

15. John Steinbrunner, *The Cybernetic Theory of Decision* (Princeton, Princeton University Press, 1974).

16. Adam Ulam, *Expansion and Coexistence: The History of Soviet Foreign Policy, 1917–1967* (New York, Praeger, 1968); Vojtech Mastny, *Russia's Road to the Cold War: Diplomacy, Warfare, and the Politics of Communism, 1941–1945* (New York, Columbia University Press, 1979).

17. György Konrád, *Antipolitics*, Richard E. Allen, trans. (San Diego, New York and London, Harcourt, Brace, Jovanovich, 1984), pp. 1–2.

18. Citations can be found on both sides of the issue: Stalin allegedly said on one occasion that Communism fits Poland the way a saddle fits a cow. On another he told Milovan Djilas that every country would seek to impose its social system as far as its armies extended. Another indication that reading a politician's lips is hardly a guide to his long-term behavior.

19. For a useful starting point, see John Lewis Gaddis, "The Long Peace: Elements of Stability in the Postwar International System," in Gaddis, *The Long Peace: Inquiries into the History of the Cold War* (New York, Oxford University Press, 1987), pp. 215–245; see also Lawrence Friedman, *The Evolution of Nuclear Strategy* (New York, St. Martin's, 1981) and McGeorge Bundy, *Danger and Survival* (New York, Random House, 1988).

20. Werner Link, "Building Coalitions: Non-Governmental German-American Linkages," in Charles S. Maier, ed., *The Marshall Plan and Germany* (Oxford, Berg Publishers Limited, 1991); also Federico Romero, *Gli Stati Uniti e il sindacalismo europeo 1944–1951* (Rome, Edizioni Lavoro, 1989).

2

Thomas J. McCormick

America's Half Century: United States Foreign Policy in the Cold War

Thomas McCormick is professor of American diplomatic history at the University of Wisconsin-Madison and, in effect, heir to a tradition of revisionist or "progressive" historiography exemplified by the late William Appleman Williams. McCormick has demonstrated a continuing interest in theoretical issues in the history of American foreign relations. His 1983 article, "Drift or Mastery? A Corporatist Synthesis for American Diplomatic History," in Stanley I. Kutler, ed., *The Promise of American History,* looked to models of state-business-labor collaboration as an explanatory framework for recent foreign-policy formation.

In the book from which this selection is taken, McCormick takes as a starting point the vision of capitalist development sketched by the noted French historian Fernand Braudel, and what has become known as world-system analysis—a model of global capitalist development since the sixteenth century advanced principally by Immanuel Wallerstein, which sees economic development in the "core" Western European and North American states as dependent upon the extraction of material and cheap labor power from the semi-periphery of Eastern Europe, and the periphery of Third-World societies. For McCormick the Cold War resulted from the restless capitalist energies of the United States, the most recent heir to the successive candidates for economic hegemony that world capitalist development continually throws up. The U.S. had fought World War II to integrate Asia and Europe into a global economy—"hegemonic goals, awesomely global and omnipresent in nature." (p. 33)

The historian differs from the theorist, however, in recognizing that such aspirations did not automatically come to pass. The capitalist agenda ran into real resistance—once the Axis collapsed, from the Soviets and later nationalist forces in Asia. The selection excerpted here is chapter 3, "Cold War on Many Fronts, 1945–1946," pp. 43–71, and exemplifies how McCormick seeks to yoke together his wide-ranging long-term analysis and the immediate diplomatic reactions to United States ambitions in the wake of World War II. The explanatory framework is in line with earlier "revisionist" models of how American capitalist imperatives forced policies of confrontation on the Soviet Union. Like these earlier accounts, it raises the issue of whether a process of reciprocal escalation can be understood by considering the supposed systemic needs of only one actor. One also wonders whether the recurrent "needs" of capitalism allowed for real policy choices or whether statesmen were marionettes in the hands of abstract economic imperatives.

Cold War on Many Fronts, 1945–1946

In July 1945, at the Potsdam (Berlin) conference with Britain and Russia, President Harry S. Truman received official word that the first testing of an atomic bomb had been "successful beyond the most optimistic expectations of anyone." The military administrator of the atomic bomb project, Major General Leslie R. Groves, estimated "the energy generated to be in excess of the equivalent of 15,000 to 20,000 tons of TNT; and this is a conservative estimate." Science director of the project, J. Robert Oppenheimer, later recalled the impact of the test on those observing it at Alamogordo, New Mexico.

> We knew the world would not be the same. A few people laughed, a few people cried. Most people were silent. I remembered the line from the Hindu scripture, the *Bhagavad-Gita:* Vishnu is trying to persuade the Prince that he should do his duty and to impress him he takes on his multi-armed form and says: "Now I am become Death, the destroyer of worlds."

For President Truman, however, the atomic bomb meant not merely death but life. It meant not only the military capacity to be "destroyer of worlds," but the political capacity to help create a new world, unitary and open, under America's protective aegis. Thus, with an excessive casualness that badly concealed his cockiness, Truman informed Stalin of the American achievement. Atomic diplomacy had begun. The Cold War would not lag far behind.

Atomic Diplomacy

For nine gestating months, President Roosevelt and his successor had anticipated the news Truman received at Potsdam. As early as September 30, 1944, Secretary of War Stimson had told Roosevelt, "There is every reason to believe that before August 1, 1945, atomic bombs will have been demonstrated and . . . that one B-29 bomber [will be able to] accomplish with such a bomb the same damage against weak industrial and civilian targets as 100 to 1,000 B-29 bombers." Indeed, he knew (as would Truman after April 1945) that both the director of the Office of Scientific Research and Development, Vannevar Bush, and the chairman of the National Defense Research Committee, Charles Conant, president of Harvard, believed that the first generation fission bomb would be superseded by a hydrogen "super-super bomb" in which the energy released would be increased by "a factor of a thousand or more . . . equivalent in blast damage to 1,000 raids of 1,000 B-29 Fortresses, delivering their load of explosive on one target." They even alerted the President to the possibility of delivering atomic or hydrogen bombs "on an enemy target by means of a robot plane or guided missile."

Five days after the end of the Potsdam conference, the United States dropped the first atomic bomb on Hiroshima. It was August 6, 1945. Russia entered the Far Eastern war on August 8, the Americans dropped the second atomic bomb, on Nagasaki, on August 9, and Japan sued for peace on August 10. President Truman called those war-ending atomic raids "the greatest thing in history." In two blinding glares—a horrible end to a war waged horribly by all parties—the United States finally found the combination that would unlock the door to American hegemony.

With the atomic bomb, the Truman administration, like Oppenheimer's multiarmed Vishnu, could accomplish several goals simultaneously. Struck by fanatical Japanese resistance at Iwo Jima and Okinawa and unpersuaded by navy and air force arguments that Japan could be bombed and blockaded into submission, Truman unquestionably believed that the atomic raids saved many American lives, by eliminating the need for a land invasion of Japan. Important for obvious reasons of sentiment and humanitarianism, that conviction also had great domestic political significance. The American government had consistently waged World War II in a manner that minimized, as much as feasible, the human and economic sacrifices asked of the American people. To have done otherwise might have jeopardized public support for the war's internationalist objectives and risked revival of prewar isolationism; and to have ended the war with a quantum jump in American casualties, especially after spending two billion tax dollars on a weapon that made such a battlefield price unnecessary, was no way to sustain popular support for American policy. Conversely, a graphic demonstration of the bomb's military power was a means of suggesting to Americans that the role of postwar policeman could be played on the cheap ("More bang for the buck," as a later secretary of defense would say) and at little cost in American lives. Power with perquisites but few prices.

Another goal of the atomic raids was to shock the world, for two diametrically different purposes. The more benign was to give the world "adequate warning as to what was to be expected if war should break out again," as Arthur Compton, one of the bomb project's top researchers, told Secretary of War Stimson. The bomb "must be used" so that it would never be used again. But the shock also was to make clear to the world that the United States was ruthless enough to drop the bomb on live targets. A prearranged demonstration of the atomic bomb on a noninhabited target, as some scientists had recommended, would not do. That could demonstrate the power of the bomb, but it could not demonstrate the American will to use the awful power. One reason, therefore, for American unwillingness to pursue Japanese peace feelers in mid-summer 1945 was that the United States did not want the war to end before it had had a chance to use the atomic bomb.

This less benign purpose sought principally to shock the Soviet Union and Western Europe. From the beginning of the Manhattan Project, which built the bomb, Russia had been excluded from participating in it or sharing the fruits of it, even though Britain and Canada had played significant collaborative roles. The elaborate security programs connected with the project were aimed less at German spies than Soviet sympathizers. It was hoped that the Americans' atomic monopoly (and demonstrated willingness to use it) would make the Russians, as Secretary of State James F. Byrnes phrased it, "more manageable in Europe." Either in tandem with or in place of economic diplomacy, atomic diplomacy might inhibit potential Soviet expansionism and even intimidate Soviet leaders into softening their policies on Eastern Europe and Germany. Put another way, atomic diplomacy might resolve the ambiguity of the Yalta accords in America's favor. It might sufficiently shift the balance of forces that the United States could up the ante in the power game that inevitably occurred in the rearrangement of a shattered world. Such hopes were to be disappointed. If anything, atomic diplomacy reinforced Russia's security fears, strengthened its disposition to control its Eastern European buffer zone more tightly, undermined soft-liners on German policy, and led Soviet leaders to create a crash atomic bomb project of their own.

Western Europe, even more than Russia, was the target of the atomic shock treatments. Persuading Europe to discard its own nationalism and accept American internationalist hegemony was expected to be no easy matter. It would likely prove even more difficult when, as anticipated, American public opinion required the postwar demobilization of the American army and its partial withdrawal from Europe. With the Red Army still mobilized east of the Elbe River, Western Europe might be intimidated into making separate political and economic arrangements with the Soviet Union. The atomic bomb, however, gave the United States a diplomatic tool more powerful than the Red Army presence. If Europe cooperated with the United States, that tool could provide Europe with a nuclear umbrella that would shield it from Red Army diplomacy and provide a psychologically secure environment so that America could get on with the primary task of rebuilding European industry, a vital component of a revivified world-system. In that purpose, atomic diplomacy was no small success. It might not have made Russia more manageable, but it did make Europe more malleable.

Finally, the atomic bomb as diplomatic weapon enabled the United States to exclude Russia from the development of postwar policy toward Japan and to monopolize that sphere itself. While the United States did not want the war to end too quickly, before the bomb could be used, it also did not want it to go on too long. If war in the Far East lasted well beyond Russian entry on August 8, it would not only facilitate Russian military expansion in Northeast Asia but would permit the Soviet Union to stake a substantial claim to sharing in the postwar occupation and governance of Japan. At that early juncture the United States was still unsure what role Japan would be allowed or asked to play in postwar Asia. Few Americans, however, doubted that Japan, with its vast industrial resources at Osaka, Nagoya, and Tokyo, would play an important role. Whatever the role, however, the United States wanted a monopoly on its determination. Viewed in this context, the timing of the atomic raids becomes more explicable. Not only does it help explain the Hiroshima raid on August 6 (two days before the Russian entry), but it suggests an even more pervasive reason for the unseemly haste with which the bomb was dropped on Nagasaki—on August 9, before Japanese authorities had time to make sense of the first raid. Quite simply, the United States wanted the war ended within days (not weeks or months) in order to limit the size and scope of Soviet involvement.

American Power and the American Dream

In his historical novel *Washington, D.C.*, Gore Vidal described the last days of a fictionalized Franklin Roosevelt and the first days of his successor.

> The ravaged old President, even as he was dying, continued to pursue the high business of reassembling the fragments of broken empires into a new pattern with himself at center, proud creator of the new imperium. Now, though he was gone, the work remained. The United States was master of the earth. No England, no France, no Germany, no Japan left to dispute the Republic's will. Only the mysterious Soviet would survive to act as other balance in the scale of power.

Vidal's fiction mirrored reality. There was indeed a giddiness among postwar American internationalists that came from possessing vast, preponderant power while the rest of the world possessed so little.

Economic might was the more obvious component of that power. After a decade of depression and underutilized capacity, American industry was running full-bore, while wartime demand and government aid had stimulated extensive capital spending on additional productive capacity. Spurred on by having an integrated, continental market in its forty-eight states, America's industry was the most rationalized in the world. It most approached optimal size and the economies of scale, so it enjoyed advantages over all its global competitors in all of the high-value product lines; steel, farm machinery, machine tools, electrical equipment, construction machinery, and automobiles and trucks. Only in the less profitable lines of nondurable consumer goods, such as textiles, was it unable consistently to out-produce and out-sell its commercial rivals. Compounding U.S. economic supremacy, the American farm belt, in the face of the war's devastation of European agriculture, enhanced its historic position as the world-system's major breadbasket. Likewise, American bankers transcended their previous parity with British counterparts as New York clearly surpassed London as the dominant financial center of the world-system. Thus, unscathed by the ravages of war and only mildly distorted by its limited mobilization for war, the American economy by 1946 was the workshop, the bakery, and the banker of the postwar world. In contrast, Great Britain, the Soviet Union, Germany, and Japan had all been devastated by war and their economies grotesquely distorted by the awful strains of more extensive mobilization.

Military might was the other element of the power that was breeding arrogance among American leaders. Despite the rapid demobilization of the wartime army in 1945–1946, the United States remained the most powerful military force in the world-system. The monopoly of the atomic bomb was central to that superiority—the Aladdin's lamp tucked away in the folds of the American cape, ready to be withdrawn and rubbed if circumstances demanded. Also important were American naval supremacy and continued leadership in strategic air power, providing the greatest mobility and firepower. In contrast, the German and Japanese military machines were defeated and dismantled. The British war engine was significantly reduced and sorely strained in the attempt to project British interests in the Indian Ocean and the Mediterranean Sea. Even the mighty Red Army, conqueror of the *Wehrmacht* and occupier of Eastern Europe, was partially demobilized in 1946 as the Soviet Union threw itself into the task of postwar economic reconstruction at home. Possessing no atomic bomb, no modern navy, and no strategic air command; decimated by terrible losses of life and equipment in the war with Germany; and handicapped by a poor transport system and technological backwardness (the horse was still on a par with the internal combustion engine as the army's source of power and movement), the Soviet Union was in no position to challenge the United States if the latter chose to play the role of world policeman. Even assuming the worst of Soviet intentions, American military intelligence had already concluded by November 1945 (before partial Soviet demobilization) that the USSR would not have the military power to risk a major war before 1960.

If there was a certain arrogance discernible in American leaders, it was an arrogance of righteousness as well as of power. In the last analysis, American leaders assumed that American power was constructive simply because they believed American intentions self-evidently just and generous. Looking back over the sweep of a half-century, they thought they understood why the world-system had hovered on the brink of self-immolation through two world wars, the great depression, and epic social revolutions. Moreover, they had a vision of how to reorder and manage the world-system in ways they thought would negate its self-destructive tendencies and usher in a golden age of economic profitability, political stability, and social tranquility. While they acknowledged the self-interest that would be served by their new order, they were firm in their proud conviction that other core powers would participate in the benefits of that order, and that even the periphery ultimately stood to gain from "trickle down" effect. In a cost-benefit analysis, the rest of the world would win more than it would lose by acquiescing in American hegemony; greater security and material rewards in exchange for diminished autonomy. The great trade-off!

The postwar American vision was not a new intellectual construct but one largely borrowed from British thought. The old hegemonic power tutored the new. It was Britain past, not Britain present, that did the teaching—not the declining Britain of the twentieth century, of John Maynard Keynes, but the ascending Britain of the eighteenth and nineteenth centuries, the Britain of Adam Smith. The envisioned goals were material rewards and physical security for both the United States and the world as a whole. America had to make a plausible case that its hegemony served systemic interests as well as self-interests if others were to defer to it voluntarily.

The general physical security was contingent in part on nations enjoying adequate material rewards. If the rewards were reasonably satisfactory, then there was less likelihood of nations or peoples using war or revolution to effect some economic redistribution. But security was also contingent on having an umpire or policeman for the system as a whole. American leaders, of course, were determined that the United States should play the role, but changing circumstances would dictate how and to what degree it shared the role with other powers. It might be shared with other Great Powers through the UN Security Council, as the Yalta-Potsdam plan originally envisioned. It might be shared with the UN General Assembly, as it would be during the Korean War. It might be shared through regional alliances such as NATO (the North Atlantic Treaty Organization), SEATO (Southeast Asia Treaty Organization), ANZUS (a mutual defense pact among Australia, New Zealand, and the United States), and the OAS (Organization of American States). But however it was shared, America would be the nexus.

Material rewards, in turn, depended on a certain amount of physical security. Trade and capital would not flow into areas made inhospitable by anticapitalist regimes or made dangerous by war or revolution. As John C. Calhoun noted a century earlier, speaking of slavery's future in America's western territories, "property is inherently timid."—It would go only where the political climate was stable and receptive. The same was true of other forms of property, of goods and gold, in the mid-twentieth century. Capital would not venture into parts of the world-system that were not physically safe and politically stable. The earlier case China in the 1920s was an instructive example. All the Western powers and Japan had accepted the open door principle of free market competition in China. All recognized the independence of China and agreed to forego further efforts at partitioning or colonizing it. And all looked forward to the profitable exploitation of China and to its transformation from Marco Polo's dream to the reality of Asian riches. Yet foreign capital would not enter that free market because the Chinese revolution, with its disunity, xenophobia, economic nationalism, and violence, made China wholly uninviting. American diplomacy and the Washington treaty system had opened the door to China, but none would pass through the portals unless a "fair field and no favor" could be made a safe field as well. From such examples American postwar leaders concluded that global prosperity depended in part on a hegemonic America maintaining global law and order.

Security per se, however, did not guarantee prosperity. To an equal degree, American internationalists believed, the global economy had to be organized on the basis of classic liberal principles of free trade, comparative advantage, and economies of scale. Only a free market economy on a worldwide level, they argued, could maximize profits for the whole system as well as for its specific parts. At the heart of these principles was the concept of "productionism." In essence it was an internationalized version of Say's Law. A nineteenth-century French economist, J. B. Say, had posited that "in an economy characterized by specialization, each producer makes goods, not for his own consumption, but in the expectation of exchanging them for other goods. . . . It follows that the aggregate supply of goods produced is the same thing as the aggregate demand. *Total demand and total supply are identical.* That is Say's Law."

That classic economic theorem had repeatedly broken down in the twentieth century, especially in the depression of the 1930s. National economies were not "characterized by specialization," but by self-sufficiency. They attempted to produce everything needed by their populaces, even those products for which they possessed no natural advantage and which could have been imported more cheaply, and even those goods whose production runs were too small to realize the savings that came with economies of scale. The result was uneconomical production runs of overpriced goods for undersized markets. A further consequence was the very thing Say's Law deemed impossible—supply in excess of available demand that resulted in overproduction crises and industrial depressions of increasing severity and length.

The American dream of a unitary free world reinvoked Say's Law at the global level after it failed at the national. If nations gave up efforts at self-sufficiency (autarky) and specialized in those products they could make as well as and sell for less than anybody else (comparative advantage), and if they produced those items in large volume (economies of scale) for a global market rather than a national market, the end result would be a world economy in which everything that was produced would be consumed. Crises of overproduction would become a thing of the past; production would create its own demand. Maximizing global production would maximize global consumption and per capita standards of living. That was the essence of productionism: producing the largest volume of specialized goods for sale in the widest possible world market.

This international growth strategy employed two favorite metaphors: the world economy as a pie and a rising tide lifting all ships. Scarcity (non-growth) economics had regarded the economic pie as fixed in size (zero-sum) and had espoused national economic planning as a way to slice the pie in favor of this class as opposed to that class, or for this nation as opposed to some other—for winners and losers. The result was class conflict at home in the first case or confrontation abroad in the second. As Cordell Hull, secretary of state from 1933 to 1944, put it, "When nations cannot get what they need by the normal processes of trade, they will continue to resort to the use of force." Making the pie bigger (productionism), however, offered a way out. Even if a given class or nation retained the same percentage of the pie, the pie's absolute increase meant that each slice's size would grow as well. Even if unequal, the material rewards would be sufficiently large to assure that social and international peace would be the natural companions of prosperity.

On the rising economic tide, some ships, to be sure, were bigger than others, and the American ship was the biggest of all. Specialized production for a free worldwide market clearly favored the American economy, since it possessed the natural advantage of being able to outcompete the rest of the world in a wide range of the most profitable products. As a consequence, other core nations suspected American economic policy of being a self-serving device to steal away their old empires and intrude into their home markets. Likewise, peripheral nations feared it as a self-serving means to perpetuate the gap between "rich lands and poor," as Nobel economist Gunnar Myrdal termed them, and to keep the raw material economies of the Third World dependent on the industrial economies of the First.

Given their perception of American intentions, core capitalist nations in postwar Europe were inclined to regulate and limit their trade with dominant America and to plan their domestic economies so that supply and demand were balanced. Giving the powerful influence of the working-class in most European governments, that planning generally involved elaborate welfare programs and the nationalization of decaying industries like coal and steel. Similarly, peripheral nations were inclined to regulate and limit their trade with all core countries and to launch planned industrialization programs of their own that substituted indigenous production of goods previously imported (import-substitution policies).

While acknowledging the self-serving character of productionism, American leaders argued that a global growth strategy would not only lift all ships in absolute terms but in relative terms as well. It would do what welfare capitalism or import-substitution could not do. It could enable other core countries to close the gap between the American standard of living and their own, and it would facilitate the transformation of the periphery from raw material production to industrialism. Welfare capitalism that redistributed wealth from capital to labor would, they claimed, prompt domestic capitalists to leave and foreign capitalists not to enter. Capital underinvestment, coupled with higher wage costs, would price such a core nation's goods out of the world market, result in heavy trade deficits, and ultimately depress the economy and the per capita income. Similarly, import-substitution and state-planned industry in the periphery would discourage the import of capital and technology, prompt domestic capitalists to flee in search of higher profits, and rely upon national markets that were too small or poor to generate adequate local demand.

Alternatively, productionism would argue that the way for European working classes to gain was to sacrifice, and the way for the periphery to industrialize was to specialize even further in nonfinished raw materials. If labor in the core made short-term sacrifices (austerity, balanced budgets, diminished welfare programs), the savings would ultimately make it possible for their nations to compete with the United States for a larger share of the world market. Profit rates would be maintained, domestic capital would stay at home, foreign capital would be attracted, and labor's fixed share of an expanding economy would be more remunerative than a larger share of a stagnant one.

Similarly, if the periphery gave up its short-term, uneconomical efforts at forced industrialization, it could make its specialized agricultural and raw materials production more large-scale, more mechanized, and ultimately more profitable. Anticipating the modernization theory of the 1960s, American economists and public figures argued that such primary commodity specialization would attract foreign capital to the road, rail, and harbor improvements that would later have industrial uses. They also pointed out that the profits from raw materials and agricultural sales in an expanding world market could be used to capitalize the next stage of development in light industry and semi-finished manufacturing. Specialized production for the world market rather than self-sufficient production for the national market was the better road to modernity. Writing for the powerful, elitist Council on Foreign Relations, famed Harvard economist Alvin Hansen acknowledged that the "legitimate goals" of the periphery included the right to industrialization. That right, however, was limited to "a moderate degree of industrialization consistent with their resources, especially the manufacture of light consumer goods." His view echoed the consensus articulated as early as 1944 by the interdepartmental Executive Committee on Economic Foreign Policy, which praised the virtues of "balanced development" that realized "productivity and . . . income by making economic use of those resources in which a country has a comparative advantage."

Future Secretary of State Dean Acheson summarized America's free market vision of productionism in 1943 when he told a congressional committee that what would be required after the war was "an arrangement which has the effect of increasing production in the world, of consumption and employment, and reducing the barriers of trade and doing away with discrimination." A year later, at the Bretton Woods conference, the United States created the institutional infrastructure essential to the arrangement Acheson envisioned. The International Bank for Reconstruction and Development (the World Bank) was to provide long-term funding for the reconstruction of postwar Europe and, later, for Third World development. Dominated by the United States (which subscribed to one-third of its $9.1 billion capital and held one-third of its directorships), its lending policies were expected to favor those nations that played by the American rules of internationalism and to penalize those that leaned toward economic nationalism and managed trade.

Institutional twin to the World Bank was the International Monetary Fund (IMF). Operating with a $7.1 billion budget, it was designed to induce deficit trading nations to avoid currency devaluation as a means to correct their imbalance and to opt instead for deflationary spending cuts that would make their exports more price competitive. Also dominated by the United States, the IMF aimed at a world of free convertibility. Essential to the maximization of world trade, foreign exchange earned by sales to one trading partner had to be freely convertible to gold or any other foreign currency if it was to be used to buy from yet another trading partner. Aiming also at stable and predictable exchange rates, the IMF sanctified the U.S. dollar as the benchmark against which all other currencies would be valued. No one in 1944 anticipated the events of three decades later when the Bretton Woods system would collapse and the American dollar and American trade would begin their long decline. For the moment, the more pressing issue was how to transform the World Bank and the IMF from paper institutions into functioning ones, how to change the American dream of free trade and free convertibility to the reality of a free world.

Selling the American Dream to Western Europe

Selling the American vision to other members of the world-system was no mean chore. The European core and much of the periphery, especially Asia, had compelling reasons to resist American plans. Similarly, the Soviet Union, with its ambivalent relationship to the world-system, eventually chose not to play by American rules, especially when American policy hardened and made the rules more stringent than those established earlier by the Yalta system. The Soviets ultimately proved the greatest obstacle to American hegemony and its blueprint for a new world order, hence the Cold War. One can make the case, however, that Western Europe was of even greater concern to American policymakers in 1945 and 1946.

Some European leaders endorsed economic internationalism and invited America's hegemonic efforts to impose it on Europe; "empire by invitation," it has been called. Robert Schuman, Georges Bidault, Jean Monnet, and others saw transnational economic institutions and eventual European economic unification as the wave of the future. International control of the Ruhr, the European Coal and Steel Authority, and the European common market sprang, in part, from the minds of such leaders. They reflected three motivations. They sought to stifle the dangerous tendencies of German nationalism by integrating the German economy into a larger European context. They sought to induce Britain to eschew its special relationship to the old British empire and to use its still considerable financial power to stimulate European productivity. Finally, they sought to become competitive with the United States in world markets. These unificationists saw their own historic nationalism as their worst economic enemy. The quest for national self-sufficiency had spawned and artificially protected inefficient and unprofitable industries that sold into limited national markets too small to permit large-scale production and at prices too high to be competitive in a free market. Imperialism had attempted to overcome the handicap by enlarging the market, which made larger production runs possible, and by providing cheap raw materials from within one's own trading bloc. But imperialism's monopolistic character also shut European producers out of global competition, at home and in their empires, that might have forced them to be more efficient. European economic integration, therefore, could become the postwar means to overcome the nationalistic obstacles preventing Europe from wresting its share of world markets from the dominant American economy.

Despite such advocacy of European internationalism, most European governments reembraced their prewar doctrines of economic nationalism and resisted American efforts to change their minds. Such preference grew from pressures at home and from their assessment of their situation abroad. As the American concept of productionism anticipated, much of the internal pressure on these countries came from the European working classes. Empowered by their key role in the war effort and embittered by fifteen years of economic deprivation, they were determined to use their political clout to get government commitment to full employment and social safety net programs. As a consequence, European governments were under great pressure to regulate the economy in ways that insured a larger share of national income for labor. On the other hand, those governments doubted they could generate labor's share through free competition in the world market, at least not in the short run. Free market competition served the United States well, for it possessed comparative advantages in a whole range of high-profit enterprises; but the free market severely penalized those less blessed with such advantages. Forced to compete with the United States in an open, free market world, Europe feared being stripped of its overseas colonies and economic spheres of influence and being threatened even in its own home markets.

Responding to labor pressure from within and fearful of American competition from without, Europe began in 1946 to experiment with nationalistic policies that smacked more of the prewar order than the postwar one desired by the United States. At home, European governments moved toward greater regulation (sometimes even management) of the economy, attempting to raise labor's share of income while restraining the flight of capital. Included in that economic regulation were brief flings with higher tariffs and currency controls to protect the home market for domestic producers, minimize the trade deficit with the United States, and ward off external pressure for deflation and spending cuts. At the same time, they tried to insure themselves of a share of the periphery by exempting their formal administrative colonies from the American open door. Even when they moved toward acceptance of political independence for the colonies (for example, the British in India in 1947), they attempted to retain some arrangement that favored their own trade and capital and discriminated against others, like the Americans. In short, the Europe of 1946 seemed to be moving toward a semiautarkic system somewhere between the German bilateralism of the 1930s and the American multilateralism of the 1940s, but probably closer to the former. European leaders envisioned not a unitary free world but a system divided into compartments and spheres (the Americas, the Russian empire, and Europe and its overseas dependents in Asia and Africa). And while trade among those regional blocs would remain important, individual states would regulate and limit trade in ways that would maintain a trade balance and protect the integrity of their domestic programs.

If all that were so, why then did Europe eventually accept American hegemony and the multilateral vision that went with it? The diplomacy of the British loan in 1946 suggests an answer. Great Britain had an enormous need for American dollars in 1946. Although desperate to import American machinery, electrical equipment, and raw materials for its own industrial revitalization, it lacked sufficient dollars to pay for them and had no immediately prospective means to earn such dollars. The United States, for its part, regarded the British sterling bloc, the Commonwealth, as the chief bottleneck to world trade. The collective sense among American leaders was that eliminating British restrictions on converting Commonwealth pounds to dollars would, in one giant step, unplug the stoppage that kept postwar trade at depression levels.

The British loan of 1946 was the trade-off that gave dollars to the British and greater access to the sterling bloc to the Americans. To describe the loan's essentials, the United States gave Great Britain a long-term, low-interest loan of $3.8 billion. The British paid for that loan with a promise that pounds sterling would be made freely convertible to dollars within a year. That seemingly innocuous concession literally implied the demise of British economic management at home and economic control of its dominions. Up to this juncture, the British had used convertibility controls as the chief means of minimizing their trade deficit with the United States while protecting their labor programs against deflationary tendencies. Having been faced with the options of cutting back on domestic spending or cutting back on American imports, Britain had chosen the latter. It had rationed the pounds that could be converted to dollars in order to limit how much British consumers could spend on lower-priced American goods. Free convertibility now ruled out that option and left the Labor Party government with no alternative save the ironic and deflationary one of cutting government spending and prolabor programs. In effect, American internationalism required that, when the dictates of the world market and the policies of individual states came into conflict, the former had to prevail.

Free convertibility also threatened British control of its overseas client-states. World War II ended with Great Britain owing significant amounts of money to India, Egypt, Australia, and other overseas dependencies for goods and services provided during the war. Britain had paid for them with a series of paper transactions that deposited funds in what were known as blocked currency accounts. In effect, this practice created a special form of sterling similar to the German aski mark of the 1930s, one that could not be converted to dollars and could be spent only on purchases from Great Britain. It was one way for the British to continue economic dominion even as they lost political dominion over colonies, like India, and protectorates, like Egypt. With the end of convertibility controls, the British faced the certain prospect that India, Egypt, Australia, and others would convert the newly unblocked sterling to dollars in order to buy comparable goods and services from the United States at prices cheaper than Great Britain could offer. Along with this might come a drift of British dependencies out of the sterling trade bloc into a multilateral system dominated by the United States. If that occurred, then the Soviet prediction might well come to pass: that Great Britain would "be reduced to second-rate power" and the "United States . . . then remain the only capitalist Great Power."

Despite the implications of free convertibility, the British accepted it as a necessary price. Unwilling to adopt a painful, Soviet-style forced reindustrialization, Britain found the transfer of American technology, goods, and raw materials essential to British reconstruction. And borrowing the dollars seemed the only way to pay for them. As it turned out, the British did not have to pay the full freight for the 1946 loan. Free convertibility created such a mass run on the pound sterling by its domestic and foreign holders that it brought the British economy to the brink of financial ruin. So, in order to save its major trading partner, the United States had to let the British revert to controlled semiconvertibility. Indeed, more than a decade passed before, in 1958, the British pound and other European currencies became freely convertible to dollars. So the 1946 loan revealed something of the prematurity of the American effort to convert Europe to its vision of internationalism. Yet it showed some of the potency of American dollar diplomacy in winning over reluctant European critics, and it revealed much about which way the wind was blowing.

Confronting the Periphery: The China Tangle

Converting the periphery to the American way of viewing and doing things presented problems of a different nature. In the immediate postwar period, the issue was less the periphery's dissatisfaction with its specialized role as primary commodity producer (though that would soon become apparent) than the political instability that prevented much of the periphery from playing any economic role at all. This was especially true in Asia where anticolonial uprisings and political independence movements destabilized French Indochina, the Dutch East Indies, and British Malaya and stymied the resumption of traditional core-periphery trade. Most especially was this true of China, where the long-running civil war that began in the 1920s accelerated, nullifying American hopes for the role China might play in the political, military, and economic life of postwar Asia.

Asia presented a dilemma for the United States that it did not face in Europe. In confronting it in 1946, America was forced to make some serious revisions to its postwar dream of an ideal world. The problem with Asia was that it possessed only one industrial nation, namely Japan. That meant that any postwar reindustrialization of Japan presented potential dangers not apparent in German reindustrialization. A reconstructed Germany might be counterbalanced by a reconstructed Britain, France, Belgium, and Netherlands. It could be subsumed within the framework of a larger European industrial core. A reconstructed Japan, however, would have no natural counterweights in Asia. Possessing singular power in the region, it would tend to regain great freedom of action as it regained industrial strength. Past Japanese behavior in the 1920s and 1930s made American leaders fearful that a revivified Japan would be tempted to try unilateral expansion in Asia whenever world circumstances permitted it.

Economic logic had to give way to strategic considerations. Japan seemingly could not be reindustrialized without its becoming an Asian policeman that could not be trusted or easily controlled. So, in 1945–

46, America leaned toward a strategy that would contradict Japan's comparative advantage. Japanese industry would be decentralized and scaled down through the break-up of the prewar monopolies and the forfeit of industrial reparations to its wartime Asian victims. Some American policymakers favored the creation of alternative industrial centers in China and perhaps Indonesia, the Philippines, or Korea, partly financed by Japanese reparations. In this Asia of multiple, semi-developed industrial centers, economic power would be somewhat equalized; so political-military power would depend more on population, size, and geography. China, not Japan, would be the logical Asian peacekeeper, performing the role first envisioned for it in Roosevelt's concept of the Four Policemen.

The Chinese civil war wrecked all. Waged between the Kuomintang (KMT—the Chinese nationalists) and the Chinese Communist Party (CCP), this decades-long struggle renewed itself in scale and ferocity after Japan's defeat in 1945. In this internecine encounter, the KMT enjoyed the moral approval of the United States and a billion dollars of war and postwar aid. It even benefited from the 1945 Treaty of Friendship and Alliance with the USSR and Stalin's efforts to discourage the CCP from a revolutionary attempt to seize power. Nonetheless, the KMT fared poorly, partly because of the burdens of uncontrollable inflation and its own corruption, and partly because of the mass peasant support and superior tactics of the CCP.

By early 1946, American hopes of an outright nationalist victory were dead, and the only hope for China lay in a negotiated stabilization agreement. Consequently, President Truman sent General of the Army, General George C. Marshall on his famous mission to China, to arrange formation of a coalition government dominated by the KMT but with communist participation. The proposed union disintegrated before the incompatible parties even got to the altar. A February cease-fire broke down by mid-spring, and by the fall the KMT and CCP were waging wholesale war in Manchuria with the latter seeming to have the upper hand. By the end of 1946, it was clear that the nationalists could not win the civil war, and the best the United States could hope for was a long, stalemated struggle that at least avoided a communist triumph. The USSR concurred in that hope, but out of fear that a unified China, even a communist one, might be more of a danger than an aid to Russian interests in Asia. In any case, it was clear that no acceptable Chinese regime would play the role desired for it by American leaders. Spurred on by that realization, in 1947 those policymakers reassessed their Japanese policy and eventually followed the reverse course, reindustrializing Japan after all. Even that flip-flop, however, did not mean that the United States had given up on China. As John Foster Dulles, future secretary of state, put it: "[The United States] must get away from the idea that this . . . is the last word as to what is going to happen in China. There has never been those final last words as regards China in the past, and I do not think it is so now."

Russia and Its Options

The effort to integrate Russia into the world-system on American terms has properly received great scholarly attention, for the failure of that effort produced the Cold War—a prolonged state of belligerency without actual fighting. By the end of 1946, the Yalta system had collapsed and the Cold War had begun. The ambiguity over Germany and Eastern Europe did not produce a softer Russian policy on Germany nor its acceptance of democratic capitalist regimes in Eastern Europe. Ambiguity instead devolved into a more hardened bipolarization between Russia and America over the future organization of Europe and of its Middle Eastern periphery. Neither economic diplomacy nor atomic diplomacy by the United States persuaded the Soviet Union to make its accommodation with American preeminence and American prescriptions. Indeed, both strategies might have been counterproductive. By reviving the specter of "capitalist encirclement," they may have strengthened the political power of those Soviet authorities who wished to tighten Russian control over its new postwar spheres, build atomic weapons, modernize the military, and encourage disturbances in the world-system that would preoccupy the United States and make it less threatening to Soviet security.

The USSR per se was not then very important to the United States. Its importance derived from the fact that its very existence complicated the overarching American task of reconstructing Western Europe and integrating it into a global free market. Russia did, after all, control Eastern Europe, an historic source of food, raw materials, and markets for Western Europe, and thus important to the latter's recovery. It did possess political and ideological ties with some political parties and trade unions in Western Europe and it did possess substantial military power, making it automatically of concern to Europeans. In addition, Russia's example of five year economic plans and forced industrialization offered Europe an alternative model of state capitalism and economic autarky to the American model of economic internationalism. To a Europe, leaning to the left and nationalist options, these factors constituted an inducement to work out barter arrangements and closer political relationships with the Soviet Union. They tempted Europe to play the Russian card in ways that might further circumscribe American access to the Eurasian land mass.

In that context, the issue in 1945 and 1946 was whether or not Russian international goals and policies would be reconciled with the

American goal of rebuilding and reintegrating capitalist Europe. On what terms, if any, should Russia be readmitted to a world-system that had expelled it after the Bolshevik Revolution of 1917? To properly understand the issue one must realize that it was not a new issue but a recurring one. Russia, both czarist and communist, had always possessed an ambivalent relationship to the world-system. Historically, Russia had evolved as an empire, fueled by migration and colonization both eastward and westward. Although imposing in size and numbers, Russia was economically backward, and imperial czars had often tried to nullify the consequences of that backwardness by attempting to insulate Russia from more modern Europe. As a result, in modern history the Russian empire often functioned as an area outside the world-system. At other times, Russian leaders self-consciously opted for closer ties to the West, either out of military necessity (the Napoleonic Wars, for example), or out of nascent modernization impulses, borrowing from the West (capital and technology) in order to catch up with the West. In effect, prerevolutionary Russia vacillated between contrary impulses to isolate itself from or integrate itself into the world-system. And the system itself reacted with equal ambivalence. Modernizing Russia as part of the system looked to be a profitable undertaking, but Russian size and military power made it a risky one.

Central Europe's failure to follow Russia's revolutionary example led the USSR to partially withdraw from the world-system and attempt to create a socialist enclave—an external world. But foreign intervention and capitalist encirclement, the decimation of the working class by civil war, and the opposition of the peasantry all exacerbated an existing distortion in the Russian economy dubbed *war communism:* inordinate amounts of scarce resources went into a modern military industry while all too little went into agriculture and civilian industry. This created a society at once modern and fearsome yet backward and ineffectual.

Under Stalin, this war communism devolved into another variant of state capitalism. The state simply replaced private corporations in accumulating capital, disciplining workers, appropriating surplus, and making investments. This state capitalism, in turn, coexisted in shifting tension and tolerance with "black capitalism" in consumer goods and services (a black market version of free enterprise). In effect, Russia was experimenting with its own varieties of economic nationalism as a strategy to catch up with and overtake Western capitalism. Save for a radical ideology, which it used to legitimize its actions, the Russian state under commissars was not unlike the Russian state under czars. Stalin had more in common with Peter the Great than with Karl Marx.

Next to the emergence of American hegemony, the reemergence of Russia as an actor in world affairs was the most significant consequence of World War II. Its reentry into the world-system left Stalinist Russia with two options. It could remain inside that system and attempt to realize Russian ambitions through peaceful coexistence with internationalist America, or it could insulate itself from that world-system, integrate its wartime gains into an enlarged Russian empire, and pursue its goals through an adversarial relationship with the capitalist world. A number of factors, both foreign and domestic, pulled the Soviet Union and Stalin in both directions in 1945 and 1946.

Staying inside the world-system offered greater rewards for the USSR in the first twelve months after the final end of World War II. The greatest reward was the possibility of influencing public policy and future choices for the western, industrialized two-thirds of defeated Germany. So long as coexistence remained the norm, Russia had a chance of benefiting from German industry, by receiving either dismantled equipment or a significant share of industrial production. Once the Iron Curtain descended, however, the West would be the sole beneficiary of German productivity. It would also be in a position, if it so chose, to rearm the Germans and integrate them politically and militarily, as well as economically, into a transnational framework. Western Europe would be safe from German revanchism, but would Russia be?

In addition, staying inside the system offered the Soviet Union a better chance for realizing the traditional Russian geopolitical desire for warm-water access to the oceanic highways of the world. Russia had historically sought access to the Persian Gulf and the Mediterranean Sea only to be blocked by Britain's containment policy in Afghanistan, Iran, and Turkey. In 1944, Stalin had agreed to respect the British sphere of influence in Greece (a commitment he largely honored), but he had made no such commitments on points east of Greece. Given Russian anticipation of Britain's decline as a world power, the chance to expand Russia's presence in Iran and Turkey was more propitious than it was likely to be in the foreseeable future. But the prospects might improve if Russia maintained a peaceful relationship with the United States. Given American hostility to Britain's closed door policies, the United States might even welcome an Anglo-Russian competition that might reduce British influence in the Near East while keeping Russia's expanded presence within reasonable bounds. On the other hand, a clearly confrontational relationship between Russia and the West would assuredly lead Britain and the United States to bury the hatchet and make common cause against any Russian encroachment. In the end, the USSR would face an American opponent in the Persian Gulf and the Mediterranean far more powerful than prewar Britain had been.

Extending wartime cooperation was also a way for the Soviets to strengthen communist parties in Western Europe. The political left had enjoyed an enormous postwar resurgence, especially in France and

Reasons for Russia
wanting good relations w/ West. - Western Communism
                                  - Access to Med
United States Foreign Policy in the Cold War — Growth & Modernization   41

Italy. With its stature enhanced by its wartime role in anti-Nazi resistance movements, and that of many conservatives tarnished by pro-Nazi collaboration, the European left was in a position to challenge centrist reformers for the opportunity to lead the construction of the war-torn continent. Often winning 20 to 30 percent of the popular vote, European communists were powerful enough to demand and often get cabinet positions in coalition governments, like de Gaulle's in France. This postwar renewal of popular front governments was likely to enhance the power of the left and put it in a position to influence public policy on reconstruction. Given the traditionally close ties between western European communist parties and Moscow, this was tantamount to saying that Russia could have some say in European policy choices.

All this was partly contingent on Russia's remaining inside the world-system and enjoying a certain legitimacy that then could rub off on its European comrades. If, however, Russia retreated into Stalin's earlier "socialism in one [bloc]," the European left and Soviet influence would face likely demise. First, western European communist parties would become open to charges of disloyalty, of collaborating with an external, alien world whose existence was threatening to European security. Second, it was eminently predictable that any Russian self-isolation would be followed by instructions to western European communist parties to abandon popular front coalition politics and reembrace the revolutionary militancy of the early 1930s (the so-called Third Period of the Communist International). If this happened, the tactic of working outside the system would only isolate European communists on the radical fringe of European politics and further open them to charges of marching to Moscow's orders rather than meeting the needs of their own working classes.

A final reason for Russia to stay on good terms with the West was that sustaining the spirit of Yalta and allied unity would offer more means for promoting Russian growth and modernization. Self-isolation and a hostile relationship with the West would necessitate continued, massive military spending that would further distort the misshapened Russian economy and delay the material rewards ("bread and butter socialism," as Khrushchev later called it) long promised to the Russian people. Peaceful coexistence, however, might not only redirect capital from the military to the civilian economic sector but maintain access to Western economies whose technology transfers were essential if Russian modernization was not to lag hopelessly behind core capitalist countries. Crucial here was atomic technology. Setting aside the issue of military usage, many Russians viewed nuclear power at the cutting edge in the future of industrial energy and propulsion. An adversarial relationship with the West would perpetuate not only an American atomic bomb monopoly but a significant Western technological lead in the refining of fissionable materials and the development of peaceful industrial uses of atomic energy. Coexistence, however, might mean a Russian share in that technology.

While all these factors produced cooperationist tendencies in Russian policy during 1945 and 1946, other elements pushed Stalin in the other direction—toward withdrawal from the world-system—primarily the desire to protect Russian control in Eastern Europe. The problem with coexistence was its two-way character. While cooperation facilitated Soviet input into the German issue and European reconstruction, it also made it possible for the West to insist on some say in Eastern Europe. Anglo-American demands for free elections or for economic open doors kept alive the option of democratic capitalism in Eastern Europe. And that option was anathema to many Soviet leaders who feared that historic hostilities and pro-Western economic ties would ultimately produce governments in Eastern Europe that were not only anticommunist but anti-Russian. The former might be tolerable, but the latter was not. The region was simply too vital as a defensive buffer to be spared, a fact attested to in 1939 when Russia had conquered and absorbed the Baltic republics and the eastern third of Poland. From this viewpoint, withdrawing from the world-system into self-containment offered a seemingly sure means of imposing "Red Army socialism" in Eastern Europe and creating a series of satellite protectorates that would act as a Great Wall between the capitalist world and the Russian empire.

A second factor that favored Russian isolationism was Stalin's enduring need to maintain social control in Russia itself. He had sought to do so through coercion in the purges of the late 1930s, but the exigencies of waging war later forced him to stress consensus-building instead. The basis of that consensus was Russian parochialism—defense of the holy homeland against alien invaders. It was in the name of Russian nationalism rather than international communism that Stalin led his warring country. That sufficed nicely so long as the war was one of self-defense fought on Russian territory, but the transition to an offensive war and the movement of millions of Russian soldiers and their intellectual cadres into Eastern and Central Europe altered circumstances dramatically. Its revolutionary ideology dulled by four years of neglect, Russian national parochialism had no ally in confronting the cosmopolitan forces it encountered in its victorious march. New cultures, new ideologies, new ways of viewing and doing things were strewn in the path of the Russian army, until it met the ultimate "other" when American and Russian soldiers embraced on the banks of the Elbe River. These encounters reinforced parochial suspiciousness, but they also provoked curiosity, and curiosity can kill consensus. The longer the Russian army maintained routine contact with Westerners, friends and foes alike, the more susceptible it would be to variegated, pluralist influences. In that context, dropping an Iron Curtain between Russia and the West and imposing more conformist regimes in the East seemed a way of keeping the other world fearsome rather than fascinating, and a way of buttressing the Stalinist regime inside Russia.

Finally, Russian tendencies to withdraw from the world-system were reinforced by the doomsday thinking prevalent in some Russian intellectual circles at the end of World War II. It held that postwar capitalism would cause the world to drift back into another 1930s-style great depression and that the consequent autarkic tendencies and nationalistic rivalries would produce another global crisis, perhaps yet another global war. If that happened, then Russia would face anew, as it had from 1939 to 1941, the possibility of internecine conflict in the West being redirected against the Soviet Union. To prevent that eventuality, proponents of such theories advised Stalin to consolidate Russia's wartime gains, integrate its new territories into the Russian empire, step up its military spending—to make the Soviet world so impregnable that capitalists would fight only amongst themselves and leave Russia in a position to affect the future direction of a world destroyed by capitalism's third and finally successful try of the century at suicide.

The Beginnings of the Cold War

Such end-of-capitalism millenialism had little impact on Stalin in late 1945 and early 1946. Inherently cautious, the Soviet leader believed "the bourgeoisie is very strong" (as he told Tito) and that capitalism had great resilience as a world economy. Indeed, Western Europe, aided by the lower fuel costs of a mild winter, showed signs of surprising economic recovery rather than of imminent collapse. Moreover, as late as May 1946, Russia still retained some hope that it would influence and benefit from Western policy in Germany and that it might yet share in nuclear technology. The ratio of rewards to liabilities seemed better for coexistence than for confrontation.

Nowhere was this more apparent than in the Russian strategic sphere in Eastern Europe. American demands for political pluralism and market economies proved less substantive than rhetorical and tactical. American leaders invoked them to satisfy domestic voters or as a stalling device to deflect Russian pressure on other issues. For example, the London Foreign Ministers Conference in September 1945 saw the United States bring the meeting to a stalemate partly over the lack of free elections in Bulgaria. Its real purpose, however, was to prevent Russia from adding Japan to the agenda in an effort to secure Russian participation in its occupation. Secretary of State James F. Byrnes privately admitted that the United States was "going off in the same unilateral way [in Japan] as the Russians were going off in the Balkans."

Two months later at the Moscow Foreign Ministers Conference, after the Japanese issue was safely resolved in American favor, the United States recognized the Bulgarian government without a murmur of disapproval about the means of its election.

The superficial nature of America's Eastern European policies made them more a nuisance than a threat to Soviet regional interests. That permitted Russia the luxury of approaching Eastern Europe in a more pragmatic way, rather than having to make an all-or-nothing choice between open doors or a closed curtain. As a consequence, Soviet policy differed from country to country. In Poland, Romania, and Bulgaria, the Iron Curtain (Winston Churchill gave it the name) descended harshly and rapidly in 1945–46. Geography and history determined their fate. Poland's northern plains were the natural avenue of invasion into Russia and the one used by the bulk of the *Wehrmacht* in 1941. Romania's and Bulgaria's seacoasts faced Russia across the Black Sea. Both had allied themselves with Nazi Germany, and Romania's Danube River delta had been a jumping-off point into southwestern Russia. Elsewhere in Eastern Europe the Russians operated in more cautious ways. In Finland they tolerated (as they still do) a noncommunist regime that maintained economic ties with the West while it remained firmly committed to a foreign policy friendly toward the USSR. In Hungary they accepted a conservative rout of the communist party at the polls and peaceful relations with a noncommunist government until the spring of 1947, after the Cold War had begun. In Czechoslovakia they lived with a coalition government dominated by independent, democratic socialists until 1948 when a domestic crisis, partly generated by America's Marshall Plan, led to a communist takeover. In Yugoslavia Stalin advised his fellow communist, Josip Tito, to forego a communist revolution and share power with noncommunists—an unwanted piece of advice that helped provoked Yugoslavia's break with Russia in 1948. In its occupied third of Austria, the Russians rang down the Iron Curtain in 1947 only to ring it up again in 1955 by, surprisingly, signing a peace treaty with that country. In many ways, Russian policy in Eastern Europe reminded one of traditional American policy in the Caribbean, where the United States used formal control in some countries and informal control in others, depending on geographic circumstances and local conditions—foreign policy that was more utilitarian than doctrinaire.

This cautious Russian commitment to coexistence eroded throughout much of 1946, chiefly because American policy hardened in ways that implicitly upped the ante for Russia's admission to the world-system, President Truman declared that Yalta was simply a wartime "interim agreement," subject to reassessment in light of the realities of postwar power redistribution. Moreover, he made clear that in any necessary new arrangements he would follow a tough negotiating line. "I am tired of babying the Soviets," said Truman in January 1946. The attitude carried over into American policy on the Middle East, atomic energy, and Germany.

In the Near East, Russian probes into the old British sphere quickly corrected the USSR's mistaken assumption about American policy. While the United States might not have minded some loosening of British control in the area, it had no intention of letting any other nation fill the vacuum. Instead, it wished to supplant the British and to continue their policy of keeping Russia bottled up in the Black Sea and the Caspian Sea. In Iran, Russia used political pressure and military threats to coerce from that country a share of oil concessions comparable to that given the English and Americans. However, American invocation of the UN Security Council and a stern demand that Russia fulfill its wartime pledge to leave northern Iran were sufficient to effect Russian withdrawal—without an Iranian oil concession. In Turkey, Russian pressure to get a share of strategic control over the Dardanelles (an historic Russian objective) produced another American warning and the first postwar dispatch of a carrier task force to the region. The result once more was a Russian tactical retreat. And in Greece, Russia lent only moral support to the civil war waged by Greek communists and other antimonarchists, though it feared that communist Yugoslavia's material aid to that revolution might signal a Pan-Balkan movement independent of Stalin's control. Even Stalin's nominal and indirect involvement, as we shall see, would be sufficient to justify the stern Truman Doctrine response in early 1947.

Nineteen forty-six witnessed a toughening of America's atomic diplomacy as well, after three months of vacillation in late 1945. Most American leaders continued to see America's atomic bomb monopoly as something to hoard and exploit in postwar power brokering with the Soviets. A few, however, shared Secretary of War Stimson's belief that "if we fail to approach [the Russians] now and merely continue to negotiate with them, having this weapon rather ostentatiously on our hip, their suspicions and their distrust of our purposes and motives will increase."

The embodiment of this vacillation was Truman's new secretary of state, James F. Byrnes. At the London Foreign Ministers Conference, Byrnes had warned his Russian counterpart, V. M. Molotov, in humor too black to be funny, that if he did not "cut out all this stalling and let us get down to work, I am going to pull an atomic bomb out of my pocket and let you have it." Sobered by the failure of that conference and the apparent ineffectualness of atomic diplomacy, Byrnes went to the Moscow conference at the end of 1945 in a very different frame of mind. Voicing his opposition to "using the bomb for political purposes," he called for the international control of atomic energy. Promising that the American bomb monopoly would "not be unnecessarily prolonged," he affirmed the ultimate objective of "unlimited exchange of scientific and industrial information."

Byrnes' deviant venture in depoliticizing the atomic bomb brought the whole weight of the American foreign policy establishment down upon him. The bipartisan powers on the Senate Foreign Relations Committee, Arthur H. Vandenberg, Republican from Michigan, and Tom Connally, Democrat from Texas; the State Department professionals, like Roosevelt's former under secretary, Sumner Welles, and Russian expert George F. Kennan; military spokesmen, like Secretary of the Navy James Forrestal and Admiral William Leahy; and a host of leaders from elite organizations like the Council on Foreign Relations, all agreed that the atomic bomb monopoly was crucial to Europe's sense of security and therefore to the success of American reconstruction policies. The monopoly, therefore, was to be sustained until the task was completed.

Providing the rationale for that unyielding approach was George F. Kennan's "long telegram" from Moscow in February 1946 (later the basis for his famous "Mr. X" article in 1947). Kennan characterized the USSR as an insatiably expansionistic society driven by its revolutionary Marxist-Leninist ideology, its paranoid sense of national insecurity, and its Stalinist totalitarianism. Western reasonableness, he argued, would only whet the Russian appetite in much the fashion that appeasement had done with Hitler in the 1930s. Only Western strength and resolve, applying a counter-force at every weak point between the Russian empire and the free world, could "contain" the Soviet Union. Its expansionism thus frustrated, the communist regime would eventually collapse, be overthrown, or mellow into a form more like those in the West.

That containment policy consensus resulted in Byrnes' fall from favor with President Truman and ended any Soviet hopes that coexistence could lead to a share in atomic technology. The Acheson-Lillienthal plan, put forward in the spring of 1946, still retained some of Byrnes' flexibility, but it sharply upped the price that Russia would have to pay: international control of Russia's essential uranium supplies, international determination of the number and location of nuclear power plants in the USSR, international on-site inspection, and, finally, suspension of the Russian atomic bomb project. In the meantime, the American atomic bomb monopoly would continue, and not until all other stages had been achieved would the United States destroy its nuclear weapons. In turn, the Acheson-Lillienthal proposal was altered and subsumed by the far more rigid Baruch plan. It insisted that Russia give up its UN veto power where atomic energy issues were concerned, and it refused to establish any timetable for the accomplishment of the stages. Bernard Baruch, the plan's author, neither expected Russia to accept the plan nor regretted that it would not. Predictably, Russia said no, and it stepped up the pace of its own atomic bomb project.

Neither the unhappy denouement of this attempt to address the atomic energy issue nor the Middle Eastern competition, in and of themselves, was sufficient to cause the Cold War. The former was as much consequence as cause, and the latter was a predictable part of the power probes and territorial readjustments that take place after any major war that produces a rapid and dramatic shift in the balance of power. But there were other fundamental causes for Cold War, and by 1946 one had emerged from the ashes of World War II that was so crucial as to be irreconcilable. The issue was Germany's future. No one issue would so polarize East and West, in 1946 and on through the Berlin blockade of 1948, the Berlin crisis of 1961, and the missile deployment controversy of the 1980s. Indeed, one can argue without much exaggeration that, before 1950, Germany was considered the *causa belli* of the Cold War, and it has never since been far removed from center stage.

For both the USSR and the United States, Germany was central to their concepts of national security. Two world wars had amply demonstrated to the Soviets the grave dangers and possible consequences of allowing Germany to reindustrialize and rearm, while it perhaps still harbored notions of realizing the German amibitions of 1914 and 1939. Even the unlikely prospect of a German resolution, so dear to Russian hopes in 1919, no longer struck a responsive chord. Given a quarter century to ossify, the communist revolution had become a Russian empire. Communist internationalism had been nationalized into Stalin's "socialism in one country," and new centers of world radicalism were not welcome unless they were clearly subordinate to the Soviet Union. That was true of Mao's China, Tito's Yugoslavia, and of communist guerrillas in the Greek civil war. It would be even more true of a core colossus like Germany.

For the United States, the logic of economic internationalism quickly carried it away from the Treasury Department's hard policy. Germany pastoralized would be a Germany of radically reduced living standards and per capita income, perhaps ripe for a move to the left and rapprochement with Russia. Germany reindustrialized would be Europe's most cost-competitive producer and its most effective consumer. Without full German participation in the European economy there could be no European recovery; without that, there could be no revitalization of the world-system; without that, there could be no American prosperity or any permanency to American free enterprise. Not unmindful of the German role in past intracapitalist wars and aware that France especially shared Russia's fears of German revanchism, the United States thought that reindustrialization (and even remilitarization) could safely be accomplished if Germany were integrated into a collective Atlantic community via a common market or a multinational armed force.

Those contradictory perspectives on Germany clashed frontally in 1946. The key issues were reparations to the USSR and the level of German industrial productivity. Russia actually decreased productivity in its occupation zone and pressured the West to keep its productivity levels as low as possible. At the same time, Russia stripped the meager industrial capability from its eastern zone while prodding the West to deliver to the Soviets plant and equipment from its more industrialized areas of control, all for shipment back to the Soviet Union. In May, any semblance of compatibility vanished when the United States stopped all shipments of industrial reparations from the western zones to Russia and adopted the so-called First Charge Principle: namely, that German productivity and its capacity to pay for Western imports took precedence over Russian reparation demands. By late summer, Secretary of State Byrnes made his famous Stuttgart speech (in the heart of the German industrial region) and publicly affirmed a new priority. It boosted the Germans' right to control their own destiny, withheld approval of Poland's absorption of East Prussia, and promised that American troops would remain in Germany. Finally, in December, the Americans and the British integrated their occupation zones, creating Bizonia and laying the foundation for what would soon be the Federal Republic of Germany. Faced with this fait accompli, Russia stopped its removal of German industry to the east and began producing German goods on German soil. Clearly, the Russians were there to stay as well. By the end of the year, the outlines of two Germanys were visible to one and all. The Russian-American Cold War had begun.

The Cold War at Home

If Russia was now the external devil, there was also an "enemy within" that threatened America's hegemonic internationalism in 1946. It had appeared in 1945 when popular pressure had forced the American government to commence a rapid demobilization of the American armed services. But it became more dramatically apparent in 1946 with the emergence of heterogeneous political groups that did not buy the logic or accept the imperatives of American hegemony, either for their constituents or for the nation as a whole. Representing both the political left and the political right, they seemed, to the centrist liberals who dominated the Democratic party of Harry Truman, to be frightening precursors of a new isolationism.

On the left were labor leaders from the more radical industrial unions, who pushed for Keynesian programs of deficit spending and full employment at home and limited, regulated trade abroad; also New Deal mavericks, like Henry Morgenthau and Harold Ickes, who entertained similar views and who assigned higher priority to German and Japanese deindustrialization than to the restoration of postwar trade; and finally internationalists, like Secretary of Commerce Henry Wallace, who did assign great value to world trade but who feared that the emerging containment policy toward Russia might needlessly sacrifice potential markets in so-called socialist countries. These groups clashed repeatedly within the administration in 1946 over its response to the wave of postwar labor strikes, its equivocation over the full employment act, its failure to prevent the hostile Taft-Hartley labor relations act, and its dismissal of Wallace from the cabinet for his public espousal of renewing Soviet-American cooperation. The clash climaxed in September 1946 when representatives of these groups formed the Progressive Citizens of America (PCA) and collectively criticized the government for retreating from New Deal domestic reform and opting for overseas adventurism instead. The organization was the nucleus of the left-wing Democrats who would bolt the party two years later and run Henry Wallace as the Progressive party candidate against President Truman.

Far more imposing were the groups on the right, whose power was evident in the congressional elections of 1946, which returned control of the legislature to the Republican party for the first time in nearly two decades. Tied closely to local chambers of commerce and to businessmen selling largely in the home market, they stressed the need for protective tariffs to safeguard that home market. Distrustful of Europeans and doubtful of America's power to restrain their autarkic tendencies, they saw more danger than promise in an American globalism and made their wariness clear by speaking against foreign aid, tariff liberalization, and participation in international banking and monetary agencies. The most principled and eloquent of these conservative critics was Senator Robert A. Taft of Ohio ("Mr. Republican"). "Our fingers will be in every pie," said he in his condemnation of American internationalism. "Our military forces will work with our commercial forces to obtain as much of world trade as we can lay our hands on. We will occupy all the strong strategic-points in the world and try to maintain a force so preponderant that none shall dare attack us. . . . Potential power over other nations, however benevolent its purposes, leads inevitably to imperialism."

Most conservatives did not share Taft's concern for potential American imperialism. Moreover, they did believe that the American free enterprise economy needed foreign outlets for its goods and capital if it was to survive. However, they saw that need best served not through a unitary world-system but through creation of an American-monopolized sphere of strategic-economic influence in one part of the planet. For them, the Monroe Doctrine was a more appropriate guide for American policy than the Open Door policy. Most, however, no longer limited their vision of an American-dominated New World simply to the Western Hemisphere (the old Fortress America policy of the 1930s). They added another arena to that of North and South America, enlarging the American sphere to include the so-called Pacific rim, meaning all those economies located on the rim of the Pacific Ocean—North America on the east and Southeast Asia, China, Korea, and Japan on the west. Spearheading this enlargement was a group called the China lobby, a loose coalition of missionary-reform groups, with sentimental attachments to China, and of West Coast businessmen (like freshman senator William Knowland), whose commercial horizons followed the course of the setting sun. Already critical of the administration's policy of trying to force the Chinese nationalists into coalition government with the communists, they would later attempt to embarrass the executive branch for its alleged loss of China.

These threats from the left and right badly frightened centrist liberals and threatened their control of mainstream politics in postwar America. Rebuilding the European core, integrating the periphery, and holding Russia in purgatory were formidable tasks even for a country of awesome power. They were impossible tasks unless the executive branch had the consensus support of Congress and the public to provide American policy with necessary laws, dollars, weapons, personnel, and moral approval. The last was the key to all the others. Anything was possible if the government and its foreign policy had the public's blessing of legitimacy. Nothing was ultimately possible without it. So in a real sense, 1946 was the beginning of a battle for legitimacy waged by liberal internationalists against the specter of born-again isolationism. The battle tactics would become clearer a year later, but they were foreshadowed by the creation in late 1946 of the Americans for Democratic Action (ADA). Proclaiming liberal internationalism as the "vital center" of American life, the ADA saw the Truman administration as the embodiment of American pragmatism and political give-and-take, committed to defending that American way against the doctrinaire extremism of both the radical left and the conservative right. Portraying themselves as tough-minded liberals or realists with a heart (a sort of sensitive-macho hybrid), they characterized the right as uncompassionate and the left as utopian. Militantly anticommunist on one hand and pro-New Deal reform on the other, the ADA perfectly embodied what later would be called Cold War liberals. It also anticipated centrist tactics in the battle for legitimacy: use anticommunism to both muzzle the left and co-opt the right. The Cold War with Russia was not the only cold war that began in 1946.

II

DIVIDING EUROPE

3

W. Averell Harriman and Elie Abel

Special Envoy to Churchill and Stalin

Averell Harriman was almost 50 when he arrived in London to serve as expediter for Lend Lease assistance in 1941–42. He then became Ambassador to Russia in autumn 1943 and remained at that critical post until January 1946. His career continued through the Truman Administration, during which he served the President briefly as Ambassador to Great Britain, then as Secretary of Commerce, director of the European Recovery Program within Europe, and finally as Special Assistant during the Korean War. After a term as Governor of New York, Harriman returned to aid President Kennedy in negotiating a settlement in Laos, and helping to smooth the way for the Test Ban Treaty. Few careers in American diplomacy have been so notable.

Harriman was not at ease with reflective literature; he never had George Kennan's philosophical and historical depth, nor Dean Acheson's urbane and sovereign style. Nonetheless, he shone in cutting through difficult conflicts, arguing for practical solutions, and energizing staff assistants who had to negotiate complex continuing issues. He moved at ease among the British elite, earned Soviet respect as a representative of capitalism (his father had founded the Union Pacific railroad), and exemplified the patrician strand in the Democratic Party that Roosevelt had also embodied. He wrote this memoir of his World War II service in conjunction with the journalist Elie Abel late in his eighties. Harriman wanted to make sure that it fully utilized his own collection of papers and carefully reported the complexity of the issues he had to deal with. He asked the present editor to help him with the project, and the recollections of the Polish issue were among the most crucial we drafted and edited together. The selection here includes chapter XIV, pp. 315–334 of *Special Envoy to Churchill and Stalin, 1941–1946* (Copyright© 1975 by W. Averell Harriman and Elie Abel) and is reprinted by permission of Random House, Inc.

The wartime conflicts over Poland—its contested postwar frontiers with the Soviet Union, and the regime it would be allowed to have—lay at the origins of U.S.-Soviet disagreement. The Polish government in London was an uneasy broad coalition of Social Democrats, democratic peasant representatives, and highly nationalist military leaders. Some had exaggerated ambitions for their postwar land; all feared Soviet intentions to dominate the country. Churchill, whose Tory political inclinations would ordinarily have favored these patriotic exiles, urgently wanted to compose wartime differences with Stalin and repeatedly urged the London Poles to come to terms on the cessions of territory that the Soviets were demanding. The London Poles' resistance enraged the Prime Minister; their accusations that the Soviets had murdered thousands of Polish officers during the brief Soviet occupation of the eastern third of their country in 1939–41 enraged the Soviets. (Of course, as Moscow finally confirmed in the spring of 1990, the suspicions were all too true.) Stalin was evidently content to see the London Poles' resistance forces within occupied Poland—the so-called Home Army—overcome in their uprising against the occupying Germans. The Soviets' delay in taking Warsaw until the Germans had finished their repression (which might have been legitimately attributed to strategic prudence); their reluctance to let the British and Americans drop relief supplies (which appeared pure cynicism); and their subsequent recognition of a virtually unknown communist exile group as the "Government" of Poland instead of the London Poles deeply distressed President Roosevelt in the fall of 1944—all the more since he wanted to be certain of Polish-American votes in the 1944 Presidential elections. On the other hand, Soviet armies continued to engage millions of Germans on the Eastern front, and Russian forces might be needed to help with the subsequent offensive against Japan. The Grand Alliance could not be disavowed; cooperation must not be endangered. Roosevelt and Churchill thus sought to work out a compromise on these painful issues at Yalta in February 1945.

The chapter selected here documents these first shadows upon Soviet-American collaboration. The view from the American embassy during these difficult months is a useful contrast to the abstract model of a capitalist world system. The history of Poland in the War is laden with controversy: first, Poles have been condemned for a rife anti-Semitism that made many of them apparently indifferent onlookers to the Nazi extermination of almost 3 million Polish Jews; second, their political representatives in London have been condemned for stubborn refusals to cooperate for the sake of the Alliance. More recently, their champions have endeavored to refute the accusations of anti-semitism, or at least to remind us how much non-Jewish Poles also suffered in this cruelest of Nazi occupations. And as Soviet condemnations of the Stalinist period grow, the preoccupations of the London Poles appear increasingly justified. The issue recurs: what sacrifices of small peoples were the Big Three prepared to countenance to preserve their own harmony? What sacrifice was required to defeat Hitler? Was there any alternative to the alliance of expediency that Soviet policy seemed to demand as the price of its immense war effort? These are all painful and difficult issues, not easily resolved even in dispassionate debate, and often subject to demagogic exaggeration on both sides. But the student is now very well served by a joint study that examines both the international context and the internal politics of the Resistance and of postwar Poland: John Coutouvidis and Jaime Reynolds, *Poland, 1939–1947* (Leicester, Leicester University Press, 1986).

Poland, the Touchstone

Again the Poles," Stalin growled. "Is that the most important question?" Those troublesome Poles, he complained to Harriman, kept him so busy that he had no time for military matters.

The date was March 3, 1944. Harriman, who had requested the Kremlin meeting on instructions from Roosevelt, replied that he too would prefer to discuss military questions, but Poland had become a pressing problem. He promised to be brief. It was not a question of time, Stalin said. The Russians had taken their position and would not recede from it: "Isn't it clear? We stand for the Curzon Line." The trouble was that the Polish government in London (he called it "the émigré government") took the Russians for fools. It was now demanding Wilno as well as Lwow. Happily, the people of Poland, who were not the same as the London émigrés, would take a different attitude. He was certain they would welcome the Red Army as liberators.

Harriman did not doubt that Stalin believed this would happen. Only later, when he learned that his troops were widely regarded as foreign invaders, did Stalin find it necessary—in Harriman's view—to impose rigid controls on Poland and Rumania. For the moment, Harriman's task was to persuade Stalin and Molotov that they should resume discussions with the Poles in London and try to negotiate a settlement instead of imposing one by brute force. It was hard going.

Roosevelt feared, Harriman said, that if the problem was not soon resolved, there would be civil war in Poland. Stalin saw no such danger. "War with whom?" he asked. "Between whom? Where?" Mikolajczyk had no troops in Poland. What about the underground force known as the Home Army? Harriman inquired. Stalin grudgingly acknowledged that the London government might have "a few agents" in Poland, but the underground, he insisted, was not large.

Harriman asked what kind of solution Stalin could envisage. He replied, "While the Red Army is liberating Poland, Mikolajczyk will go on repeating his platitudes. By the time Poland is liberated, Mikolajczyk's Government will have changed, or another government will have emerged in Poland."

Roosevelt was concerned, Harriman said, lest a new regime, formed on the basis of the Soviet proposals, should turn out to be "a hand-picked government with no popular movement behind it." Denying any such intention, Stalin nevertheless proceeded to rule out the return from exile of Polish landlords—"Polish Tories," as he called them. "Poland," he said, "needs democrats who will look after the interests of the people, not Tory landlords." Stalin added that he did not believe Churchill (a British Tory, after all) could persuade the London Poles to reshape their government and modify its policies; he was sure that Roosevelt agreed with him on the need for a democratic government in Poland.

Stalin assured Harriman, however, that he would take no immediate action on the Polish matter. The time was not ripe, he said. When Harriman remarked that there were some good men in the London government, Stalin replied, "Good people can be found everywhere, even among the Bushmen."

Not for the first time, Harriman mentioned the President's worries over public opinion in the United States. Stalin responded that he had to be "concerned about public opinion in the Soviet Union." Harriman remarked, "You know how to handle your public opinion," to which Stalin replied, "There have been three revolutions in a generation." Molotov, who had been silent through most of the interview, added without smiling, "In Russia there is an *active* public opinion which overthrows governments." When they spoke of three revolutions, Stalin and Molotov meant the uprising of 1905, the Kerensky revolution of February 1917, and the Bolshevik Revolution the following autumn. Stalin, the revolutionist, was always alert to the possibility of a new revolution, which would have to be stamped out before it got started.

Harriman's bleak interview with Stalin on March 3 was the second in a long series on the intractable Polish problem. He had gone to Moscow as ambassador in 1943 with another set of priorities in mind, military cooperation first among them. But in the months that followed Teheran, Poland was to use up much of his energy and patience. There was no end, he recalled, "of indignities and disagreeable incidents unrelated to political issues." The Russians, for example, had two broadcasting stations in the vicinity of Moscow whose location was important to American pilots in order to triangulate their approach to the Soviet capital. In spite of repeated requests, the Russians refused to disclose to the embassy more than the one well-known location. The issue disappeared when an American pilot flew over the second transmitter accidentally and marked the location.

"We were treated as potential enemies," Harriman recalled. "Our Russian staff—servants, office staff and chauffeurs—had their food-ration cards taken away because they worked for the American embassy. Kathleen had to feed them all after that, but our supplies ran short at times when a convoy was delayed or our shipments sunk. Then we would send someone out of Moscow to buy potatoes and cabbages from a collective farm."

It was the Soviet attitude toward Poland, however, that was to shake Harriman's hopes for Soviet-American cooperation more profoundly than the daily frustrations of Soviet secrecy, inefficiency and general high-handedness as they affected Lend-Lease negotiations, joint military planning, such as homely matters as potatoes, cabbages or the issuance of exit visas to Russian women who had been unpatriotic enough to marry American citizens. Yet Harriman continued to believe, long after George Kennan had given way to these frustrations, that each small victory at the expense of the Soviet bureaucracy was worth the fight; limited agreements were better than none. He accepted even minor concessions in the belief that small steps forward could lead to longer strides toward cooperation once the enveloping suspicion, as much traditional Russian as Communist, had been pierced.

But Poland was to become the touchstone of Soviet behavior in the postwar world, the first test of Stalin's attitude toward his less powerful neighbors. It was to raise troubling questions in Harriman's mind about differing war aims within the alliance and about the differing meanings attached to such simple words as "friendly" or "democratic." His role at this period surpassed the conventional bounds of ambassadorial duty. His personal convictions, which he did not hesitate to make clear in communications to the President and the State Department, were often at variance with his instructions from Washington. During his first days in Moscow, Harriman had come to believe that all the earnest talk about a free, independent Poland was likely to become academic once the Red Army occupied the country. Cordell Hull was not disposed to listen when Harriman urged upon him the supreme importance of pressing the London Poles to come to terms with the Kremlin before it was too late. Roosevelt, looking ahead to the 1944 election and the predictable wrath of the Polish voters, had pleaded with Stalin to give the Poles "a break," and above all, not to jeopardize his own re-election prospects by unilateral action. Washington treated Poland as a British problem in the first instance, one that Churchill alone might be able to solve by pressing the London Poles to reorganize their government.

Churchill and Eden had talked sternly to Mikolajczyk after Teheran, pressing him to "accept the so-called Curzon Line (prolonged through eastern Galicia) as a basis for negotiations with the Soviet Government." The Prime Minister reported to Stalin and to Roosevelt:

> I said that although we had gone to war for the sake of Poland, we had not gone to war for any particular frontier line but for the existence of a strong, free, independent Poland, which Marshal Stalin had also declared himself supporting. Moreover, although Great Britain would have fought on in any case for years until something happened to Germany, the liberation of Poland from the German grip is being achieved mainly by the enormous sacrifices and achievements of the Russian armies. Therefore Russia and her Allies had a right to ask that Poland should be guided to a large extent about the frontiers of the territory she would have . . .
>
> I advised them to accept the Curzon Line as a basis for discussion. I spoke of the compensation which Poland would receive in the North and in the West. In the North there would be East Prussia; but here I did not mention the point about Koenigsberg. In the West they would be free and aided to occupy Germany up to the line of the Oder. I told them it was their duty to accept this task and guard the frontier against German aggression towards the East . . . in this task they would need a friendly Russia behind them and would, I presumed, be sustained by the guarantee of the Three Great Powers against further German attack.[1]

Churchill appeared to draw the line, however, at forcing the Poles to reconstruct their government by a purge of the so-called reactionaries. "Do you not agree," he wrote to Stalin, "that to advocate changes within a foreign government comes near to that interference with internal sovereignty to which you and I have expressed ourselves as opposed?" Stalin did not, of course, agree.

> I think you realized [he replied on February 4] that we cannot re-establish relations with the present Polish Government. Indeed, what would be the use of re-establishing relations with it when we are not at all certain that tomorrow we shall not be compelled to sever those relations again on

account of another fascist provocation on its part, such as the "Katyn Affair"?[2]

Nor had Stalin's offer of territorial compensation at Germany's expense reconciled the Polish government to the loss of territory in the east. The Poles had seen their country partitioned in 1939 between Germany and Russia, and they looked to the Western powers to restore it. For them, the Soviet effort to annex one third of Poland looked like another cynical repartition, the evil fruit of the Hitler-Stalin pact of 1939. The Russians, understandably, had a different perspective. Poland was the foreign invader's route to Moscow (a point Stalin had made repeatedly to Harriman), not a country like any other. Both Napoleon and Hitler had marched into Russia across the Polish plain and Stalin, believing in defense in depth, was determined that it should not happen again. The Russian leadership had not forgotten or forgiven the prewar Polish government's refusal to let Soviet troops traverse Polish territory, even in the hypothetical event of their joining the British and French against the Germans. Nor had it forgotten the humiliations inflicted upon the young Red Army in 1920 by the Polish forces of Marshal Jozef Pilsudski. In taking back the strip of territory they had lost to Pilsudski after World War I and briefly reoccupied in 1939, they proposed to fix a new boundary close to the Curzon Line, itself the product of an unsuccessful earlier British effort to mediate between Poles and Russians in December 1919 and January 1920.

At the Paris Peace Conference in 1919 the Allies had decided to reconstitute a Polish state out of the wreckage of the old Austro-Hungarian, German and Czarist empires—a decision that raised serious questions about the undefined eastern frontier. In December 1919 the Supreme Council of the Allied Powers suggested a line that roughly followed the ethnic divisions of Eastern Europe: Poles living to the west of the line, White Russians to the east. The proposed new boundary would run from the East Prussian frontier in the north to the edge of eastern Galicia in the south. No effort was made at the time to push the boundary line through eastern Galicia. That fragment of Austro-Hungary, with its major city Lwow, was supposed to become a League of Nations mandated territory under Polish administration.

Neither the Polish nor the Soviet governments, however, would accept the proposals of the Peace Conference. In the spring of 1920 the new Polish republic, encouraged by the French (who hoped to build up Poland as an ally against both the Germans to the west and the Bolshevik Russians to the east), struck against the Soviet Union. Despite early successes in the field, the Polish offensive collapsed and soon the Red Army was pushing deep into Poland. For a time, in the summer of 1920, it appeared that Poland might be bolshevized at the point of a

Russian bayonet. The Poles then appealed to the Allies and, as a condition of mediation, accepted a British proposal that they withdraw to the suggested boundary of December 1919. The British terms, though, were unclear about who would control Lwow. This proposed armistice line, bearing the signature of Lord Curzon, the British Foreign Secretary, was dispatched to the Soviets on July 11, 1920. But the Soviets rejected it, continuing their advance toward Warsaw and East Prussia until they outran their supply lines. At this point the Poles, with French assistance, counterattacked and by autumn they were advancing into Russian territory.

Lenin's new Bolshevik regime—increasingly aware that the Russian people had been totally exhausted by three years of intervention and civil war, famine and economic disruption—agreed to negotiate in the winter of 1921. The result was the Treaty of Riga, which ceded to Poland a large area east of the Curzon Line, including a 150-mile-wide belt of White Russian and Ukrainian territory. It was this belt of contested land—earlier administered by czarist Russia and Austria-Hungary—that the Soviets had reoccupied in 1939, part of Stalin's price for the nonaggression treaty with Hitler.

At Teheran, after Roosevelt had made clear to Stalin that he could take no public position on the Polish dispute, Churchill had tried to draw out Stalin on the details of a frontier settlement. There was no quarrel between them on the Curzon Line, only some debate about its application to Lwow. In fact, the Curzon note of 1920 had left the future of Lwow and Galicia in limbo. Stalin returned to Moscow having accepted the Curzon Line, but insisting that Lwow must be Russian. Churchill had agreed to the Curzon Line, with Polish territorial compensation in the west, but deferred the fate of Lwow for future negotiations. Beneš, meanwhile, assured Churchill (as he had earlier assured Harriman in Moscow) that Stalin would be willing to resume relations with the London Poles, but only if they purged the anti-Soviet elements from their government and accepted the Curzon Line.

On January 6, 1944, as the Red Army was about to crash into the disputed territory, the Polish government in London issued a declaration ignoring the whole issue of new boundaries. It promised military cooperation by the underground Home Army on condition that the Soviet Union resumed diplomatic relations with the London government. Five days later, Harriman and Clark Kerr were called to the Kremlin after midnight to be handed a reply by Molotov, who explained that "as everyone else is talking about Poland it would be wrong for us to remain silent." The Soviet response gave the London Poles no quarter. It accused them of "not infrequently" playing into the hands of the Nazis, while the Union of Polish Patriots and the Soviet-sponsored Polish Army Corps under Major General Zygmunt Berling were already "operating hand in hand with the Red Army on the front against the Germans." The "emigrant Polish Government," by contrast, had shown itself "incapable of organizing the active struggle against the German invaders," the Soviet government contended.

Finding Molotov "most anxious and hopeful" for Washington's reaction, Harriman sent a message the same day pleading for a more active American role behind the scenes:

> I recognize that we should not become directly involved in attempting to negotiate this question between the two Governments. On the other hand, I cannot help but be impressed by the chaotic conditions adversely affecting our vital war interests that will probably result as Soviet troops penetrate Polish territory unless relations are re-established promptly between the two Governments.
>
> It would seem that the Poles can make a better deal now than if they wait, living as they appear to be in the hope that we and the British will eventually pull their chestnuts out of the fire.
>
> If it is clear, and I believe it is, that we will not be able to aid the Poles substantially more than we already have in the boundary dispute, are we not in fairness called upon to make plain the limitations of the help that we can give them and the fact that, in their own interest, the present moment is propitious for them to negotiate the re-establishment of relations with the Soviets?

Mikolajczyk, meanwhile, had approached Hull through his ambassador to Washington, apparently in the hope of strengthening his own hand against Churchill through a reaffirmation of the American policy of opposing territorial settlements before the end of the war. Hull's noncommittal response was that the Administration's policy against wartime settlements did not rule out negotiated agreements by mutual consent. Hull, in short, was neither as frank with the Poles as Harriman would have wished, nor as totally opposed to negotiations as Mikolajczyk may have hoped. Thus Roosevelt and Hull left the main responsibility to Churchill and Eden, even though the proposals they kept pressing on the London Poles would have raised a storm across the United States had they been made public.

When Harriman saw Molotov again on January 18, the Soviet Foreign Minister for the first time gave some indication of the Cabinet changes the Russians wanted to see before they would deal with the Poles in London. The London government must be reconstructed, Molotov said, to include Poles now living in England, the United States and the Soviet Union. These must be "honest men" who were "not tainted with fascism; men with a friendly attitude toward the Soviet Union." As possible members of the new government he volunteered the names of Dr. Oskar Lange, a Polish economist who was then teaching at the University of Chicago; Father Stanislaus Orlemanski, an obscure priest of an obscure Catholic parish in Springfield, Massachusetts; and Leo Krzcki, a trade-union leader who was then national chairman of the American Slav Congress. Mikolajczyk could remain, Molotov added, though he had doubts about the Polish Foreign Minister, Tadeusz Romer.

On January 21 Harriman sent another telegram to Washington suggesting that in his opinion, the Soviets would recognize a reconstituted London government under Mikolajczyk if it was ready to accept the Curzon Line as "a basis for the boundary negotiations." It was his impression that the Russians would not insist on a total purge; Mikolajczyk could pass muster "by eliminating the irreconcilably anti-Soviet members and bringing in at least one Polish leader from the United States, one now in Russia, and perhaps one from Poland." Harriman wounded a prophetic warning:

> Unless the Polish group in London proceeds along the above line, I believe the Soviets will foster and recognize some type of Committee of Liberation. Then one of two alternatives would face us:
> (1) Continued recognition of the Polish Government in London, the practical effect of which would be to give the Russians a free hand to do what they wish in Poland, at least until after the hostilities are terminated.
> (2) Insistence on our being given representation in setting up administrative machinery within Poland similar to what has been given to the Russians in Italy by us. Withdrawal of recognition from the Polish Government in London would be one consequence of this course.

That painful choice could only be averted, Harriman argued, by quickly persuading the London Poles to reconstruct their government and negotiate with the Russians before the Red Army crossed the Curzon Line. This would require "the strongest pressure" that Churchill and Eden could bring to bear. "I would not feel qualified," Harriman added, "to say how far the American Government should go." He asked Hull for his reaction and "any information as to the line of thinking you have in mind."

All the Ambassador got in return was a request from Hull that he should see Molotov and go back over the old ground, warning the Russians again that their unilateral actions in the case of Poland ran the risk of alienating American public opinion. Believing this approach to be fruitless, Harriman sent the Secretary of State his own capsule version of Molotov's predictable responses: that the Soviets "perceive no reason why Poland should be liberated through the efforts of the

Red Army so that there may be placed in power a group which has shown a basically antagonistic attitude toward the Soviet Union"; that the Curzon Line "has had the sanction of the British Government and no recorded objection from the United States Government"; and that the Soviets would allow the people of Poland to select a government of their own choosing. "I make no attempt to argue the Soviet case," Harriman wrote on January 24, "but I want to put before you as clearly as I can what I am satisfied is, and will be, the attitude of the Soviets." In order to be useful at the Moscow end, Harriman added, he needed clear answers to a number of policy questions:

- Was the United States prepared to accept as "reasonably warranted" the Soviet position that the present Polish government was so unalterably hostile as to justify Moscow's refusal to deal with it?
- If so, was Washington ready to say as much to the Russians, the British and the Poles, and to decide "how far are we ready to involve ourselves in negotiations" on reconstructing the London government?
- If not, would the United States be prepared to claim in Poland the same rights to participate in occupation policy-making as it had granted the Russians in Italy?

Until Washington defined its policy and was ready to present specific suggestions, Harriman concluded, it would not be in an effective position to argue against any unilateral Soviet action. But Hull and Roosevelt were not prepared to take hard, unpopular decisions.

When Harriman saw Stalin again on February 2, he took the occasion to express the President's hope that some way might be found to settle the Polish dispute. In reply, Stalin reached for a bulging briefcase on his table, pulled out a six-month-old copy of *Niepodloglosc*, an underground paper printed in Wilno, and thrust it angrily in front of the Ambassador. The headline, in Polish, read: "HITLER AND STALIN— TWO FACES OF THE SAME EVIL." It was difficult to deal with people who could publish such a paper, Stalin said. The Poles in London might be able to fool Mr. Eden but now they had shown their true character.

When Harriman, nevertheless, stressed the high importance of reaching a Polish settlement, Stalin said he would be glad if relations with the Polish government could be improved. He was convinced, however, that it could not be done so long as people like General Sosnkowski and Stanislaw Kot, the former ambassador to the Soviet Union, remained in the government. "These people would have to be removed before the Soviet Government could deal with the Polish Government in London," Stalin said. The Poles liked to think, he added, that "Russians were good fighters but fools. They thought they could let the Russians carry the burden of the fighting and then step in at the end to share the spoils. But the Poles would find out who were the fools."

Clark Kerr reported that Stalin sounded slightly less negative later the same evening, when he in turn called at the Kremlin. In response to a series of written questions, Stalin promised that Poles living east of the Curzon Line would be permitted to migrate westward and that democratic elections would be allowed in Poland after the liberation. It was Clark Kerr's impression, Harriman reported, that "although Stalin manifested a firm determination not to establish relations with a government he could not trust, he indicated no desire to 'hand-pick' a new Polish Government."

Churchill continued to press the London Poles for concessions to reality. In a meeting at Chequers on February 6 he warned Mikiolajczyk and Romer that "the Curzon Line was the best that the Poles could expect and all that he would ask the British people to demand on their behalf." If they persisted in their present course, Churchill added, they would lose everything "while the Russian steamroller moved over Poland, a Communist government was set up in Warsaw and the present Polish Government was left powerless to do anything but make its protests to the world at large."[3]

Mikolajczyk, however, rejected the Curzon Line in the name of the underground leaders inside Poland as well as his own government. He had gone a long way toward meeting the Russian demands, he said, by agreeing to negotiate all questions, including frontier changes. He had issued orders to the underground movement to enter into friendly contact with the Russians. But he could not announce, the Polish Premier said, "that he would accept the Curzon Line and give away Wilno and Lwow." To do so would only undermine his government's authority with the Polish people. On February 22 Churchill told the House of Commons: "I cannot feel that the Russian demand for a reassurance about her Western frontiers goes beyond the limits of what is reasonable or just." His statement failed to sway Mikolajczyk's government, nor did it satisfy Stalin. When Clark Kerr saw Stalin on the last day of February, trying once again to discover whether the Kremlin would yield an inch on its demands, he found that "no argument was of any avail." It was, the British ambassador reported, "not a pleasant talk."

Harriman's second talk with Stalin on March 3 went no better. "Again the Poles," Stalin had said, in a mood of aggravated annoyance with the exile government. Harriman had come away with no encouragement other than Stalin's promise to take no immediate action because, as he said, the time was not ripe.

In the days that followed, Harriman put his mind to various ways of breaking the deadlock. With Clark Kerr's advice and agreement, he drafted a proposal that would get around the Soviet refusal to deal directly with the London Poles. The Western Allies could, on the one hand, take their cue from Stalin's statement that the time was not ripe for action on Poland and resign themselves to a period of "watchful waiting." The great disadvantage of this course, he pointed out in a draft never sent on to Washington, was that the Red Army, meanwhile, would move into Poland, leaving the Soviets free to do as they pleased. He felt that the Russians in time were likely to surface a new Polish regime of their own, led by Communists who had sat out the war in Moscow, and extend to it the recognition they had denied the London government. The cost of waiting, in short, would be high: "The solution to the Polish question would be a completely Soviet one."

The second course, which Harriman clearly preferred, was to try for agreement between the British, the Americans and the Russians on a set of ultimate objectives for Poland. The three powers would commit themselves to the restoration of a strong, independent Poland and to assuring the Polish people's right to freely select a broadly representative government of their own after the war. The Soviets would be authorized to administer the disputed territory east of the Curzon Line, leaving the final frontier settlement to be concluded after the war. As for the liberated areas west of the Curzon Line, an Advisory Council representing all three powers could be set up to consult with the Soviet military authorities on "questions of a political character," to make certain that the long-suffering population received relief assistance and to promote conditions which would permit the early transfer of governmental responsibility to Polish bodies.

The second course had its advantages, Harriman argued. It would restore faith in the agreements of Moscow and Teheran, demonstrating that the Big Three were searching together for an honest solution; moreover, the participation of Western representatives might "operate as an automatic restraint upon Soviet excesses." He conceded the disadvantages as well: the danger that by participating in the proposed commission, the United States and Britain would find themselves obliged to underwrite "at least tacitly" whatever the Soviets did on Polish territory—either that or contemplate a serious breach in the alliance. He also foresaw an undermining of the London government's authority, which could sharpen disunity among Poles overseas and damage morale among Polish servicemen fighting with the British.

"I knew that only the British government could bring about the changes that I believed to be essential in the composition and attitude of the Polish government-in-exile," Harriman recalled. "For that reason I kept urging Clark Kerr to send vigorous telegrams to his government. The reason I did not send some of the messages I dictated late at night to Meiklejohn was that when I read them again in the morning I felt they might do more harm than good. I knew I couldn't influence Hull. I had to reach the President and Hopkins. And I kept coming back to the realization that the main effort would have to be made in London, not Washington."

Churchill was still pressing Mikolajczyk hard in the spring of 1944 and being reproached by Stalin for not pressing harder. Increasingly exasperated, Churchill notified Stalin on March 21 that he proposed to make a statement in the House of Commons suggesting that all territorial changes be postponed for the duration of the war. "Of course, you are free to make any speech in the House of Commons—this is your affair," Stalin wrote back. "But if you make such a speech I shall consider that you have committed an act of injustice and unfriendliness toward the Soviet Union."[4]

As Harriman in Moscow thought about these unhappy developments he became more convinced than ever that the territorial dispute would, in the end, prove less of an obstacle than the determined anti-Soviet character of the London government. Torn between his long-standing view that nothing would be gained by appeasement of Stalin and a desire to understand the Soviet position, he set down his thoughts in a memorandum on March 24:

> I realize that the Polish situation does not look the same to me as it does in Washington, but I do not consider that my view is entirely colored by the Moscow atmosphere. I knew Sikorski intimately, had a number of long talks with him and have seen a number of the Poles, both important and lower rank, in London and elsewhere. The majority of them, with the exception of Sikorski, are mainly committed to a policy of fear of and antagonism to the Soviet Government. There is no doubt in my mind that the policies of the [Polish] Government are dominated by the officer group who are convinced that a war with Soviet Russia is inevitable.
> Sikorski himself, shortly before he was killed, when I asked him why he could not consolidate his Government on a policy which he favored of working with the Soviet Union, said to me: "This is impossible for me to accomplish at the present time. The only constituents I have now are the Army."
> Stalin is convinced that there is no hope for a friendly neighbor in Poland under the leadership of the controlling group in London, and he is unwilling to have the Red Army re-establish them in power. I believe he is basically right. In spite of the conjectures to the contrary, there is no evidence that he is unwilling to allow an independent Poland to emerge.

Harriman's disagreements with Churchill had been few during the London years. Now he felt that the Prime Minister was mistaken in threatening to withhold recognition of territorial changes until after the war. Although Churchill, in fact, did not make the speech which in prospect had so greatly alarmed Stalin, Harriman found him filled with bitterness when he dined at 10 Downing Street on May 2 on his way to Washington for consultations with Roosevelt.

Churchill arrived late and visibly tired at the end of a long Cabinet meeting. He asked some perfunctory questions about life in Moscow and did not appear to be much interested in Harriman's answers. But the vigor and the passion came flooding back when Harriman raised the Polish question. The Prime Minister argued that he had done a great service for Stalin as well as the London Poles. With great effort he had persuaded the Poles to accept the Curzon Line as a temporary demarcation for administrative purposes, leaving the final determination to the peace conference. He had committed the British government to support the westward expansion of Poland's frontiers at the expense of Germany. And all he got in exchange, he said, was "insults from Stalin—a barbarian."

Harriman quietly took issue with Churchill, explaining his belief that the Soviet government worried less over the boundary issue than over the composition of the Polish government and its political attitudes. "I explained that Mikolajczyk was not unacceptable to the Soviets as an individual, nor were others coming from the Polish democratic parties, but that Stalin was convinced that the group in London were under the domination of Sosnkowski and the military, who saw in the future only war with the Soviet Union," Harriman noted in his memorandum on the dinner conversation with Churchill.

The Prime Minister made no promises to reconsider his position. But as Harriman was leaving he showed signs of a new mood. He asked Harriman to tell Stalin "how earnestly he had tried to find a solution, how much progress he had made and how hurt he was that Stalin had not believed in his good intentions."

Two days later, at a garden party for the visiting prime ministers of the British Dominions, Churchill sent for Harriman and reopened the subject. "He made me listen to a fifteen-minute fight talk," Harriman remembered, "on how badly the British had been treated by the Soviet government beginning with the Ribbentrop treaty, during the period when Britain stood alone, the insults that had been hurled at him by Stalin consistently, and his determination that the Soviets should not destroy freedom in Poland, for which country Britain had gone to war. He asked that I present this attitude to the President and asked for the President's support in this policy 'even if only after he is re-elected to office.'"

Harriman had encountered the same attitude of sour disenchantment in a talk with Eden on May 3. There was a serious question, Eden said, whether Britain could ever again work with the Soviets. Harriman argued the contrary proposition: that by patience, understanding and readiness to be firm on matters of principle, the Western Allies could still develop "reasonably satisfactory relationships" with the Russians. "For example," he said, "we should have dealt with the political side of the Polish question at Moscow and Teheran. The fact that we did not register opposition to the Soviet Government's unwillingness to deal with the Poles in London had been accepted by the Soviets as acquiescence, even though [it was] understood to be reluctant. The Soviets' own policy was to react violently against any statement of ours, and they expected us to do the same. This technique of theirs is one that we should bear in mind at all times and not allow ourselves to drift into difficulties as a result of indecision. On the other hand, we should attempt to understand their basic objectives and not make issues where we are not on firm ground."

Harriman, in short, was thoroughly aware of the sharp swing in official British opinion when he looked up Lord Beaverbrook. He found his old friend in improved health and far less vehement than in his War Cabinet days, "fussing with civilian aviation and watching developments" from the sidelines. Beaverbrook announced with dramatic effect that everyone in the British government except himself was anti-Russian now. His own view was that the Soviets ought to have a free hand in Eastern Europe but should be excluded from Allied councils in Italy and Western Europe generally. "In other words," Harriman noted, "he believes in spheres of interest."

On his way back from Washington, Harriman stopped again in London to find that Churchill's rage against Stalin had blown itself out, "Due largely to Stalin's recent civil messages," he reported to Roosevelt on May 29, "the sun is shining again on the Soviet horizon." Something more substantial than a change in Stalin's tone had affected the Prime Minister, as he soon explained. During Harriman's absence in Washington he had tried his hand at a sphere-of-interest arrangement with the Russians, and it appeared to be working. The British had agreed to keep hands off Rumania while the fighting there continued, Churchill said, and the Russians in turn were willing to leave the British a free hand in Greece. Already the Greek Communists were being more cooperative, to the point of indicating that they would join rather than oppose a new coalition government of all the main resistance groups and political parties, then being organized in Cairo, with George Papandreou as Prime Minister. The Soviets were being so cooperative about Greece, Churchill added, that he was now hopeful of resolving even the Polish problem.*

---

*Churchill's enthusiasm was running ahead of events. The possibility of a temporary sphere-of-interest arrangement had been mentioned to the Soviet ambassador, Fedor T. Gusev, on May 5 by Eden. On May 18 Gusev informed

Back in Moscow, Harriman assured Molotov on June 3 that the President would urge Mikolajczyk, who was about to visit the United States, to drop Sosnkowski and his followers from the Polish Cabinet. The President, he said, considered it of paramount importance that permanent, friendly relations be established between the Soviet Union and Poland; for that reason Mikolajczyk would have to reconstruct his government. Roosevelt remembered Stalin's reassurance at Teheran that Poland's independence would be respected, Harriman added. With the election five months off, the President "thought it best to keep quiet on the Polish question," as he had explained to Stalin at Teheran, and he had insisted that Mikolajczyk make no public speeches during his American visit. "It was a time to keep barking dogs quiet," Harriman said. The Soviets could be helpful by not airing the question for a time.

Molotov inquired whether there had been any change in the President's views on the Polish question since he had discussed it with Stalin at Teheran. No, Harriman replied, adding that the President was confident that Stalin too would stand by his statements at Teheran. Molotov put several questions about American reactions to the Moscow visit of Father Orlemanski and Professor Lange, whom the Soviets had put forward as possible candidates for a reconstructed Polish government, at which Harriman remarked that neither had an "especially large" following in the United States.

When Harriman saw Stalin on June 10, there was more talk of the Normandy landing than of Poland. He raised the subject with the appearance of hesitation, saying that he knew Stalin did not like to talk about the Poles. "Why not?" Stalin responded in obvious good humor. Harriman had never seen Stalin in a more agreeable mood. The success of the Second Front doubtless affected his attitude, although he was cordial even in discussing Poland. Stalin expressed gratitude for the President's reaffirmation of his statements at Teheran, adding that he fully realized how difficult it was for the President to speak out during the election campaign. He also undertook to keep Roosevelt informed of any new development in Polish-Soviet relations. Harriman remarked that the President was puzzled about the status of Lwow but believed it was a matter to be worked out between Russians and Poles.

The unanswered question was "Which Poles?" While Mikolajczyk was in Washington seeing Roosevelt, Stalin had been meeting in

---

the British Foreign Office that his government favored the idea but would like to know whether Washington had any objection. Hull objected strongly. Thus it was not until mid-July, following repeated appeals from Churchill to Roosevelt, that the United States gave its lukewarm assent to a three-month trial period. Stalin let the proposal drag and Churchill, sensing fresh Russian encouragement to the Communist resistance group in Greece, did not press the matter for several months.

Moscow with a delegation from the so-called Polish National Council, a body of uncertain origin recently formed inside Poland. Stalin urged Harriman to talk with them. These, he said, were "living people," not émigrés, and they would have a great deal to tell him regarding conditions in Poland. Harriman agreed to meet the delegation unofficially the following day. The principal spokesman for the group turned out to be Edward Boleslaw Osubka-Morawski, who described himself as a Catholic, an economist and a member of the Polish Socialist party. He had changed his name four times during the German occupation, he said, and was now Vice President of the Polish National Council. The others were a Colonel Turski, the only acknowledged Communist in the group; a former Lodz industrialist called Hanecki; and a young man who called himself Hardy. He had been a student in Warsaw before the war, he said, an active partisan and a member of the Peasant party, although his wing of the party had broken away from Mikolajczyk's leadership.

Osubka-Morawski, who did most of the talking, denounced Sosnkowski and his "reactionary Fascist clique" at length, insisting they had no real support in Poland except for an underground force of perhaps 30,000 men. He appealed for arms from the United States for what he described as the "People's Army." Questioned by Harriman about the Council's position on frontiers, he said that it hoped Poland would be able to keep Lwow and the Galician oil fields, but he personally saw little prospect of holding Wilno "because of its geographic position." The Council, he added, was trying to be practical. It recognized the great power of the Soviet Union and felt the chance of getting a reasonable settlement from the Russians was bound to increase if its own demands were reasonable. He acknowledged that the National Council was "in agreement on fundamentals" with the Union of Polish Patriots in Moscow but insisted there had been no contact between the two organizations before his visit to the Soviet Union.

Harriman found it curious that Osubka-Morawski and the London Poles appeared to feel much the same way about keeping Lwow and the Galician oil fields. "It seemed to me at the time," he recalled, "that if the best of the London Poles had gotten together with the National Council people, they could at least have saved Lwow and the oil fields."

When Harriman asked his visitors what the outcome of a present-day election in Poland might be, Osubka-Morawski replied that Mikolajczyk's Peasant party would run ahead of the others. It was axiomatic, however, that after the war the large estates would have to be broken up, the land distributed to the peasants and the principal industries placed under national control.

Mikolajczyk, meanwhile, had met four times with President Roosevelt in the week of June 7–14. The President told him, among other things, that Lwow ought rightfully to belong to Poland and that he should avoid "any final or definite settlement of the frontiers now." Roosevelt added that "it might be desirable to find an opportunity to bring some changes in your cabinet in order to make an understanding with the Russians possible."[5] Roosevelt stressed, however, that the Poles would have to negotiate their own settlement with Stalin. He urged Mikolajczyk to fly to Moscow without delay for a "man to man" discussion with the Soviet leader. Mikolajczyk agreed to go if invited, as he was, after both Churchill and Roosevelt intervened with Stalin.

A four-day visit to Soviet Central Asia with Vice President Henry Wallace offered Harriman a welcome break from his Polish preoccupations in mid-June. Wallace had undertaken a brief, enthusiastic study of Russian in preparation for his trip. But Roosevelt did not want Wallace to talk with Stalin. At the President's direction, Wallace flew from Alaska across Siberia to Tashkent and Alma Ata, then on to China. The president was perfectly willing for Wallace to see Chiang Kai-shek," Harriman recalled. "Indeed, he thought that the Vice President's liberal influence might do some good with Chiang. But he was taking no chances of confusing Stalin about American policy."

On June 14 Harriman flew to Tashkent, accompanied by Tommy Thompson; the Chinese ambassador to the Soviet Union, Foo Pingsheung; and the Mexican ambassador, Luis Quintanilla, a personal friend of Wallace's. He met Wallace there and together they visited several agricultural experiment stations, where Soviet scientists were trying to develop improved strains of cotton, potatoes and melons. Wallace, who had made a considerable fortune as a developer of hybrid corn, was in his element. "All his life, Wallace had been trying to get American farmers to accept science," Harriman reported on his return to Moscow. "In the Soviet Union he saw scientific methods being forced on the farmers, and it was heaven for him. Here he found capable agricultural scientists with the authority to compel farmers to follow their orders."

Throughout the trip Wallace was totally absorbed in matters agricultural. Harriman and Thompson took more interest in the social and political attitudes of a region normally closed to foreign diplomats. They found the people refreshingly hospitable, the fruits displayed in local markets both succulent and abundant, and the evidence of economic uplift in what had been an isolated, backward region compelling. They discovered, among other things, that few of the Uzbek population (whose devotion to Moscow was not being taken for granted in the Kremlin) had seen service in the Red Army at the beginning of the war. As the fighting raged on, however, and the casualties multiplied, the Uzbeks were called to combat like other Soviet citizens and suffered heavy losses in the Battle of Stalingrad.

Wallace got to deliver a short speech in Russian, Harriman noting that the crowd in the Tashkent theater "managed to understand" him. The American guests also were treated to the first performance of Bizet's *Carmen* in the Uzbek language. Thompson dryly observed in his report to Washington that "fortunately for the guests, only one act of the opera was given."

Harriman returned to Moscow on June 19 and was soon again absorbed in Polish problems. Two days later he warned the State Department that the London Poles were about to be outflanked. The Ambassador's "best guess" was that with the Red Army now rolling into Poland proper, the Russians "in consultation, no doubt, with the Polish National Council" would install local administrations in the liberated areas. "Mikolajczyk and certain other representatives of the democratic parties of the London Government will then be asked by the Polish National Council to return to Poland and associate themselves in the formation of a government," he predicted. "Individuals of the Union of Polish Patriots in Moscow, and perhaps Dr. Lange and one or two other Poles in the United States, will be similarly invited. A government will be formed, based on the 1921 constitution and repudiating the constitution of 1935, regardless of who accepts these invitations."*

Moscow would promptly recognize the new government, having made certain that "real influence in Polish affairs will be exercised by the Soviet Government," and would then call upon London and Washington to follow suit. "We will [then] be faced with a *fait accompli*," Harriman wrote, "and with the difficult decision as to what will be our relations with the Polish Government in London and our attitude toward the new government in Poland."

That forecast was confirmed the following evening, July 22. Radio Moscow announced, from liberated territory, the formation of a Polish Committee for National Liberation, which was to serve as the executive authority of the Polish National Council (four of whose members had so recently and so modestly called upon Harriman to plead for American arms). The Committee's mission was anything but modest: "to direct the fight of the people for liberation, to achieve independence, and to rebuild the Polish state." The announcement had been issued from Chelm, the first large town liberated by the Red Army on territory that

---

*The Polish Constitution of 1921 established the new state as a parliamentary democracy. By the late twenties, however, power reverted to the military, General Pilsudski and his colonels. In 1935 the Pilsudski regime instituted a frankly authoritarian constitution more nearly in step with the rise of Fascist regimes elsewhere in Europe. Overwhelming power was now concentrated in the President, and Parliament lost effective control. Civil liberties were restricted, and the rights of political organizations curtailed.

was Polish beyond dispute. The Committee moved on to Lublin after a few days and came to be known as the Lublin Committee. The Russians, moreover, had already signed an agreement with the Chelm-Lublin Committee, assigning to it "full responsibility in matters of civil government" behind the Red Army's lines.

The Polish government-in-exile in short, was suddenly confronted with a rival Polish regime, bearing out Harriman's early warnings to Roosevelt and Hull; a rival already established on Polish soil and enjoying full support from the Russians. Exactly six weeks earlier Stalin had assured Roosevelt, through Harriman, that he would keep him informed of any new Polish developments. As he explained to Harriman on another occasion, he never broke a promise but sometimes he changed his mind.

When Mikolajczyk at last reached Moscow and asked for a meeting with Stalin, Molotov replied that he had better see the Lublin representatives. They were, Molotov said, better informed than Stalin about conditions in Poland. The Polish Premier insisted. He had, after all, been invited to Moscow by Stalin, however grudgingly. Molotov told him on July 31 that he would try to arrange a meeting with Stalin in three days. He added that the Red Army was only ten kilometers from Warsaw. The next day Warsaw rose up in arms against the Germans.

"Warsaw will be free any day," Mikolajczyk said to Stalin, when they finally met on August 3. "God grant that it be so," Stalin replied. But he went on to sneer at the underground army: "What kind of army is it—without artillery, tanks, air force? They do not even have enough hand weapons. In modern war this is nothing . . . I hear that the Polish Government instructed these units to chase the Germans out of Warsaw. I don't understand how they can do it. They don't have sufficient strength for that."

Mikolajczyk asked Stalin whether he would help the Warsaw uprising by supplying arms. "We will not permit any action behind our lines," he said. "For this reason you have to reach an understanding with the Lublin Committee. We are supporting them. If you don't do it, then nothing will come out of our talk. We cannot tolerate two governments."[6]

The scene was being played out much as Harriman had prophesied on January 21. Washington had chosen the course of sitting tight to await developments. Feeling powerless to alter the course of events inside Poland, it watched with rising alarm as the Russians installed their friends in power. Only the Russians were by reason of geography in a position to liberate Poland. And as Stalin said to Tito* in 1945,

---

*It was actually Milojan Djilas with whom Stalin spoke.—Ed. note.

"Whoever occupies a territory also imposes on it his own social system. Everyone imposes his own system as far as his army can reach. It cannot be otherwise."[7]

Harriman continued to believe, however, that in Poland it might have been otherwise—if the British government, backed strongly by the United States, had pressed the Polish government-in-exile to swallow the Curzon Line and get rid of its bitter-end generals like Sosnkowski. It was, he felt, the only hope (a slender hope, admittedly) of preventing a wholly Russian solution to the Polish question.

Endnotes

1. FRUS (Foreign Relations of the United States), 1944, Vol. III, The British Commonwealth and Europe (1965), pp. 1240–43.

2. Stalin's Correspondence, Vol. I, p. 196.

3. FRUS, 1944, Vol. III, pp. 1249–57.

4. Ibid., pp. 1268–70.

5. Rozek, Allied Wartime Diplomacy, p. 22.

6. Ibid., pp. 237–42.

7. Milovan Djilas, Conversations with Stalin (New York, Harcourt, 1962), p. 114.

Radomír Luža

Czechoslovakia between Democracy and Communism

The nations of Eastern Europe were both the source and the principal victims of the Soviet-American antagonism. In modern times these small lands remained subject to heavy foreign influence even after they had won their right to exist as states at the close of World War I. With the collapse of German power in 1944–45 and the advance of the Red Army, it was unlikely that they could escape deep infringement of their newly recovered independence.

Nonetheless, it was not foreordained that they must be communized. In Czechoslovakia a precarious independence was maintained for almost three years. And even today Finland provides the example of a country that has preserved a democratic political life while clearly accepting an international role that respects Russian interests. Was "Finlandization" excluded for the East European nations? Stalin's own thinking remains hard to reconstruct. On the one hand, he reportedly told the Yugoslav communist, Milovan Djilas, that the country that sent its troops into a liberated area would also inevitably impose its own social system. On the other hand, he allegedly reassured the Czech leader Edvard Beneš (among others) in regard to his intentions toward Warsaw that "communism fit Poland like a saddle fits a cow." Perhaps the Russian leader never intended to allow a free choice of regimes in Eastern Europe, or perhaps he interpreted the formulae of democratic governments and free elections, which he accepted at Yalta, at being tantamount to a choice for communism. At the least he expected a strong communist role in Hungary and Czechoslovakia and worked to assure a preponderant communist influence in Poland and Rumania from late 1944 on, if not earlier. And even if the final totalitarian result was not planned at the outset of the process, the logic of conflict with Washington meant that every dispute between the two great powers led to further repression in Eastern Europe and thus to more irreconcilable Soviet-American polarization.

But what were the United States' stakes in this relatively distant area? Our economic intercourse with Eastern Europe was minimal, although neo-Marxist critics assert that if Washington was to assert the "open door" as its general stance, it had to fight for this right in Eastern Europe as well. More plausible a factor in my judgment was the ideological commitment generated within America as part of the national mobilization for World War II. After waging a messianic struggle on behalf of oppressed peoples, how could American leaders simply surrender the region where World War II had begun to a new repression? (This was all the less likely in view of the millions of votes in major industrial states that the ethnic groups from Eastern Europe represented.) "Realist" critics of American foreign policy could well answer that we ended up surrendering the region in any case and that it was illusory to believe there was an alternative. By refusing to recognize Soviet preeminence, and likewise failing to develop credible threats to deter it, we both "lost" the area to communism and envenomed relations with Moscow. Nonetheless, the wisdom of renunciation is not usually learned with difficulty. At the end of Roosevelt's war, acquiescence in the division of Europe would have demanded an implausibly rapid psychological re-education of Americans—even apart from the moral elements involved.

Most accounts of Eastern Europe in English focus upon the region as part of the larger Soviet-American struggle. For an able summary of East European developments in terms of their ramifications upon American policy, the student might well employ Bennett Kovrig's, *The Myth of Liberation: East-Central Europe in United States Diplomacy and Politics since 1914* (Baltimore, Md.: The Johns Hopkins University Press, 1973); and see also Lynn Ethridge Davis, *The Cold War Begins: Soviet-American Conflict over Eastern Europe* (New York, 1974). The essay included here offers a different perspective—namely a focus upon the difficulties of the Czechoslovak republic from the viewpoint of Prague. Czechoslovakia was the country of Eastern Europe most akin to the West in terms of social and economic structure; it had enjoyed the greatest success between the wars in maintaining democratic government; it was least ravaged by the war itself; and it was the most successful in combating postwar inflation. It gave the greatest promise of being able to preserve friendly relations with Moscow and a pluralist regime at home. Thus its communization in early 1948 especially dismayed Westerners, convincing them of the gravity of the Cold War much as the fall of France had pressed home the earnestness of the Second World War. But the account instructively highlights the burdens placed upon Czech democracy from its own internal problems. And it also suggests that failures of will and resolve also played a crucial role—in short, Czechoslovaks made history as well as suffered from it.

Radomír Luža teaches history at Tulane and with Victor S. Mamatey is the editor of the volume, *A History of the Czechoslovak Republic, 1914–1948*, from which this essay is taken with the permission of Princeton University Press and the author. Professor Luža has also written *The Transfer of the Sudeten Germans: A Study of Czech-German Relations, 1933–1962* (New York: New York University Press, 1964) and *Austro-German Relations in the Anschluss Era* (Princeton: Princeton University Press, 1975).

The Government of the National Front

The fate of postwar Czechoslovakia, like that of other small nations of East Central Europe, did not depend on the will and actions of her people alone. It was also affected by the actions of the great powers and their postwar relations.

In the winter of 1944–45, while the Red Army was fighting its way to Prague, Vienna, and Berlin, the Soviet Union, the United States, and Britain were making final preparations for the meeting of their leaders at Yalta. They were aware that the presence of the Soviet military might in Poland, Rumania, Bulgaria, Hungary and Czechoslovakia meant a basic shift of power in Europe. Nonetheless, both East and West still clung to the concept of postwar coalition and were exploring the basis for a series of agreements on European and Far Eastern problems.

The policy of President Edvard Beneš, developed while he was in exile in London, had been to restore Czechoslovakia to her pre-Munich territorial integrity and reinstitute her democratic institutions. The success of this policy depended on the continued cooperation of the Allied Powers, not only until the end of the war but afterward. Only in these circumstances could Czechoslovakia hope to recover her independence and territorial integrity and restore her traditional parliamentary-democratic system. Throughout the war, therefore, Beneš had tried to promote a cooperative effort of the anti-Nazi alliance to find a permanent settlement in Europe. Alone among the exiled leaders of East

Central European countries he sought both the support of the Western powers and an accommodation with the Soviet Union. The signing of the Soviet-Czechoslovak alliance treaty in Moscow in December, 1943, was conclusive proof of his determination to come to terms with Moscow, and appeared to be a guarantee of the success of his policy.

Beneš was, therefore, deeply disappointed and even shocked when reports reached him late in 1944 that Soviet authorities were promoting a movement in Ruthenia (Carpathian Ukraine)—which had been the first Czechoslovak province liberated by the Red Army—for its secession from Czechoslovakia and its attachment to the Soviet Ukraine. As early as 1939, in conversations with Ivan Maisky, the Soviet ambassador in London, Beneš had voiced his willingness to solve the question of Ruthenia in full agreement with the Soviet Union,[1] and had reiterated this view in his last talk with Stalin in Moscow in December, 1943. At the time the Soviet leaders did not regard the question as pressing, but they now apparently were determined to force a solution favorable to the Soviet Union. Czechoslovak complaints lodged with the Soviet government against Soviet activity in Ruthenia during December, 1944, proved to be of no avail.

At the same time Beneš became alarmed about the ultimate fate of Slovakia, which had been partially liberated by the Soviet army. Although the Communist Party of Slovakia (KSS) had abandoned its earlier agitation for a "Soviet Slovakia," it continued to press—with the approval of the leadership of the Communist Party of Czechoslovakia (KSČ) in Moscow—for a loose federation between Slovakia on one hand and Bohemia and Moravia on the other.

Beneš's tense concern was ended by a personal letter from Joseph Stalin on January 23, 1945, assuring the Czechoslovak government of his full support. The Soviet leader suggested, however, that the problem of Ruthenia should be solved by negotiations between the two countries that would take into account the desire of the province's Ukrainian population to join the Soviet Union. The underlying concern of Beneš, that the Soviet Union would use its control of Czechoslovak territory in disregard of its commitments, was thus relieved.[2] Soviet-Czechoslovak relations had for some time been regarded as an index of Soviet-Western relations. Undoubtedly, Stalin's decision to ease Beneš's fears on the eve of the Yalta conference was motivated, in part, by a desire to dissipate the suspicions of President Franklin D. Roosevelt and Prime Minister Winston S. Churchill, already aroused over Soviet designs in Poland and the other countries of East Central Europe occupied by the Soviet army.

Just before writing his letter to Beneš, Stalin discussed with Klement Gottwald, the exiled Czech communist leader in Moscow, the policy the KSČ should follow during and after the liberation of Czechoslovakia.

Stalin advised Gottwald to accept Beneš as president, and to come to an understanding with him and his government.[3] This flexible Soviet policy essentially reflected the line set forth in the Comintern declaration of 1943, which asserted that "the great differences in the historical development of individual countries determine the differences of the various problems that the workers' class of every country has to cope with." Until the next reexamination of communist strategy in the summer of 1947, Stalin set the stamp of his approval on this thesis of national roads to socialism: "In private he even expressed the . . . view that in certain instances it was possible to achieve socialism without the dictatorship of the proletariat."[4]

During its Moscow exile the top echelon of the KSČ (Gottwald, Rudolf Slánský, Jan Šverma, and Václav Kopecký) worked out a policy line in terms of a special Czechoslovak road to socialism.[5] After broadening their reexamination to include a review of past mistakes, they determined that the party should lead and organize the national liberation struggle of the Czech and Slovak people against Nazism. In thus assuming the role of a responsible mass movement, the party acted upon the belief that after the end of the occupation it could win popular confidence under the banner of national independence.[6] In short, the communist leadership in Moscow envisioned liberation as a means of winning a predominant share of power. The irony of such an approach was that it visualized economic and social reform as being subordinate to the achievement of the primary political task: becoming the leading political force in the country. In conformity with this aim, the party tended to move cautiously. It set up broad national and democratic—instead of narrow socialist—demands. In fact, the program of the Czech home resistance—nationalization of industry, banks, and insurance companies—was much more far-reaching than the initial communist platform, which merely involved confiscation of the property of Czech and Slovak traitors and hostile Germans and Magyars.[7]

During the war the principal Czech and Slovak political forces at home and abroad held lively discussions on the future form of the country. In the winter of 1944–45, as the Soviet army overran a large part of Czechoslovakia, the balance of the pendulum between the democratic parties represented by Beneš in London and the communists led by Gottwald in Moscow swung in favor of the communists. It was a foregone conclusion that, at the end of the war, the London cabinet would be replaced by a new government with strong communist participation.[8] In 1945, with the Soviet armies advancing across Czechoslovakia, it became urgent for Beneš to implement this agreement and to return to the liberated part of the country with a newly constituted cabinet. To determine the composition of the new government and adopt a program, it was decided to hold a conference of Czech and

Slovak political parties in Moscow. The choice of Moscow rather than London for the conference was undoubtedly motivated by the fact that the Czechoslovak government needed the consent and assistance of the Soviet government to return to its homeland. It also gave the communists a considerable advantage in the ensuing negotiations.

After taking leave of Churchill and Anthony Eden on February 24,[9] Beneš, accompanied by some members of his cabinet, left London for Moscow, where he arrived on March 17. A delegation of the Slovak National Council (SNR), composed equally of Slovak Democrats and Communists, also arrived in Moscow from the liberated parts of Slovakia. However, since Bohemia and Moravia were still firmly in the grip of the Germans, the Czech home resistance was unable to send representatives. Altogether, the Czech Communist (KSČ), National Socialist, Social Democratic, and People's parties and the Slovak Democratic and Communist (KSS) parties were represented. All other prewar political movements were excluded from the conference, primarily because of their past anticommunist attitude.

Gottwald assumed the initiative at the conference, which opened on March 22 and lasted eight days, with the presentation of a draft program as the basis of the negotiations.[10] Beneš did not take part in the meetings, on the ground that as a constitutional president he stood above parties.[11] This left the London democratic exiles leaderless, since they were used to deferring to him in London, even in minor matters. It also weakened their position, because Beneš enjoyed tremendous prestige, particularly in the Czech provinces. Out of fear of arousing "suspicion on the part of the communists,"[12] they discarded any joint political platform to counter the communist program. To the bewilderment of the disunited democratic camp, it soon became apparent that the negotiations were a controversy between two political groups, one based in London and the other in Moscow: "Here for the first time there was joined the battle of two political worlds."[13] What started out as negotiations for a governmental blueprint broadened into a survey of a program of action that would change almost every aspect of Czechoslovak life.

The democratic leaders received some satisfaction from the fact that the communist draft, to some extent, incorporated points agreed upon during previous exchanges of opinion between the parties. In the main, it reflected Gottwald's conception of the necessity for agreement with the democratic parties and articulated some of the aspirations of the Czech and Slovak people. Although the democratic and communist leaders clashed on many points, in the end their common interests proved strong enough to produce a final text that was not very different from the original draft.

The sharpest controversy during the negotiations occurred between the London group and the Slovak delegation, in which Gottwald assumed the role of benevolent arbiter.[14] The Slovaks brought to Moscow a resolution passed by the SNR on March 2, which demanded what amounted to attributes of sovereignty for Slovakia: a Slovak government, parliament, and distinct army units. The London group rejected this demand. It based itself on Beneš's speech of February 23, 1945, in which the president had recognized the special needs of the Slovaks but had insisted that the definition of Slovakia's place in the Czechoslovak state—like, indeed, all constitutional questions—should be left to the elected representatives of the people at home to decide after the war.[15] In the end the Slovaks yielded and accepted as a compromise a somewhat ambiguously worded statement proposed by Gottwald, which he later called grandly the "*Magna Carta* of the Slovak Nation."

In the negotiations to form a new government, the communists likewise imposed their will, but managed skillfully to camouflage their victory in a seeming compromise. They did not claim the premiership or a majority of posts in the cabinet. Instead, Gottwald proposed, and the other party leaders agreed, that the government should represent a "broad National Front of the Czechs and Slovaks." In strict conformance with the rules of parliamentary arithmetic, this decision was implemented by awarding three posts in the cabinet to each of the six parties participating in the conference. The prime minister and five vice-premiers, who were the heads of the six parties, were to form an inner cabinet to direct and coordinate the government's activities. It was further decided to give posts to four non-partisan experts and to create three state-secretaryships, thus bringing the total membership of the cabinet to twenty-five.

Upon the conclusion of the Moscow conference, President Beneš and the party leaders departed for Košice, a modest eastern Slovak town recently liberated by the Red Army. They arrived there on April 3 and stayed until after the liberation of Prague on May 9. On April 4 the new government was formally installed and the next day it announced its program, which, despite its origin in Moscow, came to be known as the "program of Košice."[16]

The Košice program proposed no radical transformation of Czechoslovak society along socialist lines. It was quite free of characteristic Marxist language. On the other hand, unlike the Czechoslovak declarations of independence issued in Washington and Prague in 1918, which had been idealistic professions of faith in democracy, it said little about freedom. Its tone was sober. It threatened more than it promised.

The program opened with a government tribute to the Soviet Union and a pledge to support the Red Army until final victory. For this purpose the government announced the formation of a new Czechoslovak army, trained, organized, and equipped on the model of the Red

Army, with Czech and Slovak units under a unified command, and educational officers introduced into all units to extirpate fascist influences. Czechoslovak foreign policy, it said, would be based on the closest alliance with the Soviet Union on the basis of the 1943 treaty and on practical cooperation in the military, political, economic, and cultural fields, as well as in questions concerning the punishment of Germany, reparations, frontier settlements, and the organization of peace. It promised to maintain friendly relations with Poland, Yugoslavia, and Bulgaria on the "basis of Slavic brotherhood," to seek reconciliation with a democratic Hungary (after correction of injustices), and to promote a rapprochement between Hungary and Austria and their Slavic neighbors. Finally, almost as an afterthought, it thanked Britain for the aid extended during the war and promised to consolidate relations with her and the United States and promote close relations with France.

In the field of domestic policy the government pledged to hold elections at the earliest possible time for a national constituent assembly that would determine the precise form of the Czechoslovak government. In the meantime, the government guaranteed the people their political rights and set up new administrative machinery, in the form of popularly elected national committees, to administer public affairs at the local, district, and provincial levels.

The Slovaks were recognized as a distinct (*samobyntný*) nation and the SNR as their legal representative and "carrier of state power in Slovak territory." The question of Ruthenia was to be settled as soon as possible according to the democratically expressed will of its people. The German and Magyar minorities were given the right of option for Czechoslovakia, with the understanding that disloyal German and Magyar citizens would be removed. The property of those who had "actively helped in the disruption and occupation of Czechoslovakia" was to be placed under national control pending a final disposal by the legislative authorities. Their land would be placed in a National Land Fund and distributed to deserving Czechs and Slovaks.

Czech and Slovak collaborators were to be deprived of voting rights and barred from all political organizations. The former agrarian party and all prewar parties not represented in the new National Front were accused of collaboration and proscribed. War criminals, traitors, and "other active, conscious helpers of the German oppressors" were to be punished without exception. President Emil Hácha and all members of the Protectorate government, as well as Jozef Tiso and all members of the Slovak government and parliament, were to be charged with high treason and brought before a "National Court." Finally, the Košice program provided for a broad system of social welfare.

In the new cabinet, according to a communist participant at the

Moscow conference, the communists captured "positions which were a starting point for the assault on the actual fortress of capitalism. . . . The balance of power was such . . . from the beginning of the liberation, that the influence and weight of . . . KSČ was predominant and decisive."[17] At the Moscow conference, the communists had successfully promoted Zdeneǩ Fierlinger, a left-wing Social Democrat, as prime minister. From their point of view, the choice proved an excellent one. As wartime ambassador to Moscow, Fierlinger had won the confidence of the Soviet government by his display of an uncritically pro-Soviet and anti-Western attitude. As premier, he collaborated with the communists so closely that he won the popular epithet of "Quislinger."

Thanks to separate representation, the combined KSČ and KSS held eight seats in the cabinet and controlled the ministries of interior, information, education, agriculture, and social welfare.[18] The police, security, and intelligence services were in their hands. The Ministry of Defense was entrusted to Gen. Ludvík Svoboda, commander of the Czechoslovak army in Russia, as a nonparty expert. (Although a noncommunist at that time, Svoboda was a loyal friend of the Soviets.) As a concession to the democratic parties, the communists agreed to the reappointment of Jan Masaryk as minister of foreign affairs. A genuinely nonpartisan personality, dedicated only to the defense of his country's interests, the son of the first president of Czechoslovakia was by family tradition, education, and experience a thoroughly Western man. Therefore, as Masaryk's assistant and watchdog the communists insisted on appointing Vlado Clementis, a Slovak communist, to the newly created post of state-secretary of foreign affairs.

Thus far the "circumspect and purposeful course of the KSČ"[19] proved to be of particular advantage to the Communist party, whose chairman, Klement Gottwald, had given proof of his political maturity and craftsmanship. The less colorful democratic leaders let themselves be outmaneuvered. Since the central issue was one of power, it is surprising that neither Beneš nor his colleagues found it advisable to prevent the communists from assuming control of the police and security organs. A reasonable compromise on this question would have helped those forces in both camps who were willing to face up to problems affecting their common commitment to a democratic Czechoslovakia. Despite some apprehensions, however, the democratic leaders had no reason to contradict Fierlinger's observations before their departure from Moscow that "It is an immense achievement that we can return home united. . . . The ideological borderline between Moscow and London has been removed. I am aware of the fact that not a few would criticize the composition of the new cabinet . . . but I consider it an immense success that unlike other emigrations . . . we are the first to be able to put order into our affairs abroad."[20] Neither side regarded the Moscow agreement as a final settlement; both were aware that the final battle was yet to come—at home after the war.

In the Czech provinces the approaching end of the war coincided with a rising tide of guerrilla activities. Early in 1945 the largest resistance group—the Council of the Three—the illegal trade unions, and the underground KSČ established the Czech National Council as the center of Czech resistance. The council was strengthened during the first days of May by a spontaneous popular uprising that spread through those parts of the country still occupied by the Germans. The movement reached Prague on May 5, where a fierce battle broke out with German army and SS units that raged even after the official dates of German surrender at Theims and Berlin (May 7 and 8, respectively). In the early morning hours of May 9 the first Soviet tanks arrived in Prague. On May 10 the government returned to Prague. It was followed by President Beneš amid frenetic acclamation on May 16.

The Nazi occupation was terminated. The war was over.

Between Democracy and Cominform, 1945–1947

On its return to Prague, the Czechoslovak government took quick and firm hold of the levers of command. Under the Moscow agreement President Beneš had been given emergency powers to issue decrees with the validity of laws, at the request of the government, until the convocation of the National Assembly. These powers were first used to assert government authority throughout the country. The Czech National Council was dissolved.[21] The Slovak National Council, on the other hand, continued to function at Bratislava.[22] It soon became apparent, however, that it was necessary to define its jurisdiction and the basis of its relationship to the central government at Prague, a matter that the Košice program had noted only in very general terms. The SNR took the initiative in the matter. On May 26 it adopted a proposal for the fundamental organization of the republic, in the drafting of which both Slovak communist and democratic leaders shared. The proposal envisaged a dualistic, symmetrical organization of Czechoslovakia into two federated states—Slovakia and Bohemia-Moravia—each with a government and diet of its own. A federal government and parliament were to be centered in Prague.

The previous Czechoslovak experiment in federalism—the ill-fated Second Republic in 1938–39—had not been a happy one. The proposal of the SNR therefore encountered opposition from the Czech parties, both communist and democratic. On May 31, just before the government at Prague began a discussion of the SNR proposal, the leaders of the KSČ invited the KSS leaders to a meeting at which the KSS submitted to the "unified leadership" of the KSČ and agreed to abandon the SNR plan.[23] At the cabinet meeting on May 31 and June 1, only the Slovak Democrats defended the proposal for federalization, while the Czech National Socialists and Populists pressed for the restoration of the republic's pre-Munich centralist organization; the KSČ and KSS adopted a halfway course. The discussions ended in a compromise. Federalism was discarded, but Slovakia's autonomy was assured. The resulting "First Prague Agreement" both defined and circumscribed the jurisdiction of the SNR.[24]

The government delayed a full year before implementing its pledge, given in the Košice program, to hold general elections for a constituent assembly at the earliest possible time. Meanwhile it covered the naked strength of its power in a temporary constitutional garb. On August 25, 1945, a presidential decree provided for the formation of a single-chamber, 300-member provisional national assembly. It was to be chosen not by general elections but by a complicated system of three-stage elections through the local, district, and provincial national committees—thus allowing the parties of the National Front to determine its composition.[25] The Provisional National Assembly met for the first time on October 28, 1945, the national holiday, and confirmed President Beneš in his office. In the next few days the cabinet was formally reorganized, but no significant changes were effected in its composition.

The Provisional National Assembly's initiative remained limited. Usually, it approved unanimously and without discussion the decisions made by the party leaders at meetings of the National Front. Thus on February 28, 1946, it approved, also unanimously and without discussion, the ninety-eight presidential decrees issued from May to October, 1945, many of which affected the fundamental structure of the Czechoslovak state and society.

The delay in holding elections, however, did not indicate indifference on the part of the party leaders to public opinion. Quite the contrary. After the overthrow of Nazism all of Europe was swept by an intense popular demand for immediate reform and a certain disillusionment, or impatience, with constitutional procedures when they threatened to delay reform. Under these circumstances, to defer the pressing tasks of reconstruction and reform in order to engage in an electoral contest appeared almost frivolous to the Czech and Slovak party leaders. Their decision to preserve the interparty truce offered by the National Front and "get to work" had full public approval.

Air attacks, military operations, and the German occupation had made World War II more destructive for the Czechs and Slovaks than any previous conflict. According to an official government estimate 250,000 persons had died. In Bohemia, 3,014 houses were destroyed and over 10,000 were badly damaged; in Moravia the respective figures were 11,862 and over 19,000. In Silesia 34,986 buildings were ruined. Slovakia, because of the prolonged fighting in 1944–45, was the most seriously hit.[26] In the Czech provinces the total war damage per person was estimated at 17,000 Czechoslovak crowns (about $2,400), but in Slovakia it amounted to 35,000 crowns (about $4,900).[27] In eastern Slovakia alone 169 villages were razed and 300 damaged; 24,000 buildings were ruined or heavily damaged. The transportation system was seriously dislocated. Almost all the large factories had been badly bombed.[28] Livestock suffered heavily. Nevertheless, a large amount of food and raw materials stockpiled by the Germans during the occupation remained in the country.

The end of the war closed a struggle for the Czech nation's very existence. Since 1938 the Czechs had been humiliated and persecuted. They had also suffered from Nazi cruelties and the bloody fighting of the last days of the war. The radical mood of the country transformed resentment against the Nazis into demands for the permanent removal of all Germans. Popular support for the idea of expelling the Sudeten Germans caught even the Communist party by surprise. However, it swiftly went beyond the Košice program and espoused popular demands. A presidential decree on June 21, 1945, provided for the expropriation without compensation of the property of the Germans and Magyars as well as that of Czech and Slovak collaborators and traitors. The land that came within the scope of the decree involved about 270,000 farms covering 6,240,000 acres, which provided the communist minister of agriculture with a rich pork barrel from which to reward those who were willing to serve the party. By the spring of 1948 some 1,500,000 people had moved to the Czech borderlands left vacant by the Sudeten Germans, who had been removed to the American and Soviet zones of occupation in Germany in accordance with the mandate given Czechoslovakia by the Allied powers at Potsdam. After June 15, 1949, only 177,000 Germans were left in the Czech provinces.[29] This national adjustment wrought a profound change in the economic and social structure of the country. There was much disorder and violence—yet this is present in every revolutionary process. In the final analysis, the expulsion of the Sudeten Germans was a Czech national response—neither communist nor Soviet inspired—to a situation created by Nazi war policy and the Sudeten Germans themselves.

The Slovaks, led by the KSS, pressed for a similar removal of the Magyar minority from Slovakia. But it was one thing to press a claim against the Germans, who at that time were regarded as outlaws in all of Europe, and quite another to press one against the Hungarians, who were regarded as minor culprits. The Soviet Union tended to regard Hungary as a future satellite, like Czechoslovakia, and was not anxious to complicate its tasks by contributing to dissension between two of its prospective clients. At the Potsdam conference it failed to back the Czechoslovak demand for the removal of the Magyar minority. The matter was left to bilateral Czechoslovak-Hungarian negotiations. Under a mutual exchange agreement concluded between the two countries on February 27, 1946, 68,407 Magyars out of some 500,000 did leave for Hungary and a somewhat smaller number of Slovaks returned to Slovakia.[30] No large fund of land comparable to that in the Czech borderlands became available in Slovakia, a factor that had important repercussions in Czechoslovak politics.

Partly for this reason, the Czechoslovak delegation at the Paris Peace Conference in 1946 raised the demand for authorization to remove 200,000 Magyars from Slovakia. But by then, the Western powers were adamantly opposed to any further population transfer, and the matter was dropped.[31] They did, however, accede to the Czechoslovak demand for a small enlargement of the Bratislava bridgehead on the south bank of the Danube River at the expense of Hungary.[32]

Meanwhile, in June, 1945, the Poles suddenly reopened the Těšín (Teschen) question. On June 19 Polish troops under General Rola-Zymierski moved up to the city of Těšín. Possibly the Poles were encouraged to revive this old thorn in Polish-Czechoslovak relations by the Soviet government, which was anxious to prod Czechoslovakia into settling the Ruthenian question. In any event, on the same day the Soviet government invited Czechoslovakia and Poland to send delegations to Moscow to discuss outstanding questions affecting their relations. On June 29, after a week of discussions, the Czechoslovak and Soviet governments signed an agreement formally transferring Ruthenia to the Soviet Union.[33] When the Czechoslovak delegation returned to Prague, Prime Minister Fierlinger announced that the Polish-Czechoslovak discussions had been indefinitely adjourned. Apart from the loss of Ruthenia and the enlargement of the Bratislava bridgehead, the pre-Munich boundaries of Czechoslovakia remained intact.

The internal position of Czechoslovakia appeared to be fully consolidated. The withdrawal of Soviet and United States troops from Czechoslovakia as early as November and December of 1945 heralded a return to normalcy. By the fall of 1945 the country had also made considerable progress in economic reconstruction. Almost everyone agreed that it had bright prospects, provided that the wartime grand alliance and the internal balance between the communist and democratic forces could be maintained.

Since it had to compete with the democratic parties, the Communist party sought to be a mass party. The KSČ readily admitted members of former parties, drawing a line only at admitting former fascists and collaborators who, in Czech opinion, stood beyond the pale. The KSS, on the other hand, readily admitted even members of the former Hlinka People's party—indeed, it strenuously courted them. It posed as a Slovak nationalist party and did not hesitate to exploit religious prejudice by pointing out to the Slovak Catholic majority that the leadership of its competitor, the Slovak Democratic party, was largely Protestant. At the end of 1945 the KSS claimed a membership of 197,000, while in March, 1946, the KSČ claimed to have over 1,000,000 members.[34]

The growing strength of the Communist Party was reflected in its high moral and internal consolidation. Between 1945 and 1948 the leadership of the KSČ (with Klement Gottwald as chairman and Rudolf Slánský as secretary-general) remained remarkably stable, and the party was unusually free of factional strife. The KSS experienced some internal stress, however, as its nationalist posture came into conflict with the strategy of the parent party, the KSČ. At a joint meeting of the central committees of the KSČ and KSS in Prague on July 17–18, 1945, the Czech communists sharply criticized their Slovak comrades for viewing the development from a "nationalist," instead of a "class," point of view and for allying themselves with the "reaction" in the SNR, that is, the Slovak Democrats. A resolution, passed at the meeting, demanded that the "policy of the KSS must not be to separate but to orient the party towards the progressive forces in the Czech provinces and in the central government" and delegated Viliam Široký, a dour internationalist communist, to take charge of the KSS.[35] The separation of the two parties, which was maintained for tactical reasons, thereafter became nominal.

While the Communist party was united, the Czechoslovak Social Democratic party (chairman: Zdeněk Fierlinger; secretary-general: Blažej Vilím), which had a long and distinguished history of defending the cause of the Czech working class, was increasingly rent by a tug-of-war between its right and left wings, representing its liberal-democratic and Marxian-socialist traditions, respectively. The Czech National Socialist party (chairman: Petr Zenkl; secretary-general: Vladimír Krajina), which claimed to be a socialist but non-Marxist party, suffered from no such dilemma. It came increasingly to the fore as the most resolute adversary of the communists among the Czech parties. The Czech Populist party, under the leadership of Msgr. Jan Šrámek, the wartime premier in London, was a progressive Catholic party that before the war had received its greatest support among Czech peasants, especially in Moravia. After the war it had difficulty in finding its bearings in the radical atmosphere, which affected even the countryside. The Slovak Democratic party (chairman: Josef Lettrich; secretary: Fedor Hodža), which was largely a continuation of the Slovak branch of the proscribed agrarian party, suffered from the polarization

of Slovak opinion after the war between the radical revolutionary movement and the conservative Catholic anticommunist movement. It could
not compete with the communists in appealing to the former and found
it distasteful and dangerous to appeal to the latter, for fear of exposing
itself to the charge of catering to cryptofascists.

In retrospect it is clear that the prolongation of the provisional regime
benefited the Communist party more than the democratic parties, by
allowing an unusual measure of influence in public affairs to various
extraconstitutional mass organizations, such as worker, peasant, youth,
resistance, and other nationwide associations, that sprang up after the
liberation of the country. The general European "swing to the left"
immediately after the war undoubtedly helped the Communist party
gain a preponderant influence in these organizations. No instrument
was more important to it than the united Revolutionary Trade Union
Movement (ROH) and workers' factory councils (závodní rady). This
was true at least in the Czech provinces. In Slovakia, where the working
class did not have the same importance,[36] the Communist party relied
more on its influence in the resistance organizations, especially the
association of former partisans.

The communist plans had emphasized the necessity of gaining leadership of the working class, a traditional domain of the Social Democratic movement. In the first postwar days the communists occupied
positions of power in the ROH and the workers' councils in all large
factories. In this situation, the predominant influence of the Communist party with the working class,[37] combined with its control of important levers of the state apparatus, became the central fact of politics.

After the party consolidated its grip on the political structure in the
early summer of 1945, its initial moderation in economic affairs began
to fade. President Beneš and the two socialist parties viewed the nationalization of the principal industries, banks, and insurance companies as inevitable. Moreover, the corresponding pressure exerted by
the workers found widespread popular support. Under these circumstances the expropriation of German capital evolved into a wider trend
that reflected a consensus of all responsible political forces. Thus, the
first postwar measure of large nationalization in Europe[38] became a
demonstration of a common resolve to establish collective ownership
and direct state control over the chief means of production. The presidential decrees of October 24, which were mainly prepared by the
Social Democratic controlled Ministry of Industry, resulted in the
creation of a nationalized sector containing 61.2 percent of the industrial labor force.[39]

The nationalization decrees were the last great measures adopted
without parliament's authorization. After the convocation of the Provisional National Assembly four days later, the democratic parties sought

to limit the influence of the ROH and other extraconstitutional mass organizations and to confine policy-making to parliament. This encountered the opposition of the communists, who had found it advantageous to promote their aims through these organizations. They lent themselves more easily to manipulation than did the parliament, which had an orderly procedure and in which, moreover, they were a minority. The National Front began to experience increasing strains, and early in 1946 it was decided to hold general elections for the constituent assembly. May 26 was set as the date for the elections.

All parties committed themselves to maintain the National Front and the Košice program. This seemingly left no divisive issues. The electoral contest was nevertheless lively, though orderly. The difference between the parties lay in the accent they placed on specific aspects of the common program. The communists and Social Democrats stressed its social aspects and hinted that there were more to come. The democratic parties, on the other hand, maintained that the social goals of the program had largely been attained and placed a greater accent on freedom and democracy.

In Slovakia two new parties came into existence. Some of the old Slovak Social Democrats regarded the fusion of their party with the Communist party during the Slovak uprising in 1944 as a shotgun marriage, and now wished to go it alone. In January, 1946, with the assistance of the Czech Social Democrats, they formed the Labor party.[40] The other new party, the Freedom party, came into existence as a byproduct of electoral strategy by the Slovak Democratic party (DS). On March 30 Lettrich, the chairman of the DS, concluded an agreement (incorrectly known as the "April Agreement") with the Catholic leaders under which the Catholics were promised representation in all organs of the DS in a ratio of 7:3 in their favor.[41] The April Agreement promised to bolster the electoral strength in the DS, because the Catholic clergy had a powerful influence in Slovakia, especially in the rural areas, but it was fraught with dangers for the party. Many Catholic politicians were unreconstructed ľudáks. Their entry pulled the party sharply to the right and proved more than some of its leaders could stomach. The dissidents, among whom was notably Vavro Šrobár, formed the Freedom party on April 1.[42] Even more important was the communists' reaction to the April Agreement. In direct retaliation for its conclusion, the KSČ, with the concurrence of the Czech parties and the KSS, pressed through a further limitation of SNR prerogatives. Under the "Second Prague Agreement" on April 11, 1946, the SNR was deprived of the important power of making personal appointments without the approval of the Prague government.[43]

While the United States remained studiedly aloof during the electoral campaign, the Soviet Union gave a pointed reminder of its interest. On

May 22, almost the eve of the elections, it was announced the Soviet troops would be moved across Czechoslovak territory from Austria and Hungary to the Soviet zone of occupation in Germany. At the outcry of the democratic leaders over this crude attempt at intimidation, the troop movement was postponed, but its psychological purpose had already been attained—it reminded the Czechs and Slovaks that the Soviet army was close by and could return on short notice.[44]

The communists approached the elections with confidence. They hoped to win an absolute majority, but were not worried if they did not. On February 4, at the outset of the campaign, Gottwald assured the party workers: "Even if it should happen, which is improbable, that we should not gain a favorable result . . . the working class, the party, and the working people will still have sufficient means, arms, and a method to correct simple mechanical voting, which might be affected by reactionary and saboteur elements."[45] In other words, if the results of the election were favorable to the communists, they would be accepted; if not, they would be "corrected."

The elections on May 26, which proved to be the last free Czechoslovak elections, passed without incident and, according to foreign observers, without any attempt at intimidation or manipulation. The ballot was secret. All citizens over eighteen years of age, except political offenders, were not only allowed, but were obliged to vote, thus assuring a heavy turnout. The results did not basically alter the existing party balance. In the Czech provinces the KSČ obtained 40.1, the National Socialists 23.5, the Populists 20.2, and the Social Democrats 15.6 percent of the vote. In Slovakia the DS obtained 62, the KSS 30.3, the Freedom party 3.7, and the Labor party 3.1 percent.[46] In the whole country the communists (the combined KSČ and KSS) secured 37.9 percent of the vote. This fell short of their hopes but was still impressive. The most surprising development was the failure of the Social Democratic party, which had at one time been the largest party in Czechoslovakia but was now the smallest. Its Slovak branch, the Labor party, likewise made a poor showing. During the electoral postmortem the democratic wing blamed the defeat on the campaign strategy of the party leadership, which had adopted an almost identical position on many issues as the communists, and demanded that in the future the party follow an independent course of action.

The most impressive gains were made by the Slovak Democrats. There is no doubt, however, that the large vote cast for the DS represented less a show of confidence by the Slovak electorate in the DS than a rebuke to the KSS. Several factors accounted for the communists' modest showing in Slovakia compared with their good record in the Czech provinces: the relative importance of the Slovak working class; the absence of a large reserve of confiscated land with which to entice the land-hungry peasantry, such as existed in the Czech borderlands; the greater war damages in Slovakia and consequently greater problems of reconstruction (in the winter of 1945–46 there were acute food shortages in the province); the influence of the conservative Catholic clergy, who did not hesitate to warn in their sermons against the perils of "godless" communism; and the bitter memory of the many excesses committed against the civilian population by the Red Army during its operations in Slovakia in 1944–45, for which the injured took revenge by voting against the "Russian party," that is, the communists.[47]

The communists did not mistake the fact that the large vote for the DS was really a vote against them, and at once took steps to correct the situation. "We have not won yet, the struggle continues," said Gottwald in reporting the results of the election to the central committee of the KSČ on May 30,[48] and he made it clear that the first target in the continuing struggle must be the DS. In order to limit its influence. Gottwalk proposed to abolish what was left of Slovak autonomy—"even if we thereby violate formal national rights or promises or guarantees. . . . The Slovak comrades will no doubt understand."[49]

For the assault against the DS, Gottwald proposed four concrete steps: to limit further the prerogatives of the SNR, to launch a drive against the ľudáks camouflaged in the DS, to punish Jozef Tiso, and to take steps against the Slovak Catholic clergy, for the adoption of which the KSČ secured the concurrence of the National Front of the Czech parties on June 12 and the National Front of the Czech and Slovak parties two days later.[50] The first step was implemented in the "Third Prague Agreement" on June 27–28, 1946, which placed the legislative powers of the SNR under government control and the Slovak commissioners under the appropriate ministers in Prague.[51] In practice, Slovakia reverted to the position that it had held before the Munich agreement in 1938: that of a simple administrative unit, like Bohemia and Moravia. This latest advance of centralism placed added strains not only on the relations between the KSS and DS but also—since it was supported by all Czech parties—between the Czechs and Slovaks as a whole.

The National Front had been somewhat shaken by the electoral contest. However, all parties still professed loyalty to it and it was continued. The Eighth Congress of the KSČ in March, 1946, had endorsed the strengthening of the National Front and had directed the party to implement further the national and democratic revolution.[52] (The KSČ never failed to stress that whatever the future model of the republic, it would correspond closely to special Czech and Slovak conditions.[53]) On July 2 the cabinet was reshuffled to conform with the results of the elections. Fierlinger yielded the premiership to Gottwald, as the representative of the largest party. Of the twenty-five cabinet

posts, the KSČ received seven, the KSS one and one state secretaryship, the National Socialists four, the DS three and one state
secretaryship, and the Czech Populists and Social Democrats three
posts each.[54]

The parties were impelled to maintain a solid front by, among other
things, the opening of the Paris Peace Conference on July 29. Three
days earlier Gottwald and a delegation had returned from Moscow with
the good news that the Soviet government had not only promised to
support Czechoslovak claims at the conference but had also waived the
provision of the Potsdam agreement that entitled it to claim German
"external assets" in Czechoslovakia. Moreover, Gottwald revealed that
the Soviet government had promised to support Czechoslovak economic plans by concluding a long-term trade treaty. On the other hand,
the United States government had granted Czechoslovakia a credit of
$50 million in June to buy American surplus war supplies in Europe.
However, in September, before the credit was exhausted, the United
States abruptly suspended it because the Czechoslovak delegates at the
peace conference had applauded the Soviet delegate when he inveighed
against American "economic imperialism."[55]

Czechoslovakia had been caught in the first cross fire of the cold war.
On July 10, Soviet Foreign Minister Vyacheslav Molotov fired the first
shot in the East-West struggle for Germany, by calling for the formation
of a German national government and questioning the French right to
the Saar. United States Secretary of State James F. Byrnes replied in his
famous Stuttgart speech on September 6, by also calling for a German
national government and by repudiating—in effect—the Potsdam
agreement on the Oder-Neisse boundary and thus, by implication,
reopening the whole question of the eastern settlement. Czechoslovak
isolation from the West and dependence on the East had increased.

This development boded ill for the first important measure of the
Gottwald government—the Two-Year Economic Plan for 1947–48,
which the National Assembly approved on October 24.[56] The plan,
which proposed to raise the standard of living ten percent above the
prewar level, was oriented toward the long-range coexistence of the
private and nationalized sectors of the economy and was predicated on
the assumption that Czechoslovakia's traditional trade ties with the
West would continue. At that time the Soviet Union faced gigantic
problems of reconstruction and was in no position to provide economic
aid to Czechoslovakia or to furnish, in exchange for Czechoslovak
exports, the kind of goods and services she needed to realize her
economic plans. The promised Soviet-Czechoslovak trade pact did not
materialize until December, 1947.

The next important measure of the Gottwald government was political: it staged the trial of Monsignor Tiso as a deterrent to Slovak

separatists. The trial, which opened in Bratislava on December 3, 1946, ended in March of the following year with Tiso's conviction of treason and a sentence of death. As calculated by the communists, the sentence placed the DS in a difficult position. The leaders of the party, chairman of the SNR Lettrich and Vice-Premier Ján Ursíny, were Protestants and former agrarians. They had led the Slovak resistance against Tiso's government during the war and had little sympathy for him, but they were put under pressure by the party's Catholic wing to save him. When the government considered Tiso's appeal for mercy on April 16, the DS ministers moved to commute the sentence to life imprisonment. They were seconded by the Czech Populist ministers, who demurred at hanging a fellow priest. However, the other ministers held firm for execution.[57] On the recommendation of the cabinet, President Beneš declined the appeal for mercy, and on April 18 Tiso was hanged.

Since the removal of the Sudeten German minority the "Slovak question," that is, the problem of satisfactorily adjusting relations between the Czechs and Slovaks, had become the foremost internal question in the country. The trial of Tiso, by deeply offending conservative Catholic opinion in Slovakia, aggravated this concern. It was to trouble the Third Czechoslovak Republic until its end—and, indeed, continued in a different form afterward.

In the spring of 1947 the Communist party adopted the goal of winning at least fifty-one percent of the votes in the next elections and thus gaining a majority in the National Assembly. This angered the other parties, but it did indicate that the communist leadership did not yet wish to take over all power, but was committed to the maintenance of the National Front. There were radical elements in the party that criticized the leadership for not following the Bolshevik way. Simultaneously, there were anticommunist groups in the country, biding their time. Both segments, however, represented politically insignificant forces. The predominant majority of the people wholeheartedly endorsed the objectives of the National Front to liberate men from economic and social domination within a democratic society.

These hopeful expectations, predicated on the belief that Czechoslovakia could eventually become the show window of a new, more humane system and the bridge between East and West were shattered in the summer of 1947 by Stalin's new policy line,[58] which called for consolidating the Soviet hold on Eastern Europe and drawing clear lines of combat with the West. On June 5, at Harvard University, U.S. Secretary of State George C. Marshall made his historic offer of American aid to Europe. Czechoslovakia was eager to share in the American aid, which it needed to complete the Two-Year Economic Plan successfully. On July 4 and 7 the cabinet and inner cabinet, respectively, voted unanimously to accept an invitation to send a delegation to a preliminary conference of European states in Paris to discuss the Marshall Plan.[59] Immediately after the cabinet made its intention known, a government delegation led by Premier Gottwald left for Moscow where it was scheduled to negotiate mutual trade problems and to discuss the possibility of concluding a Franco-Czechoslovak treaty. When the delegation arrived in Moscow on July 9, it was given an ultimatum by Stalin to choose between East and West. On the following day the Prague government reversed its decision to send a delegation to Paris.[60] It had chosen the Soviet alliance.

At the end of September, the Information Bureau of the Communist parties (Cominform), including the KSČ, was founded at Szklarska Poreba in Poland as the institutional device of the communist international control system.[61] The delegates aimed "to apply the final touches to a general plan for easing the 'National Front' allies out of power and establishing a Communist dictatorship" in Eastern Europe.[62] The Cominform, then, was founded at the moment when "the Soviet Union had finally decided to take under her direct control a number of East European states," particularly Czechoslovakia.[63] The secretary general of the KSČ, Rudolf Slánský, informed the conference that the first task of the party was "to deal a death blow to reaction in Slovakia,"[64] and added ominously: "It will be necessary to throw reactionary forces out of the National Front."[65] The road was opened for the Stalinist takeover in Czechoslovakia.

From the Cominform to the Prague Coup

By the fall of 1947 the struggle for power in East Central Europe was almost decided. Czechoslovakia remained the sole exception. It still had a coalition government. During the summer her hitherto favorable economic development suddenly ceased. A severe drought caused the harvest to fall to one-half of its normal level. As the leading party in the government, the communists received the major blame for the deteriorating economic situation. Feeling that the tide of public opinion was turning against them, they sought to postpone the elections that they had proposed in the spring. The democratic parties, on the other hand, aware that their chances in an electoral contest had improved, pressed for holding them at an early date. After much bickering it was decided to hold them in May, 1948.

As the parties girded for another electoral struggle, the communists displayed a wide arsenal of political and psychological weapons. In August they proposed that the owners of property in excess of one million Czechoslovak crowns pay a "millionaires' tax" to provide aid to the ailing rural districts. Millionaires had never been numerous in Czechoslovakia and their ranks had been further reduced by the war and the subsequent expulsion of the German minority. Even the Social Democrats demurred at supporting so demagogic a measure. However, when communist propaganda succeeded in arousing popular support for it, the Social Democrats hastened on September 11 to conclude an agreement with the KSČ providing for their cooperation. The social democratic leadership thus sought to bind the KSČ to their own democratic practices. However, a large number of party members sharply criticized the agreement and Minister Václav Majer even tended his resignation.[66]

A strident note crept into communist propaganda. The communist press began systematically to impugn the loyalty of the other parties to the republic and to vilify their leaders. The public was shocked by the revelation on September 10 of an abortive attempt on the lives of noncommunist ministers Jan Masaryk, Petr Zenkl, and Prokop Drtina, who had received parcels containing bombs. The communist Minister of Interior Válav Nosek and the communist-dominated police showed a curious lack of interest in the case. Instead, with much fanfare, the Slovak Commissioner of Interior, Mikuláš Ferjenčik, announced on December 14 the discovery of a plot by the ľudák underground to assassinate President Beneš and overthrow the republic. Subsequently, the police linked the alleged plot to the ľudák exiles Karol Sidor and Ferdinand D'určanský. Widespread arrests, ultimately of more than 500 persons, followed. Among the arrested were three DS members of the National Assembly and a secretary of Vice-Premier Ján Ursíny. Although Ursíny himself was not implicated in the plot, he was forced to resign from the cabinet.

The affair served as a smoke screen behind which the communists prepared to purge the Slovak board of commissioners of its DS majority and to restructure the National Front of Slovak parties to make it more responsive to their wishes.[67] To set the stage for this coup, they arranged for the Slovak Trade Union council (SOR—the Slovak counterpart of ROH) to meet in Bratislava on October 30 and for the Slovak Peasant Union to meet there two weeks later. At its October 30 meeting the SOR passed a resolution blaming the board of commissioners for the breakdown in food distribution and a failure to safeguard the security of the state and calling for its dismissal. Another resolution called for the reorganization of the Slovak National Front to include trade union, resistance, and peasant organizations. On the following day, in response to this "voice of the people," the communist chairman of the board of commissioners, Husák, four other communist commissioners and the nonparty Commissioner of Interior Ferjenčik resigned from the board. Husák declared that the board was thereby dissolved and opened negotiations with the minute Freedom and Labor parties, until then unrepresented on the board, to form a new one. The DS leaders naturally protested against this novel constitutional concept whereby a minority could dismiss the majority from the cabinet. They refused to resign from the board or to admit the mass organizations into the National Front.

The government in Prague then stepped into the situation, but to the dismay of the communists the National Socialists and Populists refused to associate themselves in a communist measure of coercion against the DS. On November 18, after prolonged negotiations, a new board of commissioners was formed in which the DS was deprived of its majority and the Freedom and Labor parties received representation.

The Slovak "November crisis" proved to be a dress rehearsal for the Prague "February crisis." The communists had effectively used their control of the police and mass organizations and had ruthlessly exploited every weakness in the ranks of the DS to achieve their objective. The democratic parties were alerted to what was in store for them. An early symptom of their reaction was the reassertion by the Social Democratic party of its independence of the KSČ. At its congress at Brno on November 16 the procommunist Fierlinger was removed as chairman of the party and replaced with centrist Bohumil Laušman.[68] The democratic parties were encouraged by this development to believe that the Social Democratic party would cooperate with them. Laušman, however, personified the inability of the party to decide whether to fight on the side of the Communist party for social demands or on the side of the democratic parties for democracy. Under his leadership the party wavered in Hamlet-like indecision between the communist and democratic parties.

The communists increased their pressure on the other parties through the winter of 1947–48, with each issue exacerbating the political atmosphere and widening the divergences between the two camps.[69] The noncommunist parties made common complaint about police use of false confessions and *agents provocateurs*. Accusations levelled at the KSČ for attempting to monopolize control of the police engendered popular demands for the preservation of basic democratic freedoms. The time remaining for any possible settlement was running out. In November, 1947, the upper echelons of the KSČ began concerted action according to a plan based on their experience in the Slovak crisis. This involved a call by the ROH for a meeting of the workers' factory councils and peasant committees to formulate new popular demands. The party would then endorse their program, which would be adopted subsequently by all the mass organizations and those personalities within the existing parties who had secretly been won over by the communists. The ensuing "renovated" National Front would draw up a unified list of candidates for the elections.[70] The new alliance would then mount an electoral campaign aided by the mass media of communication, national committees, and police machinery—all controlled by the party.[71]

On February 12, 1948, the ROH issued a call to the workers' factory councils to meet in Prague on February 22, an action that convinced the democratic leaders that the communists were about to move. In a cabinet meeting the following day, the National Socialist ministers precipitated a crisis by protesting against the demotion and transfer of eight high noncommunist police officers by Minister of Interior Nosek. All ministers except the communists approved a motion introduced by the National Socialists to instruct Nosek to reinstate the police officers and desist from further personnel changes in the police forces. The communists were placed in a minority position in the cabinet and appeared isolated. Encouraged by their success, the National Socialists decided to take the offensive against them and try to upset their timetable. On February 20 the National Socialist ministers, followed by the Populist and Slovak Democratic ministers, resigned from the cabinet in protest against the failure of Nosek to carry out the cabinet decision of February 13 in the police matter. The "latent crisis" was thus transformed into "open crisis."[72]

The dramatic return of two old adversaries, U.S. Ambassador Laurence A. Steinhardt and Soviet Deputy Minister of Foreign Affairs and former ambassador to Czechoslovakia Valerian A. Zorin, to Prague on February 19 appeared to give the crisis an international dimension. Steinhardt declared to the press that the door to the Marshall Plan was still open to Czechoslovakia.[73] Zorin arrived ostensibly to expedite deliveries of grain, which the Soviet government had promised in December to alleviate the food shortage. The Western press speculated widely that he had really come to Prague to direct the communist takeover. Actually, no evidence ever turned up indicating that he had directly intervened in the crisis.[74] He did not have to. Gottwald and his associates had matters well in hand.

The ministers who had resigned constituted a minority, since neither the Social Democrats nor nonparty ministers Jan Masaryk and Ludvík Svoboda had been consulted and thus had not resigned. Consequently, Gottwald remained legally in power. The ministers who had resigned counted on President Beneš to refuse to accept their resignations. In that case, they would compel Gottwald either to call new elections or to carry out the decision of the cabinet in the police matter. They thought in strictly parliamentary terms, regarding their resignation as a mere cabinet affair, and called on their supporters "to remain calm under all circumstances." But the communists refused to abide by the rules of parliamentary democracy. While the democratic ministers and parties passively awaited Beneš's decision, the communists used their control of mass organizations and the police to take over power.

On the morning of February 21 Gottwald addressed an organized mass meeting in the Old Town Square in Prague. He accused the resigned ministers of having formed a "reactionary bloc" in the cabinet to obstruct the popular policies of the communists. They had precipitated the crisis, he alleged, to prevent the holding of elections, the outcome of which they feared. By their action they had "excluded themselves from the National Front," and the communists could have no further dealings with them. They would be replaced "with new people, who had remained faithful to the original spirit of the National Front." Gottwald put his proposal for the "renovation" of the cabinet into a resolution that was approved by acclamation, and on the spot a workers' delegation was "elected" to carry this expression of the "will of the people" to the president.

At the same time the communists deployed the instruments of their takeover—party activists, workers' militia, the police, and "action committees"—in Prague and outside it, according to a carefully prepared plan. On February 24 armed workers lent Prague a certain spurious aura of Petrograd in 1917, but their military value was slight, if any. In the event of an armed conflict with the other parties, the communists relied on the police, particularly on specially trained police regiments composed exclusively of communists. On the morning of February 21 the police assumed guard over the Prague radio station, post and telegraph offices, and railway stations. The most original instrument of the communist takeover was the action committees, which had been secretly organized earlier among men within and outside the KSČ whom the party could trust. Action committees sprang up in every government bureau, factory, and town—in fact, in every organized body in the country—and proceeded to purge them of democrats.[75]

By mass demonstrations centered on Prague and the mere threat of violence, the communists isolated and silenced the democratic parties, split the Social Democratic party, and awed the president. In such an unprecedented situation, naturally, the majority of the population expected word from Beneš—word that never came. After resisting the communist demands for five days, Beneš yielded. On February 25 he accepted the resignation of the democratic ministers and simultaneously appointed a new cabinet handpicked by Gottwald, which—in addition to communists and Social Democrats—included some members of the National Socialist, Populist, and Slovak Democratic parties, who had secretly agreed to cooperate with the communists. The façade of the National Front was thus maintained.

The only force that could have prevented the communist takeover was the army. But the army under General Svoboda, a friend of the communists, remained neutral throughout the crisis. In any event, Beneš never considered opposing force by force. The behavior of the noncommunist party leaders was, if possible, even worse. While the communists were brilliantly using the instruments of power, "the non-Communist parties . . . had no organization, no plan"[76] and finished in complete disarray, despite the support they enjoyed from the helpless and baffled majority of the Czech and Slovak people. By their precipitate and ill-considered resignation, the democratic ministers had made it possible for the communists to take over power by constitutional means. They were not forced out of the government by the communists; they had walked out of it.

Meanwhile, the zealous Husák had anticipated Gottwald's coup at Prague with one of his own at Bratislava.[77] But the events in Bratislava lacked the drama of those in Prague, because they constituted, more or less, only a mopping-up operation, designed to complete what had been left undone in November. Unlike Gottwald, Husák did not have to contend with Beneš. Moreover, while Prague was swarming with foreign correspondents who had come to observe and report on the death of Czechoslovak democracy, none troubled to go to the provincial backwater of Bratislava. Husák, therefore, dispensed with the elaborate *mise en scène* that Gottwald felt compelled to arrange at Prague. Unlike the DS ministers in Prague, the DS commissioners in Bratislava did not resign; they had to be expelled from the board. On February 21, without awaiting the outcome of the cabinet crisis in Prague, Husák wrote them that the resignation of the DS ministers from the central government bound them to resign too, and against the eventuality that they might dispute this ruling he posted policemen at the doors of their offices to turn them away. They did not choose to resist, for the DS had been emasculated and cowed in November and had nothing left with which to fight. The communists took a majority of seats on the board (eight out of fifteen), and distributed the rest among the other parties (including two pliant DS members) and representatives of the communist-controlled mass organizations. Action committees completed the mop-up.

After appointing the new government on February 25 and receiving its members when they were sworn in on February 27, Beneš retired to his country residence at Sezimovo Ústí. On June 7 he resigned and withdrew from further participation in the conduct of state affairs. The communists were left the sole masters of the republic—free to reorganize it according to their beliefs and concepts.

Endnotes

1. Edvard Beneš, *Memoirs: From Munich to New War and New Victory* (Boston, 1954), p. 139.

2. See the account of Eduard Taborsky, Beneš's former secretary, "Benešovy moskevské cesty" —"Beneš's Trips to Moscow"] *Svědectví*, 1, Nos. 3–4 (1957), 203ff. Taborsky stated that in his wartime conversations with Soviet leaders Beneš held that Ruthenia should belong either to Czechoslovakia or to the Soviet Union. "As much as he wished" this area "to be Czechoslovak again, he was by no means ready to insist on it as the price of Soviet friendship" (p. 207). On March 24, 1945, Soviet Foreign Minister Vyacheslav M. Molotov asked Beneš to repeat in writing his acceptance of the loss of Ruthenia (p. 212).

3. Gustáv Husák, *Svedectvo o Slovenskom národnom povstaní* [*Testimony about the Slovak National Uprising*] (Bratislava, 1964), pp. 554–55; Zdeněk Fierlinger, *Ve službách ČSR* [*In the Service of the Czechoslovak Republic*] (2 vols.; Prague, 1947–48), II, 599ff.

4. See Miroslav Soukup, "Některé problémy vzájemných vztahů mezi komuninstickými stranami" ["Some Problems of the Mutual Relations between the Communist Parties"], *Příspěky k dějinám KSV*, IV (Feb. 1964), 13ff.

5. Gottwald's report to the central committee of the KSČ, September 25–26, 1946.

6. Milan Hübl, "Lidová demokracie V 1946" ["Popular Democracy in 1946"], *Slovanský přehled*, No. 2 (1966), 65–70.

7. See Karel Kaplan, *Znárodnění a socialismus* [*Nationalization and Socialism*] (Prague, 1968), *passim*. This tendency was discernible in other European communist parties, notably in France and Italy.

8. See the discussion Beneš had with Gottwald and other communist exiles in Moscow in December 1943, in Beneš, *Memoirs*, pp. 268–75, and, from the communist point of view, Bohuslav Laštovička, *V Londýně za války* [*In London during the War*] (Prague, 1960), pp. 310–30.

9. See Libuše Otáhalová and Milada, Červinková, eds., *Dokumenty z historie československé politiky 1939–1943* [*Documents on the History of Czechoslovak Politics 1939–1943*] (2 vols.; Prague, 1966), II, 750–51.

10. For the minutes of the negotiations see Miloš Klimeš *et al.*, eds., *Cesta ke květnu* [*Road to May*] (2 vols.; Prague, 1965), I, 380–453. For accounts see Laštovička, *V Londýně*, pp. 496–553, and Husák, *Svedectvo*, pp. 578–89.

11. Josef Korbel, *The Communist Subversion of Czechoslovakia, 1938–1948* (Princeton, 1959), p. 114. Korbel rightly blames Beneš for his withdrawal from what the President wrongly considered to be a matter of party politics. For revealing conversations between president Beneš and U.S. ambassador in Moscow, W. Averell Harriman, on March 22 and 31, 1945, see U.S. Department of State, Foreign Relations of the United States. Diplomatic Papers 1945. Vol. IV: *Europe* (Washington, 1968), pp. 427–29 and 430–33.

12. Korbel, *The Communist Subversion*, p. 114.

13. Minister Jaroslav Stránský's recollections, ibid., p. 114.

14. Jaroslav Opat, *O novou demokracii, 1945–1948* [For a New Democracy, 1945–1948] (Prague, 1966), pp. 44–48; Jozef Jablonický, *Slovensko na prelome* [*Slovakia in Transition*] (Bratislava, 1965), pp. 227–85; Jaroslav Barto, *Riešenie vzťahu Čechov a Slovákov, 1944–1948* [*Solving the Relations Between the Czechs and the Slovaks, 1944–1948*] (Bratislava, 1968), pp. 30–34; and Samo Falťan, *Slovenská otázka v Českovslovensku* [*The Slovak Question in Czechoslovakia*] (Bratislava, 1968), pp. 186–200.

15. Edvard Beneš, *Šest let exilu a druhé světové války. Řeči, projevy a dokumentry z r. 1938–45* [*Six Years of Exile and the Second World War: Speeches, Declarations, and Documents in 1938–45*] (Prague, 1946), pp. 423–24.

16. The full text of the Košice program may be found in *Za svobodu českého a slovenského národa: Sborník dokumentů* [*For the Freedom of the Czech and Slovak People: a Collection of Documents*] (Prague, 1956), pp. 368–90, published by the Institute for the History of KSČ in Prague. For an English translation of point six of the program dealing with the Slovaks, see Jozef Lettrich, *History of Modern Slovakia* (New York, 1955), pp. 317–18.

17. Bohuslav Laštovička, "Vznik a význam košického vládního programu" ["The Origin and Importance of the Košice Government Program"], *Československý časopis historický*, VIII (August 1960), 465.

18. For the negotiations leading to the formation of the government and its composition, see Opat, *O novou demokracii*, pp. 48–50. In the SNR and its executive organ, the board of commissioners, the Communist party of Slovakia (KSS), and the Democratic party (DS) continued to share power equally.

19. Laštovička, "Vznik," p. 463.

20. Klimeš, *Cesta*, I, 447.

21. During the war both the Moscow and London exiles emphasized the primary importance of the home front. Upon returning to Prague, however, both united in refusing to offer the Czech resistance leaders any representation in the cabinet. See Josef Belda et al., *Na rozhraní dvou epoch* [*On the Frontier of Two Epochs*] (Prague, 1968), pp. 40–41.

22. Apart from the fact that the SNR was recognized in the Košice program, it had functioned continuously since February, 1945. By the time the government was established in Prague in May, the SNR was well entrenched and carried on as a quasi-government.

23. Falťan, *Slovenská otázka*, pp. 206–207; Barto, *Riešenie*, pp. 54–58.

24. Barto, *Riešenie*, pp. 67–79; Falťan, *Slovenská otázka*, pp. 207–12; Belda, *Na rozhraní*, p. 43.

25. The four Czech parties received forty seats and the two Slovak parties, fifty seats each. The remaining forty seats were distributed among representatives of mass organizations.

26. Radomír Luža, *The Transfer of the Sudeten Germans* (New York, 1964), p. 262.

27. V. Jarošová and O. Jaroš, *Slovenské robotníctvo v boji o moc, 1944–1948* [*The Slovak Workers in the Struggle for Power, 1944–1948*] (Bratislava, 1965), p. 69.

28. Luža, *The Transfer*, p. 262.

29. Ibid., pp. 271, 291; Karel Kaplan, "Rok československé revoluce 1945" ["Year of the Czechoslovak Revolution"], *Sborník historický*, 15 (1967), p. 115.

30. Juraj Zvara in *Historický časopis*, No. 1 (1964), 28–49, and in *Příspěvky k dějinám KSČ* (June 1965), 409–27.

31. U.S. Department of State, *Foreign Relations of the United States 1946*. Vol. IV: *Paris Peace Conference: Documents* (Washington, 1970), 727–28; A. C. Leiss and R. Dennett, eds., *European Peace Treaties after World War II* (Boston, 1954), pp. 93–96.

32. For Article I of the Hungarian peace treaty, defining the bridgehead, see ibid., p. 274.

33. F. Němec and V. Moudrý, *The Soviet Seizure of Subcarpathian Ruthenia* (Toronto, 1955), pp. 251–53. For the text of the Soviet-Czechoslovak treaty of June 29, 1945, on the cession of Ruthenia, see *British State and Foreign Papers*, Vol. 145 (1943–45) (London, 1953), pp. 1096–98.

34. Opat, *O novou demokracii*, p. 69. For a good survey of the strength, aims, and leadership of the KSČ and all parties after liberation, see Belda, *Na rozhraní*, pp. 22–39. For the KSČ, see Zdeněk Eliáš and Jaromír Netík, "Czechoslovakia," in William E. Griffith, ed., *Communism in Europe. Continuity, Change, and the Sino-Soviet Dispute* (Cambridge, Mass., and London, 1966), II, *passim*.

35. Barto, *Riešenie*, pp. 98–100; Jarošová and Jaroš, *Slovenské robotníctvo*, p. 97. The resolution was implemented at a conference of the KSS at Žilina on August 11–12, 1945, when Široký replaced Karol Šmidke as chairman and Štefan Bašťovanský replaced Edo Friš as secretary of the party. Neither Šmidke nor Friš was a Slovak nationalist but both had been swept along by the nationalists since the Slovak uprising. Široký had not participated in the uprising, being in prison at the time. Of Slovak origin but a Magyar by education, he was a bitter enemy of Slovak nationalists whether in or out of the party. The true spokesman of the nationalists in the KSS, Gustáv Husák, saved himself, for the moment, by abjuring nationalism—also for the moment—and turning on his wartime nationalist allies, the Slovak Democrats.

36. In Slovakia 25.58 percent of the population derived an income from industry, mining, and the trades, compared to 39.5 percent in Bohemia and Moravia. On the other hand, 52.59 percent of the Slovak population worked in agriculture, forestry, and fisheries, while only 20.37 percent of the population of the Czech provinces did. See Jarošová and Jaroš, *Slovenské robotníctvo*, p. 65.

37. June, 1945, the prominent communist trade unionist Antonín Zápotocký became chairman of the ROH. The membership amounted to 2,249,976 on December 31, 1947. See V. Pachman, "Boj o odborovou jednotu v letech 1945–1948" ["Struggle for the Unity of the Trade Union Movement in 1945–1948"], *Československý časopis historický*, VIII, No. 6 (1960), 810.

38. Czechoslovakia was the second state after the U.S.S.R. to nationalize in industry and banks.

39. Opat, *O novou demokracii*, p. 115; Kaplan, *Znárodněni*, pp. 7–58.

40. Marta Vartíková, *Od Košíc po február* [*From Košice to February*] (Bratislava, 1968), p. 71. Jaroslav Nedvěd, "Cesta ke sloučení sociální demokracie s komunistickou stranou" ["The Road to the Merger of the Social Democratic

and Communist Parties"], *Rozpravy Československé Akademie věd*, No. 8 (1968), 46–48.

41. Opat, *O novou demokracii*, pp. 162–66; Belda, *No rozhraní*, p. 70; Vartíková, *Od Košíc*, p. 78.

42. Vartíková, *Od Košíc*, pp. 74–77.

43. Barto, *Rišenie*, pp. 138–47; Falt'an, *Slovenská otázka*, pp. 216–17.

44. Hubert Ripka, *Le Coup de Prague: Une révolution préfabriquée* (Paris, 1949), p. 39.

45. Belda, *No rozhraní*, p. 60.

46. Ibid., pp. 72–73; Opat, *O novou demokracii*, pp. 178–89.

47. The same factors operated against the communist, to a smaller extent, in Moravia. The communist share of the vote in Moravia was 34.5 percent as against 43.3 percent in Bohemia.

48. Belda, *Na rozhraní*, p. 74.

49. Vartíková, *Od Košic*, p. 80; Jarošová and Jaroš, *Slovenské robotníctvo*, p. 157; Barto, *Riešenie*, p. 159.

50. Barto, *Riešenie*, p. 160; Belda, *Na rozhraní*, p. 80.

51. Belda, *Na rozhraní*, p. 83; Opat, *O novou demokracii*, pp. 193–95; Barto, *Riešenie*, pp. 170–71; Falt'an, *Slovenská otázka*, p. 222. For the Czecho-Slovak negotiations in the National Front, see the informative article by Miroslav Bouček and Miloslav Klimeš, "Národní fronta Čechů a Slováků v letech 1946–1948" ["The National Front of the Czech and Slovaks in the Years 1946–48"], *Sborník historický*, 20 (1973), 207–14.

52. Opat, *O novou demokracii*, pp. 135–36.

53. Gottwald on July 8, 1946, in presenting the "construction program" of his new government to the National Assembly. See Opat, *O novou demokracii*, pp. 197–200. Also in September, 1946, and on October 4, 1946.

54. Ibid., pp. 191–96; Belda, *Na rozhraní*, pp. 84–86. While claiming the premiership and a proportionate share of posts in the central government, the communists were extremely reluctant to accept the results of the elections in the Slovak National Council and the board of commissioners. It was not until August 7, after bitter wrangling between the KSS and the DS, that the DS was allowed to take 60 percent of the seats in the SNR and 9 out of 15 posts on the board of commissioners. The communists fought tooth and nail against relinquishing the commissariat of interior, which controlled the police. In the end they agreed to relinquish it, not to a DS member but to a nonparty expert, Gen. Mikuláš Ferjenčík. Moreover, contrary to the principle that the strongest party should get the chairmanship of the board, which Gottwald had invoked to claim the premiership, this important post was retained by the communist Husák. See Vartíková, *Od Košic*, pp. 109–11; Jarošová and Jaroš, *Slovenské robotníctvo*, p. 163.

55. James F. Byrnes, *Speaking Frankly* (New York, 1947), pp. 143–44; Ripka, *Le Coup*, p. 41. In addition to the insult at the peace conference, the Americans were angered by a Czechoslovak deal with Rumania, under which Prague resold

American goods to the Rumanians at a profit, and by the Czechoslovak failure to compensate American citizens for the loss of property in Czechoslovakia through nationalization. The American rebuff was a great blow to Masaryk, who had to explain it in a secret cabinet meeting on October 7. Se Belda, *Na rozhraní*, pp. 120–21; U.S. Department of State, *Foreign Relations of the United States 1946*, Vol. VI: *Eastern Europe: The Soviet Union* (Washington, 1969), pp. 216, 220ff.

56. Belda, *Na rozhraní*, p. 95; Opat, *O novou demokracii*, p. 204.

57. Belda, *Na rozhraní*, pp. 172–73.

58. Jaroslav Opat, "K metoď studia a výkladu některých problémů v období 1945–1948" ["On the Method of Study and Explanation of Some Problems in the Period of 1945–1948"], *Příspěvky dějinám KSČ* (February, 1965), 65–83.

59. Belda, *Na rozhraní*, pp. 121–22; Opat, *O novou demokracii*, pp. 236–38.

60. Ripka, *Le Coup*, pp. 51–55. Apparently, the Czechoslovak acceptance of the invitation to go to Paris was in part a result of a misunderstanding brought about by Soviet inefficiency. Masaryk sought advance Soviet approval for accepting the invitation, but Bodrov, the Soviet chargé d'affaires in Prague, lacked instructions. Failing to get a reply from Moscow in time, the Czechoslovak government announced its acceptance—only to be told by Moscow that it must not go to Paris. See Belda, *Na rozhraní*, pp. 122–25. Masaryk, who clung to relations with the West, was crushed by the humiliation. For more information see Josef Belda et al., "K otázce účasti Československa na Marshallově plánu" ["On the Question of the Czechoslovak Participation at the Marshall Plan"], *Revue dějin socialismu*, VIII (1968), 81–100.

61. *For a Lasting Peace, for a People's Democracy,* November 10, 1947.

62. Eugenio Reale, who participated at the conference as the delegate of the Communist party of Italy, in Milorad Drachkovitch and Branko Lazitch, eds., *The Comintern: Historical Highlights* (New York, 1966), p. 260.

63. Vladimir Dedijer, *Tito* (New York, 1953), p. 292.

64. The minutes of E. Reale in Drachkovitch and Lazitch, *The Comintern*, p. 254; Jarošová and Jaroš, *Slovenské robotníctvo*, p. 232.

65. Conference of the Nine Communist Parties, p. 118, quoted in Korbel, *Communist Subversion*, p. 186.

66. Nedvěd, "Cesta ke sloučení," p. 56; Belda, *Na rozhraní*, pp. 154–67; Opat, *O novou demokracii*, pp. 242–45.

67. For the Slovak November crisis see Jarošová and Jaroš, *Slovenské robotníctvo*, pp. 221–52; Vartíková, *Od Košic*, pp. 147–62; Lettrich, *History*, pp. 249–51. For Gottwald's formula to solve the crisis, see Václav Král, ed., *Cestou k únoru* [*The Road to February*] (Prague, 1963), p. 270.

68. Nedvěd, "Cesta ke cloučení," pp. 58–59.

69. The KSČ raised demands for the nationalization of private trade and for new land reform. In February, 1948, it was defeated in an attempt to prevent an increase in the salaries of public servants. It continued to use the security apparatus to increase pressure, and managed to hush up an investigation of the attempt against the lives of three democratic ministers.

70. According to a confidential survey of public opinion taken by the communist-controlled Ministry of Information, the KSČ faced a loss of eight to ten percent in the next election. See Ripka, *Le Coup,* p. 190.

71. Miroslav Bouček, *Praha v únoru* [*Prague in February*] (Prague, 1963), pp. 25, 149; Karel Kaplan in *Historica* (Prague, 1963), V, 241.

72. The literature on the February crisis is quite extensive. Among the communist accounts and documentary collections are: Belda, *Na rozhraní,* pp. 223–62; Bouček, *Praha,* pp. 143–254, and *Únor 1948: Sborník dokumentů* [*February 1948: A Collection of Documents*] (Prague, 1958); Král, *Cestou,* pp. 329–410; Miroslav Bouček and Miloslav Klimeš, *Dramatické dnů února 1948* [*The Dramatic Days of February, 1948*] (Prague, 1973), *passim;* Jiři Veselý, *Prague 1948* (Paris, 1958), pp. 71–190, which is a French adaptation of his *Kronika únorových dňu* [*Chronicle of the February Days*] (Prague, 1958); and Alois Svoboda *et al., Jak to bylo v únoru* [*What Happened in February*] (Prague, 1949), *passim.* A Czech National Socialist account may be found in Ripka, *Le Coup,* pp. 201–316, of which there is an English translation, *Czechoslovakia Enslaved* (London, 1950), and a Social Democratic one in Bohumil Laušman, *Kdo byl vinen?* [*Who is to Blame?*] (Vienna, n.d.), pp. 108–54. President Beneš's side of the story is told in detail by the head of his chancellery, Jaromír Smutný, in "Únorový převrat 1948" ["February Revolution, 1948"], *Doklady a Rozpravy,* Nos. 12 (1953); 19 (1955); 21 (1955); 25 (1956); and 28 (1957); published by the Institute of Dr. Edvard Beneš in London. For Steinhardt's report of the February coup, see *Foreign Relations of the United States, 1948,* 9 vols. (Washington, 174), IV, 738–756. Accounts by Western scholars may be found in Korbel, *Communist Subversion,* pp. 206–35, and Paul E. Zinner, *Communist Strategy and Tactics in Czechoslovakia, 1918–1948* (New York, 1963), pp. 204–16. The most recent analysis was given by Pavel Tigrid, "The Prague Coup of 1948: The Elegant Takeover," in Thomas T. Hammond, ed., *The Anatomy of Communist Takeovers* (New Haven and London, 1975), pp. 399–432. Among the numerous accounts by Western journalists, perhaps the best may be found in Dana Adams Schmidt, *Anatomy of a Satellite* (Boston, 1952), pp. 108–21.

73. Report of ČTK, the Czechoslovak News Agency, in Král, *Cestou,* p. 347. Steinhardt informed Czechoslovak officials that the United States would consider favorably an application for a credit of $25 million to purchase American cotton. See Schmidt, *Anatomy,* p. 110. Although Czechoslovakia experienced great economic difficulties at the time, the economic weapon was quite inadequate to affect the crisis.

74. According to Belda, *Na rozhraní,* p. 265, Zorin assured Gottwald that "the Soviet Union would not allow Western powers to interfere in the internal affairs of Czechoslovakia." Since, however, none of the Western powers intervened in the crisis, the Soviet Union did not have to do so either. Although the crisis had international repercussions, it was a purely internal one.

75. The purge involved some 28,000 persons. See Karel Kaplan, *Utváření generální linie výstavby socialismu y Československu* [*The Formation of the General Line of the Construction of Socialism in Czechoslovakia*] (Prague, 1966), p. 27.

76. Kaplan, *Historica,* V, 250ff.

77. For the Slovak side of the crisis see Vartíková, *Od Košíc, pp. 181–84;* Jarošová and Jaroš, *Slovenské robotníctvo,* pp. 265–67; Lettrich, *History,* pp. 259–60.

5

John Lewis Gaddis

Spheres of Influence: The United States and Europe, 1945–1949

John Gaddis is Distinguished Professor of history at Ohio University and probably the leading historian of United States security policy during the Cold War. His early work, *The United States and the Origins of the Cold War, 1941–1947*, was an early counter-revisionist work (New York, Columbia University Press, 1972), while *Strategies of Containment* (New York, Oxford University Press, 1982) surveyed the shifting concepts underlying American national-security policy throughout the Cold War. The essays collected in *The Long Peace* (New York, Oxford University Press, 1987), from which this chapter 3 (pp. 48–71) has been reprinted with the permission of the author and Oxford University Press, probe diverse and revealing issues: the nature of nuclear deterrence, the decision to extend military commitments to Asia, the State Department's interpretation of the Sino-Soviet relationship, among others. Gaddis has also been a leader of American efforts to seek Soviet historians' cooperation in scholarly cooperation and the opening of archives. He is about as sovereign in this field as any historian is likely to get.

Gaddis's special strength lies in dissecting the currents of contending policy that were debated within American administrations, sometimes between the military and civilians; in this case, primarily between leading foreign-service officers. His work radiates a certain assurance of American reasonableness: The occasional zany plan for rolling back the enemy, half-cocked idea for fomenting partition, ebullient confidence in the utility of nuclear hardware, all of which also litter American discussion, always emerge as safely subordinated to the statesmanship of the truly thoughtful protagonists, such as Bohlen and Kennan. Not that Gaddis is unaware of the fissionable side of American preponderance. But he conveys to us a world in which restraint and wisdom largely prevail. Looking back on forty years of the Cold War, this author agrees with Gaddis on the overall outcome (allowing for major exceptions: e.g. Vietnam), but finds the process more disorderly. Nonetheless, Gaddis' work reveals to us the elaboration of policy as we would have hoped it was debated, and he correctly insists that such ascribed causal forces as the needs of American capitalism do not automatically yield a given policy outcome.

In this study, Gaddis follows the winding path by which American policy makers learned to make their peace with the partition of Europe. The chief spur was the lesson that Bohlen perceived in the fall of 1945; the influence the Soviets claimed over a neighboring state's foreign-policy alignment seemed to require total subjugation. On the other hand, when Bohlen reached this conclusion, it was not yet true for Hungary and Czechoslovakia. Gaddis rightly emphasizes how by 1947 the German issue lay at the center of the policy debate. Nonetheless, Germany had not been the most neuralgic area of initial quarrel with the Soviets. German problems did present highly technical issues that exacerbated friction, such as reparations and the role of central administration, but the split over Germany was also a result of the overall breakdown between East and West.

When Gaddis wrote this article, most observers took it for granted that the partition of Germany and Europe had become permanent fixtures of the world's geopolitical landscape. Both assumptions have been shattered, and the era of European partition is ending. The justifications that Gaddis cites for accepting partition in the late 1940s, such as the hope that Western development would be attractive enough to help undermine the Soviet hold on the satellites, seemed hopelessly naive by the 1960s and 1970s. In fact, they have come to pass. The events of 1989–90 will doubtless prod continuing reevaluation of these early decisions that seemed almost to accumulate for lack of real alternatives in the early postwar years.

A basic conflict is . . . arising over Europe between the interests of Atlantic sea-power, which demand the preservation of vigorous and independent political life on the European peninsula, and the interests of the jealous Eurasian land power, which must always seek to extend itself to the west and will never find a place, short of the Atlantic Ocean, where it can from its own standpoint safely stop." This was George F. Kennan's depressing assessment of the situation that confronted the United States and its allies early in 1945, conveyed in a letter to his friend and fellow Russian expert, Charles E. Bohlen. Kennan went on to recognize the extent to which victory over Germany required the Soviet Union's military cooperation, even if this brought about an unprecedented projection of Moscow's influence into central Europe. "But with all of this, I fail to see why we must associate ourselves with this political program, so hostile to the interests of the Atlantic community as a whole, so dangerous to everything which we need to see preserved in Europe. Why could we not make a decent and definite compromise with it—divide Europe frankly into spheres of influence— keep ourselves out of the Russian sphere and keep the Russians out of ours? . . . And within whatever sphere of action was left to us we could at least [try] to restore life, in the wake of the war, on a dignified and stable foundation."[1]

Bohlen received Kennan's letter at Yalta on the eve of Franklin Roosevelt's last meeting with Churchill and Stalin. In his hastily composed hand-written reply, he acknowledged as valid Kennan's assessment of Soviet intentions, but dismissed as "utterly impossible" his recommendation for a division of Europe into spheres of influence. "Foreign policy of that kind cannot be made in a democracy," he continued. "Only totalitarian states can make and carry out such policies." Years later, in his memoirs, Bohlen elaborated: "The American people, who had fought a long, hard war, deserved at least an attempt to work out a better world. If the attempt failed, the United States could not be blamed for not trying."[2]

This exchange between the State Department's two most experienced Soviet specialists reflects the dilemma facing the United States as it contemplated the implications of a victory in Europe purchased at the price of an expansion of Soviet influence over Europe. Should the United States play by the Russians' rules and carve out for itself a sphere of influence over as much of the Continent as remained open to it? Or should it seek to persuade the Russians to change the rules: to build a new European order, based upon a rejection of power politics altogether? In the end, of course, Europe was divided, very much along the lines that Kennan had proposed. But Washington accepted this solution only slowly, and with considerable reluctance: Bohlen's idea of a postwar settlement based upon principles of self-determination and big power cooperation proved remarkably persistent. In its eventual decline and ultimate rejection can be traced the origins of a European settlement that has lasted, itself with remarkable persistence, down to the present day.

I

Americans had not been much inclined, prior to World War II, to think about the balance of power in Europe, but events of the early 1940's had abruptly undercut earlier isolationist arguments that whatever happened on the Continent could not affect the security of the United States. In their place, there arose the conviction that the primary American interest in postwar international affairs would be to ensure that no single state dominate Europe.[3] As an Office of Strategic Service analysis puts it in the summer of 1944: "our interests require the maintenance of a policy designed to prevent the development of a serious threat to the security of the British Isles (and of the United States), through the consolidation of a large part of Europe's resources under any one power."[4] Increasingly, as the end of the war approached, strategic planners in Washington became aware of the prospect that Germany's defeat would leave a power vacuum in central Europe into which only the Russians would be well-positioned to move. Great Britain, they noted, would be far too weak to provide a counterbalance.[5] But there was, as yet, no consensus that the United States should project its own influence into Europe to restore equilibrium.

Britain and the United States were following divergent policies in their efforts to deal with the inevitable expansion of Soviet influence into postwar Europe, another O.S.S. analysis pointed out in January, 1945: The British approach emphasized "the division of the problem areas into spheres of Soviet and non-Soviet predominance with a neutral zone between." Obviously, such a straightforward partition of the continent would be simple to accomplish, but it would be "a very primitive type of international compromise":

> [I]n its extreme form it implies that within each of the areas affected the interests of the Great Powers are essentially irreconcilable, and that the only practicable solution is to isolate geographically the fields where these interests are to operate. . . . Thus this system probably supplies each great power with the maximum of temptation and the maximum of opportunity for intervention in the domestic affairs of its neighbors. In the long run this might well lead to divergent trends of development in the Soviet and non-Soviet spheres and to a sharpening of the differences between "two worlds."

The American preference should be "to establish and maintain independent democratic regimes within both spheres and within the neutral zone. . . . In the absolute form, such a program would constitute a complete negation of the system of spheres of influence; and to the extent that it is realized in practice it will limit the authority of each Great Power within its sphere."[6]

To be sure, Washington never actually contemplated such a thorough rejection of spheres of influence. President Roosevelt's own cherished concept of a world settlement enforced by "Four Policemen"—the United States, Great Britain, the Soviet Union, and Nationalist China— clearly implied the existence of such spheres. Certainly the United States was not prepared to give up its own predominance in Latin America, or to deny itself new areas of influence in the Pacific after the war.[7] Nor was there a predisposition to challenge the Russians' obvious attempt to secure a dominant postwar influence along their western borders.[8]

But there was no great effort, as the end of the war approached, to position American forces in such a way as to counter Soviet strength in Europe: indeed it was at Yalta that Roosevelt in effect promised the withdrawal of American troops from the Continent within two years of Germany's surrender.[9A] Nor did Churchill's impassioned pleas to hold American forces in place after that event meet with a favorable response from President Truman.[10] As late as the Potsdam Conference in July, 1945, State Department planners were still worrying that the British might seek to lure the United States into supporting a spheres of influence settlement in Europe. Such a solution, they concluded, would "represent power politics pure and simple, with all the concomitant disadvantages. . . . Our primary objective should be to remove the *causes* which make nations feel that such spheres are necessary to build their security, rather than to assist one country to build up strength against another."[11]

It requires something of an effort, at this distance, to reconstruct the reasons for Washington's aversion to spheres of influence in Europe, even in the face of what were clearly Russian efforts to create their own in that part of the world. Probably most important in the minds of Roosevelt administration officials, curiously enough, was the fear of a resurgent isolationism inside the United States. "Our boys do not want to fight to rule the world, isolationist Congressman Hamilton Fish warned, "or to divide it into three parts, like ancient Gaul, between Great Britain, Russia, and the United States."[12] The President and his advisers were keenly sensitive to such arguments. In the Atlantic Charter and other wartime pronouncements, they had resuscitated the vision of a Wilsonian peace, based on self-determination, economic multilateralism, and collective security, not because they believed such a settlement to be attainable in every respect, but as a means of overcoming the isolationism that had grown out of the failure to implement that kind of peace two decades before.[13] A peace based too obviously on spheres of influence might seem to many Americans to be no peace at all, and hence result, as had the settlement of 1919, in the withdrawal rather than the projection of United States authority.

It would be unfair, though, to write off the administration's idealism in this respect solely as a way to sanctify the wielding of power. There was, as well, a sincere sense among Roosevelt, his subordinates, and much of the public at large that the "old diplomacy" had failed, and that Wilsonian methods of collective security, tempered to be sure by a regard for practical circumstances, deserved to be given another try.[14] American officials did work overtime during this period to demonstrate, at times with creative ingenuity, how the benefits of a Wilsonian settlement would accrue not just to the United States but to the rest of the world as well. But these arguments were by no means wholly cynical: to have acknowledged openly spheres of influence would have been to admit the irrelevancy of the American domestic experience, upon which so substantial a portion of this new approach to world affairs was based.

There also still existed uncertainty as to the Russians' motives for seeking spheres of influence in the first place. Despite some worry over the ideological component in Soviet policy,[15] the prevailing wartime view in Washington was that the projection of Russian power into Europe was occurring for defensive rather than offensive reasons. If Moscow could be assured of the West's peaceful intentions, then its reasons for seeking spheres of influence, it was thought, would disappear.[16] An open attempt to build countervailing power in Europe might have the effect of a self-fulfilling prophecy, reinforcing the Kremlin's suspicions and perpetuating its inclination toward unilateralism. "[W]e must always bear in mind," a State Department analysis of Soviet-American relations concluded in December, 1945, "that because of the differences between the economic and political systems of our two countries, the conduct of our relations requires more patience and diligence than with other countries." American interests had to be defended, to be sure. "On the other hand, in order to minimize Soviet suspicions of our motives we should avoid even the appearance of taking unilateral action ourselves."[17]

A year after his reply to Kennan's letter, Bohlen still considered spheres of influence an inappropriate solution to Europe's problems. It might be possible to reach a *modus vivendi* with the Russians on that basis, he acknowledged early in 1946. But such a settlement would

> reduce the United Nations organization to a façade with the real power concentrated in the hands of the United States, Great Britain, and the Soviet Union. While this policy

would perhaps offer the best means of avoiding difficulties with the Soviet Union in the immediate future, merely to state it is to demonstrate its impossibility of adoption. . . . [I]t would constitute a great step backwards from the principle of a cooperative world and would never receive the support of the American people.

Moreover, Bohlen added, such a settlement "would merely temporarily postpone an eventual clash with the Soviet Union under conditions infinitely worse for the United States and Great Britain" since, as a dictatorship, the U.S.S.R. "would be able to consolidate into an absolute bloc its sphere of influence while the Western democracies by their very nature would be unable to do the same in theirs."[18]

For Bohlen and those who thought like him, the very nature of Western political systems precluded a spheres of influence settlement: democracies could not join with dictatorships to divide the world. There would have to be, instead, a compromise between the facts of power and the obligations of justice; only on that basis could American interests in Europe be satisfied. Even after reading Kennan's pessimistic "long telegram" on the roots of Soviet behavior, Bohlen saw no reason "why the two systems cannot peacefully coexist in the same world provided that neither one attempts to extend the area of its system by aggressive and ultimately forceable means at the expense of the other." The problem for the West was "(a) to convince the Soviet Union of this possibility and (b) to make clear well in advance the inevitable consequence of the present line of Soviet policy based on the opposite thesis."[19]

II

For the next year, the Truman administration followed closely the dual approach Bohlen had recommended. On the one hand, there took place an exhaustive effort—probably insufficiently appreciated, in retrospect—to convince the Russians that a comprehensive European settlement would be preferable to a cold-blooded division of the Continent into separate spheres. At the same time, though, there was set in motion a program of gradual preparation for a division in Europe, as much in the hope that it would ward off Soviet inclinations in that direction as from a desire actually to implement it.

There was little inclination in Washington in the early postwar months to try to challenge directly the reality of Soviet hegemony in Eastern Europe. Instead, American officials made an effort to try to "educate" the Russians to the fact that outright domination would be both unnecessary and counter-productive. In October, 1945, Bohlen had actually suggested recognizing "legitimate" Soviet security interests in Eastern Europe if the Russians would agree to show the same restraint regarding the internal affairs of that region that the United States had demonstrated in Latin America.[20] Secretary of State James F. Byrnes made this idea the subject of a public speech later that month, pointing out that the disinterested and mutually beneficial Good Neighbor Policy had evolved out of the self-interested Monroe Doctrine: "We surely cannot and will not deny to other nations the right to develop such a policy."[21]

But Bohlen himself had seen the principal difficulty in this approach: "from all indications the Soviet mind is incapable of making a distinction between influence and domination, or between a friendly government and a puppet government."[22] The report of the Ethridge Committee, a delegation of American observers sent by Byrnes to Rumania and Bulgaria to report on Soviet policies there, strongly reinforced this conclusion: "[T]o concede a limited Soviet sphere of influence at the present time," it argued, "would be to invite its extension in the future."[23] With public and Congressional opinion growing increasingly hostile to the idea of any further concessions to the Russians on any grounds, it is not surprising that a consensus began to emerge within the government early in 1946 against further efforts to "enlighten" Moscow as to the disadvantages of spheres of influence, and in favor of tougher methods.[24]

The central issue here was the future of Germany. State Department planners had argued virtually without exception that there could be no stability in postwar Europe if Germany remained divided. Experiences of the interwar years had seemed to show that the Germans would never accept permanent partition of their country; moreover, a unified Germany was thought vital to the economic recovery of Europe as a whole.[25]

The failure to persuade the Russians to abandon their sphere of influence in Eastern Europe brought the German question to the forefront in two important but contradictory ways: it made all the more urgent the need to ensure that Germany could pose no threat to the Soviet Union in the future, thereby removing the Russians' principal excuse for dominating Eastern Europe in the first place; but it also raised the need for the Western powers to begin thinking about consolidating their own positions in Germany, in the event agreement with the Russians proved impossible. The dilemma was that by weakening Germany to reassure the Russians the West would leave itself vulnerable, but by strengthening its position there it would confirm Soviet suspicions. It was in the effort to resolve this dilemma that the United States in the spring of 1946 undertook two new initiatives on Germany: the proposal, in the Council of Foreign Ministers, of a four-power disarmament treaty; and, simultaneously, movement toward the consolidation of Western occupation zones.

The idea of a treaty between the United States, the Soviet Union, Great Britain, and France to keep Germany disarmed had been discussed off and on in Washington for some time, both for the purpose of reassuring allies that the United States did not propose to abandon them after the war, and as a means of alleviating Soviet fears of a resurgent Germany that had provided the justification for imposing a sphere of influence in Eastern Europe.[26B] But by the spring of 1946 the proposed treaty had become a test of Soviet intentions as well: if the Russians accepted it, the argument ran, they would have no further need for spheres of influence. If they did not, then the division of Europe would have to be accepted as a fact and the West would have to begin consolidating its own sphere. It was with these alternatives in mind that Byrnes formally proposed a twenty-five year treaty to the Russians at the end of April, 1946.[27]

Moscow's negative response seemed to confirm the fears of those who had argued that its determination to impose spheres of influence reflected offensive rather than defensive intentions. There was as yet no unanimous acknowledgment in Washington that Europe had been divided into two spheres, James Reston noted in the *New York Times* early in May, "but even the most pro-Soviet members of Mr. Truman's Administration agree that the Administration is nearer to accepting this thesis today than it has been at any other time since the end of the war."[28] It was within this context that emphasis began to be given to the other element in American policy during this period: the consolidation of a defensible Western position in Germany in the event negotiations with the Russians failed.

Convinced that the division of Europe was inevitable in any event, Kennan had for some time been arguing in favor of this approach. The only acceptable alternative, he had written in March, 1946, was for the United States and its allies "to carry to its logical conclusion the process of partition which was begun in the east and to endeavor to rescue [the] western zones of Germany by walling them off against eastern penetration and integrating them into [the] international pattern of western Europe."[29] This in fact is what Washington began to do in the spring and summer of 1946, with the termination of reparations shipments from the American zone, the initiation of talks with London looking toward a merger of American and British occupation zones and, most important, Secretary of State Byrnes's assurance at Stuttgart in September that American troops would remain in Germany as long as the occupation forces of any other power did.[30]

It is important to note, though, that these decisions of 1946 did not constitute final American acceptance of the division of Germany. The consequences of such a division, both in economic and geopolitical terms, were sufficiently unsettling to keep American negotiators at work for another year in the effort to secure a German peace treaty. At late as December, 1947, Secretary of State George C. Marshall, who spent much of that year conducting these negotiations, was still emphasizing the need to make sincere offers to the Russians on Germany rather than simply gestures in the expectation of refusals. Marshall was "most anxious in regard to the general international situation to avoid a 'frozen front,' which was tragic to contemplate."[31]

But a German settlement that risked leaving the Soviet Union in a position of dominance in central Europe was an even more unsettling prospect and by 1947 there had emerged a definite consensus in Washington that negotiated reunification was not worth that price. "I think that it amounts to this," Kennan told students at the Air War College in April of that year:

> We insist that either a central German authority be established along lines that will make it impossible for the Soviet Union to dominate Germany . . . , or that we retain complete control over the western zones. . . . I think it may mean the partition of Germany, and we all admit that is undesirable. . . . I hope we won't shrink from carrying out that partition rather than giving the Russians the chance to dominate the whole country, though.[32]

If the fear of a Germany under Soviet control served to make the idea of a divided Europe more respectable in American eyes, so too did the prospect of a power vacuum in the Near East and Eastern Mediterranean brought about by the decline of British power there. American planners had been well aware of the fact that the war had weakened Britain's world position,[33] but even so the rapidity of the collapse came as a surprise. As late as April, 1946, Truman could still speculate publicly about the possibility of a contest for world influence between London and Moscow, with Washington acting as an impartial umpire.[34] But within less than a year, American opinion had shifted to the view, as an official in the British Foreign Office noted with grim satisfaction, "that no time must be lost in plucking the torch of world leadership from our chilling hands."[35]

The threat to the balance of power in the Near East had seemed, at first something that could be handled simply by issuing statements aimed simultaneously at warning the Russians off and at arousing world opinion against them. Both the Iranian and Turkish crises of 1946 had been dealt with in this way, with Washington relying primarily upon the deterrent effect of pugnacious pronouncements.[36] The situation in

Greece, though, was something else again. Here the danger to the balance of power came not so much from the possibility of external attack as from that of internal disarray, the effects of which, it was thought, would benefit the Russians without the risks of direct military involvement. As the State Department's Office of Near Eastern and African Affairs noted late in 1946, "[i]t is vastly to the interest of the U.S. that the recognized government [in Greece] be assisted in becoming strong enough *before the fact* to handle its internal problems without requiring a sudden increase in assistance *during* a state of actual or near civil war."[37]

The British decision to cut off economic and military aid to Greece and Turkey early in 1947 forced Washington to move beyond attempts to discourage Soviet expansion by rhetoric alone. Instead, it appeared, positive action would be required to reconstitute centers of resistance to the Russians in areas vulnerable to them. This new approach would require squeezing increased appropriations out of a Congress still much attracted by the budgetary advantages of isolationism: hence, the administration's all-too-successful effort, through the Truman Doctrine, to alarm legislators by raising the specter of a world divided between antipathetic ways of life.[38] But the new situation also stimulated serious thinking in Washington as to how the United States might most effectively use its resources, not just in Greece and Turkey but in Europe as a whole, to reconstitute the balance of power left unstable by the creation and feared expansion of Moscow's sphere of influence. The collapse of Council of Foreign Ministers discussions on a German peace treaty that April further heightened the sense of urgency.[39]

The result, of course, was the Marshall Plan, an ambitious attempt to reconstitute a political balance in Europe by economic means. The plan rested upon the assumption that the Russians were not prepared to risk war to extend their influence; rather, the danger was that they might successfully exploit European psychological demoralization resulting from war damage and the discouragingly slow pace of reconstruction, whether by means of external intimidation, internal subversion, or even the possibility that Europeans might vote their own communists into office through free elections.[40] The Marshall Plan also reflected, paradoxically enough, an awareness of limited capabilities: the United States could not afford to contain threats to the balance of power in all places by all means. Maintaining European equilibrium ranked first on Washington's list of priorities; of the limited instruments available for doing this, economic assistance seemed to provide the quickest and most effective way.[41]

Even so, the traditional aversion to spheres of influence still lingered in the United States: it was partly in deference to this sentiment that Marshall initially offered aid to the Soviet Union and its East European satellites as well, with a view to placing responsibility for the division of Europe squarely on Moscow's shoulders.[42] It was the Russians' refusal of this offer—after a disquieting initial hesitation—that reconciled American officials once and for all to the inevitability of a divided Europe. As career Foreign Service officer Burton Y. Berry put it at the end of July, 1947, it was time to "drop the pretense of one world."[43C]

It was left to Bohlen, who had originally so strongly resisted the idea of a divided Europe, to draft the most thoughtful analysis of the new situation:

> The United States is confronted with a condition in the world which is at direct variance with the assumptions upon which, during and directly after the war, major United States policies were predicated. Instead of unity among the great powers—both political and economic—after the war, there is complete disunity between the Soviet Union and the satellites on one side and the rest of the world on the other. There are, in short, two worlds instead of one. Faced with this disagreeable fact, however much we may deplore it, the United States in the interest of its own well-being and security and those of the free non-Soviet world must re-examine its major policy objectives. . . . The logic of the situation is that the non-Soviet world through such measures are open to it [should] draw closer together politically, economically, financially, and, in the last analysis, militarily in order to be in a position to deal effectively with the consolidated Soviet area. Only in this way can a free and non-Soviet world hope to survive in the face of the centralized and ruthless direction of the Soviet world.[44]

Or, as Secretary of State Marshall put it with characteristic brevity at a cabinet meeting in November: "Our policy, I think, should be directed toward restoring a balance of power in Europe and Asia."[45]

III

"[T]he realisation is now widespread," the British embassy in Washington reported early in 1948, "that there is nothing reprehensible *per se* in the exercise of power. Whereas a year ago the phrase 'power politics' bore a sinister connotation in the American mind, it has since come to be accepted as a normal technical term."[46] Curiously, though, this willingness to think in "balance of power" terms did not produce a corresponding determination on the part of the United States to carve out a sphere of influence for itself in Europe, comparable to the one the Russians had imposed. Instead, Washington's preference was to try to reconstitute an *independent* center of power on the continent, strong enough to act on its own to maintain equilibrium there. As John D.

Hickerson, Director of the State Department's Office of European Affairs, described it, the idea was to create "a third force which was not merely the extension of US influence but a real European organization strong enough to say 'no' both to the Soviet Union and to the United States, if our actions should seem so to require."[47]

"The idea of a United States of Europe has, of course, long appealed to Americans, who are always prone to accept the naive and uncritical assumption that ideas and institutions that have proved their value here can be exported to provide ready-made remedies for the ills of less fortunate areas of the world."[48] It was not unusual for British diplomats in Washington to take a slightly jaded view of American enthusiasms, and this dispatch, written in the spring of 1947, was no exception. But it would be a mistake to see the Truman administration's support for European integration—in preference to the overt extension of an American sphere of influence over Europe—as a simple-minded effort to transplant what had flourished at home to stonier and less fertile soil overseas. There were in fact good reasons for Washington's reluctance, even after acknowledging the reality of a divided Europe, to impose its own control there.

One reason was that American officials did not see themselves as possessing, at that time, either the resources or the domestic support necessary to dominate large portions of the world in order to deny them to the Russians. "[P]ublic and Congressional reaction to foreign affairs is still conditioned by two main factors," a British Foreign Office analyst observed in May, 1947: "fear and dislike of Russia and aversion to the responsibility, and more particularly to the cost, of preserving the world balance of power."[49] A country still wary of international commitments could not discard its traditions overnight; rather, administration leaders argued, there would have to be a gradual expansion of responsibilities, carried out with full awareness of the need to expend limited resources efficiently and alongside obvious and convincing demonstrations from its allies that the United States would not be the only nation carrying the resulting burdens.[50]

It followed from this that a multi-polar international system, with several independent centers of power sharing the burdens of containment, would best suit American interests. Certainly this was Kennan's view: "it should be a cardinal point of our policy," he wrote in October, 1947, "to see to it that other elements of independent power are developed on the Eurasian land mass as rapidly as possible in order to take off our shoulders some of the burden of 'bi-polarity.'" Kennan went on during the next year to develop the concept of keeping key power centers—notably Great Britain, the Rhine-Ruhr industrial complex, and Japan—from falling under Soviet control, not by extending American control over them, but rather by encouraging their develop-

ment as independent forces with the strength and self-confidence necessary to defend themselves.[51] An American sphere of influence in Europe would undermine that strategy, to which Truman administration
officials were generally sympathetic.[52]

Such a solution would also conflict with the still-cherished, it imper-
fectly observed, tradition of non-intervention. Despite the collapse of
"one worldism," American officials continued to pay deference to the
principle of self-determination. "[I]t is not our intention to impose our
way of life on other nations," Assistant Secretary of State Charles
Saltzmann insisted in September, 1947. "That in itself would be undemocratic. Our only purpose is, in so far as possible, to give other
nations the opportunity to decide these matters for themselves, free
from coercion."[53] This was not simply boiler-plate rhetoric, intended
for public consumption: the view in Washington persisted throughout
the late 1940 s that the viability of political systems depended in large
part upon their autonomy, even spontaneity. For this reason, Americans
were willing to tolerate a surprising amount of diversity within the anti-
Soviet coalition: one of the more durable strains in State Department
thinking between 1946 and 1948 involved the need to cooperate with
the democratic Left in Europe, despite the fact that its programs of
nationalization and social welfare were anathema to conservatives in the
United States.[54] If one result of such flexibility was to make European
governments better able to resist Soviet pressure because of their firm
base of popular support, then that only confirmed the long-standing
American view that principle and self-interest were not always irreconcilable.

It should be recognized as well, though, that the interests of the
United States and non-communist Europe were largely congruent during this period, and that Washington as a consequence had little need to
impose its will on potential allies. If there was ever a time when one
nation was *invited* to extend its influence over another part of the world,
then surely the experience of the United States in Europe after World
War II came close to it.[D] "[W]e should be placed in an impossible
position," Foreign Secretary Ernest Bevin reminded the Cabinet, "if
the United States Government withdrew from Europe."[55] The governments of Greece, Turkey, and Iran all fervently applauded the growth of
American influence in the Eastern Mediterranean and the Near East.[56]
And certainly public opinion in Western Europe welcomed a more
active American role there as well, given the alternatives at best of
further economic deterioration, at worst of Soviet domination.[57] "It
seems evident," Secretary of State Marshall commented in November,
1947, "that, as regards European recovery, the enlightened self-interest
of the United States coincides with the best interest of Europe itself."[58]

There were other, more specific, reasons for promoting the idea of

European integration. One involved the problem of what to do with Germany now that an agreement with the Russians had become unlikely. A Joint Chiefs of Staff analysis in April, 1947, summarized the dilemma: "Without German aid the remaining countries of western Europe could scarcely be expected to withstand the armies of our ideological opponents until the United States could mobilize and place in the field sufficient armed forces to achieve their defeat." Moreover, "the complete resurgence of German industry . . . is essential for the economic recovery of France—whose security is inseparable from the combined security of the United States, Canada, and Great Britain." But all indications were that the French would "vigorously oppose any substantial revival of German heavy industry." This was unfortunate, since "the German people are the natural enemies of the USSR and of communism." It followed that the American interest was to convince both the French and the Germans "that the emergence of a principal world power to the east . . . which they can successfully oppose only if both are strong and united . . . makes them interdependent just as France, England, Canada, and the United States are interdependent."[59] European integration might provide a way to incorporate Germany into a European system without leaving Germany in control of that system. As Kennan put it early in 1948: "Only such a union holds out any hope of restoring the balance of power in Europe without permitting Germany to become again the dominant power."[60]

Finally, it should be pointed out that Americans did not see the division of Europe as something that would last forever. To an extent that is only now coming to be fully appreciated, Washington planners throughout this period were quietly considering how the Soviet Union's Eastern European satellites might be detached from the Kremlin's control.* This had been one of the additional motives behind the offer of Marshall Plan aid to the satellites in the summer of 1947; a year later Kennan was making the point that "the door should be left open for everyone in Europe to come in at the proper time so that there could be a real unification of Europe and the development of a European idea."[61] Only a viable European union would exert this kind of attraction, William Clayton pointed out: "The Russian satellite countries would then feel the pull so much stronger than the West than from the East, that Russia would find it more and more difficult and in the end impossible to hold them."[62] "Our objective," Under Secretary of State Robert Lovett wrote to Averell Harriman in December of 1948, "should continue to be the progressively closer integration, both economic and political, of presently free Europe and eventually of as much of Europe as becomes free."[63]

"If the United States entertained any idea of extending American influence or domination over Europe," Secretary of State Marshall had commented in a public speech given a year earlier, "our policy would not be directed toward ending European dependency upon this country but toward perpetuating that relationship."[64] This statement can stand as an accurate reflection of how American officials saw their own *intentions* with regard to Europe during the early days of the Cold War. There was, as the British Embassy in Washington perceptively pointed out, a distinction between seeking a balance of power and a sphere of influence:

> On a broad view, an analysis of its activities leads to the conclusion that what the United States most requires from candid observers abroad are not reproofs that it is abusing its giant power, but commendation for such wisdom and generosity as it has thus far displayed, along with encouragement bravely to persevere in the employment of its vast resources for its own and the general welfare. In the meantime, to those critics who accuse her of taking undue advantage of her own strength and of the weakness of others, America might well reply in the words of Clive when arraigned by a committee in the House of Commons for having exploited his unrivalled power in India for purposes of personal aggrandizement: "By God, Mr. Chairman, at this moment I stand astonished at my own moderation."[65]

But intentions are one thing; actual policy is something else again, as the events of 1948–49 made clear. The American vision of an independent, prosperous, and self-confident center of power in Europe proved to be more elusive than had appeared to be the case in 1947. Circumstances gradually compelled the United States to create its own sphere of influence in Europe, despite its own profound misgivings about that course of action.

IV

It is evident, in retrospect, that Washington considerably underestimated the difficulties of establishing an independent "third force" in Europe. That concept had been based upon several precariously balanced propositions: that a Soviet threat existed awesome enough to compel Europeans to submerge ancient rivalries, but not so awesome as to prevent them from acting in a self-confident and decisive manner; that American economic assistance would stimulate self-reliance without encouraging dependency; that no further initiatives would be necessary to sustain a European order whose collective interests would be compatible with, though independent of, those of the United States. It did not take long for the shakiness of these assumptions to become apparent.

"It is curious that there is so little discussion of the strategic aspects of European integration," F. B. A. Rundall, of the British Foreign Office, noted in February, 1948. "One would imagine that Mr. Lippmann or a similar pundit would have taken up the point that, for the countries concerned, the economic decisions involved in integration are inevitably bound up with considerations of strategy and common defence in which the United States are no less involved. Yet perhaps this is a hare that no one wishes to start before the elections."[66] To the extent that domestic political considerations required a step-by-step approach to the expansion of American commitments overseas, Rundall was on target. Yet, one has the impression that American planners were genuinely surprised, quite apart from their concern about public and Congressional reactions, to have the issue of military security in Europe raised in the first place.

They themselves had consistently deprecated the probability of a Soviet military attack. "The Soviet effort in Europe is a *political* one, not a *military* one," Kennan had repeatedly argued. "The Soviet aim is not to undertake a military conquest which could only be followed by Red Army occupation of Western Europe. . . . The aim is rather to establish in that area a system of indirect control which will give them power without responsibility."[67] Admittedly, no one could rule out the possibility of war altogether. "[T]he threat of war, intended or unintended, will become greater in proportion to weaknesses in the economy, military force, and foreign policy of the United States," the Pentagon's Joint Intelligence Committee noted in February, 1948. But as long as reasonable American strength was maintained—and, in particular, as long as the deterrent power of the American atomic monopoly remained in existence—then the prospect of war in Europe by anything other than gross miscalculation on Moscow's part seemed very remote.[68]

Nevertheless, the whole point of the Marshall Plan had been to restore self-confidence, so that Europe would be in a position to defend itself. From this perspective, the European state of mind was at least as important as American intelligence estimates. It came as something of a shock, therefore, to have Ernest Bevin calling Washington's attention in January, 1948 to "the further encroachment of the Soviet tide" and the need to "reinforce the physical barriers which still guard our Western civilisation," in terms Dean Acheson might have found useful in prodding obdurate Congressmen toward a grudging acceptance of international responsibilities.[69] The Russians, with their usual deftness in producing responses opposite from those intended, punctuated Bevin's point dramatically by staging a coup in Czechoslovakia the following month: this event, together with warnings from other European leaders in addition to Bevin, was sufficient to convince many in Washington that the Marshall Plan alone would not restore self-confidence in Europe; some form of explicit military guarantee would be needed as well.[70E]

Such guarantees, though, would raise problems. There was no assurance that Congress would authorize a direct military commitment to the defense of Western Europe, or what the exact nature of that commitment would be.[71] There was the question of what countries would be covered by such a guarantee: for the United States to undertake to defend everyone would be to exceed American capabilities; for it to leave certain countries out might only invite aggression against them.[72] There was concern that such a guarantee might sap the Europeans' resolve to defend themselves in the first place. "If they are not willing to defend their national independence at this risk," Kennan argued in April, 1948, "then perhaps they would indeed be beyond helping. For there are very definite limits—which people here are constantly forgetting—on the ability of this country to shoulder alone the risks and responsibilities of keeping alive the hope for a continuation of civilization in large parts of this globe."[73]

Cautious negotiations with both allies and Congressional leaders over the next year solved some of these problems. The administration assured Congress that the proposed North Atlantic Treaty involved no obligation to go to war without its consent.[74] The problem of limited resources was addressed by stressing the extent to which an explicit commitment to defend Western Europe would in itself deter the Russians without more specific measures having to be taken; indeed, Secretary of Defense Louis Johnson even suggested that NATO might make it possible to *reduce* the American defense budget.[75] Washington carefully undertook no obligation to station additional troops in Europe, reviving instead the old pre-World War II concept of the United States as an "arsenal" supplying military hardware to the Europeans, who would themselves furnish the manpower. As John Hickerson put it late in 1948: "It is a question of committing, not forces, now, but the potential of Pittsburgh and Detroit."[76F]

But the problem of reconciling self-sufficiency with reassurance was not so easily resolved. Despite official claims that the new alliance would facilitate more than it would impede European integration,[77] Kennan was quietly predicting to his colleagues that "this arrangement will come to overshadow, and probably to replace, any development in the direction of European union":

> Instead of the development of a real federal structure in Europe which would aim to embrace all free European countries, which would be a political force in its own right, and which would have behind it the logic of geography and historical development, we will get an irrevocable con-

gealment of the division of Europe into two military zones: a Soviet zone and a U.S. zone. Instead of the ability to divest ourselves gradually of the basic responsibility for the security of western Europe, we will get a legal perpetuation of that responsibility. In the long run, such a legalistic structure must crack up on the rocks of reality; for a divided Europe is not permanently viable, and the political will of the U.S. people is not sufficient to enable us to support western Europe indefinitely as a military appendage.[78]

"The doubts and criticisms he raises regarding the Atlantic Pact . . . unquestionably have a certain validity," Bohlen wrote to Acheson early in 1949 in a memorandum which, while addressed to the views of James P. Warburg, could have applied to Kennan's as well. "It is, however, the same old story—while clearly expressing the objections to it, he does not seem to offer any feasible alternative. . . . I entirely agree with him that the primary danger is political and not military, but I do not think he fully values the intimate relationship between economic recovery, political stability, and a sense of security against external aggression."[79]

This was, in fact, the essence of the problem. A European "third force" could only be built upon a foundation of European self-confidence, a fact Kennan himself had recognized in supporting the Marshall Plan. But it was Europeans, not Americans, who would determine when the point of self-confidence had been reached, and what would be necessary to sustain it. If they concluded that self-confidence depended upon a formal American military commitment, then Washington, whatever its reservations about the effect this might have upon European self-reliance, was hardly in a position to argue. "I recognize fully that military alliances aren't worth a tinker's dam," Walter Bedell Smith noted with brutal candor in the summer of 1948, "yet those people do attach far greater importance to the scrap of paper pledging support than we ever have."[80]

If the issue of military security posed problems for the "third force" idea, so too did the awkward question of who should belong to it. Germany's position raised the most obvious difficulties. The collapse of talks with the Russians on a comprehensive German settlement late in 1947 pushed the United States, Britain, and France toward a consolidation of political and economic institutions in their three occupation zones, as much as a matter of administrative convenience as by subtle geopolitical design. By the summer of 1948, they had agreed, in what came to be known as the "London Conference" program, to allow Germans "those governmental responsibilities which are compatible with the minimum requirements of occupation and control and which ultimately will enable them to assume full government responsibility."[81] What this meant, as an internal State Department policy statement acknowledged, was the reconstitution of western Germany "as a political entity capable of participating in and contributing to the reconstruction of Europe."[82]

There was no escaping the fact, though, that a divided Germany would pose profound implications for the idea of a European "third force." No one was more sensitive to these than Kennan, who as late as 1947 had been prepared to contemplate the partition of Germany with equanimity.[83] What changed Kennan's mind was his growing preference for a multipolar over a bipolar postwar order, and the importance, in that scheme of things, of having an independent center of political, military, and economic power on the European continent. A permanently divided Germany, with each half the client of a rival non-European superpower, would not only ruin chances for a mutual withdrawal of Soviet and American forces and preclude any possibility of weaning away Moscow's East European satellites; it would also, by leaving a highly skilled and highly nationalistic people artificially separated, create a volatile and unstable political balance, subject to revanchist pressures from both sides of the line. With these considerations in mind, Kennan late in 1948 proposed an approach to the Russians looking toward a pull-back of occupation forces to specific garrison areas, and the establishment, after free elections, of an independent, demilitarized, neutral, but unified German state.[84]

Kennan's "Program A," as his proposal came to be known, raised fundamental questions as to where the American interest in Europe lay. Was the balance of power there to be maintained by accepting as permanent the division of the Continent, which in turn implied permanent Soviet and American spheres of influence there? Or was Europe to be reconstituted as an entity unto itself, with a unified but presumably "tamed" Germany at its core? The latter alternative—emphatically Kennan's own choice—was by no means rejected out of hand in Washington. Dean Acheson, upon becoming Secretary of State early in 1949, found Kennan's arguments persuasive enough to appoint him to chair a National Security Council steering group charged with formulating an American negotiating position should talks with the Russians on Germany eventually take place. After listening to one Kennan presentation on the subject, Acheson wondered out loud how the London Program looking toward a divided Germany had ever been agreed upon in the first place.[85G]

And yet, despite Acheson's intellectual sympathy for Kennan's approach, the hard reality was that Britain, France, and their smaller neighbors preferred the known risks of a Europe divided into Soviet and American spheres of influence to the imponderables of a unified "third force" that could conceivably fall under German or even Russian control. Bohlen had noted the difficulty when "Program A" was first proposed in the fall of 1948:

> [T]he one faint element of confidence which [the French] cling to is the fact that American troops, however strong in number, stand between them and the Red Army. If you add to that the strong fears to be generated with the prospect of returning power to Germans at the present juncture. I am sure that the general line of approach suggested . . . would have a most unfavorable reaction in France and probably in Holland and Belgium as well.[86]

These reservations became painfully clear when "Program A" was leaked to the press in May, 1949, just before the Council of Foreign Ministers was to take up the future of Germany. Ambassador David Bruce had to reassure the French "that we did not favor withdrawal of US forces or any disposition of those forces which would weaken our influence in [the] European scene."[87]

But the abandonment of "Program A" in no way lessened Washington's determination to end the occupation of Germany; what it meant, rather, was that if the integration of Germany as a whole into Europe as a whole was not possible, then its efforts would be directed toward integrating what remained of Germany into what remained of Europe. Even Kennan recognized the force of this logic: "Either the rest of Europe tries to work with the West German state, as it is now emerging, takes a sympathetic and constructive interest in it, and learns to regard its development as a European as well as a German responsibility, or there will be soon no Germany with which the rest of Europe can cooperate, and no possibility of real unity and strength in Western Europe."[88] It was in this connection that the North Atlantic Treaty interlocked neatly with the London Conference program. Acheson described the relationship early in 1949: "it was doubtful that, without some such pact, the French would ever be reconciled to the inevitable diminution of direct allied control over Germany and the progressive reduction of occupation troops; . . . a pact of this nature would give France a greater sense of security against Germany as well as the Soviet Union and should materially help in the realistic consideration of the problem of Germany."[89H]

There remained, though, the question of where Great Britain would fit into the postwar European order. London had no quarrel in principle with the idea of a "third force" in Europe: "We should use United States aid to gain time," the Cabinet had concluded in a secret session in March, 1948, "but our ultimate aim should be to attain a position in which the countries of western Europe could be independent both of the United States and of the Soviet Union."[90] At the same time, though, Britain had its own overseas responsibilities which the Americans, however much they might have railed against "imperialism" in the past, were reluctant to see too quickly liquidated. "It is essential for the British to take the lead in working towards closer European integration," Robert Lovett argued late in 1948. "However, at least at the present time it would be unwise both for them and for us were a position of strong European leadership to require a lessening of British ties with this country and Dominions."[911]

Mindful of these complexities, and with Bevin's approval, Gladwyn Jebb, British Assistant Under-Secretary of State for Foreign Affairs, wrote to Kennan in April, 1949, proposing informal consultations, not just on the position of Britain in Europe, but on the long-term prospects for European integration in general.[92] Coming at a time when developments with regard both to NATO and West Germany seemed to be undermining the "third force" idea, Jebb's suggestion met with a favorable response from Kennan. The real question, he told the Policy Planning Staff, was "whether the emergence of a united western Europe postulates the formation of a third world power of approximately equal strength to the United States and the Soviet Union. Another way of stating this question is whether there are to be two worlds or three."[93]

There ensued, in preparation for these discussions with the British, the most thorough analysis yet carried out in Washington on the question of what the United States really wanted in Europe: an independent, self-reliant aggregation of power compromising as much of Europe as possible, or a sphere of influence closely linked to Washington.

V

"[W]e are getting here into very deep spheres of thought about the nature of ourselves as a nation and of the world we live in," Kennan told a group of consultants brought to Washington in June, 1949, to advise the Policy Planning Staff on how to answer Jebb's questions about the future of Europe.[J] The problem was more than just the achievement of peace and security: "It is a problem of man learning to manipulate his own nature in such a way as to handle effectively those sides of it which are apt to produce violence and degradation and to release in a far greater degree those sides of it which are capable of creating beauty and mastery of environment." The extent to which the United States, acting alone, could accomplish these ends was severely limited:

> [W]e must regard our role in world affairs in these coming years as a much more modest one than many of us are accustomed to think. . . . [W]e must concentrate, as all

modest people must, on our own self-respect: on keeping ourselves and our friends above water amid the genuinely great dangers that modern civilization holds, on exercising as beneficial an influence as we can abroad without claiming that we have the insight or the power to effect any vast change of human institutions on a global scale, and meanwhile to try to shape the course of our internal life in such a way as to produce in later generations people who will be able to make a better and a greater contribution to the improvement of human life. Anything more ambitious than that, and anything that bears with it universal ambitions and pretensions, seems to me to be a form of arrogance and even intolerance based on a terrifying smugness and lack of historical perspective.

"I do not believe that our great moment as a factor in world affairs has yet arrived," Kennan added. "I fervently hope that it has not."[94]

Given this preoccupation with both the limited capabilities and limited wisdom of his countrymen, it is not surprising that Kennan continued to hope for the emergence of a "third force" in Europe, strong enough to maintain the balance of power against Soviet expansionism without an indefinite dependence upon American support. A unified Germany would be the nucleus of such a system, to be sure, but the system would also constrain the Germans by preventing any link-up with the Russians, on the one hand, and by reassuring Germany's western neighbors, on the other. Such a grouping might also attract the allegiance of Moscow's unhappy satellites in Eastern Europe; certainly it would encourage European self-reliance in the area of economic reconstruction. And it would fit within Kennan's larger geopolitical assumption that a world with power distributed among several centers would be more stable than one divided rigidly into two spheres.[95]

The problem, though, was how to keep the Germans from dominating such a grouping. One possibility would be to include Great Britain in it as a counterweight, and Kennan at first leaned toward that idea.[96] But as it became apparent that the British were not prepared to liquidate Commonwealth responsibilities in order to align themselves with the Continent, and as the extent of British financial difficulties became obvious with the devaluation of the pound, Kennan came instead to favor a purely continental grouping, with Britain linked instead to the United States and Canada.[97] Germany would be the dominant power in such a system, but one might hope that the experience of defeat and occupation would have moderated German ambitions.[98] Whether this was the case or not, though, the possibility of German hegemony had to be risked because the alternative—a permanently divided Germany—would leave Europe itself divided, incapable of playing the independent role Kennan had envisaged. There was a certain "horrifying significance" in the fact that the Germans would again "get a place in western Europe which is going to be very important," Kennan admitted to Dean Acheson. "But it often seemed to me, during the war living over there, that what was wrong with Hitler's new order was that it was Hitler's."[99K]

Not surprisingly, this vision of a European "third force" dominated by Germany met with a less than cordial response in France when the British began circulating rumors there of this trend in American thinking. "It is not necessary to spell out in detail what the French think this would mean for them left alone on the continent to face Germany," Bohlen wrote Kennan from Paris in October, 1949. "[I]f it becomes evident that we are creating an Anglo-American-Canadian bloc as a political reality in our European policy we will not be able to hold on to the nations of Western Europe very long."[100] Bohlen's warning was reinforced later that month by a meeting of United States ambassadors in Western Europe, which concluded unanimously that "no effective integration of Europe would be possible without UK participation because of the belief (not without reason) held by western continental powers of potential German domination if such UK participation did not take place."[101L]

Interestingly, the British Foreign Office, which had taken care earlier in the year to disassociate Britain from participation in a continental bloc, now also questioned the viability of the "third force" concept. No possible combination of powers independent of the United States, Bevin told the Cabinet, was likely in the foreseeable future to develop the military, political, and economic cohesion necessary to resist the Russians: "The conclusion seems inescapable that for the present at any rate the closest association with the United States is essential, not only for the purpose of standing up to Soviet aggression but also in the interests of Commonwealth solidarity and of European unity." It was true that such a policy might well require the subordination of British and European interests to those of the United States. But despite "occasional violence of talk, American public opinion and the American Congress are both peace-loving and cautious, and more likely to err on the side of prudence than of rashness." If that should ever cease to be the case, "it may reasonably be expected that partnership with the United States in a Western system would increase rather than diminish the opportunities for the United Kingdom to apply a brake to American policy is necessary."[102]

"That you were right in your premonitions about the effects of talking to the British about European union I gladly concede," Kennan wrote Bohlen early in November. "The path of lesser resistance and lesser immediate trouble in this matter would have been to keep silent." Nor did he have any intention of challenging the collective opinion of the American ambassadors in Western Europe: "Even if the Secretary agreed one hundred percent with my view, I would not ask him to move in the face of such a body of opinion. Time will tell who is right." But the existing policy, Kennan warned:

> (a) gives the Russians no alternative but to continue their present policies or see further areas of central and eastern Europe slide into a U.S.-dominated alliance against them, and in this way makes unlikely any settlement of east-west differences except by war; and
> (b) promises the Germans little more in the western context than an indefinite status as an overcrowded, occupied and frustrated semistate, thus depriving them of a full stake in their own resistance to eastern pressures and forfeiting their potential aid in the establishment of a military balance between east and west.

"You may have your ideas where one goes from here on such a path and at what point it is supposed to bring us out on the broad uplands of a secure and peaceful Europe," Kennan added, with some bitterness. "If so, I hope you will tell the Secretary about them. . . . I find it increasingly difficult to give guidance on this point."[103]

Bohlen found Kennan's attitude less than helpful: "I had hoped we could profitably correspond on such subjects, but frankly I am not interested in polemics." "You know me well enough to take into account my polemic temperament," Kennan wrote back. But "I agree that there is no point in continuing the debate. A decision has fallen. . . . Perhaps it was the right one. None of us sees deeply enough into the future to be entirely sure about these things. But I find my estimate of my own potential usefulness here shaken by the depth of this disagreement . . . and I will be happier than ever if, as I hope, it will be possible for me . . . to subside quietly into at least a year or two of private life."[104]

VI

It is curious that Kennan and Bohlen, who agreed so completely on the interpretation of Soviet behavior, should have disagreed so adamantly about the future of Europe, to the point that each had wound up by the end of 1949 defending precisely the opposite position on spheres of influence from the one each had advanced at the beginning of 1945. Kennan's initial advocacy of an outright division of the Continent had been modified by the evolution of his thinking on the advantages of multipolarity as a stabilizing force, by his awareness of the limits of American power, and by his growing conviction, as he recalled in his *Memoirs*, "that we are not fitted, either institutionally or temperamentally, to be an imperial power in the grand manner."[105] Bohlen's initial resistance to spheres of influence had been eroded by the failure of negotiations with the Russians, by the success of the Marshall Plan and NATO, and by the obvious willingness of Europeans themselves to welcome an American assertion of influence over them. Significantly, it was Bohlen whose views reflected at each point the mainstream of official thinking in Washington; Kennan, on this question at least, was the perpetual critic.

It is worth asking, though, why the Kennan vision of an autonomous "third force" in Europe, which at an earlier stage had had widespread support in Washington, failed to materialize. The reason, almost certainly, is that the Europeans themselves did not want it. Confronted by what they perceived to be a malevolent challenge to the balance of power from the east, they set about inviting in a more benign form of countervailing power from the west rather than undertake the costly, protracted and problematic process of rebuilding their own. The United States, with some reluctance, went along.

Time would indeed tell, as Kennan observed, whether the Europeans were wise in choosing this alternative; even the passage of four decades provides no clear answer to that question. What can be said is that the system that did come into being in Europe after World War II, however improvised, artificial and arbitrary, has proven to be far more stable and resilient than Kennan or anyone else could have foreseen at the time.[106] How long it will last is anyone's guess, but given all the accidents, irrationalities, and perversities of history, that uncertainty hardly lessens the necessity of being grateful for small favors.

Endnotes

1. Kennan to Bohlen, January 26, 1945, Charles E. Bohlen Papers, Box 1, "Personal Correspondence 1944–46," Diplomatic Branch, National Archives. See also Charles E. Bohlen, *Witness to History: 1929–1969* (New York: 1973), pp. 174–76; also Kennan to Harriman, September 18, 1944, George F. Kennan Papers, Box 28, Seeley Mudd Library, Princeton University. This latter memorandum is printed in George F. Kennan, *Memoirs: 1925–1950* (Boston: 1967), pp. 222–23, but under the date of December 16, 1944.

2. Bohlen to Kennan, undated, Kennan Papers, Box 28. See also Bohlen, *Witness to History,* pp. 176–77.

3. See Chapter Two, of John Lewis Gaddis, *The Long Peace.*

4. OSS R & A #2284, "American Security Interests in the European Settlement," June 29, 1944, OSS Records, Modern Military Records Branch, National Archives.

5. JCS 973/1, "Fundamental Military Factors in Relation to Discussions Concerning Territorial Trusteeships and Settlements," August 3, 1944, U.S. Department of State, *Foreign Relations of the United States:* [hereafter *FR*] *1944*, I, pp. 699–703. See also Admiral William D. Leahy to Cordell Hull, May 16, 1944, U.S. Department of State, *Foreign Relations of the United States: The Conferences at Malta and Yalta, 1945* [hereafter *FR: Yalta*] (Washington: 1955), pp. 106–8. For evaluations of the significance of these documents, see Mark A. Stoler, "From Continentalism to Globalism: General Stanley D. Embick, the Joint Strategic Survey Committee, and the Military View of American National Policy during the Second World War," *Diplomatic History*, VI (Summer, 1982), 312–13; and James F. Schnabel, *The Joint Chiefs of Staff and National Policy, 1945–1947* (Wilmington, Delaware: 1979), pp. 13–16.

6. OSS R & A #2669, "Capabilities and Intentions of the USSR in the Postwar Period," January 5, 1945, OSS Records.

7. See, on these points, Robert Dallek, *Franklin D. Roosevelt and American Foreign Policy, 1932–1945* (New York: 1979), pp. 389–91, 536–37; and Wm. Roger Louis, *Imperialism at Bay: The United States and the Decolonization of the British Empire, 1941–1945* (New York: 1978), pp. 259–73.

8. Such is the central argument of Geir Lundestad, *The American Non-Policy Towards Eastern Europe, 1943–1947* (New York: 1978).

9. Bohlen minutes, Roosevelt-Churchill-Stalin meeting, February 5, 1945, *FR: Yalta*, p. 617. See also the discussion of American policy regarding postwar overseas military bases in Chapter Two, of John Lewis Gaddis, *The Long Peace*.

10. See John Lewis Gaddis, *The United States and the Origins of the Cold War, 1941–1947* (New York: 1972), pp. 206–11.

11. Potsdam briefing book paper, "British Plans for a Western European Bloc," July 4, 1945, U.S. Department of State, *Foreign Relations of the United States: The Conference of Berlin (The Potsdam Conference) 1945* [hereafter *FR: Potsdam*], I, 256–64 [emphasis in original].

12. *Congressional Record*, April 26, 1944, p. 3719.

13. For administration expressions of concern along these lines, see Cordell Hull to W. Averell Harriman, February 9, 1944, *FR: 1944*, IV, 826; a State Department Post-War Programs Committee memorandum, "Policy Toward the Settlement of Territorial Disputes in Europe," July 28, 1944, printed in Harley Notter, *Postwar Foreign Policy Preparation* (Washington: 1949), p. 593; a State Department briefing book paper prepared for the Yale Conference, "American Policy Toward Spheres of Influence," undated. *FR: Yalta*, p. 105. For further background, see Gaddis, *The United States and the Origins of the Cold War*, pp. 149–57; and Dallek, *Roosevelt and American Foreign Policy*, p. 536.

14. See, on this point, Robert A. Divine, *Second Chance: The Triumph of Internationalism in America During World War II*, especially pp. 167–74. Two influential wartime best-sellers contributing to the revival of Wilsonianism were Wendell Willkie, *One World* (New York: 1943); and Sumner Welles, *The Time for Decision* (New York: 1944).

15. Concerns about ideology surfaced, for example, in a State Department Division of European Affairs memorandum, "Current Problems in Relations with the Soviet Union." March 24, 1944, *FR: 1944*, IV, 840; in an Office of Strategic Services Research and Analysis report, #1552, "The Current Role of the Communist Party in the USSR," June 12, 1944, OSS Records; in a

conversation between Ambassador W. Averell Harriman and Secretary of the Navy James V. Forrestal, April 20, 1945, reported in Walter Millis, ed., *The Forrestal Diaries* (New York: 1951), p. 47; and in a memorandum by Raymond E. Murphy of the State Department's Division of European Affairs, "Possible Resurrection of Communist International, Resumption of Extreme Leftist Activities, Possible Effect on United States," June 2, 1945, *FR: Potsdam*, I, 267–80.

16. Such, clearly, was Roosevelt's thinking. See John Lewis Gaddis, *Strategies of Containment: A Critical Appraisal of Postwar American National Security Policy* (New York: 1982), pp. 9–13. For other assessments stressing the probable defensive nature of Soviet expansionism, see the following Office of Strategic Services Research and Analysis reports: #1337S, "Russian Intentions in the Mediterranean and Danube Basins," October 20, 1943; #2284, "American Security Interests in the European Settlement," June 29, 1944; #2669, "Capabilities and Intentions of the USSR in the Postwar Period," January 5, 1945, OSS Records; also JIC 250, "Estimate of Soviet Post-War Capabilities and Intentions," January 18, 1945, Army Staff Records, ABC 336 Russia Section 1-A, Modern Military Records Branch, National Archives.

17. Department of State memorandum, "Foreign Policy of the United States," December 1, 1945, *FR: 1946*, I, 1139. See also OSS Research and Analysis reports 2284 and 2669, cited above; and a draft report by Bohlen and Geroid T. Robinson, "The Capabilities and Intentions of the Soviet Union as Affected by American Policy," December 10, 1945, printed in *Diplomatic History*, I (Fall, 1977), 389–99.

18. Draft report by Bohlen and Robinson, undated but early 1946, Department of State Records, Decimal File 1945–1949, 711.61/2-1446, Diplomatic Branch, National Archives.

19. Bohlen memorandum, March 13, 1946, Bohlen Papers, Box 4, "Memos (CEB) 1946."

20. Bohlen memorandum, October 18, 1945, Bohlen Papers, Box 3, "Memos (CEB) 1945." See also a memorandum by Cloyce K. Huston, Chief of the State Department's Division of Southern European Affairs, "Suggested Extension of American Policy in Eastern Europe," October 24, 1945, Department of State Records, Decimal File 1945–1949, 711.61/10-245.

21. Speech to the New York *Herald Tribune* Forum, October 31, 1945, *Department of State Bulletin*, XIII (November 4, 1945), 709–11.

22. Bohlen memorandum, October 18, 1945, Bohlen Papers, Box 3, "Memos (CEB), 1945."

23. Ethridge memorandum, "Summary Report on Soviet Policy in Rumania and Bulgaria," December 7, 1945, *FR: 1945*, V, 637.

24. For this shift in attitudes toward the Russians, see Gaddis, *The United States and the Origins of the Cold War*, pp. 282–315.

25. For the background of American planning on the postwar treatment of Germany, see *ibid.*, pp. 95–132.

26. See, for example, memoranda on the subject by Llewellyn Thompson and John D. Hickerson, both dated June 22, 1945, *FR: 1945*, III, 528–31.

27. The text of the proposed treaty is in *FR: 1946*, II, 190–93.

28. *New York Times*, May 6, 1946.

29. Kennan to Byrnes, March 6, 1946, *FR: 1946*, V, 519. See also Kennan to Bohlen, January 26, 1945, Bohlen Papers, Box 1, "Personal Correspondence 1944–46"; and Kennan to Carmel Office, May 10, 1946, *ibid.*, pp. 555–56.

30. The Byrnes Stuttgart speech of September 6, 1946, is in the *Department of State Bulletin* XV (September 15, 1946), 496–501. For reparations and the merger of occupation zones, see John H. Backer, *The Decision to Divide Germany: American Foreign Policy in Transition* (Durham: 1978), pp. 96–101.

31. British notes on a conversation between Marshall and Bevin, London, December 18, 1947, *FR: 1947*, II, 824. For the negotiations on the German peace treaty, see *FR: 1946*, II, 941–65; *FR: 1947*, II, 1–112, 139–502, 676–795.

32. Transcript, Kennan post-lecture question and answer session, Air War College, April 10, 1947, Kennan Papers, Box 17. See also Walter Bedell Smith to Byrnes, January 7, 1947, *FR: 1947*, II, 141; JCS 1769/1, "United States Assistance to Other Countries from the Standpoint of National Security," April 29, 1947, *ibid.*, I, 741; John Balfour to the British Foreign Office, July 20, 1947, Foreign Office Records, FO371/61055/AN2552, Public Record Office, London; W. Averell Harriman to Truman, August 12, 1947, Harry S. Truman Papers, PSF Box 178, "Foreign Affairs: Germany (2)," Harry S. Truman Library; and Robert Murphy to Samuel Reber, November 20, 1947, *FR: 1947*, II, 725.

33. See, for example, Leahy to Hull, May 16, 1944, *FR: Yalta*, pp. 107–8.

34. Truman press conference, April 18, 1946, *Public Papers of the Presidents: Harry S. Truman, 1946* [hereafter *Truman Public Papers*] (Washington, 1962), pp. 211–12.

35. F. B. A. Rundall minute, March 10, 1947, Foreign Office Records, FO 371/61053/AN906.

36. By far the best account of U.S. actions during the Iranian and Turkish crises of 1946, as well as the subsequent Greek crisis, is Bruce R. Kuniholm, *The Origins of the Cold War in the Near East: Great Power Conflict and Diplomacy in Iran, Turkey, and Greece* (Princeton: 1980).

37. "Memorandum Regarding Greece," October 21, 1946, *FR: 1946*, VII, 243 [Emphases in original.]

38. See Joseph M. Jones, *The Fifteen Weeks (February 21–June 5, 1947)* (New York: 1955), p. 141; also p. 36, above.

39. The documentation on these negotiations is in *FR: 1947*, II, 139–471.

40. See, for example, a Joint Chiefs of Staff memorandum to Patterson and Forrestal, March 13, 1947, *FR: 1947*, V, 112; PPS/1, "Policy with Respect to American Aid to Western Europe," May 23, 1947, *ibid.*, III, 224–25; William L. Clayton memorandum, "The European Crisis," May 27, 1947, *ibid.*, 230–32; Kennan National War College lecture, June 18, 1947, quoted in Kennan, *Memoirs: 1925–1950*, p. 351; Burton Y. Berry to Kennan, July 31, 1947, Policy Planning Staff Records, Box 31, "United Nations 1947–1949," Diplomatic Branch, National Archives; Bohlen to Joseph C. Grew, August 2, 1947, Bohlen Papers, Box 1, "Correspondence 1946–1949: G"; Kennan memorandum of a

conversation with Clark Clifford, August 19, 1947, Policy Planning Staff Records, Box 33, "Chronological—1947"; CIA 1, "Review of the World Situation as It Relates to the Security of the United States," September 26, 1947, Truman Papers, PSF Box 255, "Central Intelligence Reports—ORE 1948."

41. Minutes, PPS meeting, May 8, 1947, Policy Planning Staff Records, Box 32; Marshall to Jefferson Caffery, June 12, 1947, *FR: 1947*, III, 249; Transcript, Kennan National War College lecture, June 18, 1947, Kennan Papers, Box 17; PPS/4, "Certain Aspects of the European Recovery Program from the United States Standpoint (Preliminary Report), July 23, 1947, printed in Thomas H. Etzold and John Lewis Gaddis, eds., *Containment: Documents on American Policy and Strategy, 1945–1950* (New York: 1978), p. 113; PPS/5. "Planning With Relation to a United Nations Program at the Forthcoming General Assembly," August 7, 1947, *FR: 1947*, I. 594; Forrestal to Chan Gurney. December 8, 1947, quoted in Millis, ed., *The Forrestal Diaries*, pp. 350–51.

42. Kennan, *Memoirs: 1925–1950*, p. 342.

43. Berry to Kennan, July 31, 1947, Policy Planning Staff Records, Box 31 "United Nations 1947–1949." For evidence that similar thinking was taking place elsewhere within the government, see the draft memorandum of the Executive Committee on the Regulation of Armaments, "Applying the Truman Doctrine of the United Nations," July 30, 1947, *FR: 1947*, I, 577–83.

44. Bohlen memorandum, August 30, 1947, *ibid.*, pp. 763–64. See also Bohlen's notes of Under Secretary of State Lovett's discussion with a group of War Department officials, August 30, 1947, *ibid.*, pp. 762–63; and the Forrestal Diary, August 31, 1947, Millis, ed., *The Forrestal Diaries*, p. 307. For a Policy Planning Staff effort to extend this line of analysis to Japan, see the draft paper "United States Policy Toward a Peace Settlement with Japan," September 17, 1947, Policy Planning Staff Records, Box 32, "Minutes of Meetings—1947."

45. Revised summary of PPS/13, "Résumé of World Situation," November 6, 1947, *FR: 1947*, I, 770n. See also the Forrestal Diary, November 7, 1947, Millis, ed., *The Forrestal Diaries*, p. 341.

46. Inverchapel to Foreign Office, February 9, 1948, Foreign Office Records, FO 371/68013B.

47. Hickerson memorandum of a conversation with Lord Inverchapel, January 21, 1948, *FR: 1948*, III. 11.

48. Inverchapel to Bevin, May 7, 1947, Foreign Office Records, FO 371/61047/AN1751.

49. F. B. A. Rundall minute, May 3, 1947, *ibid.*, FO 371/61054/AN1570.

50. See, on this point, the memorandum of a conversation between William L. Clayton, Lewis Douglas, and British cabinet officials in London, June 25, 1947, *FR: 1947*, III, 281; Lovett to Clayton and Caffery, August 14, 1947, *ibid.*, pp. 356–57; Truman speech at Rio de Janeiro, September 2, 1947, *Truman Public Papers: 1947*, p. 430; Lovett to Inverchapel, February 2, 1948, *FR: 1948*, III, 17–18; Bohlen to Lovett, August 9, 1948, *ibid.*, pp. 208–9; and Marshall to United States embassies in Paris and other capitals, August 27, 1948, *ibid.*, p. 223.

51. Kennan to Cecil B. Lyon, October 13, 1947, Policy Planning Staff Records, Box 33, "Chronological—1947." For Kennan's "five power" concept, see his lectures at the National War College and the Naval War College, September 17 and October 11, 1948, Kennan Papers, Box 17; also Kennan, *Memoirs: 1925–1950*, p. 359.

52. For the Truman administration's response to Kennan's ideas, see Gaddis, *Strategies of Containment*, pp. 55–65.

53. Saltzmann address to the International Council of Women, Philadelphia, September 11, 1947, *Department of State Bulletin*, XVII (September 21, 1947), 595. See also Secretary of State Marshall's testimony before the Senate Foreign Relations Committee, January 8, 1948, U.S. Congress, Senate, Committee on Foreign Relations, *European Recovery Program* (Washington: 1948), p. 13.

54. See, on this point, a draft report by Bohlen and Robinson, undated but early 1946, Department of State Records, Decimal File 1945–1949. 711.61/2-1446; Maxwell M. Hamilton to H. Freeman Matthews, February 14, 1946, *ibid.;* William D. Leahy diary, May 20, 1946, William D. Leahy Papers, Library of Congress; Robert Hooker memorandum. September 20, 1946, Department of State Records, Decimal File 1945–1949, 711.61/9-2046; John Balfour to Nevile Butler, June 9, 1947, Foreign Office Records, FO 371/61048/ AN2101; Balfour to Foreign Office, July 20, 1947, *ibid.*, FO 371/61055/ AN2552; Harriman to Truman, August 12, 1947, Truman Papers, PSF Box 178, "Foreign Affairs: Germany (2)"; Bohlen to Marshall, March 26, 1948, Bohlen Papers, Box 4, "Memos (CEB) January—June 1948"; Willard Thorp to Marshall, April 7, 1948, *FR: 1948*, I, 558–59; Carlton Savage draft paper, April 26, 1948, filed with PPS minutes, same day, Policy Planning Staff Records, Box 32.

55. Minutes, Cabinet meeting of February 15, 1947. Cabinet Records. CAB 128/9. Public Record Office, London.

56. See, on this point, Kuniholm, *The Origins of the Cold War in the Near East*, pp. 345–46, 381–62.

57. Geir Lundestad, *America, Scandinavia, and the Cold War, 1945–1949* (New York: 1980), p. 194.

58. Marshall speech at Chicago, November 18, 1947, *Department of State Bulletin*, XVII (November 30, 1947), 1025.

59. JCS 1769/1, "United States Assistance to Other Countries from the Standpoint of National Security," April 29, 1947, *FR: 1947*, I, 741. See also an Office of Military Government for Germany memorandum, "A Summarized Analysis of the German Problem," March 5, 1947, *ibid.*, II, 229.

60. Kennan to Marshall, January 20, 1948, *FR: 1948* III, 7. See also PPS/23, "Review of Current Trends: U.S. Foreign Policy," February 24, 1948, *ibid.*, I, 515–16.

61. Kennan comments at the fifth meeting of the Washington Exploratory Talks on Security, July 9, 1948, *ibid.*, III, 177. See also Kennan to Acheson, May 16, 1947, *FR: 1947*, III, 222.

62. Clayton to Lovett, September 17, 1948, Policy Planning Staff Records, Box 27, "Europe 1947–1948." See also a Clayton memorandum of January 17,

1949, Dean Acheson Papers, Box 64, "Memos—conversations Jan–Feb 49," Harry S. Truman Library.

63. Lovett to Harriman, December 3, 1948, *FR: 1948*, Ill, 301.

64. Marshall speech at Chicago, November 18, 1947, *Department of State Bulletin*, XVII (November 23, 1947), 1026.

65. Inverchapel to Bevin, May 22, 1947, Foreign Office Records, FO 371/61048/AN1986.

66. Rundall minute, February 23, 1948, *ibid.*, FO371/68018/AN1702.

67. Kennan to Marshall, January 6, 1948, Policy Planning Staff Records, Box 33, "Chronological: Jan–May 1948" [emphases in original]. See also PPS/13, "Résumé of World Situation," November 6, 1947, *FR: 1947*, I, 776–77; transcripts of Kennan lectures to the Secretary of the Navy's Council and the National War College, December 3 and 18, 1947, Kennan Papers, Box 17; Kennan to Marshall, February 3, 1948, Policy Planning Staff Records, Box 33 "Chronological Jan–May 1948." See also a Moscow Embassy staff report, "Evaluation of Present Kremlin International Policies." November 5, 1947, *FR: 1947* IV, 606–12; and Walter Bedell Smith to Marshall, December 30, 1947, *ibid.*, II, 908. See also David Mayers, "Containment and the Primacy of Diplomacy: George Kennan's Views, 1947–1948" *International Security, XI* (Summer, 1986), 124–62.

68. JIC 380/2, "Estimate of the Intentions and Capabilities of the USSR Against the Continental United States and the Approaches Thereto, 1948–1957," February 16, 1948, Army Staff Records, ABC 381, USSR 2 Mar 46 Sec 5-B. On the deterrent effect of the atomic bomb, see Forrestal to Chan Gutney, December 8, 1947, quoted in Millis, ed., *The Forrestal Diaries*, pp. 349–51; and NSC 30, "United States Policy on Atomic Weapons," September 10, 1948, *FR: 1948*, I, 626–27.

69. "Summary of a Memorandum Representing Mr. Bevin's views on the Formation of a Western Union," enclosed in Inverchapel to Marshall, January 13, 1948, *ibid.*, III, 4–6. See also the minutes of the British Cabinet meeting of January 8, 1948, Cabinet Records, CAB 128/12; C. P. (48)6, "The First Aim of British Foreign Policy," January 4, 1948, *ibid.*, CAB 129/23; and C. P. 48(72), "The Threat to Western Civilisation," March 3, 1948, *ibid.*, CAB 129/25. See also Alan Bullock, *Ernest Bevin: Foreign Secretary* (New York: 1983), pp. 513–25.

70. Marshall to Truman, March 12, 1948, *FR: 1948*, III, 49–50. For expressions of concern from other foreign leaders, see *ibid.*, pp. 6–7, 29–30, 34–35, 52–53.

71. See, on this point, the memoranda of conversations between Lovett and Inverchapel, January 27 and February 7, 1948, *ibid.*, pp. 12–13, 21–23.

72. Memorandum by George Butler, "Points for Discussion at S/P Meeting," March 19, 1948. Policy Planning Staff Records, Box 33, "Chronological Jan–May 1948"; John Hickerson comments at the second meeting of the US-UK-Canada security conversations, March 23, 1948, *FR: 1948*, III, 65; Inverchapel to Foreign Office, April 30, 1948, Foreign Office Records, FO 371/71671/N5183.

73. Kennan unsent letter to Walter Lippmann, April 6, 1948, Kennan Papers, Box 17.

74. State Department publication 3462, "The North Atlantic Pact: Collective Defense and the Preservation of Peace, Security and Freedom in the North Atlantic Community," printed in the *Department of State Bulletin*, XX (March 20, 1949), 342–50. See also Lovett's executive session testimony before the Senate Foreign Relations Committee, May 11, 1948, U.S. Congress, Senate, Committee on Foreign Relations, *Historical Series: The Vandenberg Resolution and the North Atlantic Treaty* (Washington: 1973), p. 9; and Acheson's memorandum of a conversation with the Danish foreign minister, March 11, 1949, *FR: 1949*, IV, 194.

75. Lovett comments, third meeting, Washington exploratory talks, July 7, 1948, *FR: 1948* III, 157; Hickerson to William J. McWilliams, November 27, 1948, Policy Planning Staff Records, Box 27, "Europe 1947–1948"; Bohlen memoranda of conversations with the Norwegian and Danish foreign ministers, February 8 and March 12, 1949, *FR: 1949*, IV, 70–71, 198–99; Acheson statement to the House Foreign Affairs Committee, July 28, 1949, *Department of State Bulletin*, XXI (August 8, 1949), 193. For Johnson's suggestion, see his executive session testimony before the Senate Foreign Relations Committee, April 21, 1949, The Vandenberg Resolution and the North Atlantic Treaty, p. 228.

76. Hickerson to McWilliams, November 27, 1948, Policy Planning Staff Records, Box 27, "Europe 1947–1948." See also, on the "arsenal" concept, Willard Thorp to Marshall, April 7, 1948, *FR: 1948*, I, 560. For the question of ground troops, see Bohlen to Marshall S. Carter, November 7, 1948, *ibid.*, p. 654n; Marshall to Forrestal, November 8, 1948, *ibid.*, p. 655; Acheson and Johnson executive session testimony before the Senate Foreign Relations Committee, April 21, 1949, *The Vandenberg Resolution and the North Atlantic Treaty*, pp. 216, 235.

77. See, for example, *Department of State Bulletin*, XXX (March 20, 1949), 342–50.

78. Kennan draft memorandum for Marshall and Lovett, September 26, 1948. Policy Planning Staff Records, Box 27, "Europe 1947–1948." See also the transcripts of Kennan's lectures at the National War College, the Naval War College, and the Pentagon Joint Orientation Conference, September 17, October 11, and November 8, 1948, all in the Kennan Papers, Box 17; and PPS/43, "Considerations Affecting the Conclusion of a North Atlantic Security Pact," November 23, 1948, *FR: 1948*, III, 283–89.

79. Bohlen to Acheson, February 8, 1949, Bohlen Papers, Box 4, "Memos (CEB) 1949."

80. Minutes, Policy Planning Staff meeting, June 14, 1949, Policy Planning Staff Records, Box 32.

81. London Conference communique, June 7, 1948, *FR: 1948*, II, 315. For documentation on the London Conference, see *ibid.*, pp. 1–374.

82. State Department policy statement, "Germany," August 26, 1948, *ibid.*, p. 1298.

83. See note 32, above.

84. For the most comprehensive statement of Kennan's position, see PPS 37/1, "Position to be Taken by the U.S. at a CFM Meeting," November 15, 1948, *FR: 1948*, II, 1320–38. See also Kennan's memorandum of March 8, 1949, *FR: 1949*, III, 96–102; and his *Memoirs: 1925–1950*, pp. 415–48.

85. Minutes, Acheson-Kennan discussion, March 9, 1949, *FR: 1949*, III, 102–3. For the formation of the NSC steering group, see the minutes of the Policy Planning Staff meeting of January 28, 1949, Policy Planning Staff Records, Box 32. See also, on the reception of "Program A," Wilson D. Miscramble, "George F. Kennan, the Policy Planning Staff and American Foreign Policy, 1947–1950" (Ph.D. Dissertation, University of Notre Dame, 1979), pp. 134–72.

86. Bohlen to Kennan, October 25, 1948, Bohlen Papers, Box 4, "Memos (CEB) July–December 1948." See also Hickerson to McWilliams, November 23, 1948, Policy Planning Staff Records, Box 27, "Europe 1947–1948"; Robert Murphy to Jacob Beam, December 7, 1948, *FR: 1948*, II. 1320n; Murphy to Marshall S. Carter, January 14, 1949, Policy Planning Staff Records, Box 15, "Germany 1947–8."

87. Bruce to Acheson, May 14, 1949, *FR: 1949*, III, 878. See also Kennan, *Memoirs: 1925–1950*, p. 445.

88. Kennan to Acheson, March 29, 1949 (unsent), Kennan Papers, Box 23.

89. Acheson memorandum of conversation with Senators Tom Connally and Arthur Vandenberg, February 14, 1949, *FR: 1949*, IV, 109. See also a message from Bevin read to the National Security Council on May 20, 1948, *FR: 1948*, III, 122, and Timothy P. Ireland, *Creating the Entangling Alliance: The Origins of the North Atlantic Treaty Organization* (Westport, Connecticut: 1981), especially pp. 4–8, 137–41.

90. Secret conclusions, Cabinet meeting of March 5, 1948, Cabinet Records, CAB 128/14. See also the minutes of the meeting of March 8, 1948, *ibid.*, CAB 128/12.

91. Lovett to Harriman, December 3, 1948, *FR: 1948*, III, 303.

92. Jebb to Kennan, April 7, 1949, *FR: 1949*, IV, 289–91.

93. PPS minutes, meeting of May 18, 1949, Policy Planning Staff Records, Box 32.

94. Kennan notes for introductory meeting, June 6, 1949, *ibid.*, Box 27, "Europe 1949."

95. Kennan, *Memoirs: 1925–1950*, pp. 462–64.

96. See Kennan's comments as reported in the minutes of the PPS meeting of June 3, 1949, Policy Planning Staff Records, Box 32.

97. PPS 55, "Outline: Study of U.S. Stance Toward Question of European Union." July 7, 1949, *ibid.*, Box 27, "Europe 1949"; Kennan to Acheson and Webb, August 22, 1949, *ibid.*, Box 33, "Chronological 1949."

98. See the comments of Kennan, Niebuhr, and Smith, as reported in the minutes of the PPS meeting of June 13 and 14, 1949, *ibid.*, Box 32.

99. PPS minutes, meeting of October 18, 1949, *ibid.*

100. Bohlen to Kennan, October 6, 1949, Bohlen Papers, Box 1, "Correspondence 1946–49: K."

101. David Bruce to Acheson, October 22, 1949, *FR: 1949*, IV, 343.

102. C.P. (49) 208, "European Policy: Memorandum by the Secretary of State for Foreign Affairs," October 18, 1949, Cabinet Records, CAB 129/37.

103. Kennan to Bohlen, November 7, 1949, Kennan Papers, Box 28.

104. Bohlen to Kennan, undated but November, 1949, *ibid.;* Kennan to Bohlen, November 17, 1949, *ibid.*

105. Kennan, *Memoirs: 1925–1950*, p. 464.

106. See, on this point, A. W. DePorte, *Europe Between the Super Powers: The Enduring Balance* (New Haven: 1979).

REFERENCES

This essay was originally prepared for the symposium on "European and Atlantic Defence, 1947–1953," organized by the Norwegian Research Centre for Defence History and held in Oslo in August, 1983. It appears, in slightly different form, in Olav Riste, ed., *Western Security: The Formative Years: European and Atlantic Defence, 1947–1953* (Oslo: 1985), pp. 60–91.

A. Admiral William D. Leahy, Chief of Staff to the Commander-in-Chief, had told the Combined Chiefs of Staff as early as February, 1944, that "he, personally, hoped that the United States forces in Europe would be withdrawn at the earliest possible date consistent with the stabilization of the peace." [Minutes, 144th meeting of the Combined Chiefs of Staff. February 4, 1944, Combined Chiefs of Staff Records, CAB 88/4, Public Record.

B. Senator Arthur H. Vandenberg had originally suggested the idea of a German disarmament treaty in the famous speech announcing his "conversion" from isolationism, delivered on the floor of the Senate on January 10, 1945. [See the *Congressional Record* for that date, pp. 164–67.]

C. Kennan, as it happened, had already anticipated this recommendation, as minutes for the Policy Planning Staff meeting of July 28, 1947, show: "Mr. Kennan undertook to prepare a paper setting forth the implications involved in the fact that we are presently faced with a two-world situation, whereas the UN Charter was drawn up in the hope of a one-world system." [Policy Planning Staff Records, Box 32, Diplomatic Branch, National Archives.]

D. For more on this "expansion by invitation" thesis, see Gaddis, *The Long Peace*, chapter 2, pp. 20–47; also Geir Lundestad, "Empire by Invitation? The United States and Western Europe, 1945–1952," *Journal of Peace Research*, XXIII (1986), 263–77; and John Lewis Gaddis, "The Emerging Post-Revisionist Thesis on the Origins of the Cold War," *Diplomatic History*, VII (Summer, 1983), 182–83.

E. The British Embassy in Washington had noted in September, 1947: "If it were not for the obstreperous behaviour of the Soviet Union, Marshall would never have made his suggestions, or, had he done so, they would have received almost no public support. The Soviet Union has not only succeeded in preventing the United States from retreating into its prewar isolationism but it is now ensuring that the United States will take an increasingly active part in the affairs of Western Europe," [Inverchapel to Foreign Office, September 6, 1947, Foreign Office Records, FO 371/61056, Public Record Office, London.]

F. The Americans were "only too ready to place a gun in the hands of any natural enemy of the Soviet Union," a confidential British political report had noted in the summer of 1948. "[W]ith 50% of the world's industrial capacity but only 7% of its population," the United States "must inevitably adopt a policy which the cynical might compare to the hiring of mercenaries." [Confidential Political Report #8, "Military Aid for Western Europe," June 26, 1948, Foreign Office Records, FO 371/68019.]

G. "Kennan is, as you are aware, a powerful influence in the State Department," the British ambassador in Washington reported to the Foreign Office, "and I regard his mission to Germany [in connection with the steering group discussions] as likely to be of particular importance." [Sir Oliver Franks to Foreign Office, March 4, 1949, Foreign Office Records, FO 371/74160.]

H. Walter Lippman made a similar point in a letter to Kennan on February 1, 1949: "The western anxiety about *our* leaving Europe and withdrawing across the Atlantic can be met by the North Atlantic Security Pact. In fact that is its chief advantage, that it supplies the juridical basis for remaining in Europe." [Kennan Papers, Box 28.]

I. "[T]he trouble with the British," William Clayton wrote to Lovett in September, 1948, "is that they are hanging on by their eyelashes to the hope that somehow or other with our help they will be able to preserve the British Empire and their leadership of it. . . . I think if we make it very clear to the British that, with complete cooperation on their part, we can possibly save them but that we cannot save their position as leader of the Empire bloc and do not intend to try, we will begin to see results in our Herculean efforts to pull Europe out of the hole." [Clayton to Lovett, September 17, 1948, Policy Planning Staff Records, Box 27, "Europe 1947–1948."]

J. Among the consultants invited by Kennan to participate were Hans Morgenthau, J. Robert Oppenheimer, Arnold Wolfers, Reinhold Niebuhr, John McCloy, Walter Bedell Smith, and, interestingly, Robert W. Woodruff, Chairman of the Executive Committee of the Coca-Cola Company.

K. "Mr. Kennan . . . said that he thought that we must decide whether we and our friends are strong enough as a group to hold the Russians and the Germans or decide that we are not strong enough to do so and therefore resign ourselves to the creation of a third force in Europe which might ultimately be dominated one way or another by the Germans. He added that he was inclined toward the second view and thought that EUR [Division of European Affairs] was in general inclined toward the first." [Minutes, PPS meeting of October 17, 1949, Policy Planning Staff Records, Box 32.]

L. John Hickerson had also expressed "grave doubts" as to "whether Germany can safely be absorbed in any association of nations in Western Europe to which the US and UK do not belong." [Hickerson to Kennan, October 15, 1949, Policy Planning Staff Records, Box 27, "Europe 1949."]

6

Geir Lundestad

Empire by Invitation? The United States and Western Europe, 1945–1952

As the introductory essay suggested, the concept of an American empire is difficult for many United States historians to accept. Running an empire was what other countries did: Rome, Spain, France, Britain—but the United States was a republic. I have argued elsewhere that Washington at least helped organize a system of imperial coordination, in which political decision makers in the countries of Western Europe looked to Washington for joint leadership, shared the premises of American policies, and effectively worked in tandem. Office holding in all the countries (the U.S. as well as Western Europe) might pass from the center-right to the center-left, but not further. To reject the postulates of U.S. policy in these countries was effectively to consign oneself or one's party to the political wilderness, see Charles S. Maier, "Alliance and Autonomy: European Identity and U.S. Foreign Policy Objectives in the Truman Years" in Michael J. Lacey, ed., *The Truman Presidency* The Woodrow Wilson International Center for Scholars and Cambridge University Press (Washington, 1989), pp. 273–298. Within this overarching system there was only one limited rejection of such coordination, namely that of French President de Gaulle in the 1960s, and even Gaullist France understoood that in a bipolar conflict its place must be in the Western camp. At the least, given the durable garrisoning of troops, our economic preponderance into the 1960s, the alignment of foreign statesmen upon Washington, the permeation of American models of mass production and mass consumption and the diffusion of culture, language, and films, the United States did run something very much like an empire. (And this is not to consider the more direct intervention that was employed in an area we saw as our traditional sphere of influence, Latin America, or in parts of Asia.)

United States influence in Europe rested not on conquest, but on the American role in overthrowing Nazi domination, then on perception of a new common threat, and commitment to common ideological and economic goals. As Geir Lundestad points out, it also depended on the local uses that Europeans could draw from the American presence. A common protector, relatively distant, with little interest in direct control, was preferable to the supremacy of earlier opponents within Europe. NATO, for example, precluded a dangerous German resurgence as well as deterring Soviet military pressure.

Geir Lundestad has taught at the University of Tromsoe in Norway and now serves as Secretary of the Nobel Peace Prize Committee and Director of the Nobel Institute in Oslo. He has also been a frequent visitor at American academic institutions. His works include *The American Non-Policy towards Eastern Europe, 1943–1947: Universalism in an Area not of Essential Interest to the United States* (New York, Columbia University Press, 1975), and *America, Scandinavia, and the Cold War, 1945–1949* (New York, Columbia University Press, 1980). Lundestad is a friendly critic of American writing on the Cold War, occasionally rebuking it for its provincial obliviousness to Europeans' own autonomous traditions. His article "Empire by Invitation? The United States and Western Europe 1945–1952," is reproduced from *The Journal of Peace Research* XXIII (1986): 263–277, with the kind permission of the author.

By 1952 a common sense of West European identity was emerging. Washington had helped nurture cooperation. But such notable initiatives as the Schuman Plan, proposed by the French in 1950 to institute a supranational Coal-Steel authority, and the European Common Market, founded in 1957 and broadening into the European Community, demonstrated the Europeans' own momentum. After some stagnation in the 1960s and the '70s, the process of integration is slated to advance decisively with the single market envisaged for 1992. Even as of the early 1950s, the economic recovery and vigor of the New Western Europe far exceeded what Washington policy makers expected or dared hope for. Despite some occasional concerns about economic competition, these were developments that Americans welcomed.

1. Introduction

'Traditionalist' historians have generally stressed the expansion of the Soviet Union after the Second World War. The Soviet Union did expand. It insisted on exercising near absolute control over Eastern Europe, it dominated North Korea, and it strengthened its position in Mongolia and later in Vietnam. The communists did win a momentous victory in China, but that was a victory won with little assistance from Moscow. As Mao Tse-tung himself said in 1958, with only slight exaggeration, 'The Chinese revolution won victory by acting contrary to Stalin's will' (Schram 1974, p. 102). The communist victory was also to prove a rather temporary blessing for the Soviets.

Thus, there was Soviet expansion after the war. But this article puts forward two suppositions. First, it will support the 'revisionist' argument that the American expansion was really more striking than the Soviet one. Only the United States became a global power in the years we are dealing with here. While America's influence could be felt in most corners of the world, with only a few exceptions the Soviet Union counted for little outside its border areas, however vast these border areas. The American expansion went so deep and affected so many different parts of the world that it can be said to have resulted in an American empire.

Second, and here I differ from the revisionists, if we choose to call this an empire, it was to a large extent an empire by invitation. Unlike the Soviet Union, which frequently had to rely on force, the United States was generally encouraged to take a more active interest in the outside world. The American influence often went deeper than the Soviet exactly because Washington's forms of control were more in accordance with the will of the local populations than were Moscow's. Not only that, but under this American empire many of the countries that welcomed American influence were also able to do considerably better, at least in longterm material terms, than was the United States itself.

2. America's Position of Strength in 1945

The United States came out of the Second World War by far the strongest power on earth. In constant 1958 prices the American gross national product had grown from $209.4 billion in 1939 to 355.2 billion in 1945. That constituted approximately half of the world's goods and services. Steel production jumped from 53 million tons in 1939 to 80 million in 1945. Production in agriculture increased at a similar pace. With 6% of the world's population, the United States had 46% of the world's electric power, 48% of its radios, 54% of its telephones, and its businesses owned or controlled 59% of the world's total oil reserves. American automobile production was eight times that of France, Britain, and Germany combined. 'Only' 400,000 Americans had lost their lives because of the war.

The population of the Soviet Union is estimated to have been around 194 million in 1940. At the end of the war it numbered around 170 million. In 1945 the Soviet Union produced 10.6 million tons of steel, only half of what it produced in 1941. The Soviet Union built 65,000 cars compared to seven million in the United States. In 1945 agricultural production was only half of what it had been in 1940, which was not a very good year, if there ever are good years in Soviet agriculture.

On the military side, only the United States had the atomic bomb. In 1944—at its highest—aircraft production reached 95,000. The US had a vast lead not only on the Soviet Union, but American production even surpassed that of Germany and Japan combined. The American navy was by far the biggest and most efficient in the world. In one field only could the Soviet Union compare with the United States. They both had roughly 12 million men under arms.[1]

Britain was about to lose its Great Power status, to some extent because of the costs of victory. War damage amounted to roughly £3 billion. Overseas assets of more than another £1 billion had been sold or lost and the income from foreign investment halved. In 1945 Britain was spending abroad more than £2000 million and was earning only about £350 million. The balance had to be acquired primarily from one source, the United States. Britain had a brilliant war record, but little else (Calvocoressi 1979, pp. 10–13).

Thus, in 1945 the United States had completed a triumphant war. Its technological revolution had really taken off, its rivals were exhausted economically, and it seemed that the US would more or less control world markets.

As Paul Kennedy has argued, a similar description would also fit Britain after the triumphs of the Napoleonic wars (Kennedy 1982, p. 6). Yet, in some ways, the Pax Americana after 1945 was more pronounced than the Pax Britannica of the 19th century. In 1950 no country had a GNP even one-third the size of that of the United States. In 1830 both Russia and France in fact had GNPs larger than that of Britain (Russett 1985, p. 212). While Britain had pulled away from the European Congress system of the post-Napoleonic period, the United States was generally able to set up a world order of its own.

3. *The New American Ideology*

In 1822 British Foreign Secretary George Canning wrote his famous words 'Things are getting back to a wholesome state again. Every nation for itself and God for us all'. In 1945 God seemed to be on the American side and practically every nation looked to America, at least for economic assistance.

Washington would have its doubts and there would be vacillation in its policies. Remnants of isolationism could certainly still be found. Yet, the surprising element was the rapidity of the change from isolationism to what is often called internationalism. America took it upon itself to create the world anew. America would protect the world against the evil schemes of the traditional powers. America would not speak only, or even primarily, for itself, but for justice and democracy everywhere.

Politically, most Americans thought world peace best protected through a world organization. So the United States created the United Nations. Economically, the Bretton Woods institutions, the World Bank and the International Monetary Fund, were not really meant to promote American objectives, but world economic progress and even peace. Militarily, there was no threat to anyone in a strong United States. As President Harry Truman stated about the atomic bomb in his Navy Day address on October 27, 1945, 'The possession in our hands of this new power of destruction we regard as a sacred trust. Because of our love of peace, the thoughtful people of the world know that trust will not be violated, that it will be faithfully executed'.

Franz Schurman is probably right when he argues that what took place in American foreign policy after the Second World War was a merger of the old internationalism and the nationalism which had formed such a strong part of the isolationist tradition (Schurman 1974, pp. 46–68). The isolationists had wanted to protect the uniqueness of America from the rest of the world. Now the United States had become so strong that it could not only remain uncontaminated by the evils of the Old World, but could also spread the American gospel to the rest of the world.

America was pure and America was powerful. Non-Americans were not always so sure about the purity. British Prime Minister Winston Churchill put it most succinctly in January 1945 when, tired by Secretary of State Edward Stettinius's sermons against power politics, he responded, 'Is having a Navy twice as strong as any other power "power politics"? Is having an overwhelming Air Force, with bases all over the world, "power politics"? Is having all the gold in the world buried in a cavern "power politics"? If not, what is "power politics"?' (Thorne 1978, p. 515).

4. *America's Global Role*

The term 'isolationism' as applied to the period up to the Second World War may easily give the wrong impression of American policies. Yet, there is no doubt that the American role expanded tremendously during and after the war. This development was in fact least striking in the economic field. In absolute figures there was a continued strong increase in US foreign trade and investments, but compared to earlier periods and to the gross national product, the foreign trade of the years 1945–1950 did not come out on the high side. Furthermore, both in trade and investments the Western Hemisphere was still more important to the United States than was Western Europe (US Department of Commerce 1975, pp. 871, 884, 887, 903, 905).

Developments were much more striking in the military field. In 1938 the United States had a defense budget of almost exactly 1 billion dollars. America had no military alliances and no US troops were stationed on territory it did not control. After the war the defense budget would stabilize around $12 billion. Alliances would be concluded and bases established in the most different corners of the world (Ambrose 1980, p. 13; Lundestad 1980, pp. 23–24).

And yet, as John Lewis Gaddis has argued, the big explosion would come only after 1950. The defense budget then quadrupled in the course of three years to more than $50 billion. Numerous new treaties and alliances were signed, primarily in Asia. By 1955 the United States had about 450 bases in thirty-six countries (Gaddis 1974).

In geographic terms the post-war expansion was not really that noticeable in Latin America, because this had traditionally been Washington's back yard. The American position even in the Pacific had been strong before the war, but now it was considerably expanded. The Japanese Mandated Islands were put under American control, with only the thinnest of concessions to the suzerainty of the United Nations. Japan itself was to be ruled by American authorities. American influence in South Korea remained strong despite the US forces being pulled back in 1948; in the Philippines independence did not really affect this country's ties with the United States that much.

The Second World War had indicated that both Australia and New Zealand would now look to the United States. In 1951 this understanding was formalized through the ANZUS pact. Britain was excluded from taking part, rather pointedly demonstrating the decline of Britain also in this part of the world (Thorne 1978, pp. 687–88).

The American role was increasing in other parts of the Pacific and Asia as well, although the expansion was generally less striking here. As to China, Truman remarked to his Cabinet in August 1946 that 'For the first time we now have a voice in China and for the first time we will be in a position to carry out the (Open Door-GL) policy of 1898'. America gave far more assistance to its side in the Chinese civil war than the Soviet Union did to its. It is another matter that not even three billion dollars could keep Chiang Kai-Shek afloat (Paterson 1981, p. 23).

After some years of vacillation, in 1948 the United States intervened rather decisively on the side of Indonesia against Holland. From 1950 Washington came to meet the costs of a war in Indo-China which a declining France could no longer afford. Even in India, where the United States on the whole showed great deference to Britain, America's attitude had to be taken into account (Hess 1971, pp. 157–59, 178–87).

In the Middle East American oil companies had been operating before the war in Iraq, Bahrain, Kuwait, and, most important, in Saudi Arabia. Now, as Aaron Daniel Miller has argued, 'Although the Americans had no desire to destroy British influence on the peninsula or in the gulf, in Saudi Arabia they sought nothing less than a reversal of traditional roles. No longer would the United States be content to remain Britain's junior partner, but it would now demand primacy in the economic sphere and at least an equal voice in political matters which might affect the fate of the (ARAMCO-GL) concession' (Miller 1980, p. 205). In Iran the United States quite rapidly took over the British role in opposing Soviet expansion. The American stand there in 1945–46 was to signal what would follow later in other parts of the world. When the British abandoned Palestine in 1948, the Americans again moved in to take over the British role, first in Israel and later in the moderate Arab countries as well.

In North Africa, as elsewhere, American interests expanded after the war. The United States continued to operate its base in Morocco and nationalist leader Habib Bourguiba in Tunisia came to look to America for support, although he would be disappointed after the expectations Franklin D. Roosevelt had created during the war (Gallagher 1963, pp. 101, 117, 236–39).

South of the Sahara, Liberia had long been under considerable American influence, but in this part of the world the United States played a more limited role than almost anywhere else.

5. *Western Europe's Position*

Western Europe, however, was what really counted. Latin America would be bitterly disappointed by Washington's lack of interest (Hilton 1981).

In North Africa, in India, in Indo-China Washington would soft-pedal its skepticism to colonial rule, not to disturb relations with the

European big powers. With regard to China the Republicans were right in accusing the Truman Administration of not being willing to do there what it did in Europe. But the fact of the matter was that not even the Republican right wing was willing to do in China what it favored in Europe (Patterson 1981, pp. 33–37).

In Eastern Europe, Washington tried to play an active role. Yet, again and again the Americans were to run up against the fact that the Western half of Europe counted for more than the Eastern. The Truman Doctrine did not apply even to all of Europe. In the spring of 1947 the Nagy government in Budapest, which had resulted from free elections in the fall of 1945, was still struggling to survive against Soviet pressure. With quite limited support from the United States, Nagy would soon fall. Repeatedly Washington entered into agreements or undertook actions which actually strengthened the Soviet hold on Eastern Europe. Thus, when the last of the countries in Eastern Europe, Czechoslovakia, 'fell' in February 1948, this was an event which many policy makers in Washington had predicted. The Prague coup was in part the result of the Marshall Plan. But, again, nothing could be done about it. Western Europe was simply too important for that (Lundestad 1975, pp. 75–106, 178–80, 405–08).

The American influence in Western Europe was rapidly growing in the years after 1945, militarily, politically, economically, and culturally. In many ways the last aspect was the most important, although it will not be dealt with here.

Militarily, the events of the two world wars had shown that the United States would intervene to prevent Western Europe from falling under the control of a hostile power. The same could happen again, alliance or no alliance. The American monopoly on the atomic bomb also gave the Western Europeans some protection before the creation of NATO (Lundestad 1980, pp. 15–17).

The American forces in Germany would provide the trip-wire in this context. Before NATO the United States had military bases on Greenland, the Azores, in Britain, and a civilian facility in Iceland.

Still NATO of course greatly strengthened the American role. The outbreak of the Korean war provided an equally important stimulus. Military assistance skyrocketed, the American troop commitment was increased, and a joint military apparatus and joint defense plans established under American leadership.

Politically and economically, the American influence varied from country to country, as had Britain's influence on its dominions and colonies. Washington's role was the strongest in the US zone in Germany. There General Lucius Clay and the army leadership, with support from Washington, first modified local plans for socialization in

Hesse, and then maneuvered to prevent British and local schemes for the socialization of the coal mines in North Rhine-Westphalia in the Bizone. In a similar way Clay was able to limit labor-management code-termination in the American zone and in the Bizone (Gimbel 1968, pp. 117–20, 126–28, 155–58, 170–71, 233–34).

In Greece the Americans dominated the administration to such an extent that Americans actually wrote both the Greek application for aid and the thank-you notes in connection with the Truman Doctrine. Under the Marshall Plan the national bureaucracies in Greece and Turkey broke down to such an extent that Americans were closely involved in running the two countries (Wittner 1982, pp. 73–74, 100–01, 121–28, 171–91; Arkes 1972, pp. 293–94).

In semi-occupied Italy the State Department and Ambassador James Dunn in particular actively encouraged the non-communists to break with the communists and undoubtedly contributed to the latter being thrown out of the government in May 1947. In more normal France the American role was more restrained when the Ramadier government threw out its communists at about the same time. After the communists were out, Washington worked actively, through overt as well as covert activities, to isolate them as well as leftist socialists. On the other side of the coin, the Americans tried to strengthen the political center, including social democratic forces in the political parties and in the labor unions (Miller 1983; Lundestad 1980, pp. 117–18).

US economic assistance was normally given with several strings attached. The French had to agree to promote trade with the rest of the world and to discourage the setting up of regional trading blocs. The loan agreement with Britain of December 1945 contained even stronger clauses meant to promote freer trade. The Attlee government had to make the pound convertible with the dollar and in principle to agree to remove restrictions that discriminated against imports from the United States (Lundestad 1980, pp. 112–15).

The strings attached to the Marshall Plan further limited Europe's freedom of action. Trade within Western Europe had to be liberalized; trade with Eastern Europe curtailed; American investments encouraged. The establishment of the counterpart funds represented an instrument with great potential for intervention, since the various countries could only draw upon these funds with the consent of the United States. Equally important were the indirect effects of the Marshall Plan. Policies had to be conducted with an eye on what might be the reaction in Washington. Thus, even the British cabinet feared that 'increased investment in the social services might influence Congress in their appropriations from Marshall Aid' (Brett, Gilliat & Pople 1982, p. 138; Milward 1984).

6. *Motives Behind US Expansion*

Many motives can be found for the American expansion after the Second World War. Most traditionalists have referred to America's and Western Europe's needs for security and protection of democracy; most revisionists have instead pointed to America's capitalism with its requirements for exports, imports, and investments. Post-revisionists have been more eclectic in their approaches and have thrown in an assortment of additional factors ranging from bureaucratic politics in the US to the seemingly natural fact that the US, as any other Great Power in history, was bound to expand more or less regardless of its political or economic system. The debate on this point very much resembles the debate on the origins of British imperialism in the 19th century.

I count myself among the post-revisionists and in this context I just take it for granted that the United States had important strategic, political and economic motives of its own for taking on such a comprehensive world role. This article, however, focuses on the reactions of local governments and populations to the American expansion.

The revisionist view of the United States thrusting itself into the affairs of other countries can undoubtedly be supported by examples from several parts of the world. Vietnam was to prove the prime illustration of massive intervention with a rather limited local popular basis. Yet, the basic pattern in the early post-war years, particularly in Western Europe, was a different one. The rule was that the United States was invited in.

Even outside of Europe, leaders in Iran, in Saudi Arabia, in Egypt, in India, in Australia and New Zealand were all looking to the United States. Their motives might vary; the need for economic assistance; a desire to employ America as a counterweight to the Soviet Union, to Britain, or to some other power; or admiration for what the United States stood for.

6.1 *Western Europe's Economic Invitation*

In this article, the focus is on Western Europe. The Europeans even more strongly than most others attempted to influence the Americans in the direction of taking greater, not lesser, interest in their affairs.

Britain offers the best example in this respect. Although London underestimated Britain's fall from Great Power status, the Attlee, as the Churchill, government clearly favored both financial assistance from America and a strong US military presence in Europe. In line with this, Whitehall expressed disappointment when Lend-Lease was abruptly curtailed; hoped for a credit substantially larger than the $3.75 billion it received; wished to continue wartime cooperation in atomic energy and the existence of at least some of the combined Anglo-American boards, particularly the Combined Chiefs of Staff; wanted the United States to carry a larger share of the expenses in the German Bizone. Robert Hathaway has shown that many forms of military and intelligence cooperation actually did continue between the United States and Britain after the war. The British would have preferred such cooperation to have been undertaken openly, but that was deemed politically impossible in Washington (Hathaway 1981).

With regard to the desire for economic assistance, the situation was much the same in most European countries. There was a desperate need for economic assistance, and there was really only one major source, the United States. In the period from July 1945 through June 1947 Western Europe in fact on a yearly average received a larger amount of assistance than it did through the Marshall Plan. And then the more than $3 billion which the Western Europeans received in humanitarian aid from the United States is not taken into account. Britain's share alone was $4.4 billion. France received 1.9 billion, Italy 330 million and the Be-Ne-Lux countries 430 million. In this period Eastern Europe only got $546 million. The Eastern Europeans tried to get much more, but their main stumbling block was Washington's unwillingness to grant such assistance to countries dominated by the Soviet Union (US Department of State 1947, pp. 30–32).

The Europeans also played an important role in shaping the Marshall Plan. The crucial person here was British Foreign Secretary Ernest Bevin. Although Washington was skeptical of working through the Economic Commission for Europe (ECE) and of having the Soviets participate, Washington left much of the initiative for the followup to Marshall's Harvard speech on June 5, 1947, to the British and the French. In the ensuing British-French-Soviet conference in Paris, Bevin dominated the scene. The Russian attempt to substitute a bilateral approach for the multilateral one favored by Washington was rejected. The ECE was to be bypassed. The Russians were to be left out. After less than a week the meeting broke down in disagreement. The British Foreign Secretary received unexpectedly firm support from his French counterpart Georges Bidault, considering the complicated domestic scene in Paris (Lundestad 1975, pp. 402–04).

Under the Marshall Plan the Europeans first requested $28 billion from the United States. This was far more than Washington was willing to give. The Truman Administration cut this down to 17 billion and Congress in turn appropriated approximately 14 billion. Only Moscow's opposition prevented Finland, Czechoslovakia, Poland and even other Eastern European countries from taking part. Washington's own attitude blocked Spanish participation. So, at least on the economic side, there can be no doubt that the Europeans were most interested in involving the United States closely in Europe's affairs (Lundestad 1975, pp. 379–408).

6.2 Western Europe's Military Invitation

The same was true in most European countries even on the military side. After the ending of the London meeting of the Council of Foreign Ministers in December 1947, Bevin presented his thoughts on military cooperation to Secretary of State Marshall. The British wanted to set up an arrangement for regional military cooperation in Western Europe. It was also obvious that they wanted to commit the Americans as closely as possible to this arrangement.[2]

Bevin and the British were not the only ones who tried to involve the United States quite closely in the defense problems of Western Europe. At this early stage, Belgian Prime and Foreign Minister Paul-Henri Spaak even went so far as to argue that any defense arrangements which did not include the United States were without practical value. The Dutch favored the same line.

The United States did not take any clear-cut position on these European urgings of closer involvement. Washington would undoubtedly be sympathetic to any European defense effort, but how far it would go in supporting it was to be determined at a later stage. Differences could be found within the Truman Administration and there was always the question of how Congress and public opinion would react to increasing the US commitment to Europe even before the European Recovery Program had been passed by Congress.

Nevertheless, the British, with general support from the Be-Ne-Lux countries, pressed on. On January 27 Bevin argued that 'The treaties that are being proposed cannot be fully effective nor be relied upon when a crisis arises unless there is assurance of American support for the defense of Western Europe. The plain truth is that Western Europe cannot yet stand on its own feet without assurance of support'.[3]

On February 6 the pressure was further stepped up. The State Department was informed of Bevin's opinion that a vicious circle was being created. The United States would not define its position as to participation before an arrangement had been worked out in Western Europe. The British in turn argued that an arrangement could not be worked out at all without American participation since the Western Europeans would then see little point in such plans.

The French were somewhat divided between an Atlantic and a European approach to defense, but under either model it was absolutely essential that the American contribution be stepped up. The French never tired of pressing their need for immediate military assistance from the United States. On March 4 'Atlanticist' Foreign Minister Bidault asked the Americans 'to strengthen in the political field, and as soon as possible in the military one, the collaboration between the old and the new worlds, both so jointly responsible for the preservation of the only valuable civilization' (Elgey 1965, p. 382).

The European pressure on the United States was building up. This perspective of Europe pulling upon the United States, instead of the other way around, should not be taken too far. Washington could not be, and was not, forced into anything against its will. Important groups in the American capital, for many different reasons, favored a strong military role in Western Europe. The point here is that at least the Europeans clearly speeded up the clarification process on the American side.

Finally, on March 12 Washington informed London that 'We are prepared to proceed at once in the joint discussions on the establishment of an Atlantic security system' (FRUS, 1948:3, p. 48). The coup in Czechoslovakia, Soviet pressure upon Finland, General Clay's famous warning of March 5 about Soviet intentions in Germany, the uneasy situation in Italy, and, perhaps most important, the rumors that the Soviets might come to propose a pact on the Soviet-Finnish model even with Norway constituted the international background to this change of position in Washington.

Despite the change in policy in Washington and despite the substantial results reached in the so-called Pentagon negotiations between the United States, Canada, and Britain in March, differences remained between Washington and several of the European capitals.

On March 17 Britain, France, Belgium, the Netherlands, and Luxembourg concluded the Brussels Treaty which established the Western Union. On the American side, while National Security Council (NSC) documents 9 of April 13 and 9/1 of April 23 on the position of the United States with respect to support for the Western Union and a North Atlantic military arrangement had stressed the objective of a defense agreement for the whole North Atlantic area, NSC 9/2 of May 11 put the accent on inducing additional European countries to join the Western Union. There were many reasons for this partial reversal on the American side to an earlier position. Within the State Department, Policy Planning Chief George Kennan and Counselor Charles Bohlen favored the so-called 'dumbbell' concept where the United States and Canada cooperated closely on one side of the Atlantic and the Europeans on the other. Republican chairman of the Senate Foreign Relations Committee Arthur Vandenberg also wanted to emphasize the responsibility of the Europeans to defend themselves. The military were somewhat ambiguous on integrating the US too closely with Western Europe.

In the end, as we know, the United States agreed to take part in a North Atlantic defense organization on an equal basis with the Western Europeans and the Canadians. Those in Washington who had long favored this solution won out. The key person and in many ways the main architect of NATO was the Director of the Office of European Affairs John Hickerson.

In this context of who pressed upon whom, it was important that the pressure of Britain and Canada for full American participation had to undermine the position of those in Washington who favored looser arrangements. The French and now even the Belgians had come to stress the need for maximum military coordination with and assistance from the United States. The treaty question could then wait. In September they too fell into line when they realized that a treaty could be concluded rather quickly and that arms and military coordination would depend on their assent to the treaty.

Although the differences between the United States and the Europeans kept being narrowed, they never disappeared entirely in the negotiations leading up to NATO. Washington continued to insist that the Europeans do as much as possible to defend themselves. The Europeans on the other hand wanted to make the American guarantees for assistance in case of an attack as automatic as possible. All through February 1949 the State Department kept mediating between the Europeans, with the French probably being the most insistent now, and Congress which disliked anything that smacked of automatic involvement. In the end Article 5 of the treaty simply declared that in case of an attack each of the parties will take 'such action as it deems necessary, including the use of armed force, to restore and maintain the security of the North Atlantic area'.

It is true that Norway, Denmark, and Iceland would have preferred their military ties with the Atlantic pact to have been more limited than they actually became. But they represented a minority of countries on this question. On the other extreme, Spain, Greece, and Turkey wanted to join NATO, but were not permitted to. And the sum of requests for military assistance from practically all the Western European countries far surpassed what the United States could deliver in the foreseeable future.

In fact, the pressure for closer American involvement in European military affairs did not end with the setting up of NATO. Thus, at the first session of the Council of the North Atlantic Treaty Organization in September 1949 the question of NATO's further organization was discussed. A Defense Committee, a Military Committee, and a Standing Group composed of one representative each of the United States, Britain, and France were established. Five Regional Planning Groups were also created. Crucial in this context was pressure from practically all the European nations to have the United States as a member of their particular group. This was the case within the Western Europe group consisting of the Brussels treaty countries, as well as within the Northern Europe group of Denmark, Norway, and Britain and the Southern Europe group of France, Italy, and Britain. The result was that the United States became a full member of the North Atlantic Ocean Regional Planning Group and the Canada-United States Regional Planning Group and only a 'consulting member' of the other three. As the report of the Council states with regard to the Northern, Western, and Southern European groups, 'The United States had been requested and has agreed to participate actively in the defense planning as appropriate' (FRUS, 1949:4, pp. 329–37; Kaplan & Tamnes in Riste 1985).

This set-up was to a large extent continued after the outbreak of the Korean war, but the definition of what was the 'appropriate' degree of involvement was certainly changed. Again, pressure from the European side was not important in the sense that it forced Washington to do anything against its will, but in that it helped shape developments in Washington.

Now the Europeans worked hard to establish an integrated force in Europe commanded by an American. The Europeans were also unanimous in their preference for General Eisenhower, who was then appointed. Four additional US divisions were sent to Europe and American military assistance to Europe greatly increased. The Korean war had made it necessary to tie the United States even more closely to Europe. The Europeans in return had to agree to German rearmament, which, particularly to the French, was a difficult concession. They also agreed to increase their forces and defense budgets considerably. But here we come to one of the elements that has continued to trouble the alliance: once the Americans had increased their commitment to NATO, this provided little inducement for the Europeans to do their part. The American objective of increasing Europe's own defense effort therefore met only with partial success (Wells in Riste 1985; Osgood 1962).

7. *The State of Public Opinion*

Thus, the pressure from European governments was undoubtedly in the direction of more, not less American attention to Europe. The question should be raised about the extent to which the governments represented their peoples on this point.

It is difficult to give one clear answer. The situation varied from country to country and polls are not available for all of them, entirely satisfactory polls probably hardly for any of them. The comments made here must therefore be rather tentative. In dictatorships such as Spain and Portugal, in civil war-plagued Greece, and in Turkey as well it was difficult to talk about public opinion. The growing American support to all of these countries, from 1950–51 including Spain, clearly showed that Washington was not afraid of cooperating with undemocratic forces. Conversely, the popular basis of the Czechoslovak government did not prevent the Truman administration from breaking with it in the fall of 1946 (Lundestad 1975, pp. 167–80). Increasingly anti-communism counted more than democratic sympathies, although a combination of both was to be preferred. In Western Europe, different from so many other parts of the world, Washington could have both at the same time.

I have concentrated on Britain, France and Germany. To start off with Britain, the Attlee government received the support of strong majorities for its America policies. In January 1946, 70% thought Britain should accept a loan from America. 17% said no. In April 1948 63% favored the government's attitude toward the US while 19% disapproved of it. In July 1947, 22% had stated that the United States wanted to dominate the world, but this declined to 14% in July 1948 and to 4% in August 1950. (The corresponding percentages for the Soviet Union were 78, 70 and 63). It is a different matter that the British, not surprisingly, did not want the United States to run British affairs and that strong minorities disliked certain aspects of America's foreign policy. The basic feeling was that the two countries should act together, but that Britain should remain independent (Gallup 1977, Great Britain, pp. 125, 161–62, 174, 179, 226, 239, 241–42, 269).

The picture was more ambiguous in France, although there too the sympathy for the United States prevailed. In July 1945 the United States was only favored 43 to 41% over the Soviet Union in reply to the question of what country would have the greatest influence after the war. Yet, the US was picked by 47% as against 23% for the Soviet Union when it came to whom they would *prefer* to see in this influential position. The doubt as to who would dominate lingered on until the spring of 1947, but there was less doubt about popular preferences. Majorities supported the American loan of 1946, French participation in the Marshall Plan, and the joining of the Atlantic pact, although the number of uncommitted/uninformed persons was frequently quite high (Gallup, 1977, France, pp. 27, 51, 55, 77, 88, 92–93, 113, 114, 119, 126, 133, 137–38, 139, 145, 147).

In Germany much criticism could be found of various aspects of the occupation, but at least in the American zone the sympathy for the United States was much stronger than for the other occupying powers. In October 1947 63% trusted the US to treat Germany fairly, 45% placed such trust in Britain, 4% in France, and 0% in the Soviet Union. The support for the Marshall Plan was pronounced and the same was true for the creation of a government for the three Western zones. The German population sustained America's actions, but the United States did not pursue the policies it did primarily for the sake of public opinion. The relationship is best expressed by the editors of the OMGUS Survey, 'The existence of a population that was receipt to reorientation . . . enhanced the Allies' opportunity to help shape German history' (Merritt & Merritt 1970, pp. 9–29, 43–58, 180–81).

In comparative polls from August 1947 and February 1948, no country showed such skepticism toward the United States as did Norway. In February, 23% thought the US would go to war to achieve its goals and not only to defend itself against attack. (37% responded that the Soviet Union would do so.) This was higher than in France (20%), Holland (16), Italy (16), Sweden (13), Canada (13), Brazil (9) and the United States itself (5) and reflected a definite feeling of distance to both of the Great Powers (Alstad 1969, pp. 89–90). Yet, only two months later 61% thought Norway should join a Western bloc (the US role in this bloc was not clear), 2% favored an Eastern bloc, while 37% thought Norway ought to remain uncommitted. A majority also sustained the decision to join NATO, at least after it had been made by the Gerhardsen Labor government (Alstad 1969, pp. 90–91, 93–95).

Thus little indicates that the European political leaders did not receive the tacit or even stronger support of their peoples when they brought their countries into closer economic, political and military cooperation with the United States.

8. What Happened to the American Empire?

Finally, it could be asked what happened to this American empire established in the first years after the Second World War. This is certainly a much too comprehensive and complicated question to even attempt to answer in any detail here. I shall only offer a few most tentative remarks.

Empires apparently lead shorter and shorter lives. The Roman lasted around 500 years, the British roughly three hundred, and the American empire, shall we say, around thirty years. In the 1970s several developments took place which, it can be argued, have resulted in the collapse of the American empire.[4]

The nuclear strength of the Soviet Union came to rival that of the United States and now at last the Soviets too played a role in the most distant corners of the world. The war in Vietnam ended in withdrawal and defeat. On the Asian mainland the American-led alliances broke down and SEATO and CENTO disappeared. Parts of the Bretton Woods system collapsed. The drastic measures taken by the Nixon administration in August 1971 showed the seriousness of America's economic problems, but did not in any way solve them. In the 1960s the United States was having difficulties with its balance of payments, in the 1970s with its balance of trade—for the first time since 1883—and in the mid 1980s the US in fact became a net debtor country. Everywhere from Vietnam to southern Africa and Iran, Washington was discovering that all kinds of local forces were no longer amenable to American influence, if they ever had been. Cuba, the Dominican Republic, Chile and Nicaragua illustrated Washington's problem even in its traditional backyard. Ronald Reagan resurrected much of the old imperial rhetoric, but little of the reality of empire. It was gone, probably forever.

The American influence was slipping in Europe too. The old continent got back on its feet. American economic assistance to Western Europe gradually ceased in the course of the 1950s. In the 1960s the same happened with the military assistance. From the time Britain joined the European Community in 1973, this European group, however loose, surpassed the United States in population and equalled it in the size of its production.

In the first years after the war Britain, traditionally the most American-oriented among the European countries, had been the leader among the Europeans. From the late 1950s de Gaulle's France challenged the supremacy of the 'Anglo-Saxons'. In the late 1960s West Germany, long the economic leader of Western Europe, developed a foreign policy profile of its own. No longer did Bonn rely completely on Washington. In 1962 the Kennedy administration was able to stop a comprehensive German gas agreement with the Soviet Union. Twenty years later Reagan failed in his attempt to do the same with a similar European deal with the Soviets. The Europeans were moving towards greater unity, first on economic and trade questions, but very slowly also on political matters. In the 1970s the American attitude to European integration became quite lukewarm, as a reflection of the fact that the premise which had underlain the earlier support for integration—that the United States and Western Europe had coinciding interests on all important questions—could no longer be taken for granted.

The United States was still the acknowledged leader of the Western world. The Europeans were still quite dependent on the US, particularly in the strategic field. Culturally the American influence was perhaps as strong as ever. US economic production was still almost twice as large as that of the Soviet Union.

Yet, although leadership persisted, hegemony was gone.[5] The end of the American empire was both illustrated and explained by the decline in America's power. Developments in the economic field could be most easily quantified, although the numbers that follow should be seen more as demonstrating trends than as measuring exact percentages. The British slipped from having had approximately half of the world's manufacturing production around 1850 to 32% in 1870 and only 15% in 1910 (Kennedy 1982, p. 6). The American decline was similarly marked. From having produced nearly half of the world's gross national product in 1945, the United States was down to 35% in 1969 (Pinder 1976, p. 343). Now the percentage is around 22.

During both the Pax Britannica and the Pax Americana many countries' economies grew faster than that of the 'hegemon' itself. In fact in its period of imperial greatness, America's economic growth slipped behind that of almost every major Western power. In 1950 Canada, France, West Germany, Italy and Japan had economies corresponding to respectively 6, 11, 11, 6, and 7% of the US gross national product. In 1975 these percentages had increased to 10, 16, 19, 9 and 23. Only that old imperial power, Britain, experienced slower growth than the United States. (The British GNP constituted 14% of the US GNP in 1950; in 1975 this had fallen to 12). (US Department of Commerce 1978, p. 908).

So, there no longer was an American empire. Was that because fewer invitations were issued? That was part of the explanation too. Fewer invitations were issued since the Europeans could do so much more on their own. And Washington did not have the strength or the interest to respond as favorably to European invitations as it had in the past.

The entire American-Western European relationship had to be redefined. The Europeans insisted that they be heard to a much greater extent than had been the case in the first two decades after the Second World War. The Americans argued that since the Europeans had become so affluent and demanded more influence, they should also be willing to shoulder greater responsibilities.

Yet, in some fields Western Europe was still quite dependent on the United States. In military, particularly nuclear, matters the American role, although reduced even here, remained supreme. In fact many European governments would again and again invite Washington to try to square the circle of deterring the Russians without frightening the local European populations. Most countries continued to be quite favorable to American economic investments, so much so that these increased from $1.7 billion in 1957 to more than 24 billion in 1970 and more than 100 billion in 1984 (Grosser 1980, p. 222; World Almanac 1986, p. 101).

An interesting phenomenon, which had been noticeable early on, kept growing ever stronger: the Europeans generally did not mind American assistance at all, but they certainly wanted fewer and fewer strings attached. Once the United States had become involved in a country, the benefits of the American presence were taken for granted by many. Then, if not earlier, cries about American interference would be heard loud and clear.

As Michael Howard has argued with regard to recent American-European military differences, a significant element behind these differences is even 'the degree to which we Europeans have abandoned the primary responsibility for our defense to the United States; have come to take the deterrence provided by others for granted; and now assume that the dangers against which we once demanded reassurance only now exist in the fevered imagination of our protectors' (Howard 1982/83, p. 319). The changes could be quite rapid, as seen for instance in the reactions of several European governments and parties to the problems posed by the modernization of Soviet intermediate range nuclear weapons in the late 1970s and 1980s.

One final hypothesis: it appears quite likely that part of the American decline was due to the expenses involved in maintaining the American empire. Thus, defense expenditures swallowed enormous resources, resources which in other countries could be used for more productive purposes. American yearly defense costs vastly outran those of European countries even on a per capita basis. American research and development was skewed. Even at the low point of the 1970s the United States devoted 28% of its total R&D money to defense compared to Germany's 7 and Japan's 4% (Kennedy 1982, p. 6). Military and economic assistance was expensive. When these benefits were ended, cooperation with the United States often weakened. Unilateral trade benefits stimulated growth among America's economic competitors. Few countries had been as firmly controlled by the US as occupied West Germany and Japan. Few countries benefited as much economically from being parts of the American empire. With America's economic problems in the 1970s, the American-sponsored liberal world trading order came under pressure. Quarrels erupted with Western Europe and Japan over steel and farm exports, exchange and interest rates, reciprocity in trade, etc.

The American experience resembled that of the British. Empire certainly had its advantages, but it could not be had on the cheap. And is not the Soviet Union, in its much more rigidly controlled empire, experiencing the same thing? China left the fold long ago. The time is over when the Eastern European countries could be exploited to Soviet economic advantage. Now they are being subsidized in several ways. Castro's victory in Cuba also proved rather costly in economic terms.

9. *Conclusion*

Thus, American expansion was one of the most striking phenomena of the post-war period; this expansion can be said to have created an American empire equal in scope to any the world had seen before. Yet, this was to a large extent an empire by invitation and it turned out that many of those who issued the invitations prospered more in material terms under the new order than did the United States itself.

ENDNOTES

1. The figures in the preceding paragraphs have been taken from US Department of Commerce (1975, pp. 228, 464); Paterson (1973, pp. 11–12); Paterson (1979, pp. 15–16, 72, 84, 152); Ulam (1971, pp. 4–6).

2. This account of the events in 1947–49 is based on Lundestad (1980); Reid (1977); and Wiebes & Zeeman (1983).

3. US Department of State. *Foreign Relations of the United States (FRUS)*, (1974) 1948, vol. 3, p. 14.

4. These final pages are generally based on the relevant chapters in Lundestad (1985).

5. For some interesting contributions in the 'hegemony' debate, see Russett (1985); Keohane (1984); Gilpin (1981).

REFERENCES

Alstad, Bjørn, ed. 1969. *Norske meninger, vol. 1: Norge, nordmenn og verden* (Norwegian Opinions, 1: Norway, Norwegians and the World). Oslo: Pax.

Ambrose, Stephen E. 1980. *Rise to Globalism. American Foreign Policy, 1938–1980*. Harmondsworth: Penguin.

Arkes, Hadley 1972. *Bureaucracy, the Marshall Plan, and the National Interest*. Princeton: Princeton University Press.

Brett, Teddy; Steve Gilliat & Andrew Pople 1982. 'Planned Trade, Labour Party Policy and US Intervention: The Successes and Failures of Post-War Reconstruction', *History Workshop*, Spring 1982, pp. 130–142.

Calvocoressi, Peter 1979. *The British Experience 1945–75*. Hardmondsworth: Pelican.

Elgey, Georgette 1965. *La république des illusions 1945–1951*. Paris: Fayard.

Gaddis, John Lewis 1974. 'Was the Truman Doctrine a Real Turning Point?', *Foreign Affairs*, vol. 52, no. 2, pp. 388–402.

Gallagher, Charles F. 1963. *The United States and North Africa, Morocco, Algeria, and Tunisia*. Cambridge, Mass.: Harvard University Press.

Gallup, George H., ed. 1977. *The Gallup International Public Opinion Polls.*

France 1939, 1944–75. Vol. One: 1939, 1944–1967. New York: Random House.

Gallup, George H., ed. 1977. *The Gallup International Public Opinion Polls. Great Britain 1937–1975. Vol. One: 1937–1964.* New York: Random House.

Gilpin, Robert 1981. *War and Change in World Politics.* Cambridge: Cambridge University Press.

Gimbel, John 1968. *The American Occupation of Germany: Politics and the Military, 1945–1949.* Stanford: Stanford University Press.

Grosser, Alfred 1980. *The Western Alliance. European-American Relations Since 1945.* London: Macmillan.

Hathaway, Robert M. 1981. *Ambiguous Partnership. Britain and America, 1944–1947.* New York: Columbia University Press.

Hess, Gary R. 1971. *America Encounters India, 1941–1947.* Baltimore: Johns Hopkins University Press.

Hilton, Stanley E. 1981. 'The United States, Brazil, and the Cold War, 1945–1960: End of the Special Relationship', *The Journal of American History,* vol. 68, no. 3, pp. 599–624.

Howard, Michael 1982/83. 'Reassurance and Deterrence: Western Defense in the 1980s'. *Foreign Affairs,* vol. 61, no. 2, pp. 309–324.

Kennedy, Paul 1982. 'A Historian of Imperial Decline Looks at America', *International Herald Tribune,* November 3, 1982, p. 6.

Keohane, Robert O. 1984. *After Hegemony. Cooperation and Discord in the World Political Economy.* Princeton: Princeton University Press.

Lundestad, Geir 1975. *The American Non-Policy Towards Eastern Europe 1943–1947.* Oslo/New York: Norwegian University Press-Humanities Press.

Lundestad, Geir 1980. *American, Scandinavia and the Cold War 1945–1949.* New York: Columbia University Press.

Lundestad, Geir 1985. *Øst, Vest, Nord, Søor. Hovedlinjer i internasjonal politikk 1945–1985* (East, West, North, South. Main Trends in International Relations 1945–1985). Oslo: Norwegian University Press. An English edition was published in 1987.

Merritt, Anna J. & Richard L. Merritt, eds. 1970. *Public Opinion in Occupied Germany.* Urbana: University of Illinois Press.

Miller, Aaron David 1980. *Search for Security. Saudi Arabian Oil and American Foreign Policy, 1939–1949.* Chapel Hill: University of North Carolina Press.

Miller, James E. 1983. 'Taking Off the Gloves: the United States and the Italian Elections of 1948', *Diplomatic History,* vol. 7, no. 1, pp. 35–55.

Milward, Alan S. 1984. *The Reconstruction of Western Europe 1945–51.* London: Methuen.

Osgood, Robert Endicott 1962. *NATO. The Entangling Alliance.* Chicago: University of Chicago Press.

Paterson, Thomas G. 1973. *Soviet-American Confrontation. Postwar Reconstruction and the Origins of the Cold War.* Baltimore: Johns Hopkins University Press.

Paterson, Thomas G. 1979. *On Every Front. The Making of the Cold War.* New York: Norton.

Paterson, Thomas G. 1981. 'If Europe, Why Not China? The Containment Doctrine, 1947–49'. *Prologue,* Spring 1981, pp. 18–38.

Pinder, John 1976. 'Europe in the World Economy 1920–1970' in Carlo M. Cipolla, ed., *The Fontana Economic History of Europe. Contemporary Economies-1.* Glasgow: Fontana.

Reid, Escott 1977. *Time of Fear and Hope. The Making of the North Atlantic Treaty 1947–1949.* Toronto: McClelland & Stewart.

Riste, Olav, ed. 1985. *Western Security. The Formative Years. European and Atlantic Defence 1947–1953.* Oslo: Norwegian University Press.

Russett, Bruce 1985. 'The Mysterious Case of Vanishing Hegemony; or, Is Mark Twain Really Dead?', *International Organization*, vol. 39, no. 2, pp. 207–231.

Schram, Stuart, ed. 1974. *Mao Tse-Tung Unrehearsed. Talks and Letters: 1956–71.* Harmondsworth: Penguin.

Schurman, Franz 1974. *The Logic of World Power. An Inquiry into the Origins, Currents, and Contradictions of World Power.* New York: Pantheon.

Thorne, Christopher 1978. *Allies of a Kind. The United States, Britain, and the War Against Japan, 1941–1945.* Oxford: Oxford University Press.

Ulam, Adam B. 1971. *The Rivals. America and Russia Since World War II.* New York: Viking.

US Department of Commerce 1975. *Historical Statistics of the United States. Colonial Times to 1970.* Washington, D.C.: Government Printing Office.

U.S. Department of Commerce 1978. *Statistical Abstract of the United States, 1978.* Washington, D.C.: Government Printing Office.

US Department of State 1947. *The European Recovery Program. Basic Documents and Background Information.* Washington, D.C.: Government Printing Office.

US Department of State. *Foreign Relations of the United States (FRUS).* Annual volumes. Washington, D.C.: Government Printing Office.

Weibes, Cees & Bert Zeeman 1983. 'The Pentagon Negotiations March 1948: The Launching of the North Atlantic Treaty', *International Affairs*, vol. 59, no. 3, pp. 351–363.

Wittner, Lawrence S. 1982. *American Intervention in Greece, 1943–1949.* New York: Columbia University Press.

The World Almanac and Book of Facts. 1986. New York: Newspaper Enterprise Association.

III

THE POLITICAL ECONOMY OF THE COLD WAR

7

Charles S. Maier

The Politics of Productivity: Foundations of American International Economic Policy after World War II

The five essays in this section focus on the interaction of politics and economics in the Western Europe that emerged under American auspices. My own article, published originally in *International Organization* 31 (Autumn 1977): 607–633, outlines some of the assumptions Americans held about the relationship of economic progress to political stability that Europeans also came to adopt. It is reproduced here with permission of the University of Wisconsin Press and Cambridge University Press. Further work in the archives of the European Recovery Administration and other sources as well as the findings of other scholars has reinforced the hypotheses presented in this piece. What I identified here as the politics of productivity served as a continuing ideological touchstone for aligning economic and social policies, for uniting a centrist political leadership across traditional class cleavages in Europe, for excluding the Communists, and for justifying a reliance on the private economy for recovery and growth.

For reasons suggested in the Introduction, I believe that resolving the recurring antagonisms between the organized working classes and the other interest groups of twentieth-century Western Europe was a major requisite for democratic political stability after World War II. Class conflict, at least perceived class conflict, had helped doom many of the interwar democracies and certainly strained those that did not succumb. The fight for shares of national income between capital and labor also seemed to inhibit investment decisions and thus contributed to economic stagnation. Avoiding renewed depression after the war would require cooperation; a consensus built around economic growth and productivity promised a basis for such cooperation. It offered a way of exiting from a vicious cycle of distributive conflict and slow, uneven progress, or even decline, and entering a virtuous circle of agreed-on norms for distributing the fruits of growth according to productivity, which would encourage labor harmony and attract investment.

If I were rewriting this essay today, I would stress another, less ideological aspect, of postwar Western political economy. Stability and growth also corresponded to a particular stage of dominant productive technology. By 1949–50, West European gross national product had recovered prewar levels, and the European economies were poised to begin two decades of unparalleled real economic growth. West European farmers registered significant advances in agricultural productivity, based upon the spread of tractors and the increased application of chemical fertilizers and increasing the output of the farms even as it liberated labor for urban manufacturing. The technology of mass production—exemplified by auto assembly lines and the continuous steel rolling mills which were crucial to national economic plans—furnished the vehicles, radio and television sets, and appliances that became items of mass consumption in the 1950s. Provision of standardized, relatively inexpensive, mass-produced durables was identified as the distinctive contribution of "Ford"-like or other American methods. United States "hegemony" in Europe thus coincided with the high water-mark of the industrial era in the post-war period, somewhat as British leadership earlier rested on textiles and finance. Conversely, United States leadership has tended to falter just as an economy based on coal, steel, and mass standardized output has also fragmented.

Students who find these themes of interest can consult another interpretive essay on related themes: "The Two Postwar Eras and the Conditions for Stability in Western Europe," *American Historical Review*, 86 (April 1981): 327–352, and now included in Charles S. Maier, *In Search of Stability: Explorations in Historical Political Economy* (New York, Cambridge University Press, 1987).

The theme introduced here has been taken up by other authors, especially in regard to Italy. See Pier-Paolo D'Attorre, "Aspetti dell'attuazione del Piano Marshall in Italia," in Elena Aga Rossi, ed., *Il Piano Marshall e l'Europa* (Rome: Instituto della Enciclopedia Italiana, 1983), 163–80; and Mariuccia Salvati, *Stato e industria nella ricostruzione: Alle origini del potere democristiano* (Milan: Feltrinelli, 1982). On the impact on trade unions see the essay by Federico Romero, "Postwar Reconversion Strategies of American and Western European Labor," European University Institute Working Paper, no. 85/193 (San Domenico di Fiesole, September 1985). Since this article appeared, I have continued a study of the United States and postwar reconstruction in Europe, which will develop further the argumentation and evidence introduced here.

The ground rules of a liberal international economic system may establish formal equality among participants but they also reflect the disparity of power and resources. Just as significant, they reveal the inequalities and conflicts within the dominant national societies of the system. The primary objective of this chapter is to suggest how the construction of the post-World War II Western economy under United States auspices can be related to the political and economic forces generated within American society. A second focus must be to demonstrate how those American impulses interacted with the social and political components of other nations, both European and Japanese.

The close of World War II brought American policy makers a rare and heady opportunity to reshape the guidelines of the international economic order. The pretensions of the Axis powers to organize continental Europe and East Asia had collapsed. Soviet Russia seemed preoccupied with its own huge tasks of reconstruction and the establishment of a glacis in Eastern Europe. Great Britain depended upon Washington's assistance to maintain its own international role and could not durably oppose American policies. Spared the losses incurred by the other belligerents, the United States inherited a chance to secure Western economic ground rules according to its own needs and visions.

What determined those needs and visions? Historians and political scientists have often argued that they represented either an enlightened idealism or a nationalistic and capitalist expansionism. Thus polarized, the debate remains inconclusive because the same policies could serve both aspirations. Washington's neo-Cobdenite mission did aim at higher world levels of exchange and welfare. Simultaneously, it was intended to benefit American producers who could compete vigorously in any market where the "open door" and the free convertibility of currencies into dollars facilitated equal access.[1] Both the defenders and the critics of American objectives, moreover, have recognized the traumatic legacy of a Depression that only wartime orders finally overcame. Indeed, Donald Nelson of the War Production Board and Eric Johnston of the Chamber of Commerce encouraged the Soviets to believe that American businessmen wanted their orders lest mass unemployment recur after the wartime stimulus ended. Nor was international commerce solely an economic objective: trade restrictions, argued New Deal spokesmen, brought political hostility. "Nations which act as enemies in the market place cannot long be friends at the council table," said Assistant Secretary of State William Clayton, a wealthy cotton dealer sympathetic at first hand to the needs of exporters.[2] He echoed Cordell Hull's assessment that the establishment of a closed trading bloc comprised an essential aspect of Fascism: "The political line up followed the economic line up."[3] Thus, a compelling objective in 1945 was to do away with protected trading areas outside the United States, thereby to banish domestic depression and international conflict. The United States would lead the United Nations to a lofty plateau of peaceful intercourse and economic expansion.

This eschatology of peaceful prosperity—with its amalgam of nationalist and universal aspirations usefully termed "Wilsonian"[4]—is not sufficient, however, to account fully for the ideological sources of American foreign economic policy. (Nor, I hope to show, is growing anti-Communism a sufficient ideological explanation.) American concepts of a desirable international economic order need to be understood further in terms of domestic social divisions and political stalemates. United States spokesmen came to emphasize economic productivity as a principle of political settlement in its own right. They did this not merely because of the memory of harsh unemployment, nor simply to veil the thrust of a latter-day "imperialism of free trade,"[5] nor even because wartime destruction abroad made recovery of production an urgent objective need. Just as important, the stress on productivity and economic growth arose out of the very terms in which Americans resolved their own organization of economic power. Americans asked foreigners to subordinate their domestic and international conflicts for the sake of higher steel tonnage or kilowatt hours precisely because agreement on production and efficiency had helped bridge deep divisions at home. The emphasis on output and growth emerged as a logical result of New Deal and wartime controversies, just as earlier it had arisen out of inconclusive reform movements.

The Domestic Sources of American Economic Concepts

In retrospect, it is easy to point out that the international economic arrangements the United States sought in the years after the Second World War would benefit a capital-intensive and resource-rich economy. Wartime leadership and British dependence brought the opportunity to press for the Treasury and State Department's preferred multilateralism. These policies had not originally been ascendant. At its inception, the New Deal had adopted a course of monetary unilateralism as Roosevelt refused cooperation with the London Economic

Conference in 1933 and embarked upon the almost capricious gold purchases of 1934. Such initiatives represented, in part, a reaction to Britain's floating of the pound and regrouping of a Commonwealth trading bloc in 1931–1932. They also reflected the Democrats' distrust of the New York banking elites (the Federal Reserve leadership and J. P. Morgan, Co., etc.) that had sought to work with the British toward monetary stabilization in the 1920s and seemed to emphasize international cooperation rather than domestic growth. Nonetheless, a common British and American need to limit competitive devaluation after France departed from the gold standard led to a Tripartite currency agreement in 1936. The danger of Nazi expansionism further impelled Neville Chamberlain to solicit Washington's cooperation and conclude the Anglo-American trade agreement of November 1938.[6] With the advent of World War II, Britain had to become even more insistent a suitor. For its Lend-Lease assistance, Washington pressed for further dismantling of the Commonwealth trading bloc. London finally had to rely upon shared political values and plucky sacrifices to temper American demands for the liquidation of its international financial position.[7]

Noisy disputes sometimes obscured the underlying thrust of United States policy, but foreign economic objectives generally reflected Cordell Hull's unceasing emphasis upon the virtue of lowering tariff barriers. This program was consistent with the lessons of comparative advantage and a universalist vision of economic advance, even as it served to encroach upon the British Commonwealth. Roosevelt needed Hull because of his excellent relations with Congress; and the official who offered an alternative program of international commodity bartering, George Peek, the Administrator of the Agricultural Adjustment Act, resigned in late November 1935. The disputes between Hull and Henry Morgenthau, Jr. at the Treasury appear more those of bureaucratic rivalry than fundamental policy disagreements. Hull was originally willing to allow the British monetary flexibility in return for free-trade commitments; in 1935 he dissented from the dollar's competitive devaluation against the pound. But while Hull afterward urged the postwar elimination of the Westminster system as a condition for Lend-Lease, Morgenthau was less insistent. The Treasury emphasized economic leadership through a pivotal role for the dollar. Rather than impose Section VII of the Lend-Lease agreement which committed Britain to move toward free trade, the Secretary of the Treasury sought to extract London's agreement not to rebuild its foreign currency reserves during the period of American aid.[8] Nonetheless, the Treasury's quest for monetary leadership was not fundamentally inconsistent with the State Department's stress on the "open door" and the importance of free trade. Both policies envisaged using the American abundance of food and cotton and the productivity of labor to establish a benign economic dominance that would raise the welfare of all nations. Neither agency had reason to sanction an exhausted Britain's maintaining imperial pretensions at US expense. Both policies derived from a Wilsonian globalism. In Morgenthau's concepts, for example, a Britain prosperous but on reduced monetary tether accompanied a Germany shorn of its heavy industry and a Russian reconstructed with American credits.[9] The premise for all policy makers was American economic preeminence. This preeminence was felt to arise naturally from the nation's energy and resources, not from the exercise of coercion.

Yet this very emphasis on economic potential itself emerged from deeper divisions. The productivist view of America's postwar mission arose naturally out of the domestic modes of resolving social conflict, or, rather, the difficulty of resolving conflicts cleanly. Neither an insistence upon conflict nor upon consensus adequately conveys the dialectical interplay of both social conditions, such that unresolved disputes brought contestants to apolitical areas of common endeavor. Most immediately, the emphasis on the benevolent mission of America's productive leadership reflected the stalemate of New Deal reform and even wartime politics. By the late 1930s, the New Deal thrust to displace economic power from private capital to either corporatist National Recovery Administration (NRA) institutions or to countervailing private forces (i.e., labor unions) was rapidly dissipating. The severe recession of 1937–38 intensified political infighting between "spenders" such as Harry Hopkins, Harold Ickes, Marriner Eccles, and Leon Henderson and those such as Morgenthau who urged tax cuts for business. Outside the White House, the Democratic coalition began to fray and the President failed to persuade Congress to enact several key proposals during 1938–39. In November 1938 Republicans won 81 new seats in the House and eight in the Senate. As the political situation in Europe became more preoccupying, it provided a further incentive for the President to turn back to a business community that a few years earlier he had labelled "economic royalists." Harry Hopkins, newly installed as Secretary of Commerce in early 1939, chose Averell Harriman as a close advisor, in part to reconstruct bridges to business leadership. Edward Stettinius, Jr. of US Steel, James Forrestal of Dillon Reed, Donald Nelson of Sears Roebuck, and William Knudsen of General Motors were only a few of the "tame millionaires" the Administration summoned to run the ever-shifting agencies designed to coordinate defense production. With Pearl Harbor, Roosevelt could announce that "Dr. Win the War" was replacing "Dr. New Deal."[10]

The infusion of industrialists, however, could not automatically adjourn old conflicts over social and economic policy. Critics of business found the new organizers unimpressive and laggard in the task of converting industry to wartime production. The new participants from banking and industry regarded the inveterate New Dealers as partisan and woolly-headed. As Forrestal reported about the provocative Henderson in July 1941: "He is trying to use the Office of Civilian Requirements to get a foothold and control of the defense effort and incidentally to fight a social as well as a military war."[11] The role of labor was particularly controversial. The Office of Production Management (OPM) and its successor, the War Production Board, resisted the policies of the trade union Left. The CIO and AFL sought representation in the key industry divisions of the OPM but had to be content with participation in the less central labor advisory committees. Labor delegates did become important on the War Manpower Committee, but after a production crisis in 1943, Roosevelt's solution of placing James Byrnes in charge of an overarching Office of War Mobilization again kept labor spokesmen from the center of decisions.[12]

From one perspective these struggles were bureaucratic rivalries with multi-million-dollar appropriations and unprecedented regulatory control as the important stakes. Yet it would be misleading to forget the ideological implications. The war imposed a common task upon all contenders but could not nullify the profound struggles over business and labor power that had continued for over a decade. Nor could it cleanly resolve them. Symptomatic of the continuing ideological and social disputes was the stormy career of Henry Wallace. By 1942 Wallace had established himself as the spokesman for a messianic liberalism of abundance; America's war was an act of millennial liberation that would usher in "the century of the common man." Not merely a visionary, the Vice-President and his aides had accumulated key economic supervisory positions. But the State Department resented the inroads of Wallace's Bureau of Economic Warfare. And the long, public quarrel with Jesse Jones, the conservative Texas millionaire who served as Secretary of Commerce and directed the Reconstruction Finance Committee (RFC), finally led Roosevelt to abolish the Bureau of Economic Warfare, limit the RFC's role, and establish a new Foreign Economic Agency under Jones's protege, Leo Crowley. The struggle was a bureaucratic and personal one but its upshot disheartened the New Deal Left and set back potential precedents for future economic regulation and planning. At Thanksgiving 1942 Wallace had approached FDR "in the spirit of Queen Esther approaching King Ahasuerus, only I was going to speak on behalf of the liberals rather than the Jews."[13] He did not recall that since the laws of the Medes and the Persians were immutable, the Jews won only the right to defend themselves, not the cancellation of the attacks already ordered.

In Congress the fate of New Deal reform under wartime conditions was also problematic. Price controls and rationing under the Office of

Price Administration (OPA) remained a sore point for conservatives, especially since OPA became a refuge for New Deal exponents such as Henderson and Chester Bowles. Senator Robert Wagner, chairman of the Banking and Currency Committee, managed to renew the OPA and price-control legislation. He failed, however, to secure passage of the Wagner-Murray-Dingell bill, which would have enacted an equivalent of Britain's Beveridge Plan if it had not remained a dead letter in 1943, 1944, and 1945. When the National Resources Planning Board, deeply influenced during the war years by Harvard Keynesian Alvin Hansen, brought forward its 1943 proposals for continued welfare reforms and countercyclical spending, it won applause from *The New Republic*. Congressional conservatives, on the other hand, responded by gutting the agency. By 1944, with further Republican gains at the polls, Congress reflected a taut division between Liberals and Conservatives. The result was typified by the fate of the Liberals' proposed full-employment bill. Originally designed to mandate government spending to prevent joblessness, it emerged, after much horse-trading, as the Employment Act, which merely targeted maximum feasible job levels. With the creation of the Council of Economic Advisors it remained more a technical than a political measure.[14]

This stalemate of forces precluded any consistent social-democratic trend for the American political economy. Coupled with the impressive record of the domestic industrial plant as the "arsenal for democracy," it made it easier for American leaders to fall back upon the supposedly apolitical politics of productivity. The theme of productivity as a substitute for harsh questions of allocation was a venerable one. It had emerged in the Progressive Era and pervaded the War Production Board of 1918. It was championed by Herbert Hoover under the form of a business "associationism" that would transcend wasteful competition, and be given institutional expression once again in the NRA concept of industrial self-government. The recurrent ideas all stressed that by enhancing productive efficiency, whether through scientific management, business planning, industrial cooperation, or corporatist groupings, American society could transcend the class conflicts that arose from scarcity. The coinage of politics—power and coercion—was minted only in the kingdom of material necessity and would have no function in the realm of abundance.[15]

Although the Depression discredited the claims to foresight and acumen on the part of America's business elites, the wartime experience suggested again that the United States could enjoy productive abundance without a radical redistribution of economic power. The neo-Progressives in the business community organized a Committee on Economic Development (CED) to urge continuing governmental responsibility (including advantageous tax benefits) for maintaining high investment and employment. Charles E. Wilson of General Electric and the War Production Board and Paul Hoffman of Studebaker, later head of the Economic Cooperation Administration, became major CED spokesmen for the new government-business partnership.[16] Not surprisingly, it was the emergency priorities of wartime that rendered this celebration of a business-oriented commonwealth initially acceptable to American Liberals. The wartime celebration of production and output, its rehabilitation of the large corporation, and its evocation of an overarching national commitment, all facilitated a new consensus on interventionist planning. As Harriman noted in his first unofficial press conference after becoming Secretary of Commerce in October 1946, "People in this country are no longer scared of such words as 'planning.' . . . people have accepted the fact the government has got to plan as well as the individuals in the country."[17]

It is important to emphasize, however, that planning was accepted only in a restricted sense. During the 1930s, the Department of Agriculture under the guidance of Rexford Tugwell and Mordecai Ezekiel, the National Resources Planning Board as influenced by Gardiner Means, and the Tennessee Valley Authority (TVA) had emerged as foyers for the planning enthusiasts. But the impact of the would-be planners was concentrated in natural resource issues; for in questions of environmental resources, providing ever-normal granaries, or halting erosion, planning could claim a conservation-related justification it could not in industry. Likewise, planning seemed more acceptable on the regional level: TVA became a New Deal showcase not merely because of its cheap power but its incubation of local democracy. Its exuberant director, David Lilienthal, foresaw TVA-like developments helping to leapfrog the more exploitative and wasteful stages of growth outside the United States as well:

> There seems to be a definite sequence in history in the change from primitive or non-industrial conditions to more highly developed modern industrial conditions. Whether all of those steps have to be taken and all the intervening mistakes made is open to question. . . . Don't we have enough control over our destinies to short-cut those wasted steps?[18]

The same buoyant belief in the power of economic rationality would mark Marshall Plan administrators. But precisely because they and other American Liberals usually envisaged planning as a step toward productive efficiency, it became apolitical. Planning would overcome the waste that CED industrialists saw in restrictive labor practices or needless competition, that Lilienthal measured in overpriced kilowatt-hours, or that Keynesians perceived in idle savings and unemployed workers. In each case, the mission of planning became one of expanding aggregate economic performance and eliminating poverty by enriching everyone, not one of redressing the balance among economic classes or political parties. When they turned to European difficulties after 1945, American advisors enjoyed greater opportunity to reshape the ailing economies abroad than to influence the domestic one. But even in confronting European needs, they reaffirmed the general premises of American economic thinking. United States aid was designed to remove "bottlenecks," and to clear away the obstacles left by war and political demoralization by temporary coal shortages and transitory dollar gaps. Prosperity was available for Europeans too, once the impediments to production were limited. The true dialectic was not one of class against class, but waste versus abundance. The goal of economic policy, abroad as at home, was to work toward the latter.

American opinion generally viewed the transition to a society of abundance as a problem of engineering, not of politics. Nonetheless, as Americans ended the Second World War, they recognized one major institutional impediment to peacetime prosperity—monopoly. Denunciation of monopoly was a recurring ideological theme. John Taylor of Caroline, Andrew Jackson, the Progressives, and the New Deal successively assailed monopoly as an affliction of democracy. The criticism of monopoly presented the same rhetorical advantages as the stress on productivity and efficiency. Instead of depicting political society as subject to complex interest cleavages, it posited a rallying of all productive elements against one isolated enemy. Spokesmen for reform found it easier to lead a crusade against monopoly than persevere in, or even fully confront the implications of, a contest against the more pervasive inequalities of power and wealth.

By the mid-1930s, the theme of monopoly became preoccupying anew on several grounds: the new literature on imperfect competition and oligopoly,[19] the relapse into severe recession in 1938, and, finally, the American diagnosis of the nature of Fascism. In his study for the Secretary of Agriculture, *Industrial Prices and Their Relative Inflexibility*, Gardiner Means contrasted the competitive market in agriculture with the administered markets where prices were not allowed to fall with slackening demand.[20] The result was reduced purchasing power that might explain persistent depression. When manufacturing prices rose faster than wages, Henderson and Ezekiel both correctly predicted renewed recession.[21] The setback to New Deal hopes prompted Roosevelt to propose a major investigation of the economic obstacles to recovery. An attack on monopoly was not only relatively cost-free in political terms; it seemed appropriate in the light of the latest economic analysis. In April 1938 the President asked Congress to open a major inquiry into American economic structures with a message that stressed the inequality among corporations (less than 0.1 percent of corporations owned 52 percent of the assets) and attributed unemployment to rigid administered prices.

Monopoly, Roosevelt suggested further, was politically dangerous: "The liberty of a democracy is not safe if the people tolerate the growth of private power to a point where it becomes stronger than their democratic state itself. That, in its essence, is Fascism—ownership of government by an individual, by a group, or by any other controlling private power."[22] This warning naturally reflected the anxieties of 1938. The *Anchluss* had taken place a month earlier. The idea also fit in with Cordell Hull's view of the German threat, which the Secretary interpreted as a political outgrowth of strivings for autarky. In syllogistic terms, Hull argued that economic nationalism reduced living standards, led to unemployment and despair, and, finally, provoked the use of political violence as an alternative to disorder.[23]

By the late 1930s Liberals thus connected Fascism with monopolistic economic tendencies. The Depression had obviously been instrumental in bringing Hitler to power. In addition, remarked Thurman Arnold, the new head of the Anti-Trust division of the Justice Department, the effort to protect special-interest groups, which the New Deal had pursued misguidedly under the NRA, had also been an objective of the ill-fated Weimar Republic.[24] When Roosevelt listened to Morgenthau plead for a cut in business taxes to restore industry's confidence, the President backed away. Appeasing business "would put a man in as President who," as he called it, "would be controlled by a man on horseback, the way Mussolini and Hitler are. . . . This simply would mean that we would have a Fascist President."[25]

It was foreordained that the anti-monopoly theme would weaken at home with economic mobilization. On the one hand, Keynesians themselves came to stress that persistent unemployment lay in the failure to invest and not with rigid prices or inadequate consumer power. The Temporary National Economic Committee (TNEC) hearings laboriously continued, producing dozens of monographs on industries, patents, and taxation, but without much legislative result. The Committee had begun with the assumption that a conflict-free solution to unemployment, price rigidity, and unhealthy concentration of power might be found in attacking monopoly. Instead, they encountered complexity and uncertainty about the relation of size to efficiency or monopoly to depression. Thurman Arnold's vigorous antitrust prosecutions languished as the War Production Board insisted that price competition had to be relaxed for the duration.[26]

Nonetheless, the theme of monopoly continued to play a strong role in the analysis of European developments. Robert Brady, who had earlier analyzed the Nazi regime and the German rationalization movement, which also involved growing mergers and concentration, spot-lighted the political role of the leading industrial interest groups in his *Business as a System of Power*. Franz Neumann's *Behemoth* helped to make a quasi-Marxist analysis of National Socialist power the intellec-tual basis for much of American planning for the postwar occupation of Germany. These and similar discussions in the press continued to elaborate Roosevelt's 1938 conclusions that Fascism was essentially an outgrowth of modern private economic power.[27]

Thus by 1945 the two themes of productivity and monopoly formed the conceptual axes along which Americans located economic institu-tions. At home there was the inconclusive confrontation between the popularly mandated New Deal and the long-sanctioned tradition of free enterprise, between the wartime rehabilitation of industrialists and the distrust of monopoly. This domestic stalemate made recourse to meta-political notions of economic organization natural and appealing. Mo-nopoly explained political and economic setbacks; productivity promised advance.

Nevertheless, the conjugate themes would be applied to different areas. The politics of productivity beckoned originally in the non-Axis countries. The inefficiencies of production that would be vexing in Europe after 1945 did not appear as a result of concentrated power but as the consequences of a hidebound traditionalism attributed to small and backward businessmen. Moreover, the indices of production and growth allowed supposedly apolitical criteria for dealing with the rival-ries among the postwar contenders in France, Italy, and elsewhere. They provided a justification for separating constructive growth-minded labor movements (Social-Democratic or Christian) from di-visive and allegedly self-seeking Communist ones.

Americans would draw upon the anti-monopoly orientation, on the other hand, in establishing plans for transforming the political econo-mies of defeated Germany and Japan. Until 1948–49, the Occupation authorities imposed decartelization in their German zone and moved to break up the Zaibatsu across the Pacific. As Edwin Pauley's reparation mission concluded in the months after V-J Day:

> Japan's Zaibatsu (literally, 'financial clique') are . . . the greatest war potential of Japan. It was they who made possible all Japan's conquests and aggressions. . . . Not only were the Zaibatsu as responsible for Japan's militarism as the militarists themselves, but they profited immensely by it. Even now, in defeat, they have actually strengthened their monopoly position. . . . Unless the Zaibatsu are bro-ken up, the Japanese have little prospect of ever being able to govern themselves as free men. As long as the Zaibatsu survive, Japan will be their Japan.[28]

Not only did the anti-monopoly concepts find service in the Occupation, but some of the trust-busters themselves left the unpromising Justice Department to pursue their work in defeated Germany and Japan.[29] The Axis powers offered a laboratory in which to pursue the reforms that had been shelved at home. Within a few years, of course, they would be shelved abroad. Faced with the Cold War, Americans ultimately would actually carry out one further dialectical transformation. They would subordinate their crusade against monopoly in the ex-Fascist powers precisely to advance the cause of productivity. Just as during the war the Administration had dropped antitrust prosecutions for the sake of industrial mobilization, after 1948, policy makers would tacitly abandon the anti-monopoly drive in Germany and Japan in order to spur the non-Communist economies as a whole. By that time, however, Americans had already constructed the scaffolding of the Western economic order they were seeking.

The Arena for American Policy

"Americans are inclined to believe that the period at the end of the war will provide a tabula rasa on which can be written the terms of a democratic new order. The economic and political institutions of 1939 and before are clearly in suspension and need not be restored intact after the war."[30] This assessment, which was offered during an October 1942 study group session of the Council on Foreign Relations, was typical of much American thinking. And by 1945, looking at Berlin and Warsaw, or Caen, who could doubt that Europe was a tabula rasa?

In fact, however, Europe was not a blank slate, and the economic policies that the United States thrust upon it could not avoid partisan implications even when they were deemed apolitical. The major issues Washington sought to influence in economic reconstruction concerned new monetary arrangements and trade agreements (the whole complex structure of multilateralism) and the role of foreign assistance. Also at issue were the nature of labor representation (specifically, how to organize trade union support for plans consonant with American leadership) and the total reconstruction possible in West Germany and Japan. Each of these massive and perplexing sets of issues tested the American postulates of productivity.

Multilateralism and Monetary Reorganization

The return to a system of stable exchange rates was high on the agenda for both American and British leaders from the beginning of US involvement in the war. Yet, within the Anglo-American alliance, there were sharp differences of interest. If Congress or the United States

Treasury were going to endorse unprecedented foreign aid first in the Lend-Lease agreements, then in the $3.75 billion loan of 1945–46, they saw no reason not to compel London to give up commercial advantages that excluded American producers. Section VII of the Lend-Lease agreement had insisted upon postwar trade liberalization (although specifics remained omitted). The Treasury did not want British reserves to rise, and American negotiators criticized Britain's reliance on the dominion credits held in sterling in London. The British, on the other hand, invoked the notion of "equality of sacrifice" in the common war effort. What Washington was being asked to bear appeared small in comparison to their losses, financial and otherwise.

It would be wrong to bifurcate the positions too absolutely. After their own devaluation decisions during 1933–34, Roosevelt and his advisors agreed that high employment should take precedence over the stability of international exchange. Veterans of the 1930s understood that they could not allow the cost of stable currency parities to be a wrenching deflation of the home economies. This meant that as natural postwar leader and source of the potential key currency, the United States would bear a special responsibility. It would be prepared to rediscount the deficits in international account of the weaker economies and to provide the international liquidity that would get its own goods abroad. Was Washington ready for that responsibility? And if Roosevelt himself, bound by ties of sentiment and flattery to Churchill, was, would Republican Conservatives and Western Democrats endorse the policies?

The record was mixed. From the outset the differences between Keynes's plan for a postwar clearing union and Harry Dexter White's proposed stabilization fund reflected the divergent national interests. In Keynes's concept, the burden of currency stabilization was to be shared with the creditor nation (much as later the United States would pressure West Germany and Japan for upward revaluation of their respective exchange rates). Keynes envisaged a large pool of international reserves, which, like later Special Drawing Rights (SDRs), could be created as needed. To discourage countries from maintaining an undervalued currency he proposed that the large creditors of the clearing union pay interest along with the debtors. This was a suggestion that most of his colleagues saw as more playful than serious. Finally, Keynes envisaged automatic overdraft rights on the clearing union by national banks, much as British businessmen might overdraw their own accounts. The United States plan included only a modest fund without overdraft rights; but by mid-December 1942 White proposed a "scarce currency" clause that would have allowed debtor nations to discriminate in trade against a creditor nation that persisted in piling up balances with the stabilization fund. "The Americans," noted Roy Harrod, who felt the concession truly epochal, "have, happily, played a card which according to the rules of the game we could not play."[31] The scarce currency provision was actually accepted by the Congress in the Bretton Woods Act of July 1945. This action suggested that the majority understood it could not demand that an exhausted Europe simultaneously "buy American" and maintain currency stability. In contrast with the 1920s, this represented a significant insight, or concession, on the part of the United States, albeit a limited one. The International Monetary Fund (IMF) remained inadequately funded and entrusted with procedures that enforced a deflationary unorthodoxy upon debtors; and Washington was to keep up pressure on Britain to restore the pound to a disastrous convertibility.

The ambivalent pattern of pressure and support on the West Europeans remained characteristic of United States policy from the war until the 1950s. Increasingly, the more restrictive policies became identified with the Treasury while those more sympathetic with European reflationary needs influenced the Marshall Plan administration. The policy makers in these agencies had to confront a variety of European monetary initiatives after 1945. For all the countries the root problem was the same: apportioning the costs of the war by cancelling various claims to wealth and income. In Belgium and Holland a resolute amputation of bank accounts and monetary claims facilitated quick reconstruction of stable currencies. This was a solution that America and Britain would impose upon West Germany three years later.[32] In France, equivalent measures were proposed by Pierre Mendès-France but met opposition from a Communist Party in search of middle-class votes and found no support from De Gaulle. Instead, France muddled through with a chronic inflation that amounted to a disguised capital levy. Italy's postwar financial policy initially followed the pattern of French irresolution, for the liberation of Italy restored a group of traditionalist *liberisti* economists as policy makers. They were untainted by Fascism but retained the laissez-faire convictions of the pre-1925 era. Once the Left had been forced out of the governing coalition in 1947, they embarked upon a severe scheme of monetary stabilization. Their restrictions of private credit indeed halted the inflation that had shrunk the lira to one-seventieth of its 1938 value, but also provoked a recession that bottled up potential labor in the South and left existing industrial capacity badly underutilized. Recent monetarists have judged the results as a necessary cleansing for the heady growth of the 1950s. However, Economic Cooperation Administration (ECA) critics of the time (and subsequent Keynesian-type analysts) sharply condemned a policy that seemed to waste Marshall Plan resources on building up currency reserves.[33] The heirs of Franklin Roosevelt did not really wish simply to restore the counterparts of Herbert Hoover.

On the other hand, there was American consensus on the general value of multilateral exchange and as much currency convertibility as possible. The creation of intra-European payment mechanisms that were to culminate in the European Payments Union of 1950 appeared just the logical steps toward an expansion of trade that all desired. These clearing mechanisms, however, raised new conflicts with London. Authorities there feared that the intra-European accounts would expose Britain's hazardous reserve position to further depletion, as had occurred when, under Washington's pressure, the pound had been made convertible for several weeks in the summer of 1947. Belgium especially, by dint of its early currency reform and the continuing influential role of its orthodox central bank, had achieved the strongest balance-of-payments position within Europe; London feared that Brussels might present its accumulation of sterling for conversion. British Labour spokesmen Stafford Cripps and Hugh Gaitskill also feared a renewal of Washington's earlier efforts to break into the sterling area. They felt that the United States sought to undermine the currency restrictions that allowed Britain to pursue socialist experiments without worrying about a flight from the pound. After a mini-crisis in June 1950, a compromise agreement between American negotiators and London limited the convertibility of intra-European claims, and Brussels and Washington spared London the burden of converting Belgium's accumulated sterling.[34]

The record of American policy thus remains ambivalent. On the one hand, United States negotiators pressed Britain to renounce its special protection for the pound and for its trade. This occurred between 1941 and 1945, again in 1946–47, and during 1950. On the other hand, credits did come through and the American demands were repeatedly modified in practice. US Treasury authorities pursued a rigid Bretton Woods multilateralism most vigorously, perhaps because key Treasury officials of the Truman years came not from academic economics (as had Harry Dexter White) or gentleman farming (as had Morgenthau) but from the world of banking. John Snyder (succeeding the cautious Southerner Fred Vinson) emerged from a mid-West banking milieu. His special assistant for international finance and later US executive director of the International Monetary Fund, Andrew Overby, had also begun as a banker and then served as a Vice-President of the New York Federal Reserve. In contrast, the Marshall Plan authorities who dealt with the individual European countries after 1948 derived from a more expansionist industry background and had endorsed Keynesian-type reflation. They also included labor union representatives to work with European trade union leaders. The debate between Treasury and Marshall Plan officials thus tended to reflect the unresolved differences between Keynesians and conservatives at home, between the New Deal and its critics.

Another indication of the same disputes and policy ambiguity was provided by American resistance to ratification of the International Trade Organization (ITO) draft charter. It was signed at Havana in March 1948, but it finally had to be removed from Congressional consideration by Truman in December 1950. The scuttling of the ITO, however, did not mean that the United States was turning its back on the laborious efforts to lower trade barriers; indeed the country remained committed to the interim General Agreement on Tariffs and Trade (GATT) concluded in 1947. But the more ambitious architecture of the ITO sought also to regulate commodity agreements and to make allowances for the weaker partners in the international economic system. American business critics felt it had the disadvantage of committing the United States to free trade while allowing escape clauses for less robust countries. Especially disturbing was the fact that the ITO would have allowed nations to keep exchange controls and continue inflationary policies to avoid the recessions that might attend a return to full convertibility. If American businessmen were to prolong the US commitment to low tariffs, they wanted Hull's implicit compact: the open door at home would be compensated for by the open door abroad.[35]

Foreign Aid

Crudely summarized, American policy sought to maximize currency stability and international trade. This would enhance the welfare of all and the predominance of the United States. The price of Bretton Woods, however, had to be foreign assistance. Initially, Americans did not realize or confess the full extent of support they would have to provide. Only after two years of false starts did they face up to the problem of Europe's dollar gap in its full magnitude. But the issue of expanding foreign aid beset their postulates with new difficulties. Originally an apolitical aid was thought to secure the broad range of American objectives. Once, however, the Soviet Union was acknowledged as a threat, the liberals' image of a healthy political economy became strained. It was no longer clear that simple maximization of output adequately answered American interests. Increasingly, policy makers rejected those forms of international assistance which provided no direct political dividend, such as the UN Relief and Rehabilitation Administration (UNRRA). Harriman and others criticized this form of aid early on.[36] On the other hand, foreign aid could not become purely subordinate to politics, for it followed from all the earlier axioms that problems of political stability and capitalist recovery were resolved by efficient and neutral applications of planning or social engineering.

The difficulties became significant when Léon Blum came to plead for coal and funds in Washington during March 1946. As the American Ambassador in Paris warned, a rebuff to Blum would benefit the Communists significantly. Assistant Secretary of State Clayton endorsed generous assistance on behalf of the State Department. In the meetings of the National Advisory Council on International Monetary and Financial Problems, however, Marriner Eccles objected that "he would dislike to have the Government accused of undertaking to buy a foreign election." (This was a scruple soon to vanish.) Clayton answered that "he had great difficulty in separating political from economic conditions in thinking about Europe. If he thought that country X was in danger of economic and social chaos he would favor a loan if it were reasonable in amount and there were a reasonable chance of repayment." Secretary of Commerce Henry Wallace was also willing to go along, provided that a "bad" loan would not be extended merely to stabilize political conditions.[37] Hesitation about using loans for partisan or anti-Communist goals was expressed in Council on Foreign Relations discussions as late as December 1946. Some speakers felt that Washington should decide on the groups it favored and extend aid selectively. Others found Dean Acheson's food policy "exerting too much direct pressure on European politics."[38]

It is notable that a selective policy still raised controversy at the end of a year of growing tension over Germany and Eastern Europe, atomic weapons, Iran, and the role of Communism in general. Nonetheless, the rationale for foreign aid now involved both Cold War objectives and the commitment to productivity. When George Kennan's Policy Planning Staff worked up a paper on aid to Western Europe in May 1947, it argued that "it does not see Communist activities as the root of the difficulties of Western Europe." Blame was instead placed on the effects of the war and the "profound exhaustion of physical plant and of spiritual vigor." Thus, it advocated "that American effort in aid to Europe should be directed not to the combatting of Communism as such but to the restoration of the economic health and vigor of European society."[39] When the European Recovery Program was launched, it was theoretically offered to the Communist states as well, although most in Washington probably did not expect Soviet adhesion and were probably relieved when Molotov quit the preliminary talks. But at least the Marshall Plan allowed American liberals to endorse an implicitly anti-Communist aid program on the older grounds of economic assistance. Aid could remain simultaneously apolitical in motive and political in result. The point is not to deny that the antagonism with Soviet Russia deeply influenced American objectives. It is easy to catalogue the Cold War initiatives of the period (whether ultimately they were taken in response to Soviet threats is not the issue here): they included firmness over Iran, formation of the Bizone, and exclusion of the Communists from the coalitions in France, Belgium, and Italy. Wrangling at the Foreign Ministers' Conferences, the Truman Doctrine, moving toward establishment of a West German state, and limiting Socialist outcomes in the Western zones were other important milestones. This escalation confirmed the division of Europe and Asia and the formation of a United States hegemony in "the West." Nonetheless, if the politics of the Cold War in a sense took over the economic rationale of American policy, it also logically continued the politics of productivity. Both were efforts to align universalist aspirations with United States preponderance.

The Issue of European Labor

The politics of productivity, as it set the guidelines for American policy during the formative postwar years, had necessarily to include a trade union dimension. Ultimately, the American prescriptions for Europe postulated that economic relations could be free of conflict, hence, could transcend earlier class divisions. This was never really true in the US, although observers during the war might be excused for thinking class antagonisms had been superseded. More accurately, the challenge of American labor had not shaken the society's consensus on the value of private enterprise as in Europe. After 1945, the view of Europe as a tabula rasa suggested an equivalent opportunity to build consensus there as well.

What such a perspective suggested was that those labor groups willing to endorse growth and productivity should continue as a component of the European coalitions. Those who dissented were held to be regrettably partisan, obstructionist, and by 1947, subversive. During the period of liberation, it was precisely the French and Italian Communists who insisted upon the imperatives of production and summoned striking coal miners and workers back to their jobs. At the same time, Catholic, Social-Democratic, and Communist labor representatives strenuously worked to unify their unions as they emerged from an era of Fascist suppression. But this unity proved ephemeral and broke down on both the political and the trade union levels.[40] In France Communist Party acquiescence in policies of wage restraint provoked criticism from left-wing militants as the harsh Winter of 1946–47 set back economic recovery. Following hesitating support for a strike of Renault workers, the Party was excluded from the French government, and, in constant touch with the State Department, De Gasperi performed analogous surgery in May of 1947.[41]

In the flurry of messages over American aid in the Spring of 1947, the issue of Communist participation in government had emerged as implicitly critical. It was not surprising that by the Fall of 1947, the Communist labor confederations should make rejection of the Marshall Plan a major issue in the demonstrations and strikes that shook France and Italy. The strike movement, however, further crystallized the internal divisions within the trade union movements. Non-Communist members had already organized their own journal in France, *Résistance Ouviere*, now redubbed *Force Ouvrière*. By late 1947 acceptance of the Marshall Plan became the major touchstone of division between the non-Communists and Communists, and Force Ouvrière leaders felt that the Communists had engaged labor's sacrifices to support a policy dictated by Moscow. At the end of 1947 they left the Confédération Générale de Travail (CGT) to organize their own federation the following April. In Italy, Catholic and socialist trade unionists left their federation, the General Confederation of Italian Labor (CGIL), a few months thereafter.[42]

Throughout this interval United States officials and AFL leaders encouraged the non-Communist unions to secede and establish their own federations. CIA agent Thomas Braden later estimated that $2 million was channeled to the pro-Western elements.[43] Ambassador Caffery in Paris condemned the CGT as "the fortress" of the French Communist Party. Ambassador James Clement Dunn in Rome saw the local working class demand for factory councils as a "Communist framework for fomenting disorder and attacking the authority of the state."[44] American CIO leaders were initially reluctant to join in the concerted pressure against the unified labor federations and for a while resisted official pleas that they enlist against the Communists. But by late 1948 the CIO was wracked by the struggle against Communist-led unions within their own ranks, and its leaders felt a greater Communist danger. Secretary James Carey also served on the Harriman Committee that helped outline the European Recovery Program after Marshall's famous address of June 1947, and he became angry over the obstruction to the plan that the fellow-traveling Secretary-General of the World Federation of Free Trade Unions seemed to be raising. By the Spring of 1949, the CIO and the AFL met with the Force Ouvrière and the British Trade Union Congress to charter a new non-Communist international labor federation.[45]

The Marshall Plan thus irrevocably split the European labor movement between 1947–49. More precisely, it sealed a division that was probable in any case; but it did so on the questions of economic recovery that Americans found easiest to defend. Given the United States axioms, what men of good will could legitimately reject the concept of assistance to stimulate investment and production? The Communists, in a sense, placed themselves outside the continuum of normal politics. On the other hand, the premises of the Marshall Plan, as well as the make-up of the Truman Administration, imposed limits on the political reaction of 1947–49. No Democratic Administration in the United States, especially one facing a challenge from its Left, could have alienated labor. Nor would it thereafter have been able to work with any anti-Communist government abroad that needed to preserve some working-class support. From this derived the imperative of constructing a Social-Democratic center, even if this strategy meant, as Dunn argued from Italy, that socialization would be accelerated.[46] The British Labour Party, finally, remained a key factor in organizing a "third force," and its members believed, in the words of Dennis Healey, that Europe could be reconstructed only as Democratic Socialist or Communist.[47] Far from turning out to be an infinitely malleable society, Europe and its divisions forced the American politics of productivity in a clear centrist direction.

Germany and Japan

The influence that Washington exerted through foreign aid in most of Europe could be imposed directly in the two societies that would later form the strongest building blocks of the Western economy along with America, specifically West Germany and Japan. During the very months that the division of Germany was being irremediable (Spring 1947 to Spring 1948), the future political economy of the West German state was also being decided. The outcome depended upon a complex interplay between a number of groups and individuals. General Lucius Clay was proconsul of the American zone. The Department of the Army in Washington supported Clay. The Department of State heeded the Paris Embassy's warnings about the dangers of compelling the shaky French government to accept too quick a German recovery. Finally, the British government controlled the industrial heartland of North-Rhine-Westphalia. It was clear that Clay would seek to limit Socialist initiatives inside the *Länder* of the American zone. The formation of the Bizone, moreover, allowed him to determine effectively the outcome within North-Rhine-Westphalia as well, even though it lay inside the British administrative sphere. During 1947 Clay forestalled British Labour Party intentions to establish the Ruhr mines under public German control. Once Clay's views prevailed in Washington, French and British dependence upon American aid precluded their resisting his framework for a capitalist and federalist West German state. The implications for future West German politics were crucial;

for coupled with the diminishing chances for reunification, the new constraints on West German collectivism effectively condemned the left wings of the SPD and of the CDU to a political desert. Who remembers today the vibrant Christian Socialism of the North-Rhine-Westphalian CDU before 1949?[48]

Comparable developments took place in Japan. The revival of trade unionism that Occupation authorities originally encouraged became unwelcome when labor protested against the deterioration of living conditions that had occurred after the end of the war and that had reached a crisis (in all countries) during the Winter of 1946–47. When the militant, Communist-oriented Sambetsu union federation announced a general strike for February 1, 1947, MacArthur prohibited the demonstration. The Socialist Party won a plurality in the April elections (the Liberals and Democrats had not yet consolidated) and participated in the government during 1947–48. It was the last time for a generation that they were to do so. Both Japanese business and the Supreme Allied Command-Pacific endeavored successfully to encourage a schism in the Sambetsu. They achieved a secession by the moderates and the formation, by 1950, of the Sōhyō federation. This was analogous to the contemporary formation of Force Ouvrière in France or the Social Democratic Party in Italy.[49]

In both Germany and Japan the policy of industrial deconcentration was slowly jettisoned. By the Fall of 1947, the Harriman-Draper mission to Germany recommended a new emphasis on rebuilding German industry and protests rose against dismantling and reparations (even to the Western allies). Draper visited Japan in early 1948 and made similar recommendations. He was followed by Secretary of the Army Kenneth Royall and by fiscally orthodox Detroit banker Joseph Dodge in early 1949. The campaign against the Zaibatsu faltered as did the effort to reorganize durably the German iron and steel industry.[50] The logic of the new policy was persuasive. If the United States were to commit itself to a greater effort to restore economic production in Europe and Asia, how could it plausibly persevere in crippling the most productive centers of those continents?

Indeed, West Germany and Japan remained the states where the United States' politics of productivity could be transplanted most triumphantly. Perhaps because of the visible destruction all around or the labor pool formed by the immigrants from the East, German labor demonstrated consistent restraint. The Social Democratic Party (SPD) did not press its program in Bizonia. Indeed, it reverted to the opposition. The trade union federation (DGB) accepted a far more circumscribed co-determination law than it originally wanted. As German industrial and banking leaders would themselves testify, trade union wage restraint became a major component of the economic miracle.[51] The post-Korea take-off in Japan condemned the Left in that country to a noisy but marginal status.

American policy in Germany and Japan was thus a resounding success. The whole thrust of Washington's effort in the emerging Federal Republic, the new Japan, and the members of the Organization for European Economic Cooperation (OEEC)—later the Organization for Economic Cooperation and Development (OECD)—was to ensure the primacy of economics over politics, to de-ideologize issues of political economy into questions of output and efficiency. The two occupied states offered the most promising ground for accomplishing the conversion of politics into economics. Especially in West Germany, the political structure developed as a scaffolding for economic reconstruction; the Federal Republic emerged as a proto-state built upon organs for economic administration. Even today both the Federal Republic and Japan are nations which represent massive economic forces that lack concomitant political weight. From states in which military-bureaucratic establishments, pursuing objectives of prestige and expansion, called upon the resources of production for statist ends, they have become political economies in which the concept of state has become virtually otiose.

In the last analysis, the politics of productivity that emerged as the American organizing idea for the postwar economic world depended upon superseding class conflict with economic growth. By bringing West Germany and Japan into a community of nations as dynamos of wider regional recovery, the United States aided other societies to adjourn their own distributive conflicts and to move from scarcity to relative abundance. By helping to establish West Germany and Japan as nexuses of economic transactions and the most efficient accumulators of capital, rather than as centers of political power, America most completely carried out its postwar economic postulates.

The success of this politics of productivity can be judged by the fact that the 1950s and the 1960s turned out to be periods of unparalleled growth and capital formation. Investment was a major objective of the European Recovery Program. Without capital formation, American aid might ease immediate balance-of-payment crises but would have to continue indefinitely, whereas the premise of the Marshall Plan as presented to Congress was that after four years Europe's self-sufficiency would be restored. By 1948–49, it was clear that Europe was investing 20 percent of its GNP, whereas from an equal social product in 1938, its societies had ploughed back only 12 percent. (And military expenditures in 1948–49 were only 1 percent less than 1938's 6 percent.) Indeed, the ambitious British investment levels of 1948–49, when gross domestic capital formation (less overseas deficit) reached 22.8 percent (1948) and 21.4 percent (1949), or roughly twice that of 1938, seemed excessive to American Keynesians. The memory of the Depression, when aggregate demand did not keep pace with productive capacity, sobered the observers of British efforts under the Marshall Plan.[52]

Insofar as much of post-World War II politics can be viewed as a debate between growth and equality, between collective investment or public consumption, at least until the late 1960s, the argument was largely resolved so as not to endanger investment. This can be inferred not only from electoral returns that excluded the Left, but from the slow percentage growth of wage shares as a component of national income. In the stately half-century decline of the return on capital, the 1950s represented a decade of redress. Reviewing the reverses of Socialism in 1959, Richard Titmuss found increasing privilege, inequality, and concentrations of power.[53] The other side of the story was unparalleled economic growth (albeit outside Great Britain) and the rise of real incomes. Germany and Japan, above all, achieved record growth and accumulation. These were, of course, precisely the arenas in which the American politics of productivity could be most thoroughly instituted.

In retrospect the 1950s and even the 1960s, must be judged a great era for the stabilized growth capitalism of the West. Conservative governments ruled in London, Bonn, Rome, for a time in Paris, and certainly in Washington. This was not right-wing leadership, but solid men of the center committed to growth after wartime destruction and exhaustion with ideological conflict. The United States encouraged this trend but did not have to impose it. Had these impulses not been present it seems unlikely that Americans could have built a breakwater in Europe any more than they were able to dam up different aspirations

Table 1. Gross national capital formation

	1950–58 (%)	Previous maxima (%)
UK	16.2	14.0 (1900–14)
German Federal Republic	26.8	24.1 (1891–1913)
Italy	19.8	17.3 (1901–10)
United States	18.4	21.9 (1889–1908)
Sweden	21.4	c. 20.4 (1941–49, inferred)
Japan	30.2	15.3 (1927–36)

Source: Simon Kuznets, *Modern Economic Growth: Rate, Structure, and Spread* (New Haven: Yale University Press, 1966), pp. 263–39.

in Asia. On the other hand, the social basis for the politics of productivity was present in Europe, as it was not in mainland Asia. The war and Nazi occupation had shaken, but not uprooted, a prevailingly bourgeois society with broad middle-class patterns of ownership and culture.

The Limits of American Hegemony

Perhaps the best term for the postwar Western economy would be that of consensual American hegemony. "Consensual" can be used because European leaders accepted Washington's leadership in view of their needs for economic and security assistance. Hegemony derives from Washington's ability to establish policy guidelines binding on the West. In what respects, however, did hegemony really mean influence exerted to alter European policies that might otherwise have turned out differently? Certainly in the years 1944 to 1947 the emphasis on free convertibility of currencies and stable exchange rates, as stipulated in the Bretton Woods arrangements and aid to Britain, were designed, in part, to limit London's capacity to organize a separate trading bloc. Pained British protests made American *force majeure* abundantly clear, although they did not necessarily justify British preferences in terms of broader criteria of economic welfare. In the years after 1947, when the objectives of some American policy makers became more politically conservative, Washington's continuing pressure on behalf of the dollar as an international currency, the political signals which accompanied its foreign aid, and its direct intervention in West Germany and Japan could inhibit leftist experiments in societies that might have tried alternative principles of economic organization. These would in turn have ultimately been less susceptible to United States influence. Usually Washington did not have brutally to abort a series of promising Socialist initiatives. Instead, it more subtly rewarded a generation of centrist "Atlantic" oriented European leaders (and Japanese Liberal Democrats) who found the American preferences rational and humane. Moreover, the United States could benefit from some of the economic arrangements generated in wartime Europe and Japan. For if the wartime experiences provoked a left-wing resistance mystique, paradoxically they reinforced corporatist patterns of social bargaining that persisted afterward. Labor relations in Germany, Japan, the Netherlands, and other countries were to bear the wartime impression, and the United States would ultimately benefit from the collaborative tendencies thus bequeathed.[54] In the last analysis, the means of exercising hegemony may be as critical as the fact of dominance itself: the architects of the American-sponsored international economic order exerted a gentlemanly persuasion. Moreover, it was one enjoying most of the mystical aura of an "invisible hand," which usually attends smoothly running cybernetic systems, much as had been the case with the Gold Standard before World War I.[55]

Hegemony remains successful, however, only when it achieves advances for the whole international structure within which it is exercised. Hegemony imposed in a zero-sum cockpit, that is, at the expense of the secondary members of the system, must finally prove less durable. (Alternatively, it requires overt force; viz., Hungary, 1956, and Czechoslovakia, 1968.) The quarter-century of relatively frictionless American domination depended partially upon the fact that the technologies of the era (including the capitalization of agriculture) permitted the growth that was its underlying premise. Ironically, too, the destruction left by World War II allowed rapid catch-up recovery that could be attributed to the American role. The result was that the politics of productivity rested upon the reality of productivity. The system paid off.

Indeed, once the system ceased to pay off, it began to founder. Between 1946 and 1971 the structures of American leadership could serve the United States in one of two ways: one accepted as legitimate and one as less legitimate by the secondary participants. Insofar as the United States was prepared to furnish European societies goods and services without real economic counterpart, it could ask policy compliance in return. This was the situation of the "dollar gap" in the late 1940s and early 1950s, when Washington provided more than $20 billion of assistance and secured more open trading areas. The other way that Americans could utilize the Bretton Woods framework was precisely the reverse: by exacting tribute through seignorage, i.e., accumulating dollar liabilities abroad and purchasing European assets with an overvalued currency. This was the situation of the late 1960s when, in effect, the United States taxed its allies for part of the costs of the Indochina War (combined with other public commitments) by trying to insist upon the unaltered reserve status of an eroding dollar. Since, however, the system remained one of consensual hegemony (contrasted, for example, with the German organization of continental Europe between 1940 and 1944), the United States could not easily enforce the power of unlimited overdrafts. The French refused to pay the levy from 1965 on, and it was primarily the special West German dependence upon US security presence that enabled the Bretton Woods framework to last as long as it did. (That West German need, both objective and subjective, in turn reflected the special circumstances in which the Federal Republic of Germany had emerged under US auspices.)

With the partial relinquishing of American claims to leadership, divergent patterns of foreign economic policy became more visible. While Washington's politics of productivity helped to reorient the Western economies in the postwar era, characteristic national preferences and approaches persisted. Of course, as American predominance relaxed, it would have been local for the secondary countries to revert to a more mercantilist conduct in the absence of forceful leadership. Such trends, though, were to be further reinforced by traditional historical patterns of economic policy making. For all its economic vigor, for example, the business leadership of West Germany continued to re-emphasize the primacy of exports and only secondarily the importance of domestic purchasing power and expansion. Italian and Japanese policy makers likewise tended to pursue policies in which relatively cheap labor played a major role. The American politics of productivity applied abroad had originally encouraged labor restraint to secure ultimate economic growth. As American leadership became more diffuse, entrepreneurs and political leaders in Europe tended to emphasize the restraint more than the growth.

Perhaps it is ungracious to ask whether what was originally a successful and, I believe, broad and generally beneficial policy had serious costs. But all grand policy structures must at least exclude alternatives, and this particular international economic system probably served to stabilize the inequalities of income and power within each society of the West and Japan. A contrast with the British imperial structure before 1914 may help to reveal the mechanism and also establish its proportions. Britain's financial preponderance rested upon real growth but also upon the society's willingness to live with sharply skewed distributions of income and wealth. Had there been sharper challenges to domestic inequality over the half-century before World War I, it might have proved far more difficult to generate the social savings that established the reserve position of sterling. By the 1920s, the costs of continuing were excessive, even for a society as cohesive as the British. American hegemony, on the other hand, was a child of Wilsonianism and the New Deal. Politically, it could not demand renunciation on the part of the American working classes for the sake of providing the liquidity of the West. Nor, initially, did it have to; the discrepancy in productivity and output between Europe and the US left by the Second World War made American leadership relatively painless in domestic terms. Conservatives complained about taxes, but the sacrifice even to support the Marshall Plan was comparatively slight. It was not the fiscal burden, but the departure from political traditions that represented the major domestic hurdle. When, by the end of the 1960s, real sacrifices at home in terms of taxation or restrictions on use of the dollar abroad might have been necessary to restore credibility in the dollar's reserve status, the Nixon Administration chose to renounce a degree of economic primacy.

Yet the contrary-to-fact query remains. Might the progress of reducing inequality within the United States as well as Europe not have been faster or surer without the quarter-century of economic domination? It is impossible to be confident. While periods of quick growth do not usually reduce income disparities, neither does stagnation, which might have been the result of a less forward American policy. Nonetheless, the question must be posed. "Welfare" criteria apply, most easily, to whole societies. Alone they cannot measure the costs of hegemony on particular components but can only confirm the triumph of productivity for the aggregate. But this, indeed, was all Americans sought to know. The cohesiveness of our politics lay in the reluctance to suggest alternative questions. In the terms that all significant sectors of opinion would have posed the issue, US foreign economic policy was beneficial as well as potent. This judgment should not be surprising; it followed from the ideological beliefs that rescued national cohesion in a society of great material differences.

Endnotes

1. For critical analyses, Lloyd C. Gardner, *Economic Aspects of New Deal Diplomacy* (Madison: University of Wisconsin Press, 1964); Gabriel Kolko, *The Politics of War: The World and United States Foreign Policy, 1943–1945* (New York: Random House, 1968); William Appleman Williams, *The Tragedy of American Diplomacy* (New York: Dell Publishing Co., 1962).

2. For Johnston and Nelson, see John Lewis Gaddis, *The United States and the Origins of the Cold War, 1941–1947* (New York: Columbia University Press, 1972), pp. 176–77, 185–89. Clayton cited in Thomas Paterson, *Soviet-American Confrontation: Postwar Reconstruction and the Origins of the Cold War* (Baltimore: The Johns Hopkins University Press, 1973), p. 4.

3. *The Memoirs of Cordell Hull*, 2 vols. (New York: Macmillan Co., 1948), Vol. 1, p. 364.

4. To see the implications of Wilsonianism, see N. Gordon Levin, Jr., *Woodrow Wilson and World Politics. America's Response to War and Revolution* (New York: Oxford University Press, 1970).

5. For the earlier analogue: John Gallagher and Ronald Robinson, "The Imperialism of Free Trade," *Economic History Review*, 2nd series, 6 (1953): 1–15; objections in D. C. M. Platt, "The Imperialism of Free Trade: Some Reservations," *Economic History Review*, 2nd series, 11 (1968): 196–306, and "Further Objections to an 'Imperialism of Free Trade,' 1830–1860," *Economic History Review*, 2nd series, 26 (1976): 77–91.

6. Benjamin M. Rowland, "Preparing the American Ascendency: The Transfer of Economic Power from Britain to the United States," in *Balance of Power or Hegemony: The Interwar Monetary System*, Benjamin M. Rowland, ed. A Lehrman Institute Book (New York: New York University Press, 1976), pp. 195–224, and, in the same volume, Harold van B. Cleveland, "The International Monetary System in the Interwar Period," esp. pp. 54–56; Lowell M.

Pumphrey, "The Exchange Equalization Account of Great Britain," *American Economic Review*, 32 (December 1942): 803–16.

7. Richard N. Gardner, *Sterling-Dollar Diplomacy: Anglo-American Cooperation in the Reconstruction of Multilateral Trade* (Oxford: Clarendon Press, 1956), offers the best account of this relationship.

8. Rowland, "Preparing the American Ascendancy," pp. 202–04, 213–15.

9. For Morgenthau's ideas, see John Blum, ed., *From the Morgenthau Diaries*, Vol. 3: *Years of War 1941–1945* (Boston: Houghton Mifflin Company, 1967), pp. 228–30, 324–26, 333ff; cf. Kolko, *Politics of War* pp. 323–40.

10. William E. Leuchtenburg, *Franklin D. Roosevelt and the New Deal, 1932–1940* (New York: Harper and Row, 1963), pp. 243ff.; J. Joseph Huthmacher, *Senator Robert F. Wagner and the Rise of Urban Liberalism* (New York: Atheneum, 1971); Robert Sherwood, *Roosevelt and Hopkins* (New York: Harper & Brothers, 1948), pp. 110–11.

11. Letter to Averell Harriman, July 7, 1941, in James Forrestal papers, Princeton University Library, Box 56. For a liberal, journalistic account of Washington wartime economic conflicts, see Bruce Catton, *The Warlords of Washington* (New York: Harcourt, Brace, 1948).

12. Paul A. C. Koistinen, "Mobilizing the World War II Economy: Labor and the Industrial-Military Alliance," *Pacific Historical Review*, 42 (November 1973); 443–78, esp. 446–60. Cf. Barton J. Bernstein, "American in War and Peace: The Test of Liberalism," in *Toward a New Past: Dissenting Essays in American History*, Barton J. Bernstein, ed. (New York: Random House-Vintage, 1968).

13. John Morton Blum, ed., *The Price of Vision: The Diary of Henry A. Wallace, 1942–1946* (Boston: Atlantic-Little Brown, 1937), p. 137. See also Norman D. Markowitz, *The Rise and Fall of the People's Century: Henry A. Wallace and American Liberalism, 1941–1948* (New York: Free Press, 1973), pp. 47ff.; Frederick H. Schapsmeier and Edward L. Schapsmeir, *Prophet in Politics: Henry A. Wallace and the War Years, 1940–1945* (Ames, Iowa: The University of Iowa Press, 1970), pp. 55–71.

14. Bernstein, "America in War and Peace," for Congressional conservatism; Markowitz, *Henry Wallace*, pp. 57–65, on the NRPB; Huthmacher, pp. 285–302; Stephen Kemp Bailey, *Congress Makes a Law: The Story behind the Employment Act of 1946* (New York: Columbia University Press, 1950).

15. See Ellis Hawley, "Herbert Hoover, the Commerce Secretariat and the Vision of an 'Associative State,' 1921–1928," *The Journal of American History*, 61 (June 1974): 116–40; also Hawley's own essay in *Herbert Hoover and the Crisis of American Capitalism*, Ellis Hawley et al. (Cambridge, Massachusetts: Schenkman, 1973); Barry D. Karl, "Presidential Planning and Social Science Research: Mr. Hoover's Experts," *Perspectives in American History*, 3 (1969): 347–409. See also Chapter 1, this volume, "Between Taylorism and Technocracy."

16. Karl Schriftgeisser, *Business Comes of Age: The Story of the Committee for Economic Development and its Impact upon the Economic Policies of the United States* (New York: Harper and Row, 1960); also Herbert Stein, *The Fiscal Revolution in America* (Chicago: University of Chicago Press, 1969), Chapters 8–9; Robert Lekachman, *The Age of Keynes* (New York: Random House, 1966).

17. Secretary of Commerce files in W. Averell Harriman papers, Washington, National Press Club Luncheon, October 15, 1946.

18. *The Journals of David E. Lilienthal*, Vol. I: *The TVA Years, 1939–1945* (New York: Harper & Row, 1964), p. 471, entry of April 14, 1942. On the conservation justification, see Robert F. Himmelberg essay in Hawley et al., pp. 63–82; for planning in the '30s: Ellis W. Hawley, *The New Deal and the Problem of Monopoly* (Princeton: Princeton University Press, 1966), pp. 122–27, 130–46; Lewis L. Lorwin and A. Ford Hinrichs, *National Economic and Social Planning* (Bloomington, Indiana: Principia, 1937); Charles Merriam, "The National Resources Planning Board: A Chapter in American Planning Experience," *American Political Science Review*, 38 (December 1944): 1075–88.

19. Joan Robinson, *The Economics of Imperfect Competition* (London: Macmillan, 1933); Edward H. Chamberlain, *The Theory of Monopolistic Competition* (Cambridge, Massachusetts: Harvard University Press, 1938).

20. US Congress, Senate, *Industrial Prices and their Relative Inflexibility*, by Gardiner means. Sen Doc. 13, 74th Congress, 1st. Sess. 1935; cf. Adolph Berle and Gardiner Means, *The Modern Corporation and Private Property* (New York: The Macmillan Co., 1937); also Maurice Leven, Harold G. Moulton, Clark Warburton, *America's Capacity to Consume* (Washington: The Brookings Institution, 1934), pp. 126–28.

21. David Lynch, *The Concentration of Economic Power* (New York: Columbia University Press, 1946), pp. 1–34; Hawley, *The New Deal and the Problem of Monopoly*, pp. 404–19.

22. Temporary National Economic Committee, *Hearings*, Vol. I, appendix, p. 105.

23. *The Memoirs of Cordell Hull*, p. 364.

24. Lilienthal, *TVA Years*, p. 324, entry of May 22, 1941.

25. John Morton Blum, ed., *From the Morgenthau Diaries*, Vol. 1: *Years of Urgency, 1938–1941* (Boston: Houghton Mifflin Company, 1965), p. 20.

26. Lynch describes the TNEC results; for antitrust see Hawley, *The New Deal and the Problem of Monopoly*, pp. 420–25.

27. See three books by Robert Brady, *The Rationalization Movement in German Industry* (Berkeley and Los Angeles: University of Carlifornia Press, 1933); *The Spirit and Structure of German Fascism* (New York: The Viking Press, 1937); *Business as a System of Power* (New York: Columbia University Press, 1943); Franz Neumann, *Behemoth: The Structure and Practice of National Socialism* (Toronto and New York: Columbia University Press, 1942). Cf. Lutz Niethammer, *Entnazifierung in Bayern: Säuberung und Rehabilitierung unter amerikanischer Besatzung* (Frankfurt am Main: S. Fischer Verlag, 1972), pp. 37ff.

28. Jerome B. Cohen, *Japan's Economy in War and Reconstruction* (Minneapolis: University of Minnesota Press, 1949), p. 427.

29. For the embittered reaction of one see James Stewart Martin, *All Honorable Men* (Boston: Little, Brown, 1952).

30. Council on Foreign Relations: Studies of American Interests in the War and the Peace, Memoranda of Discussion; Economic and Financial Series, E-A 36, October 27, 1942.

31. Cf. Gardner, *Sterling-Dollar Diplomacy;* Rowland, "Preparing the American Ascendancy," pp. 213–22; Paterson, pp. 159–73; Roy Harrod, *The Life of John Maynard Keynes* (New York: Harcourt, Brace, 1951), p. 547 (letter to Keynes, March 2, 1943).

32. Leon H. Dupriez, *Monetary Reconstruction in Belgium* (New York: The Carnegie Endowment for International Peace and the King's Crown Press, 1947), esp. Chapters 3–4; Fritz Grotius, "Die europäischen Geldreformen nach dem 2. Weltkrieg," *Weltwirtschaftliches Archiv,* Vol. 63 (1949 II): 106–52, 276–325; J. C. Gurley, "Excess Liquidity and European Monetary Reforms," *The American Economic Review,* 43 (March 1953): 76–100; Hans Möller, "Die westdeutsche Währungsreform von 1948," in *Währung und Wirtschaft in Deutschland 1876–1975,* Deutsche Bundesbank, ed. (Frankfurt am Main: Fritz Knapp GmbH, 1976), pp. 433–83.

33. For criticism, Marcello De Cecco, "Sulla politica di stabilizzazione del 1948," *Saggi di politica monetaria* (Milan: Dott. A. Giuffrè Editore, 1968), pp. 109–41; Economic Cooperation Administration, *Country Study (Italy)* (Washington, 1950); Bruno Foa, *Monetary Reconstruction in Italy* (New York: The Carnegie Endowment for International Peace and King's Crown Press, 1949); favorable judgments in George H. Hildebrand, *Growth and Structure in the Economy of Modern Italy* (Cambridge, Massachusetts: Harvard University Press, 1965), Chapters 2 and 8. On France, see Maurice Parodi, *L'économie et la société française de 1945 à 1970* (Paris: Armand Colin, 1971), pp. 66ff. For general coverage of postwar policies, A. J. Brown, *The Great Inflation, 1939–1951* (London: Oxford University Press, 1955), pp. 227–48.

34. William Diebold, Jr., *Trade and Payment in Western Europe* (New York: Harper and Row, 1952), esp.. pp. 64–69. I have also drawn upon an oral-history interview with Averell Harriman, Milton Katz, and others.

35. On this issue, see William Diebold, Jr., *The End of the ITO,* Princeton University, Department of Economics and Social Institutions, Studies in International Finance (Princeton: Princeton University Press, 1952).

36. Paterson, pp. 94–98.

37. US Department of State, *Foreign Relations of the United States,* 1946, V, 440–43. (Minutes of the Twenty-Fourth Meeting of the National Advisory Council of International and Monetary Problems, Washington, May 6, 1946.)

38. Council on Foreign Relations archives, Records of Groups, XII G.

39. US Department of State, *Foreign Relations of the United States,* 1947, III, 224–25.

40. Trends can be followed in Georges Lefranc, *Le mouvement syndical de la libération aux événements de mai-juin 1968* (Paris: Presses Universitaires de France, 1969), pp. 41–76; Fabio Levi, Paride Rugafiori, Salvatore Vento, *Il triangolo industriale tra ricostruzione e lotta di classe 1945/48* (Milan: Feltrinelli, 1974); Adolfo Pepe, "La CGIL della ricostruzione alla scissione (1944–1948)," *Storia Contemporanea,* 5 (1974): 591–636; Alfred J. Rieber, *Stalin and the French Communist Party, 1941–1947* (New York: Columbia University Press, 1962), Chapter 14.

41. Besides the above, see Ambassador Caffrey's report to the State Department in *Foreign Relations of the United States,* 1947, III, p. 703, and Ambassador Dunn (Rome) on May 28, 1947, in ibid., pp. 911ff.

42. Lefranc, pp. 51–76; Sergio Turone, *Storia del sindacato in Italia (1943–1969)* (Bari: Laterza, 1973), pp. 177–89; Daniel L. Horowitz, *The Italian Labor Movement* (Cambridge, Massachusetts: Harvard University Press, 1963), pp. 214ff.

43. *The New York Times*, May 8, 1967, p. 1, for Braden revelations.

44. *Foreign Relations of the United States*, 1947, III, 690–91 (Caffery cable, February 19), and 747–48 (Dunn report, December 11, 1948), III.

45. Evolution of the CIO leadership can be followed in *Foreign Relations of the United States*, 1948, III, 847–48, 867 (reports of March 10 and 24).

46. *Foreign Relations of the United States*, 1948, III, p. 863 (March 28, 1948).

47. Ibid., p. 855 (March 17, 1948).

48. For Clay's opposition to British plans, and Washington discussions, see *Foreign Relations of the United States*, 1947, II, pp. 910–11, 924ff; also Jean Edward Smith, ed., *The papers of Lucius D. Clay: Germany 1945–1949*, 2 vols. (Bloomington, Ind.: The Indiana University Press, 1975), Vol. I, pp. 341–43, 352–63, 411–13. For German political ramifications see, among others, Hans-Peter Schwarz, *Vom Reich zur Bundesrepublik. Deutschland im Widerstreit der aussenpolitischen Konzeptionen in den Jahren der Besatzungsherrschaft 1945–1949* (Neuwied and Berlin: Luchterhand, 1966), pp. 297–344, 551–64; also Eberhard Schmidt, *Die verhinderte Neuordnung 1945–1952* (Frankfurt am Main: Europäische Verlagsanstalt, 1970).

49. Jon Halliday, *A Political History of Japanese Capitalism* (New York: Pantheon Books, 1975), pp. 206–19, is useful from a Marxist perspective. See also Eitaro Kishimoto, "Labour-Management Relations and the Trade Unions in Post-War Japan (1)," *The Kyoto University Economic Review* Vol. 38, No. 1 (April 1968): 1–35, which emphasizes the role played by "seniority wages" in encouraging enterprise unions at the expense of more class-oriented labor coalitions; also Iwayo F. Ayusawa, *A History of Labor in Modern Japan* (Honolulu: East-West Center Press, 1966), pp. 257–75, 281–301, 315–23; Koji Taira, *Economic Development and the Labor Market in Japan* (New York: Columbia University Press, 1970), pp. 183–87.

50. Halliday, *A Political History of Japanese Capitalism*, pp. 182–90; John Gimbel, *The American Occupation of Germany, 1945–1949* (Stanford, Calif.: Stanford University Press, 1968), pp. 147ff., 163ff., 174–85.

51. See, for example, Herman Abs's presentation to the Council on Foreign Relations, December 5, 1949, Council on Foreign Relations Archives, Records of Meetings, Vol. 10.

52. Howard Ellis, *The Economics of Freedom* (New York: Harper, 1952), pp. 129, 135.

53. Richard Titmuss, "The Irresponsible Society," *Essays on the Welfare State* (Boston: Beacon Press, 1969).

54. These continuities in Europe comprise a major theme of my own current research; for the Japanese case, see Taira, p. 188, drawing upon the Japanese work or Ryohei Magota.

55. For the issue of whether international monetary systems do or do not require "hegemonic" leadership, see the essays in Rowland, ed., *Balance of*

Power or Hegemony; also Stephen D. Krasner, "State Power and the Structure of International Trade," *World Politics* Vol. 28, No. 3 (July 1976): 317–43. Insights into the regulatory capacity of the earlier system are derived from Arthur Bloomfield, *Short-Term Capital Movements under the Gold Standard,* Princeton University, Department of Economics and Social Institutions, International Studies No. 16 (Princeton, N.J., 1952), esp. pp. 72ff; Peter Lindert, "Key Currencies and Gold, 1900–1913," *Princeton Studies in International Finance,* No. 24 (Princeton, N.J.: Princeton University Press, 1969).

8

Michael J. Hogan

The Marshall Plan

Michael Hogan is Professor of History at the Ohio State University. His book, *The Marshall Plan: America, Britain, and the Reconstruction of Western Europe, 1947–1952* (Cambridge and New York, Cambridge University Press, 1987) is the most extensive and well-documented history of the European Recovery Program—the formal name for what originated as the Marshall Plan—that is currently available, and is likely to remain so for many years. We are grateful to the author and Cambridge University Press for allowing us to reprint chapter 2, pp. 54–87.

Most historians identify the Marshall Plan as a crucial step in European economic recovery. (See, however, the Milward essay that follows for a partial dissent.) It helped overcome the economic bottlenecks and make available the short supplies that Europeans needed from the United States but did not have the dollars to import. The Program's requirement of joint European consultation on mutual needs and the American encouragement of intra-European trade stimulated West European cooperation. The Marshall Plan also persuaded a wary France to accept German recovery as a needed motor for the European economy. (On this aspect of reconciling French and German priorities see John Gimbel, *The Origins of the Marshall Plan* (Stanford, Stanford University

Press, 1976).) Just as significant for European recovery, many historians and participants of the time credit the American initiative with overcoming political demoralization and reinfusing confidence in the long-term prospects for democracy. Certainly the Marshall Plan reinforced the political isolation of the West European Communists, as the Soviet Union perceived it as a major American political offensive and moved another step toward imposing total control over Communist parties, East and West.

Hogan envisages the Marshall Plan in effect as the product of an American corporatist vision, tentatively outlined in the 1920s, then instituted with steadier government involvement in the 1940s. According to Hogan, this American concept for reconstruction had then to be negotiated primarily with the British who had an agenda of their own to preserve their status as a residual great power. For Hogan, the ideas behind the Marshall Plan were based on the legacy of American social experiments: Herbert Hoover's "associationalism" and New Deal "neo-capitalism." Although they differed in many respects, both of these approaches to national political economy involved an active collaboration among industrial leaders, labor spokesmen, and a benign but interventionist state. In addition, the Marshall Plan staff continually urged integration of a larger European trade area, taking the internal American market as their model. On the other hand, Europeans, Hogan explains, forced modifications of the United States project: Americans set out to make Europe in their image, but did not succeed.

I

At the time of the three-power conference in Paris, the State Department had not devised a concrete *plan* for stabilizing Europe. Instead of a plan, there had emerged an emphasis on European initiative in drafting a recovery program, a determination to provide the Europeans with limited "friendly aid" in the drafting process, and a set of principles to guide European and American action. In addition to maximum self-help, mutual aid, and resource sharing, American leaders were talking about the importance of liberalizing intra-European trade, making currencies convertible, and using central institutions to coordinate national policies. A comprehensive recovery plan founded on such concepts, or so the Americans assumed, would erase the traditional territorial constraints on European enterprise, abolish old habits of bilateralism and restrictionism, and eliminate archaic concerns with national self-sufficiency and autonomy. These attributes were seen as barriers to maximum productivity, and they were to give way now to a large, functionally ordered, and organically integrated economy similar to the one that existed in the United States. This was the American way to stable abundance and social peace in Western Europe and to a fully multilateral system of world trade.

Together with supranational institutions of coordination and control, economic integration would also help to build a viable balance of power among the states of Western Europe and a workable correlation of forces on the Continent. It would create a unit coherent enough to harness Germany's industrial strength without restoring its prewar dominance and strong enough to countervail the Soviet bloc in Eastern Europe. Seen in this light, integration had emerged as both an economic and a strategic concept, and putting this concept into operation had become even more important after the Soviets turned their backs on the second American effort to rebuild Europe in the image of the United States.

Obstacles to the American design existed in other quarters as well, however, and these would become more apparent when non-Communist leaders from both sides of the Atlantic met in Paris and Washington to draft a recovery plan. Indeed, the very process of planning worked like a superheated crucible to agitate differences only intimated earlier. The Europeans were skeptical of a recovery strategy that meant transcending sovereignties and subordinating national interests to the needs of Europe as a whole. Their recovery planning often aimed to re-create the Continent's segmented prewar economic structure, a development that eventually forced American policymakers to modify their emphasis on European responsibility and play a greater role than expected in drafting the European program. In the American camp, on the other hand, there were disagreements over the political constraints on policy, over the best way to optimize output and integrate economies, and over the degree of free-market initiative and supranational control that should be involved. Out of these disagreements finally emerged a composite strategy that relied on both market forces and administrative mechanisms. This strategy would remain a central component of the New Deal policy synthesis that guided American Marshall Planners once the recovery program went into operation. And because previous accounts have failed to describe its development or to explore fully the European and American differences involved, it is important to discuss both issues with care.

II

Following Molotov's retreat from the Paris conference, Western leaders speculated on the motives behind Soviet policy and the meaning of this policy for the future of Europe. Marshall's proposal had been popular, which meant that Molotov's withdrawal had isolated the Communists. Bevin and Bidault wondered if the Soviets had miscalculated. Or did they consider Europe's economic condition beyond repair? Did they believe that congressional tardiness, economic recession, or resurgent isolationism would prevent the United States from acting swiftly? Were they holding themselves aloof in order to reap the benefits of a failed American initiative? Whatever the answers, Marshall's proposal and Molotov's retreat had divided the Continent into hostile blocs. Policymakers on both sides of the Atlantic now expected the Soviet Union, together with its Communist supporters in the West, to do everything possible to retard recovery and sabotage the Marshall Plan.[1]

This realization lent new urgency to policy planning in Europe and the United States. In Washington, President Truman had already appointed three fact-finding committees to investigate the resources available for an aid program and the impact of this program on the American economy. The most important of these was the President's Committee on Foreign Aid, a nonpartisan group headed by Secretary of Commerce Averett Harriman and composed of university experts and representatives from organized business, labor, and agriculture. All three boards established liaisons with the State Department, where policymakers hoped the new committees, especially the so-called Harriman Committee, would help to dissipate public doubts about the capacity of the United States to sustain a massive recovery program and mobilize congressional and public support behind the Marshall Plan.[2]

In the State Department, meanwhile, planning for European recovery went forward in George Kennan's Policy Planning Staff and in the new Committee on the European Recovery Program. The Recovery Committee, known informally as the "Board of Directors" or the "Tuesday-Thursday Group," had been organized in late June to consider Marshall's recent proposal. Chaired by Willard Thorp, the assistant secretary of state for economic affairs, it met every Tuesday and Thursday evening in the Old State Department Building and was composed of representatives from every departmental office concerned with European recovery. Among its members there was broad agreement on the need to integrate economies and put Western Europe on a self-supporting basis over a three- or four-year period. To achieve these goals while limiting the financial burden on American taxpayers, those involved thought the United States should concentrate on short-term commodity assistance, leave the World Bank responsible for long-term modernization loans, retain a veto over the distribution of its aid, and negotiate bilateral agreements binding each of the participating countries to the principles of self-help and joint programming.[3]

Beyond these points, however, there were important disputes between free-traders and planners over the best way to enhance production and foster integration. Advocates of free trade wanted to replace the patchwork pattern of nonconvertible currencies and bilateral commercial agreements with a currency-clearing scheme and a customs union. These reforms would presumably liberate enterprise from the shackles of a segmented economy and allow normal market mechanisms to forge a rational pattern of European production and trade. For the planners, on the other hand, neither a customs union nor a clearing scheme would be practical until production had revived. Negotiating them now would only lead to enervating controversies over the internal financial reforms and national tariff adjustments that would be needed to bring such mechanisms into existence—controversies that could further destabilize Western European politics and work to the advantage of the Communists. To avoid these dangers, the planners wanted to concentrate on restoring Europe's existing industries, increasing production in bottleneck areas, reducing the most flagrant restrictions on intra-European trade and payments, and building supranational coordinators to engineer a functional integration of the European economies.[4]

These debates finally resulted in a compromise that favored the planners approach—in other words, one that looked to both transnational planning and market incentives to integrate economies and increase production. The United States would support a European customs union and currency-clearing scheme. But these were long-term reforms to be achieved once the present obstacles to production and trade had been removed. In the short term, the United States should insist on a supranational planning authority with the power to allocate resources, set production targets, and foster integration. It should also provide basic grants for essential commodities and capital equipment that would bring immediate gains in production. And as production increased, it should encourage European leaders to perminormal market mechanisms to eliminate uneconomic forms of production and apportion resources on a rational basis.[5]

Thinking in the Policy Planning Staff ran along similar lines. By mid-July, the staff had finished a hefty paper entitled "Certain Aspects of the European Recovery Problem from the United States Standpoint." The paper reviewed the causes of Western Europe's distress and the factors that impeded recovery. It noted how continued deterioration there could strengthen the Communists and imperil American interests, explained why these interests made a comprehensive aid program imperative, and went on to offer recommendations that generally paralleled those emerging from the Recovery Committee.[6] The United States, as Kennan had explained earlier, should follow the "functional approach" and concentrate its aid on "key" sectors that lent themselves to "treatment on an overall European basis."[7]

The Policy Planning Staff and the Recovery Committee also adopted similar positions toward Great Britain and western Germany, stressing in each case the familiar themes of production and integration. They agreed that Britain must occupy a unique position in the recovery program, partly because of its great dependence on extra-European trade, partly because it would be difficult to reconcile the British system of imperial preference with American designs for an integrated Europe, and partly because any shortage of outside assistance might compel the financially beleaguered British to adopt restrictive commercial policies that would retard recovery and wreck American efforts to build a multilateral system of world trade. But they also wanted to incorporate the British into a *European* recovery program, taking the position, as Clayton had done earlier, that special assistance or some form of North Atlantic union should be considered only if Marshall Plan aid failed to solve Britain's balance-of-payments problem.[8]

The emphasis on restoring existing industries and increasing output applied with particular force to western Germany, where economic recovery was still deemed essential to recovery in other areas of Western Europe, to political stability in the occupation zones, and to the restoration of a "balance of power" in Europe that Marshall had proclaimed as one of the strategic goals of American policy. The Policy Planning Staff and the Recovery Committee therefore stressed the need for new measures to revive production and make the Bizone self-supporting. Although this recommendation corresponded with thinking in the War Department, both groups also thought it important to reverse the army's policy of treating the Bizone as an American "enclave." The United States, they continued to insist, should balance recovery there against recovery in the liberated areas. It should adjust western Germany's production and trade to the requirements of a European recovery program and win support from other participating countries for the "supranational" approach to economic planning favored in the State Department.[9]

In line with this thinking, American leaders launched two important initiatives on the German front during the second half of 1947. The State and War departments finally persuaded the British to suspend temporarily their plans to socialize the Ruhr coal mines, placing them instead under a private German management that American officials found more compatible with their commitment to private enterprise and their plans to raise German production as an aid to European recovery.[10] At the same time, General Clay and his counterpart in the British zone completed work on the new level-of-industry plan that Secretary Marshall and Foreign Secretary Bevin had authorized following the failure of the Moscow Foreign Ministers Conference. Although the plan aimed to put the Bizone on a self-supporting basis, the State Department had tried to tailor this goal to its own approach by persuading General Clay and his superiors in Washington to dovetail bizonal requirements with the general European recovery program being drafted in Paris.[11] Both initiatives grew out of bureaucratic negotiations between the War and State departments, whose relations resembled those between sovereign states and whose compromise represented an uneasy reconciliation of the two directions in American diplomacy: the one toward a self-supporting Germany that would pull the rest of Europe along in the wake of its own recovery, the other toward a stabilization that would integrate German and European requirements within the framework of a comprehensive recovery program.

These successes were tempered by developments in Paris, where both European and American leaders were taking positions opposed to the State Department's strategy. Among the Europeans, there was great reluctance to accept the principles of mutual aid and joint programming or to sacrifice national interest to American plans for an integrated market. In the American camp, on the other hand, Under Secretary of State Clayton and other American officials in Europe did not support the supranational planning called for in the State Department. They put their faith instead in unfettered market mechanisms and, like the free-traders on the Recovery Committee, were more inclined to stress the importance of organizing a European customs and clearing union. These developments, as we will see, led to a showdown between the State Department and its agents in Paris and to a larger American role in recovery planning than accorded with Marshall's original emphasis on European responsibility.

III

On July 12, 1947, British and French leaders convened another conference in Paris to survey European resources and needs and draft a comprehensive recovery scheme. The results were to be presented to the American government no later than September 1.[12] Altogether, sixteen nations—Austria, Belgium, Denmark, France, Great Britain, Greece, Iceland, Ireland, Italy, Luxembourg, the Netherlands, Norway, Portugal, Sweden, Switzerland, and Turkey—were represented.[13] The occupation authorities provided the conference with information concerning the Bizone.[14] The Poles and Czechs, bowing to Soviet pressure, refused to attend. The Scandinavians were present only on condition that the conference not bypass the United Nations, interfere with their trade in Eastern Europe, or compromise their neutrality.[15]

The harmonious spirit of the conference's first days soon gave way to acrimonious debate over the nature and purposes of the recovery program. Following an Anglo-French plan, the conferees easily agreed to establish the Committee on European Economic Cooperation (CEEC), composed of all participants, four technical committees to investigate the key economic sectors of food and agriculture, coal and steel, power, and transportation, and an Executive Committee to direct the work of the conference.[16] The British and French dominated the Executive Committee and tried to steer the CEEC toward their version of the recovery program. They urged the conferees to draft a program that concentrated on long-term measures of industrial reconstruction and modernization, arguing that only measures of this kind would put Western Europe on a self-supporting basis within three or four years.[17]

The French were particularly determined to safeguard their security by bringing the Monnet Plan into the continental recovery scheme. This maneuver would give their requirements priority over those of the Bizone and make France, rather than Germany, the economic and political center of an integrated Western European system. As a result, the French delegation in Paris objected strongly when the bizonal authorities provided an estimate of German steel production based on the revised level-of-industry plan. The plan called for increasing Germany's steel production to nearly eleven million tons by 1951, and for production increases ranging from 80 to 95 percent of prewar levels in such industries as metals, heavy machinery, and chemicals.[18] In operation, the French complained, the new bizonal plan would reduce Germany's reparation transfers, curtail its coal exports, and undercut the steel-production targets set in the Monnet Plan. It would revive Germany at their expense, they warned, which in turn would antagonize public opinion in France, strengthen the Communist Party there, and lessen the chances for French cooperation in the European recovery program. To lend weight to these warnings, the French delegation to the CEEC refused to accept the estimates of bizonal steel, coal, and coke production, halting all work on the conference reports dealing with these commodities until British and American leaders agreed to tripartite talks on Germany's level of industry.[19]

The State Department wanted to meet this demand, although Marshall apparently counted on a British initiative to circumvent opposition from General Clay and his superiors in Washington, who were ready to deny the French even if it meant wrecking the negotiations in Paris. Bevin fell in with this strategy. He persuaded the Cabinet to postpone the level-of-industry plan temporarily and agreed to host a tripartite conference on the German problem. This is not to say that British and American leaders would make substantive concessions when the conference opened in London on August 22. The British had decided against granting the French a voice in bizonal policy, lest they use it to further their own ambitions at the expense of German workers and British taxpayers. The War Department had held the State Department to terms that ruled out concessions on Germany's level of industry. As a result, the American negotiators in London deflected French demands for stricter limits on Germany's steel production and guarantees concerning German coal and coke exports. Nor would they approve the proposal for international control of the Ruhr that now supplemented, if it did not fully supplant, the earlier French demand for international ownership. Their only concessions were renewed promises to integrate Germany's resources into a European-wide recovery program and to consider sympathetically a French plan for international supervision of the Ruhr coal and steel industries. Even these concessions squared less with French hopes for hegemony than with Marshall's statements at the Moscow Conference and the State Department's support for a balanced approach to European recovery and security. They dovetailed, in other words, with an American strategy that relied on economic integration and supranational regulators to harmonize Franco-German differences and build a Western European framework large enough to produce abundance and contain the Soviets.[20]

The London talks failed to bring France into a three-power consensus on the German problem. The appearance of consultation and the prospect of future concessions on the Ruhr were enough to end French obstructionism in Paris, where the CEEC began using the new level-of-industry plan to calculate the rate of recovery in the Bizone and the part that Germany's resources would play in a comprehensive scheme. But the French still demanded a recovery program that emphasized industrial reconstruction and modernization. They refused to adapt the Monnet Plan to the revised level of German steel production and the concomitant decline of German coal and coke exports that the new level implied. Nor would they endorse a Benelux plan to revive Germany's production and trade, seeking instead, as they had with Anglo-American policy in the Bizone, to remold this plan to fit the contours of French foreign policy.

From the start of the CEEC meeting, the Benelux delegates, with some support from the Scandinavians and the Italians, had complained that French policy amounted to seeking American assistance for national stabilization schemes. It offered little to those countries that counted on increased trade with Germany, to those that had escaped war damage, or to those that had achieved a substantial degree of recovery. On the contrary, they said, it would enable France and other states with ambitious modernization programs to monopolize American assistance and dominate European markets after recovery had been achieved.[21] As an alternative to the French plan, the Benelux delegates wanted to divert American aid to purposes more in tune with their national interests. Their proposals would revive Germany as a market for Benelux exports, yield less support for the Monnet Plan, and postpone the day when modernized French industry could challenge the lead that Belgium enjoyed in intra-European trade.

The Dutch, in particular, hoped to restore their prewar markets in

Germany, and the Belgians sought to loosen the whole network of bilateral payments agreements and quantitative import restrictions that governed trade between participating countries. Belgium ran a large surplus in intra-European trade. But the credit margins in most bilateral payments agreements were too narrow to sustain a further expansion and debtors, whose margins were exhausted, sought to safeguard their gold and dollar reserves by raising quantitative restrictions on imports from their creditors. These developments threatened the large intra-European surplus that helped to finance Belgium's recovery. The Belgians therefore wanted to use Marshall Plan dollars to widen bilateral credit margins and make credits transferable from one debtor to another. Initiatives of this sort, they said, would help to reduce quantitative import restrictions and multilateralize intra-European payments, which would then speed the process of economic recovery and hasten the day when participating countries could balance their accounts with the Western Hemisphere. At a meeting of financial experts in London, however, the British and French would go no further than a decision to appoint a special CEEC group that was to study ways of making intra-European trade more flexible.[22]

Although the British, as we will see, had their own reasons for opposing these measures, it was the French who raised the most strenuous objections to the Benelux proposals. The French took a dim view of efforts to divert Marshall aid from the Monnet Plan to the revival of German production and trade, as the Benelux had suggested, and their plan for liberalizing trade pointed away from the Belgian scheme to a strategy of integration more appropriate to the ambitions of the French government.

During and after the war, General Charles de Gaulle, Georges Bidault, Jean Monnet, and a wide range of other French leaders, including Hervé Alphand and a number of key officials in the Quai d'Orsay, had come to believe that a European economic union would be needed to support the French economy and tame the Germans in the postwar period. As we have seen, policymakers in the French government and the British Foreign Office had looked to close Anglo-French economic collaboration as the cornerstone of a wider European association. The two governments had established a committee of officials to study the prospects for such cooperation. Bidault had even gone so far as to predict that an Anglo-Western European bloc would emerge as an independent "Third Force" in world affairs, equal in power to both the United States and the Soviet Union. Similar ideas were popular with important policymakers in the British Foreign Office, and with none more so than Ernest Bevin. But Anglo-French differences over how to handle the Germans, together with British concerns about political instability in France and about preserving the Commonwealth connection and close ties to the United States, had forced Bevin to take a more cautious approach toward Anglo-Western European economic integration than one favored in France. Indeed, the Monnet Plan led many in Paris to the conclusion that only rapid progress toward some form of European economic integration would give France access to the raw materials and labor resources required to modernize French industry. Added to this was their determination to devise a strategy of integration that would enable France to control Germany's recovery, a determination that grew as American leaders laid plans to rebuild the bizonal economy and bring western Germany into the European recovery program.[23]

The direction of French strategy became clear in the early days of the CEEC meeting, when the French delegation urged the formation of a European customs union. It would take years to organize such a union, the French admitted. Nonetheless, they wanted the conferees to commit themselves to this goal and begin negotiations looking toward a harmonization of national tariffs. A customs union, they said, would appeal to integrationist sentiment in the United States, assure congressional support for the Marshall Plan, and bring the gains in trade and production needed to raise living standards and put Western Europe on a self-supporting basis.[24] Left unmet were the special advantages that would accrue to the French, whose proposals for a customs union and for international control of the Ruhr pointed to a line of policy that would lead from the CEEC meeting of 1947, through the Finebel and Fritalux negotiations of 1949, to the Schuman Plan of 1950. In the case of a customs union, the success of this strategy depended more on international control mechanisms than on two other factors. Through a customs union, the French could work to reduce Germany's prewar tariffs and yet retain the quantitative restrictions on competitive German imports that would be eliminated under the Benelux proposal. This was one way to contain Germany and safeguard the Monnet Plan, the other being a customs union large enough to balance Germany's power against the combined power of Britain, Italy, and the Benelux countries.

If the proposal for a customs union pointed to a persistent strain on the strategy of French policymakers, then the reaction of the other delegates at Paris suggested the difficulties that would dog and finally defeat the proposal in the years ahead. The response of the British, Italian, and Belgian delegations depended inevitably on the extent to which the French proposal dovetailed with their own aspirations. The Italians wanted to negotiate a tariff union with the French, seeing this and the larger project as a partial solution to their economic problems and as a route to Italy's political reassimilation into the Western community. Although the Belgians preferred their own plan for liberalizing payments and eliminating quantitative import restrictions, their decision ultimately turned on the verdict of their Dutch partners. And the Dutch would join a union only if it included Great Britain and western Germany. Such a union would enable the Netherlands to reconstitute its important prewar trade with both countries and prevent France from dominating the group. For different reasons, then, both the Dutch and the French saw British membership as the sine qua non of any union—the key to a viable balance in the West and to a rational pattern of European production and trade.[25]

In the British government, however, there had been no resolution of the earlier disputes over the merits of an Anglo-Western European customs union. Bevin remained alive to the political advantages of this idea, and in August Sir Edmund Hall-Patch, an under secretary in the Foreign Office, suggested that European economic integration along lines "comparable to the vast industrial integration of the United States" might "go far to solve our own economic difficulties."[26] But policymakers in the economic ministries still thought this course more likely to exacerbate current difficulties than to solve them. Repeating arguments rehearsed the previous January, they saw it leading to transnational economic coordination of a kind that would prevent the Labour government from pursuing an independent course at home. Of particular concern was the government's ability to harbor British labor and industry from the competitive currents of the marketplace. This concern had led British policymakers to reject proposals, coming from the CEEC, for the coordination of national production. The same concern prompted sepulchral predictions of the destructive dislocations that would ensue if national tariffs were lowered and British industries, particularly the steel, chemical, and textile industries, faced ruinous competition from lower-cost producers on the Continent.

Adding to these concerns was a solicitous regard for the Commonwealth, with which the British did twice as much trade as they did with Western Europe. According to officials in the Board of Trade and the Treasury, joining a European union would surely bring a decrease in Commonwealth trade without compensating gains on the Continent, where British exporters faced stiff competition from producers in similar industries. Nor could this situation be avoided by incorporating the whole of the Commonwealth into a European union. Such a course meant scrapping the network of commercial and currency arrangements that tied the Commonwealth into a large multilateral market where British exporters had preferential advantages and where payments were made in sterling rather than in dollars. It meant impeding recovery at home, aggravating the Treasury's already serious dollar drain, and increasing Britain's dependence on American aid. These conclusions, coming from the economic ministries and the Colonial

Office, were reaffirmed in a report issued in August by the special committee of experts that Bevin had persuaded the Cabinet to establish the previous January. The Foreign office would seek to reverse these judgments in the weeks ahead. But given the current opposition, neither Bevin nor the British delegation in Paris could do much to support the French proposal.

This position put the British delegation under heavy pressure from the French, who still viewed European integration as a way to curry favor in Washington and tie Germany's economy to the cause of French hegemony. The British countered by insisting that French policy established the wrong priorities. European recovery planners, they insisted, should concentrate on raising production and controlling inflation before tackling such long-term issues as tariff policy and a customs union. They also tried to steer the CEEC away from the French proposal, first by proposing a customs-union study group that would conduct its work outside the scope of the conference, then by giving qualified support to some variant of the Benelux plan for liberalizing intra-European payments and eliminating quantitative import restrictions. In their view, however, the Benelux plan would have to be guided by the amount of American aid available, by the stability of national price structures, and by what each country could afford to import without dislocating its economy or risking its gold and dollar reserves. The British talked about eliminating import quotas gradually, starting with those on non-competitive commodities, and about achieving convertibility through a series of stages that would not culminate until 1951. They also warned that American dollars could extend bilateral credit margins, and thus increase intra-European trade, only if France and other countries adopted fiscal and monetary policies that curbed inflation and prevented them from absorbing a disproportionate share of Marshall Plan aid. In this field, as in others, moreover, the British were reluctant to give participating countries as a group the right to dictate national policies.[28]

These reservations hardened as the British economy deteriorated in the second half of 1947. The worldwide scarcity of dollars, the fuel and grain shortages that followed the winter crisis, and the rising cost of imports from the United States combined to slow the pace of British recovery and confront the British Treasury with a major dollar crisis. So did the Treasury's decision in July to abide by the terms of the 1946 Anglo-American loan agreement and make sterling convertible into dollars. By early August, Britain's dollar reserves were dwindling at the rate of $176 million a week, a clip that would exhaust the balance of the American loan by October and force the Treasury to draw down its final reserves. In these circumstances, the British delegation in Paris became more leery than ever of the Benelux proposal. They were in no mood to multilateralize intra-European trade and payments at a time when their own government was considering new bilateral commercial and exchange-control arrangements in order to reverse Britain's trade deficit and protect its shrinking reserves.[29]

By mid-August, progress at the CEEC meeting had been disappointing. The Benelux and French delegations had advanced proposals that came close to some of the recommendations emanating from the State Department, and following their lead the conference had appointed special committees to study the prospects for currency convertibility and a customs union. But these studies would not be finished before the conference adjourned. In the meantime, the British were dragging their feet on trade and payments policy, the French were refusing to modify their Monnet Plan, and the conferees as a group were unable to agree on a comprehensive program that incorporated the American principles of maximum self-help, mutual aid, and resource sharing. Unwilling to subordinate national interests to European needs, the conferees were following the approach Molotov had recommended earlier, compiling uncoordinated lists of separate national requirements and doing so without regard to the resources available.

Given these developments, Under Secretary of State Clayton and other Americans in Europe began urging the State Department to adopt a more aggressive policy toward the CEEC. Because their recommendations did not always fit with thinking in Washington, where policymakers were more sensitive to congressional expectations and less inclined to stress the primacy of a European customs or clearing union, the State Department was compelled to spend much of its time negotiating policy differences with its own representatives abroad. This situation made it difficult for the Americans to give consistent guidance to the Europeans and probably contributed to the lack of satisfactory progress in Paris. Nevertheless, out of these policy disputes eventually came a compromise similar to the one hammered out between free-traders and planners in Washington—one, in addition, that finally set the stage for more vigorous efforts to bring the CEEC's work into line with congressional expectations and American hopes.

IV

Clayton had been on hand for the opening of the CEEC conference and in subsequent talks with European leaders had reiterated arguments first put forward in his meetings with Bevin and other British officials in London. He urged actions that would boost production and put Western Europe on a self-supporting basis within three or four years. The United States would help by providing essential commodities and capital equipment to restore existing industries. But the Europeans would have to do their part by seeking long-term modernization loans from the World Bank and by devising sound production programs, balancing budgets, and abolishing exchange and trade controls. They should also develop "in broad lines a type of European federation" that would "eliminate the small watertight compartments" into which the Continent had become divided, and should begin, Clayton insisted, by agreeing to eliminate all tariffs over a ten-year period.[30] Together with the champions of free trade in Washington and Lewis W. Douglas the American ambassador to the United Kingdom, Clayton made the same points in a new round of talks with the British. In all of these discussions, the parties involved placed particular stress on the need to reduce tariffs and make currencies convertible, giving the impression that these were immediate items on the American agenda and inspiring the French campaign against Britain's opposition to a European customs union.[31]

The differences between these views and those in the State Department became apparent in early August, when Clayton and Douglas met in Paris with Jefferson Caffery, the American ambassador in France, Robert Murphy, the American political adviser in Germany, and Paul H. Nitze, the deputy director of the State Department's Division of Commercial Policy and a member of its Committee on the European Recovery Program.[32] Nitze summarized the thinking in the Recovery Committee and reviewed the Policy Planning Staff's recent paper, whereupon Clayton and the ambassadors approved the paper but went on to express views not fully parallel with the policy compromise that had emerged in Washington. Clayton and the others placed greater emphasis on the possibility that supranational planning could be used to revive prewar cartels or extend statist controls, and on the need for trade and monetary reforms that would set the stage for a European customs and clearing union. The Europeans, they insisted, should abandon costly social programs, "stabilize their money," fix "proper exchange rates," and agree in principle to reduce and eventually eliminate "all tariffs and trade barriers."[33]

These goals were the remedies for Europe's malaise, and they were the ones that Clayton and the ambassadors thought the United States must now prescribe. European leaders were slighting the American principles unwilling, so it seemed, to transcend sovereignties and make the "hard-core" adjustments needed to revive production, increase trade, and integrate economies. They were adopting instead the "Molotov approach" and treating American aid as a "pork-barrel." As a result, Clayton and the ambassadors agreed, the State Department must discard its commitment to European initiative, list the reforms it expected, and make these reforms the "*quid pro quo*" of American aid.[34] For Clayton, in particular, the billions of dollars that the United States was investing in European stabilization gave it the right, even the "duty," to demand the internal adjustments and cooperative action that would lift European trade and production out of the "morass of bilateralism and restrictionism."[35]

Under Secretary of State Robert A. Lovett, who now directed the chorus of recovery planners in Washington, carefully delineated the lines of harmony and discord between his views and those of the Americans in Paris. One of several Wall Street bankers on loan to the government from Brown Bros., Harriman, Lovett knew the terms of a good investment when he saw them. He did not doubt that European leaders were paying too little attention to the integrating principles of self-help, mutual aid, and joint programming. Nor did he quarrel with Clayton's emphasis on a three- or four-year recovery program that would revive production, restrain inflation, and limit the financial demands on the United States. The American people, he believed, could not be expected to support costly modernization schemes or a grab bag of national "shopping lists" that did little to balance European and American accounts by the end of the Marshall Plan period.[36]

At the same time, however, Lovett outlined differences with Clayton that were similar to those between free-traders and planners on the Recovery Committee. Like the planners, Lovett did not believe that the CEEC should get bogged down in such complicated issues as a customs union and clearing scheme. These issues should be considered eventually, but the potential for dislocating economies and exacerbating political division made it better to begin by increasing production in bottleneck areas, reforming finances, curbing inflation, and reducing bilateral barriers to inter-European trade. This was a course calculated to halt the economic decline that fostered communism. It was also one on which the Europeans might agree and to which long-term reforms could be appended.[37]

Lovett and other policymakers in Washington were also more sensitive than Clayton to the domestic political constraints on American initiative. They wanted to preserve the appearance of European responsibility and avoid any impression of dictating to the CEEC, lest this be interpreted as a commitment in advance of congressional action. Behind the scenes, they had discussed methods of providing more American direction and were assembling, "as unobtrusively as possible," a small group of economic experts in Paris. But actual intervention could not come within a formal request from the conference and any discussion of the specific conditions for American aid, or of the reasons that might prompt its termination, must wait until Congress had authorized

Marshall funds and the State Department had begun to negotiate bilateral aid agreements with the participating countries. Congress "must not again be presented on a crisis basis with a virtual commitment to any precise course of action," as had happened in the Greco—Turkish crisis. To avoid this, Clayton must stay clear of specific conditions, simply reassert American principles, and count on Europe's need for outside assistance to produce a unified and realistic recovery program.[38]

The results were disappointing. Clayton, Caffery, and Douglas continued to worry that a permanent organization would cartelize the European economy and to insist that American aid be conditioned on measures to reduce tariffs and organize a clearing union. The Europeans, on the other hand, still refused to transcend national sovereignties, permit the CEEC to examine country requirements critically, or adjust national production and investment programs to the needs of Europe as a whole. Neither would they take those measures of self-help that meant reducing living standards below prewar levels and thus risking political difficulties at home. Their work instead amounted to "an assembly job of country estimates," which, as Caffery pointed out, would merely re-create Europe's prewar "economic pattern" with all the "low labor productivity and maldistribution of effort which derive from segregating 270,000,000 people into 17 uneconomic principalities." By mid-August, moreover, the conferees were thinking in terms of a whopping $29 billion in American aid, and, according to their own estimates, even this amount would not make Europe self-supporting at the end of the Marshall Plan period.[39]

More than anything else, it was this estimate of American aid that prompted a shift in the State Department's strategy. The figure, which equaled the aggregate dollar deficit of participating countries over a four year period, stunned the Europeans as much as the Americans. Sir Olive Franks, who led the British delegation to the CEEC, rushed back to London for consultation with Bevin. He subsequently convened a special meeting of the Executive Committee in Paris, discussed the estimate with his colleagues, and finally decided to let the Americans suggest where adjustment might be made. This decision launched the process of "friendly aid." In Paris, Clayton told Franks that the figure was far too high to be acceptable to Congress. He urged the CEEC countries to reduce their food import even if doing so meant lowering living standards, and to show greater progress toward European viability by the end of the recovery period. Love and other policymakers in Washington made similar points, stressing, in particular, the need for more effective screening and coordination of national requirements by the CEEC. Because meeting this need would involve the kind of supranational planning that Clayton and the Europeans had been opposing, Lovett also sent Clayton and Caffery a long telegram reviewing American policy and dispatched his special assistant, Charles Bonesteel, along with George Kennan, to discuss outstanding issues with the Americans in Paris. The goal was to forge a consensus that would clear the way for forceful presentation of the American "requirements" to the CEEC.[40]

In his long telegram of August 26, Lovett distilled the main points of agreement between all American officials and then reasserted the key priorities in the planners' approach to European stabilization. The Europeans, he said, should enumerate "concrete proposals for mutual aid," set national production targets, and establish vigorous procedures for screening individual country requirements and for "correlating" these on an "area-wide basis." They should also establish a supranational organization to oversee this work and to coordinate, direct, and modify their plans during the recovery period. Clayton would have to swallow his objections on this score and proceed slowly in pressing for monetary reform, a clearing scheme, and a customs union. The last two would "contribute little to [the] immediate restoration of production," which was the best way to protect participating governments against the danger of Communist subversion. As for monetary reform, Lovett argued that Europe's chaotic monetary structure was really a "symptom rather than a cause" of the Continent's distress, that reforms in this area must wait until production had revived, and that any reforms not grounded "in increased production" could actually retard recovery, widen "the cleavages among producer and consumer groups," and play into the hands of the Communists. The importance of securing these reforms would increase "as production expands and economies are stabilized," but for now, Lovett insisted, production was the first priority.[41]

Kennan and Bonesteel repeated the same arguments during their meeting in Paris with Clayton, Caffery, and Douglas, the result this time being a "common position" similar to the compromise worked out earlier between free-traders and planners on the Recovery Committee. The goals were a speedy revival of production and, as production revived, a stabilization of finances, a reduction of monetary barriers, and a "further liberalization of trade." Through the setting and meeting of production targets, the Europeans would reduce their requirements for outside assistance, place their economies on a self-supporting basis, and thus clear the way for long-run modernization projects and for such schemes as a customs or clearing union. Managing this process would require "concerted action" through a continuing European organization with powers to review national programs, adjust these programs to European needs, and direct "production, trade, and manpower in the most efficient and economic manner."[42]

On August 30, the Americans communicated these "essentials" to the Executive Committee of the CEEC. So far, they said, the conference results were "disappointing." The expectations of $29 billion in American aid and of a continued deficit at the end of the aid period reflected both an absence of concerted self-help and mutual aid by the conferees and unrealistic ideas about resource availabilities in the United States and consumer needs in the participating countries. The United States did not wish to dictate to the Europeans, the Americans insisted, but the conferees should realize that anything short of the American "essentials" would "prejudice the success of the entire Marshall program" in the United States.[43] Similar warnings came from the State Department's economic experts, known as the "Friendly Aid Boys," who arrived in Paris during the last week of August. They went over the CEEC's technical reports, found the results "unacceptable," and offered the Europeans a good deal of "very blunt criticism."[44]

Nevertheless, the conferees remained as reluctant as ever to take measures that meant transcending national sovereignties or reducing living standards. The Scandinavians were opposed to a continuing organization that would circumvent the United Nations or create a Western European economic bloc. The British were opposed to action that might subject their internal policies and foreign trade to supranational control. The French were still refusing to adjust the Monnet Plan in the interest of Europe as a whole and the conferees as a group were still compiling "individual country statements" that added up to more than the Americans thought they could afford.[45]

In the eyes of American leaders, further reliance on European initiative could not produce the ends desired. The Europeans, as Lovett told the Cabinet, were not being realistic.[46] As the Friendly Aid Boys saw it, the conferees were engaged in actions that would lead to "US rejection" of their recovery program or to a prolonged congressional debate that would "embitter European peoples" and cause untoward "repercussions" on the Continent.[47] As Kennan viewed it, the conferees did not have the political strength or "clarity of vision" to draft a new "design" for Europe. The Scandinavians were "pathologically nervous about the Russians," the British were "seriously sick," and all the other delegations in Paris were infected by the same lack of resolve and realism that afflicted the British. The State Department, Kennan concluded, would have to "decide unilaterally" what was best for the Europeans.[48]

This was the argument that Clayton had made earlier, and it was one that Lovett could now accept. Early in September, Lovett helped to establish the Advisory Steering Committee, an interdepartmental group that was to coordinate recovery policy in the executive branch. At its first meeting on September 9, he took the position that the United

States could not support the recovery program emerging from the CEEC and must therefore fill the vacuum created by the failure of European leadership. To do so, the Steering Committee established a number of subcommittees to bring the CEEC work into line with the American "essentials" and the State Department decided simply to tell the Europeans that greater sacrifices and "some mutual delegation of the exercise of sovereignty" would be necessary to produce a "workable program."[49] The result was a new phase in recovery planning.

V

The assumption seemed to be that the Paris conferees were handicapped by restrictive instructions from their foreign offices. On September 7, therefore, the State Department appealed directly to the home governments, urging them to accept the American "essentials" and instruct their delegates accordingly. They were also urged to postpone their planned reception of the CEEC's report, now scheduled for September 14; to continue the conference long enough to bring the general report, if not its technical supplements, into line with American thinking; and then to transmit the results as a "preliminary" document subject to emendations and corrections by economic experts in Washington and Paris. The conferees, according to the State Department, had not done enough to incorporate national requirements into an integrated recovery plan for Western Europe as a whole. The new procedure would give them an opportunity to correct this shortcoming and avoid the harsh criticism that might otherwise accompany publication of the report in the United States. At the very least, it would enable the State Department to describe the report as "preliminary" in form and "correct in principle," blame its deficiencies on the lack of time, and claim that revisions would render the final document acceptable.[50]

In a related initiative, policymakers in the State Department decided to submit the bizonal level-of-industry plan to critical examination by the CEEC. They had been disappointed when the occupation authorities, in responding to questionnaires from the conference, had failed to adjust Germany's recovery plans to the needs of Europe as a whole or to permit the conferees to alter bizonal requirements. This failure had made it difficult for the CEEC to consider the sort of supranational approaches that the State Department saw as essential steps to a cohesive Western European order capable of maintaining a stable political equilibrium on the Continent. The new initiative was designed to correct this problem. By permitting the CEEC to scrutinize bizonal requirements and make recommendations concerning the use of facilities, the allocation of scarce materials, and the reactivation of industrial plant, the State Department hoped to encourage other participating countries to submit their own requirements to careful screening. They too should fit their national production plans into a regional recovery program and thus move toward a more efficient system integrated along functional lines.[51]

Opposition to these American proposals came primarily from the British. Although the State Department had hoped for British support in placing the bizonal level-of-industry plan before the CEEC, Bevin told Ambassador Douglas that western Germany had been brought into the recovery program on the same footing as other countries; its requirements had been adequately discussed at Paris and reintroducing them now would amount to criticism of the conference. Bevin had no interest in permitting the CEEC to determine the rate at which German industry would be reactivated. From the American point of view, he was just as reluctant to establish a precedent that might require the British to subordinate their national interest to American demands for European integration. Britain, as Secretary of State Marshall complained, wanted to "benefit fully from a European program . . . while at the same time maintaining the position of not being wholly a European country," a position the United States would justify if it sanctioned special treatment for western Germany.[52]

Despite American pressure, the British refused to budge on the German question and the State Department had to concentrate instead on its larger proposal to extend the Paris conference and revise its general report.[53] Bevin opposed this as well. He told Douglas on September 9 that time did not permit further revisions, that prolonging the conference would be tantamount to admitting its failure, and that neither Britain nor the other participating countries could make the additional sacrifices required to satisfy American demands. Further pressure from the United States, he also insisted would "impair national sovereignty," lending credence to Molotov's earlier charges and provoking opposition from nationalists and Communists across Europe.[54] British representatives repeated the same arguments to each of the participating governments as both they and the Americans worked frantically to rally the Europeans behind their respective positions. The Dutch and the Norwegians seemed sympathetic to the American proposals, but nonetheless deferred to British leadership. The Italians took the same position, while the French found it "quite intolerable that the Americans should suddenly address themselves in this manner direct to the sixteen participating powers and in this way risk wrecking the whole conference in its final critical stages." Only when the United States "made concrete offers of substantial assistance could they legitimately expect to discuss terms and conditions." Until then, Bidault told the British ambassador in Paris, France would not yield to American "pressure."[55]

Bolstered by the British and French delegates, the Executive Committee confronted Clayton and Douglas at a meeting on September 11. The Americans had by this time scaled down their original "essentials" to several, somewhat milder points. They asked the conference to continue its work and label its report a preliminary document in which participating countries would pledge to form a continuing organization, seek modernization loans from the World Bank, meet established production targets, and take concurrent steps to liberalize trade and stabilize finances. Following the British lead, the Executive Committee repeated the arguments Bevin had made to Douglas earlier, whereupon the meeting adjourned in what appeared to be a hopeless deadlock.

Later that day, however, Bidault suddenly reversed course. Apparently worried that Congress might turn its back on the Marshall Plan, he now urged the conference to continue for another month and to bring all of Clayton's original essentials into its final report. The British, Dutch, and Norwegians continued to oppose this course. But in a second meeting of the Executive Committee on September 11, they were coaxed into a compromise that the Americans then accepted. Under this compromise, the committee promised to continue the conference for another week, modify its report to reflect the points Clayton and Douglas had enumerated earlier in the day, and label the results a provisional document. The committee also agreed to recess rather than adjourn, to review the provisional report with officials in Washington, and then, if necessary, to reconvene the full conference and reconsider its report in light of the Washington conversations.[56]

The British were disappointed. Although Bevin agreed to the new procedure, he did so only after delivering an angry denunciation of American meddling and a fresh warning against further "external pressure." The "clumsy American intervention" had created "an unfortunate impression of high-handedness," which he urged Marshall to correct through renewed expressions of confidence in European responsibility.[57] But no such expressions would be forthcoming, if only because they might imply a commitment to a conference report that still fell short of American expectations and might hamper American leaders at a time when they had decided to scuttle the emphasis on European initiative in favor of a more aggressive role in recovery planning.[58]

During the last days of the CEEC meeting, American officials worked as full participants in the deliberations. The Friendly Aid Boys labored with their European counterparts to correct details in the technical reports; Clayton, Caffery, and Douglas discussed major issues with the heads of the European delegations; and with the threat of congressional disapproval hanging like a shadow over the conference, the Europeans now bowed to the American requirements. The conferees agreed to revise the report preamble, saluting in it the American principles of self-help, mutual aid and joint programming, and using it to proclaim "a new era of European economic cooperation" in which programs of "concerted action" would ensure full use of available resources and productive facilities. They also agreed to reduce their estimates of trade deficits during the aid period and to finance long-term modernization projects through loans from the World Bank and private commercial channels. As production increased, moreover "all possible steps" would be taken to restrain inflation, fix realistic exchange rates, and "reduce the tariffs and other barriers to the expansion of trade. Also included in the report was a French declaration proclaiming the benefit of a European customs union and inviting the participating countries to join in such a union once their payments difficulties had been resolved and currencies were stabilized.[59]

The major stumbling block turned out to be Lovett's demand for a supranational organization. The Swiss still worried that a strong, continuing organization would take on the characteristics of a Western European economic alliance and compromise their neutrality. Nor did they or the British want a supranational authority to dictate trade and production policies. Such an authority, they said, would impair national "sovereignty," drive several countries from the recovery plan, and widen the "schism in Europe." To get around these objections, the British delegation suggested a joint declaration calling merely for mutual and voluntary consultation after the recovery program came into operation. Neither this proposal nor the objections behind it carried much weight in Washington. But Clayton, Caffery, and Douglas seized on European concerns in order to make another pitch for the free-traders' approach to economic revival and integration. The Europeans, they warned Lovett, would never consent to a continuing organization that had the power to allocate materials and design a new European industrial pattern without regard for national boundaries. Although the policy compromise emerging in Washington assumed that a permanent organization would work in tandem with free-market mechanisms to forge a regional economy organized along productive lines, Clayton and his colleagues in Europe thought the results more likely to be a "dangerous degree" of "planned" economic activity and new cartelistic arrangements that "frustrate[d] the ultimate restoration of natural economic forces." In view of these dangers, they said, it would be "much wiser" to reduce "trade barriers," fix "appropriate exchange rates," and thus permit natural market forces, rather than supranational regulators, to "bring about a community of economic interests and responsibility."[60]

Given this opposition, the State Department backed away from its initial position and settled for a weakly phrased provision in the CEEC's report. Under this provision, the participating countries agreed to form a joint organization once the recovery program had been launched. But the new organization would have none of the supranational powers for which Lovett and the planners had called. Instead, it would merely review the progress of the recovery program, make studies, issue reports, and generally "encourage" member states to take those measures required to meet the broad objectives of the program.[61]

On September 22, the CEEC finished its work and sent its provisional findings to the State Department. In addition to the various pledges enumerated in the general report and its preamble, special committees had been appointed by the participating countries to study the feasibility of currency convertibility and a customs union. The conferees had struck a compromise on the German question, one under which Germany's revival was declared essential to European recovery but was to be carefully controlled so as to protect the economic and security interests of its neighbors. They had all agreed to the cooperative development of hydroelectric resources, the pooling of freight cars, and the standardization of certain kinds of equipment, and had established such goals as rebuilding Europe's merchant fleet, restoring prewar levels of agricultural production, boosting the production of fertilizers and agricultural machinery, and achieving increases ranging from 33 to 250 percent of prewar levels, in the output of coal, electricity, refined oil, and steel.

European leaders offset these pledges and projections with numerous qualifications, all of which reflected their inability to reconcile national aspirations with the State Department's goals of economic integration and supranationalism. The general pledges to the American principles and all such objectives as trade liberalization and financial stabilization remained empty declarations grafted on the report in response to pressure from Washington. They were not backed by concrete measures to achieve them or by a supranational authority that could guarantee compliance. Neither could the compromise on the German question conceal the unresolved tension between the divergent French and American policies toward Germany's role in the recovery program. According to the report, moreover, restoring existing productive facilities would have to go hand in hand with modernizing plant and equipment; fixing realistic exchange rates would require special stabilization loans from the United States; achieving internal financial stability must be balanced against the need to maintain high levels of employment; and realizing production targets would depend on American assistance sufficient to cover Europe's four-year trade deficit with the dollar area. The report estimated the deficit, exclusive of World Bank loans, as $19.3 billion. This sum was still greater than the Americans considered realistic, yet smaller than what participating governments thought necessary to become self-supporting by the end of the Marshall Plan period.[62]

Despite these shortcomings, the last-minute revisions in the CEEC report were important to policymakers in the Truman administration. At least they acknowledged the American principles and the American vision of an integrated and productive European economy. They also established procedures for continuing consultation between American and European leaders in Washington, which could be used to correct the flaws in the report and further advance American goals. In these ways, the report set the stage for congressional action on an interim aid program that had become increasingly important to American officials in the summer of 1947. Indeed, the importance of this program helps to explain the State Department's intervention in Paris and its subsequent approach to the European-American consultations in Washington. Through both initiatives, the State Department sought to shape a European policy that guaranteed favorable legislative action on a program of interim aid that was widely perceived as the first installment on the Marshall Plan.

VI

As the summer of 1947 drew to a close, policymakers in Washington became increasingly preoccupied with the deteriorating economic and political conditions in Europe. A British negotiating team arrived in Washington in mid-August armed with dire warnings of an imminent collapse of world trade and an immediate retrenchment of Britain's global commitments unless prompt measures were taken to halt the drain on its dollar reserves. The measures they had in mind amounted to suspending the convertibility of pound sterling, an action that would violate the convertibility pledge in the 1946 Anglo-American loan agreement.[63] American leaders, including Lovett and Secretary of the Treasury John Snyder, were sympathetic to Britain's predicament. Although they did not have much faith in the "low grade of [its] leadership" and were reluctant to encourage any "move further to the left" by the Labour government, they nonetheless thought it essential to keep "England in the picture," as Bernard Baruch put it, "in order to hold the rest of the world." Meeting this need meant arresting the decline of Britain's dollar reserves, because failure to do so would weaken the British position around the world, provide new opportunities for Soviet expansion, and make American "objectives in Western Europe and elsewhere" unattainable.[64] The problem was that suspending convertibility would embarrass the Truman administration in Congress, where elements in both political parties were critical of the Anglo-American loan agreement and hesitant to support further aid to Europe. To circumvent this problem, the tired negotiators finally concluded two days of round-the-clock discussions with an accord that effectively suspended both the obligations and the benefits of the 1946 agreement. Under its terms, the British would postpone further drawings on the American loan and then protect their reserves by suspending convertibility and negotiating exchange-control agreements with their creditors.[65]

Although this accord enabled the British to manage their balance-of-payments difficulties, the situations in France and Italy were more intractable and could not be handled without resorting to Congress. The governments in both countries faced chronic inflation, high unemployment, a shortage of grain, and serious trade deficits. Their shrinking reserves would soon be exhausted and both would be forced to curtail imports and further restrict production. Such a course would almost certainly lead to political challenges from the Left and the Right. It might even lead to the collapse of existing governments and the emergence of Communist regimes, a development, in the opinion of policymakers in Washington, that would wreck the Marshall Plan and the related efforts to contain Soviet expansion. Remedial action was essential. But during the summer and early fall, such short-term expedients as post-UNRRA relief, Export-Import Bank loans, increased grain shipments, and the return of blocked assets and gold looted by the Germans had failed to stabilize the situation in either country.[66]

The Marshall plan offered a solution, but because it could not begin much before the spring of 1948, the only immediate recourse seemed to be a special program of interim aid during the "Marshall Gap." Such a program had been under consideration in the State Department for some time. In mid-September, Secretary Marshall announced that interim aid would be necessary and would be "correlated into the general [recovery] program." Truman made the same points in a discussion with selected congressional leaders on September 29. Shortly thereafter, he asked a special session of Congress to consider new measures of stop-gap relief for Europe.[67] Congress eventually approved these measures, but the point to be emphasized here is the administration's decision to sell interim aid as the first step in a comprehensive recovery program that embraced American principles. This was deemed the best way to overcome congressional opposition to further measures of piecemeal assistance. To effect this strategy, however, the administration had to present Congress with a European plan that came close to American guidelines. This need helps to explain the State Department's pressure for last-minute revisions in the CEEC report and the decision, taken by the Advisory Steering Committee, to parallel and review the work of the

Paris conference. The same consideration also explains the negotiating posture American leaders adopted in their talks with the CEEC delegation that arrived in Washington during the second week of October.[68]

The Washington conversations again brought to the fore the familiar conflict between the integrationist ideals that inspired American policy and the concerns with national sovereignty that motivated so much of European diplomacy. During talks with members of the presidential fact-finding committees and the Advisory Steering Committee, the CEEC delegates sought assurances that the funds of local currency accumulated through their sale of American-provided commodities—the so-called counterpart funds—would not be controlled by the United States and used to impair the sovereign right of participating governments to manage their economies. They also urged the Americans to accept a continuing European organization with advisory rather than executive authority, guarantee aid sufficient to cover their deficits with North America, and provide this aid in the form of dollars, rather than commodities, without restrictions as to its use by the participating countries.

On none of these issues were the Americans very reassuring. They said that aid would consist mainly of commodities. Purchases outside the United States would be limited and restrictions on the local-currency counterpart of American aid would be determined mutually by the United States and each of the participating countries. Although the details of European programming and the functions of a continuing organization would have to wait until Congress decided the form and amount of aid, the Americans also made it clear that a strong organization, with some allocation authority, would be necessary during the recovery period. In addition, they whittled away at the CEEC's aid estimates.[69]

At the same time, American policymakers urged the Europeans to adopt the policy compromise worked out between planners and free-traders on the Recovery Committee and use it to forge the sort of integrated market that had been a factor accounting for the greater productivity and higher living standards in the United States. In addition to an allocation authority, they wanted realistic production targets, a bottleneck approach, and the fitting of national recovery plans into a European pattern of production and exchange—even if it meant, as Lovett told the CEEC delegation, "some sacrifice of national customs and tradition." They also wanted commitments to fiscal reform, currency convertibility, the elimination of quantitative import restrictions, and the eventual reduction of intra-European tariff rates. "American thought," as the CEEC delegates explained to the participating governments, was "much pre-occupied with the extent to which the reduction

or elimination of quantitative restrictions and tariffs might bring benefits to Europe through the creation of a larger market and concentration
of productive effort."[70]

The Washington talks ended without European-American agreement
on such basic issues as the use of counterpart funds, the functions of a
continuing organization, the details of trade and payments policy, and
the scope of financial and monetary reform. These and other outstanding issues would have to be considered after Congress had acted and the
Marshall Plan had been launched. So far as the Americans were concerned, however, the talks had been aimed less at producing a European-American accord on key points than on tailoring the CEEC's
report to congressional expectations. With this purpose in mind, the
State Department had simply lectured the Europeans on American
requirements and had then made the Paris report, as one CEEC official
recalled, "as attractive as possible for presentation to Congress."[71]

VII

Like the transatlantic debates during the Paris conference, the Washington talks had served to clarify the divergent American and European
views over the nature and purposes of what eventually became the
European Recovery Program. American thinking continued to emphasize the related ideas of economic integration and greater productivity.
Lovett and the advocates of economic planning assigned priority to
making the most efficient use of Europe's existing resources, both to
revive production and to block Communist encroachments. They urged
policies that would break bottlenecks, liberalize trade, and integrate
national stabilization schemes along functional lines. Clayton and the
advocates of free trade argued for a currency-clearing scheme and a
customs union, stressing in their argument how such measures would
integrate economies and create a market large enough to stimulate mass
production. The former strategy seemed to require supranational controls and economic planning to achieve its goals; the latter would rely on
normal market mechanisms. But both converged on the twin concepts
of production and integration, and out of this convergence had come a
central component of the policy synthesis that would characterize
American diplomacy in the years ahead. Although a customs union and
clearing scheme would have to wait until production had revived, gains
in production were to be accompanied by greater European efforts to
stabilize finances and multilateralize intra-European trade. In the
emerging American policy synthesis, such free-trade strategies were to
work hand in hand with supranational coordinators to create an integrated Western European system.

The Europeans resisted both directions in American thinking. They would not make specific commitments to a customs union or clearing scheme, arguing, as Lovett had, that such reforms would have to come after American aid had revived national production. But neither would they make the sacrifices Lovett considered essential to optimize output. They refused to engage in genuine joint programming, adapt national production plans to European needs, or subordinate national sovereignties to the authority of a supranational organization. Europeans favored the "Molotov approach" and sought a recovery program that would limit the scope of cooperative action, meet their separate requirements, and preserve the greatest degree of national self-sufficiency and autonomy. Americans, on the other hand, wanted to refashion Western Europe in the image of the United States. They urged European leaders to replace old patterns of national competition and autarky with a new economic system in which transnational coordinators and natural market forces would combine to integrate markets, control contested resources, enhance production, and thus lay the foundation for a new era of stable abundance. These were the points of departure in European and American paths to peace and plenty on the Continent, and they would remain so throughout the subsequent history of the Marshall Plan.

Endnotes

1. See, for example, Ambassador Jefferson Caffery, Paris, tel. to Marshall, July 3, 1947 and Ambassador Lewis Douglas, London, tel. to Marshall, July 4, 1947, *FRUS*, 1947, 3:308–9, 310–12; Douglas tels. #3719 and #3743 to Marshall, July 8, 1947, RG 59, file: 840.50Recovery/7-847; and Douglas tel. to Marshall, undated (received July 19, 1947), RG 59, file: 840.50Recovery/7-1947. For similar thinking in the United States, see Robert G. Hooker, Jr., memorandum for Mr. Thompson, July 14, 1947, RG 59, file: 840.50Recovery/7-1447; and memorandum by the Policy Planning Staff, July 21?, 1947, *FRUS*, 1947, 3:335–7.

2. For the origins and work of these three committees, see PPS/3, "Studies Relating to the Impact of Aid to Foreign Countries on U.S. Domestic Economy and Natural Resources," June 19, 1947, RG 59, PPS Records, box 3, *Reports and Recommendations, 1947*, Vol. I; Marshall and Harriman Memorandum for the President, June 19, 1947, Truman Papers, President's Confidential File (hereafter cited as CF with folder designation), folder: State Department, 1946–47; Statement Issued to the Press by the White House, June 22, 1947, *FRUS, 1947*, 3:264–6; and Thorp memorandum to Kennan, June 30, 1947, RG 59, PPS Records, box 9, folder: Economic Policy.

3. For the origins and membership of the Recovery Committee, see Ben T. Moore letter to Clair Wilcox, July 28, 1947, Records of the Committee on the European Recovery Program, RG 353, Lot 122, box 26, folder: 5.17.10, ERP

Subject File, Board of Directors; and Committee on the European Recovery Program, Minutes of Meeting, June 25, 1947, RG 353, Lot 122, box 26, folder: REP Minutes. For the agreement on substantive issues among members of the Recovery Committee, see the source cited in notes 4 and 5.

4. This analysis is based on the discussions in the Recovery Committee's first six meetings and on several of the many documents that the committee considered. See Committee on the European Recovery Program, Minutes of Meetings, June 25 and July 1, 3, 8, 10, and 15, 1947, RG 353, Lot 122, box 26, folder: REP Minutes; and Charles I. Kindleberger, "Scope of Secretary Marshall's Suggestion to Europe," July 2, 1947 (REP D-4/8), Thorp undated memorandum to Kennan (REP D-4/12), unsigned, undated "Impediments to Intra-European Trade" (REP D-3/2), and unsigned, undated "Note on a European Customs Union" (REP D-3/5), all in RG 353, Lot 122, box 27; folder: REP Documents.

5. In addition to the Minutes of Meetings cited in note 4, see Committee on the European Recovery Program, Minutes of Meetings, July 24 and 31, 1947, RG 353, Lot 122, box 26, folder: REP Minutes; and undated memorandum by Kindleberger, "Problems of Procedure in U.S. Aid to Europe" (REP D-15, later renumbered as REP D-16/11 and undated Kindleberger memorandum, "Problems of Procedure in U.S. Aid to Europe" (REP D-15/1, later renumbered as REP D-16/11a), RG 353, Lot 122, box 28, folder: REP Documents.

6. PPS/4, "Certain Aspects of the European Recovery Problem from the United States Standpoint," July 23, 1947, RG 59, PPS Records, box 3, *Reports and Recommendations*, 1947, Vol. I. See also Kennan memorandum for Under Secretary of State Robert A. Lovett, June 30, 1947, RG 59, PPS Records, box 33, folder: Chronological, 1947.

7. Kennan memorandum to Thorp, June 24, 1947, *FRUS, 1947*, 3:267–8.

8. Kennan memorandum for Lovett, June 30, 1947, RG 59, PPS Records, box 33, folder: Chronological, 1947; PPS/4, July 23, 1947, RG 59, PPS Records, box 3, *Reports and Recommendations, 1947*, Vol. I; Committee on the European Recovery Program, Minutes of Meetings, July 10, 17, and 24, 1947, RG 353, Lot 122, Box 26, folder: REP Minutes; and undated memorandum, "Special Consideration for Britain under the Marshall Plan" (REP D-3/3), RG 353, Lot 122, box 27, folder: REP Documents.

9. Committee on the European Recovery Program, Minutes of Meeting, June 25, 1947, RG 353, Lot 122, box 26, folder: REP Minutes; and Millis, *Forrestal Diaries*, 341. See also Kennan memorandum for Lovett, June 30, 1947, RG 59, PPS Records, box 33, folder: Chronological, 1947; PPS/4, July 23, 1947, RG 59, PPS Records, box 3, *Reports and Recommendations, 1947*, Vol. I; Committee on the European Recovery Program, Minutes of Meetings, July 17, 22, 24, and 29, 1947, RG 353, Lot 122, box 26, folder: REP Minutes; Kindleberger, "Problems of Procedure in U.S. Aid to Europe"; and Melvin L. Manfull, Secretary to the Committee, to the Committee on the European Recovery Program, July 2, 1947, enclosing "Questions concerning the Relation of the US-UK Zones in Germany to the General Problem of European Recovery" (REP D-2/1), and the enclosures (REP D-2/2) in Manfull to the Committee, July 9, 1947, RG 353, Lot 122, box 27, folder: REP Documents.

10. For this story, see the documents in *FRUS, 1947*, 2:924–5, 927–33, 940–

2, 946–66; Gimbel, *Origins of the Marshall Plan*, 207–15; and Department of State, *Bulletin* 17 (September 21, 1947): 576–84.

11. Gimbel, *Origins of the Marshall Plan*, 225–6, 249–50.

12. Caffery tel #2667 to Marshall, July 3, 1947, *FRUS, 1947*, 3:308–9; and Caffery tel. #2668 to Marshall, July 3, 1947, RG 59, file: 840.50Recovery/7-347.

13. Caffery tel. to Marshall, July 13, 1947, RG 59, file: 840.50Recovery/7-1347.

14. Caffery tel. to Marshall, July 3, 1947, RG 59, file: 840.50Recovery/7-347; and unsigned Memorandum of Conversation, July 25, 1947, RG 59, file: 840.50 Recovery/7-2547.

15. The Polish and Czech stories can be followed in the documents in *FRUS, 1947*, 3:313, 313–14, 318–19, 319–20, 320–2, 322, 327; and in Llewellan E. Thompson Memorandum of Conversation, July 11, 1947, RG 59, file: 840.50Recovery/7-1147. On the policy of the Scandinavian countries, see Caffery tel. to Marshall, July 10, 1947, *FRUS, 1947*, 3:316–17; American Embassy, Denmark, dispatch #234 to Marshall, July 11, 1947, RG 59, file: 840.50Recovery/7-1147; American Embassy, Norway, dispatch #1220 to Marshall, July 15, 1947, RG 59, file: 840.50 Recovery/7-1547; American Embassy, Norway, tel. to Marshall, July 16, 1947, RG 59, file: 840.50Recovery/7-1647; and Memorandum of Conversation, July 15, 1947, enclosed in American Embassy, Norway, dispatch #1236 to Marshall, July 22, 1947, RG 59, file: 840.50Recovery/7-2247.

16. Caffery tel. to Marshall, July 13, 1947, RG 59, file: 840.50Recovery/7-1347; Caffery tel. to Marshall, July 14, 1947, RG 59, file: 840.50Recovery/7-1447; and the British Charge letter to Marshall, July 15, 1947, and Caffery tel. to Marshall, July 20, 1947, *FRUS, 1947*, 3:331, 333–5.

17. Caffery tel. to Marshall, July 18, 1947, RG 59, file: 840.50Recovery/7-1847; Alexander Kirk, American Ambassador to Belgium, tel. to Marshall, July 19, 1947, RG 59, file: 840.50Recovery/7-1947; Caffery tel. #2884 to Marshall July 20, 1947, RG 59, file: 840.50Recovery/7-2047; and Caffery tel. #2886 to Marshall, July 20, 1947, *FRUS, 1947*, 3:333–5.

18. Ambassador Robert Murphy, American Political Adviser in Germany, tel. to Marshall, July 15, 1947, *FRUS, 1947*, 2:988–90; and Gimbel, *Origins of the Marshall Plan*, 225.

19. For French complaints, see "Conversation between M. Bidault, Mr. Harriman, and Ambassador Caffery," July 15, 1947, in Caffery dispatch #9273 to Marshall, July 21, 1947, RG 59, file: 840.50Recovery/7-2147; and Caffery tel. to Marshall, July 11, 1947, French Foreign Minister Georges Bidault letter to Marshall, July 17, 1947, Bidault communication to the State Department, July 17, 1947, Caffery tels. (2) to Marshall, July 18, 1947, and Caffery tel. to Marshall, July 20, 1947, *FRUS, 1947*, 2:983–6, 991–2, 992–3, 993–6, 997–9. For French policy at the Paris conference, see Caffery tel. to Marshall, July 17, 1947, RG 59, file: 840.50Recovery/7-1747; Caffery tel. to Marshall August 6, 1947, RG 59, file: 840.50Recovery/8-647; Caffery tel. to Marshall, August 8, 1947, RG 59, file: 840.50Recovery/8-847; Caffery tel. to Marshall, August 13, 1947, RG 59, file: 840.50Recovery/8-1347; and Caffery tel. to Marshall, July 20, 1947, *FRUS, 1947*, 3:333–5. See also United Kingdom delegation (here-

after cited as UK del.) tel. to FO, August 6, 1947, FO 371, 62579, UE697; and UK del. tel. to FO, August 13, 1947, FO 371, 62416, UE8106.

20. British Embassy, Washington, tel. to FO, July 22, 1947, Bevin memorandum to the Cabinet, July 22, 1947, and CM (47) 63rd Conclusion, July 23, 1947, PREM 8/495; *FRUS, 1947*, 2:983–1067; and Gimbel, *Origins of the Marshall Plan*, 231–42, 25:3. A State Department memorandum made the connection between the American approaches to the Ruhr and the problem of European economic recovery: "It appears that the basic conception behind the American approach to the Ruhr problem . . . may be realized, at least in Western Europe, through the Marshall Plan which aims at a coordinated and equitable utilization of key industrial resources in the interest of European economic recovery." See the memorandum attached to John D. Hickerson's memorandum to Lovett, August 23, 1947, *FRUS, 1947*, 2:1050–4.

21. Kirk tel. to Marshall, July 18, 1947, RG 59, file: 840.50Recovery/7-1847; Kirk to Marshall, July 19, 1947, RG 59, file: 840.50Recovery/7-1947; James Clement Dunn, American Ambassador to Italy, tel. to Marshall, July 29, 1947, RG 59, file 840.50Recovery/7-2947; and Caffery tel. to Marshall, July 20, 1947, and Caffery tel. to Marshall, July 27, 1947, *FRUS, 1947*, 3:333–5, 338–9. See also UK del. tel. to FO, July 17, 1947, FO 371, 62413, UE6153.

22. Caffery tel. to Marshall, July 20, 1947, *FRUS, 1947*, 3:333–5; Caffery tel. to Marshall, August 2, 1947, RG 59, file: 840.50Recovery/8-247; Caffery tels. to Marshall, July 31 (#3044) and August 1, 1947, *FRUS, 1947*, 3:341–3; Caffery tel. #3043 to Marshall, July 31, 1947, RG 59, file: 840.50Recovery/7-3147; and Caffery tel. to Marshall, August 9, 1947, RG 59, file: 840.50Recovery/8-947. See also UK del. tel. to FO, July 17, 1947, FO 371, 62413, UE6153; UK del. tels. to FO, July 18 and August 6, 1947, FO 371, 62579, UE697; Roger Makins, Assistant Under Secretary of State, memorandum to Bevin, July 31, 1947, FO 371, 62632, UE6877; UK del. tel. to FO, July 31, 1947, FO 371, 62579, UE6804; UK del. tel. to FO, August 13, 1947, FO 371, 62416, UE8106; and Milward, *Reconstruction of Western Europe*, 66–7, 76–7.

23. Young, *Britain, France, and the Unity of Europe*, especially 26–51.

24. UK del. tel. to FO, August 4, 1947, and B. A. C. Cook minute, August 5, 1947, 371, 62552, UE6911; UK del. tel. to FO, August 10, 1947, FO 371, 62552, UE6911; UK del. tel. to FO, August 10, 1947, FO 371, 62552, UE 7116; and Caffery tel. to Marshall, August 9, 1947, RG 59 file: 840.50Recovery/8/947.

25. Regarding Italy's position, particularly its proposal for a Franco-Italian tariff union, see the documents in RG 59, file: 651.6531/8-747, /8-1147, /8-1247, /8-1547, and /8-2247; and UK del. tel. to FO, August 8, 1947, FO 371, 62552, UE7090. For the Benelux position, see Caffery tels. to Marshall, August 9 and 14, 1947, RG 59, file: 840.50Recovery/8-947 and /8-1447; UK del. tel. to FO, August 4, 1947, FO 371, 62552, UE6911; and UK del. tel. to FO, August 11, 1947, FO 371,62552, UE7194. See also Caffery tel. to Marshall, August 20, 1947, *FRUS, 1947*, 3:364–7.

26. Hall-Patch memorandum to Bevin, August 7, 1947, FO 371, 62552, UE7147.

27. Tim Martin, British delegation to the Geneva trade talks, letter to L.

Barnett, Economic Relations Department, Foreign Office, July 18, 1947, FO 371, 62552, UE6282; Sir Stafford Cripps, Minister for Economic Affairs, memoranda of July 16 and 1947, T236/808/OF265/2/4; UK del. tel. to FO, August 2, 1947, FO 371, 62552. UE6852; UK del. tel. to FO, August 4, 1947, FO 371, 62552, UE6911; UK del. tel. to FO, August 6, 1947, FO 371, 62579, UE697; UK del. tel. to FO, August 10, 1947 FO 371, 62552, UE7116; UK del. tel. to FO, August 13, 1947, FO47 371, 62416 UE8106; UK del. tel. to FO, August 16, 1947, FO 371, 62552, UE7405; UK del. tel. to FO, August 18, 1947, FO 371, 62416, UE7440; Commonwealth Relations Office tel. to Dominion Governments, August 21, 1947, FO 371, 62416, UE7798, and Sir Sidney Caine, Deputy Under Secretary, Colonial Office, undated memorandum, "The Colonies and a Customs Union," FO 371, 62553, UE8359. See also Milward, *Reconstruction of Western Europe*, 235–41.

28. Cook minute, August 5, 1947, FO 371, 62552, UE6911; Note by the UK delegation on progress of the CEEC meeting, August 13, 1947, FO 371, 62416, UE8106; UK del. tel. to FO, August 15, 1947, FO 371, 62552, UE7393; UK del. tel. to FO, August 15, 1947, FO 371, 62552, UE7393; UK del. tel. to FO, August 15, 1947, FO 371, 62632, UE7395; FO tel. to UK del., August 15, 1947, FO 371, 62632, UE7282; UK del. tel. to FO, August 18, 1947, FO 371, 62552, UE7394; Commonwealth Relations Office tel. to Dominion Governments, August 21, 1947, FO 371, 62416, UE7798; and UK del. tel. to FO, August 30, 1947, FO 371, 62553, UE8053.

29. For the British economic situation and American concern, see *FRUS, 1947*, 3:17–49. See also Milward, *Reconstruction of Western Europe*, 260–2.

30. Clayton tel. to Marshall and Lovett, July 10, 1947, *FRUS, 1947*, 3:317–18. See also Clayton tel. to Marshall and Lovett, July 9, 1947, Caffery tel. to Marshall and Lovett July 11, 1947, Clayton tel. to Marshall and Lovett, July 29, 1947, and Clayton tel. to Lovett, July 31, 1947, *FRUS, 1947*, 3:315–16, 328–30, 339–41, 341–2; Dunn dispatch #1341 to Marshall, July 25, 1947, RG 59, file: 865.50/7-2547; Clayton tel. to Lovett, July 11, 1947, RG 59, file: 840.50Recovery/7-1147; UK del. tel. to FO, July 30, 1947, FO 371, 62418, UE6666; and UK del. tel. to FO, August 1, 1947, FO 371, 62418, UE6837.

31. In addition to the last two documents cited in note 30, see Balfour tel. to FO, July 31, 1947, FO 371, 62415, UE6810; Makins Record of Conversation [with Ambassador Douglas], August 15, 1947, Hall-Patch minute, August 16, 1947, and UK del. tel. to FO, August 19, 1947, FO 371, 62552, UE7560 and UE7461; and Harold Wilson, President of the Board of Trade, note of a conversation with Clayton, August 18, 1947, FO 371, 62416, UE7709.

32. Nitze had been sent over as a result of a recommendation by the Committee on the European Recovery Program. See its Minutes of Meeting, July 24, 1947, RG 353, Lot 122, box 26, folder: REP Minutes. See also Marshall tel. to the American Consulate, Geneva, for Clayton from Nitze, July 30, 1947, RG 59, file: 840.50Recovery/7-3047.

33. Memorandum by Wesley C. Haraldson of the Office of the United States Political Adviser for Germany, August 8, 1947, *FRUS, 1947*, 3:343–4, 345–50. See also Clayton, Caffery, Douglas, Murphy, and Nitze tel. to Marshall and Lovett, August 6, 1947, *FRUS, 1947*, 3:343–4; and Nitze's report on his conversations in Paris in Committee on the European Recovery Program, Minutes of Meeting, August 12, 1947, RG 353, Lot 122, box 26, folder: REP

Minutes. For a summary of Ambassador Douglas's views, see Douglas tel. to Lovett, July 18, 1947, RG 59, file: 841.51/7-1847.

34. Committee on the European Recovery Program, Minutes of Meeting, August 12, 1947, RG 353, Lot 122, box 26, folder: REP Minutes; and Haraldson memorandum August 8, 1947, *FRUS, 1947*, 3:345–50. See also Clayton, Caffery, Douglas, Murphy, and Nitze tel. to Marshall and Lovett, August 6, 1947, *FRUS, 1947*, 3:343–4.

35. Clayton tel. to Lovett, August 15, 1947, RG 59, file: 840.50Recovery/8-1547.

36. For the quotation, see *FRUS, 1947*, 3:357, footnote 1. For Lovett's views, see Lovett tel. to Clayton and Caffery, July 10, 1947, Lovett tel. to Clayton and Caffery, August 14, 1947, Lovett tel. to Douglas, August 20, 1947, and Lovett tel. to Caffery, August 24, 1947, *FRUS, 1947*, 3:324–6, 356–60, 367–8, 376–7; Lovett Memorandum of Conversation, July 25, 1947, RG 59, file: 840.50Recovery/7-2547; and W. Wallner Memorandum of Conversation, August 21, 1947, RG 59, file: 840.50Recovery/8-2147. For Lovett's concern about the cost of the Marshall Plan, see also Millis *Forrestal Diaries*, 279, 282.

37. Lovett tel. to Clayton and the Ambassador, July 10, 1947, and Lovett tel. to Clayton and Caffery, August 14, 1947, *FRUS, 1947*, 3:324–6, 356–60.

38. Committee on the European Recovery Program, Minutes of Meeting, July 29, 1947, RG 353, Lot 122, box 26, folder: REP Minutes; and Lovett and Wood tel. to Clayton and Caffery, August 11, 1947, *FRUS, 1947*, 3:350–1. See also Hickerson memorandum of August 11, 1947, and Lovett tel. to Clayton and Caffery, August 14, 1947, *FRUS, 1947*, 3:351–5, 356–60; and Committee on the European Recovery Program, Minutes of Meetings, July 10 and 15 and August 7 and 12, 1947, RG 353, Lot 122, box 26, folder: REP Minutes.

39. Caffery tel. to Lovett, August 26, 1947, *FRUS, 1947*, 3:380–3. See also Caffery and Clayton tel. to Marshall, August 20, 1947, Clayton tel. to Lovett, August 25, 1947, and Caffery tel. to Marshall, August 25, 1947, *FRUS, 1947*, 3:364–7, 377–9, 379–80; Caffery tel. to Marshall, August 22, 1947, RG 59, file: 840.50Recovery/8-2247; and Caffery tel. (#3452) to Marshall, August 26, 1947, RG 59, file: 840.50Recovery/8-2647.

40. UK del. tel. to FO, August 19, 1947, FO 371, 62580, UE7575; Makins minute August 23, 1947, and UK del. tels. to FO, August 24 (2), 26 (2), and 27, 1947, 371, 62632, UE7796, UE7792, UE7926, and UE7851; Bonesteel memorandum, "Minutes of Meeting on Marshall 'Plan,'" August 22, 1947, and Lovett tel. to Marshall at Petropolis, Brazil, August 24, 1947, *FRUS, 1947*, 3:369–71, 372, *FRUS, 1947*, 3:375, footnote 5; Lovett tel. to Caffery, August 25, 1947, and Caffery tel. to Marshall, August 25, 1947, RG 59, file: 840.50Recovery/8-2547; and Lovett tel. to Clayton and Caffery, August 26, 1947, RG 59, file: 840.50Recovery/8-2647.

41. Lovett tel. to Clayton and Caffery, August 26, 1947, *FRUS, 1947*, 3:383–9.

42. Clayton tel. to Marshall and Lovett, August 31, 1947, *FRUS, 1947*, 3:391–6.

43. Ibid.

44. Ben Moore letter to William Phillips and Paul Nitze, September 1, 1947,

and William Bray letter to Phillips, September 9, 1947, RG 353, Lot 122, box 38, folder: ERP Subject File, Paris Conference—Comments and Correspondence. The "Friendly Aid Boys" from the State Department included Moore, Bray, Victor Longstreet, Harold Speigel, and William Terrill.

45. Department Economic Advisers tel. to Lovett, Thorp, Ness, and Nitze, September 5, 1947, *FRUS, 1947*, 3:405–8. See also Clayton tel. to Marshall and Lovett, August 31, 1947, *FRUS, 1947*, 3:391–6; Department Economic Advisers tel. to Ness, Nitze, and Kindleberger, September 6, 1947, RG 59, file: 840.50Recovery/9-647; and Department Economic Advisers tel. to Ness and Nitze, September 7, 1947, and Lovett tel. to Clayton and Caffery, September 7, 1947, both in RG 59, file: 840.50Recovery/9-747.

46. Lovett Notes on Cabinet Meeting, August 29, 1947, RG 59, file: 811.5043/8-294 and Matthew Connelly Notes on Cabinet Meeting, August 29, 1947, Matthew Connelly Papers (Truman Library), box 1, folder: Notes on Cabinet Meetings, Post-presidential File.

47. Department Economic Advisers tel. to Lovett, Thorp, Ness, and Nitze, September 5, 1947, *FRUS, 1947*, 3:405–8.

48. Memorandum by the Director of the Policy Planning Staff, September 4, 1947, *FRUS, 1947*, 3:397–405.

49. Advisory Steering Committee, Minutes of Meeting, September 9, 1947, RG 353, Lot 122, box 26, folder: ASC Minutes. The quote is from Caffery tel. to Marshall, September 7, 1947, RG 59, file: 840.50Recovery/9-747.

50. Lovett tel. to Clayton and Caffery, September 7, 1947, *FRUS, 1947*, 3:415–17. In addition to the sources cited in note 49, see Lovett tel. to Marshall at Petropolis, Brazil, August 31, 1947, Department Economic Advisers tel. to Lovett, Thorp, Ness, and Nitze, September 5, 1947, Lovett tel. to Certain American Diplomatic Offices, September 7, 1947, and Lovett tel. to Douglas, September 11, 1947, *FRUS, 1947*, 3:396–7, 405–8, 412–15, 423–5.

51. Hickerson memorandum to Marshall and Lovett, August 11, 1947, Douglas tel. to Lovett, August 21, 1947, Kennan memorandum, September 4, 1947, Marshall tel. to Douglas, September 5, 1947, Caffery tel. to Douglas, September 5, 1947, Lovett tel. to Certain American Diplomatic Offices, September 7, 1947, and Marshall tel. to Douglas, September 8, 1947, *FRUS, 1947*, 3:351–5, 368–9, 397–405, 409–10, 411–12, 415–17, 418–19; Committee on the European Recovery Program, Minutes of Meeting, August 19, 1947, RG 353, Lot 122, box 26; folder: REP Minutes, Bonesteel memorandum to Lovett, August 27, 1947, RG 59, Bohlen Records, box 6, folder: European Recovery, 1947–48; and Murphy tel. to Marshall, September 8, 1947, RG 59, file: 840.50Recovery/9-847.

52. Marshall tel. to Douglas, September 8, 1947, *FRUS, 1947*, 3:418–19; Bonesteel memorandum of telephone conversation with Ambassador Douglas, September 8, 1947, RG 59, file: 840.50Recovery/9-847; and FO tels. (2) to UK del., September 8, 1947, FO 371, 62580, UE8350.

53. See Douglas tels. to Marshall, September 9, 12, and 17, 1947, *FRUS, 1947*, 3:42, 429–30, 434–5.

54. Douglas tel. to Marshall, September 9, 1947, *FRUS, 1947*, 3:420; and FO tel. to UK del., September 9, 1947, FO 371, 62580, UE8385.

55. UK del. tel. to FO, September 11, 1947, FO 371, 62582, UE8451; FO tel. to UK del., September 9, 1947, FO 371, 62580, UE8385; British Embassy, The Hague, tel. to FO, September 10, 1947, British Embassy, Oslo, tel. to FO, September 10, 1947, and UK del. tel. to FO, September 11, 1947, FO 371, 62582, UE8431, UE8432, and UE8443.

56. American Embassy, Lisbon, tel. to Marshall, September 10, 1947, RG 59, file: 840.50Recovery/9-1047; Caffery tel. to Marshall, September 10, 1947, RG 59, file: 840.50Recovery/9-1047; Dunn tel. to Marshall, September 11, 1947, RG 59, file: 840.50Recovery/9-1147; Caffery tel. to Marshall, September 13, 1947, RG 59, file: 840.50Recovery/9-1347; Clayton, Caffery, and Douglas tel. to Marshall and Lovett, September 11, 1947, Caffery tel. to Marshall and Lovett, September 12, 1947, Caffery tel. to Marshall, September 12, 1947, and Douglas tel. to Marshall, September 12, 1947, *FRUS, 1947*, 3:421–3, 425–8, 428, 429–30. See also UK del. tels. (5) to FO September 11, 1947, FO 371, 62582, UE8452, UE8487, UE8488, UE8489, and UE8505.

57. FO tel. to British Embassy, Washington, September 12, 1947, FO 371, 62582, UE8507. See also Douglas tels. (2) to Marshall, September 12, 1947, *FRUS, 1947*, 3:428–9, 429–30.

58. Lovett tel. to Douglas, September 13, 1947, *FRUS, 1947*, 3:430–1.

59. Caffery tel. to Marshall, September 15, 1947, RG 59, file: 840.50Recovery/9-1547; and Caffery tel. to Marshall, September 18, 1947, RG 59, file: 840.50Recovery/9-1847. See also Caffery tel. to Marshall, September 14, 1947, Caffery tel. to Lovett and Bonesteel, September 17, 1947, *FRUS, 1947*, 3:431–2, 434; Caffery tel. to Marshall, September 19, 1947, RG 59, file: 840.50Recovery/9-1947; UK del. tels (2) to FO, September 14, 1947, FO 371, 62582, UE8556; UK del. tel. to FO, September 16, 1947, PREM 8/495; and C. T. Crowe of the Foreign Office, "Report of the Commission on European Economic Co-operation," September 18, 1947, FO 371, 62586, UE8966.

60. Douglas tel. to Marshall and Lovett, September 17, 1947, and Caffery, Clayton, and Douglas tel. to Marshall and Lovett, September 15, 1947, *FRUS, 1947*, 3:434–5, 432–3. See also Caffery tel. to Lovett and Bonesteel, September 17, 1947, and Caffery tel. to Marshall, September 17, 1947, *FRUS, 1947*, 3:434, 435–7; Caffery tel. to Marshall for Bonesteel, September 8, 1947, RG 59, file: 840.50Recovery/9-847; and FO tel. to UK del., September 4, 1947, and UK del. tels. to FO, September 6(2) and 8, 1947, FO 371, 62580, UE8355, UE8300, UE8309, and UE8349.

61. Caffery tel. to Marshall and Lovett, September 19, 1947, RG 59, file 840.50Recovery/9-1947. See also the official summary of the conference report Caffery tel. to Marshall, September 20, 1947, RG 59, file: 840.50Recovery/9-2047.

62. See Committee on European Economic Cooperation, *General Report*, Vol. 1, and *Technical Reports*, Vol. 2 (London, 1947). See also the summaries of the reports in Caffery tel. to Marshall, September 20, 1947, RG 59, file: 840.5Recovery/9-2047; Department of State, *Bulletin* 17 (October 5, 1947): 681–7; and "European Proposals for a Recovery Program," *International Conciliation* 436 (December 1947): 803–27.

63. Meeting of Ministers (GEN.179/12th Mtg.), August 11, 1947, Chancellor of the Exchequer Hugh Dalton, CP (47) 233, "Balance of Payments," August 16, 1947, and CM (47) 71st Conclusion, August 17, 1947, PREM 8/489.

64. Under Secretary of the Treasury A. L. M. Wiggins, Daily Log, August 22, 1947, A. L. M. Wiggins Papers (Truman Library), box 1, folder: Daily Log, 1947, July and August; Connelly Notes on Cabinet Meeting, August 8, 1947, Connelly Papers, box 1, folder: Notes on Cabinet Meetings, Post-presidential File; Baruch memorandum to Snyder, August 21, 1947, Snyder Papers, box 56, folder: International Monetary Fund and Bank—London Trip to Second Annual Meeting, 1947; and Haraldson memorandum, August 8, 1947, *FRUS, 1947*, 3:345–50. See also Policy Planning Staff memoranda of July 21? and August 14, 1947, and Douglas tel. to Marshall, July 25, 1947, *FRUS, 1947*, 3:335–7, 360–3, 43–4; and Douglas tel. to Marshall, August 1, 1947, RG 59, file: 841.50/8-147. American officials did not think the British were doing enough to solve their own problems. See, for criticism of the British, Douglas tel. to Marshall, July 18, 1947, RG 59, file: 841.51/7-1847; Bernard Baruch memorandum for Secretary Snyder, August 21, 1947, Snyder Papers, box 56, folder: International Monetary Fund and Bank—London Trip to Second Annual Meeting, 1947; and Wiggins, Daily Log, July 29 and 31 and August 1 and 4, 1947, Wiggins Papers, box 1, folder: Daily Log, 1947, July and August.

65. This story can be followed in *FRUS, 1947*, 3:61–9. See also W. S. Surrey, "Discussions with the British with Respect to Section 8 of the Anglo-American Financial Agreement," September 11, 1947, RG 59, file: 841.51/9-1147; Ness memorandum to Lovett, September 10, 1947, RG 59, file: 840.50Recovery/9-1047; British Embassy, Washington, tel. to FO, August 19, 1947, and CM (47) 72nd and 73rd Conclusions, August 19 and 20, 1947 (and tels. attached to 73rd Conclusion), PREM 8/489.

66. French and Italian developments can be followed in *FRUS, 1947*, 3:716–90 and 920–1000. See also Advisory Steering Committee, Minutes of Meeting, October 10, 1947, RG 353, Lot 122, box 26, folder: ASC Minutes; Lovett memorandum to Truman, October 13, 1947, *FRUS, 1947*, 3:478–81; and Ness memorandum to Lovett, September 10, 1947, RG 59, file: 840.50Recovery/9-1047.

67. See the documentation in *FRUS, 1947*, 3:344–5, 345–50, 360–3, 410–11, 411 (footnote 2), 415–17, 472–7, 477–8, 478–81. The quotation is from Lovett tel. to Truman, September 6, 1947, *FRUS, 1947*, 3:410–11. For additional thinking in various government agencies and for Truman's initiatives, see Frank Southard, Director, Office of International Finance, Treasury Department, memorandum to Snyder, September 19, 1947, Snyder Papers, box 11, folder: European Recovery Program, Adm. File; Wiggins, Daily Log, October 2, 1947, Wiggins Papers, box 1, folder: Daily Log, 1947, October; Advisory Steering Committee, Minutes of Meetings, September 17 and 25 and October 2, 10, and 14, 1947, RG 353, Lot 122, box 26, folder: ASC Minutes; Committee on the European Recovery Program, Minutes of Meeting, September 18, 1947, RG 353, Lot 122, box 26, folder: REP Minutes; Connelly Notes on Cabinet Meeting, September 24, 1947, Connelly Papers, box 1, folder: Notes on Cabinet Meetings, Post-presidential File; Truman letter to Senator Styles Bridges, September 30, 1947, Truman Papers, OF, folder: 426 (Jan.–Nov. 1947); Charles S. Murphy, Administrative Assistant to the President, undated Memorandum for the President, Truman Papers, PSF, folder: General File—European Emergency; and White House Press Release, October 24, 1947, Truman Papers, OF, folder: 426 (Jan.–Nov. 1947).

68. See, for example, Committee on the European Recovery Program, Minutes of Meeting, September 18, 1947, RG 353, Lot 122, box 26, folder: REP

Minutes; Lovett tel. to Clayton and Caffery, September 20, 1947, and Clayton and Douglas tel. to Lovett, September 23, 1947, *FRUS, 1947*, 3:442–4, 445–6; Advisory Steering Committee, Minutes of Meetings, September 9, 19, and 25, 1947, RG 353, Lot 122, box 26, folder: ASC Minutes; and Committee on the European Recovery Program, Minutes of Meetings, September 11, 16, and 18, 1947, RG 353, Lot 122, box 26, folder: REP Minutes. See also the documents labeled D-16/4, /7a, /8a, in RG 353, Lot 122, Box 28, folder: REP Documents; ASC D-1, D-3, D-1/1a, in RG 353, Lot 122, box 24, folder: ASC Documents; Snyder undated memorandum for the President, Truman Papers, CF, folder: State Department, 1946–47; and Lovett memorandum for President, September 18, 1947, RG 59, file: Memoranda for the President, box 1.

69. Chairman, CEEC del. to Lovett, October 22, 1947, CEEC del. to the State Department, October 27, 1947, CEEC del. to the Participating Governments, October 31, 1947, Lovett to Chairman, CEEC del., November 3, 1947, and Record of a Meeting between Members of the Advisory Steering Committee and the CEEC Delegation, November 4, 1947, *FRUS, 1947*, 3:446–50, 452–70; Mulliken memorandum to Kotschnig and Rusk, October 23, 1947, RG 59, file: 840.50Recovery/10-2347; Memoranda of Conversations, October 15 and 16, 1947, RG 353, Lot 122, box 28, folder: REP Documents; Memoranda of Conversations, October 21, 22, and 23, 1947, RG 353, Lot 122, box 24, folder: ASC Documents; and Paul Nitze letter to Douglas October 29, 1947, Records of the Foreign Service Posts of the Department of State (Washington National Records Center, Suitland, MD), Record Group 84, London Embassy Records, box 1018, file: 850 Marshall Plan (hereafter cited as RG 84 London Embassy Records, with appropriate box and file designations). For a British account of the Washington talks, see the Foreign Office paper "European Reconstruction: Documents Relating to the Washington Conversations on European Economic Co-operation (6th October–7th November)," FO 371, 62675, UE12282.

70. See the documents cited in note 69. The quotation is from CEEC del. to Participating Governments, October 31, 1947, *FRUS, 1947*, 3:456–61.

71. Van Der Beugel, *From Marshall Aid to Atlantic Partnership*, 93.

9

Alan S. Milward

The Reconstruction of
Western Europe

Alan Milward, who has been based at the European University
Institute in Florence and then the London School of Economics, is a
leading economic historian of twentieth-century Europe. He has published several important works concerning the economic effects of
World War II and the impact of the German occupation. His recent
volume, *The Reconstruction of Western Europe, 1945–51* (Berkeley and
Los Angeles, University of California Press, 1984) is a fundamental
contribution to understanding the economics of European recovery.
Together with Michael Hogan's work, excerpted above, it stands as a
major analysis of the United States' postwar contribution. The selection
included here includes pages 90–113 and 123–125 from *The Reconstruction of Western Europe*, reprinted with the permission of the University
of California Press.

Perhaps more easily as a British national, Milward dissents from the
usual celebrations of American policy. He stresses the Europeans' own
contribution to recovery and tends to assess United States initiatives as
repeatedly falling short of their objectives. The original American plan
for postwar currency convertibility and multilateral trade, which was
formalized at the Bretton Woods Conference of 1944, could not be

sustained. Currencies remained a shambles, and postwar trade was conducted by unwieldy barter arrangements. Marshall Plan assistance, in effect, appeared necessary because Bretton Woods multilateralism could never have gotten off the ground without it. But the Marshall Plan in turn, so Milward argues, was not really necessary. Only the rapid tempo of European recovery already under way led to the bottlenecks that were interpreted as so dangerous. As for the integration of Western Europe, the continental countries' own initiatives, especially the Schuman Plan, represented the decisive advance. Milward does not deny that the Marshall Plan brought considerable assistance to Europe, and on other occasions he has praised the ERP as a thoughtful multilateral policy. But he insists on divesting U.S. policy of any retrospective heroic aura.

For a careful explanation of how Marshall Plan transfers and intra-European payments actually functioned, the reader can profitably consult Imanuel Wexler: *The Marshall Plan Revisited: The European Recovery Program in Economic Perspective* (Westport, CT, Greenwood Press, 1983). An interesting set of brief memoirs and analyses was gathered at a thirty-fifth anniversary conference at the Harvard University Center for European Studies and published as *The Marshall Plan: A Retrospective*, Stanley Hoffmann and Charles S. Maier, eds. (Boulder, CO, Westwood Publishers, 1984). An international group of scholars, including Milward, Hogan and others, has contributed to *Germany and the Marshall Plan*, Charles S. Maier, ed. (Oxford: Berg Publishers Limited, 1991).

The European Recovery Programme

The aspect of the economic reconstruction of Europe to which most energy and attention has been given and the one which still seems to awaken the most interest is that of the impact of the ERP on European economic and political life. To what extent is modern Western Europe the creation of the Marshall Plan? Could it have been otherwise? These are questions repeatedly mulled over in conferences and newspapers. At the height of the Cold War American scholars sought to demonstrate that the Marshall Plan was the cause of Western Europe's remarkable economic performance and that it had 'saved' western Europe for democracy.[1] International economists in the United States, whose subject the Marshall Plan had made important to American government policies, wrote more guardedly in much the same vein.[2]

When in reaction a 'revisionist' school of historians appeared in the United States, attributing the Cold War as much to American policies as to those of the Soviet Union, the Marshall Plan came to be seen in an opposite light, as an act of imperialistic foreign policy by the United

States.[3] In extending its great power interests to the river Elbe, and even beyond, the United States narrowed the range of economic and political choice for European societies, it was argued, and tried to turn them into political and economic satellites. Marshall Aid was interpreted as a device for furthering American exports and capital investment. Although they might have revised everything else, however, the 'revisionist' historians in no way revised the earlier views of the economic effectiveness and importance of the Marshall Plan. They were simply less pleased by its results.

Until very recently few doubts have been expressed about the overall importance and effectiveness of Marshall Aid in promoting European recovery. In general it has been seen as the indispensable starting-point of Western Europe's remarkable subsequent prosperity.[4] But with the beginnings of a more methodical history of the period the focus of the debate has changed, so that the question now posed is whether Marshall Aid was as important in contributing to the post-war settlement as everyone, Cold War historians and 'revisionists' alike, had assumed.[5] The length of time needed before this debate could be seriously begun is in itself an interesting phenomenon because the earlier works which argued for the central importance of the Marshall Plan certainly did not do so from any profound analysis of the Western European economies at the time, but more from a set of rather glib political and economic assumptions. The main reason for the scepticism about the overall importance of the ERP has been that quantitative measures of its impact on the European economies suggest that its contribution to them was greatly exaggerated by Cold War historians and that it also brought few, if any, of the economic advantages to America which 'revisionist' historians suggested. As a total sum Marshall Aid does not look large in terms of Western Europe's total foreign trade or investment. American exports to Europe did not increase but fell during the European Recovery Programme and American capital exports to Western Europe were at one of their lowest ebbs.

Similarly, many of the dramatic political changes in Western Europe which were once ascribed to American interference and alleged to be the price of Marshall Aid, the departure of the Communist Party from the French government in 1947, for example, or the defeat of the more radical aspirations for economic and social change which were noticeable in Western Europe between 1945 and 1947, have been shown to be part of the course of internal political development in the European countries concerned, rather than the result of American intervention. The ERP and its ideas appealed to powerful sections of political opinion in every Western European country and their influence was much stronger than anything brought to bear from outside. The political and economic influence of the Marshall Plan must in any case be seen as parts of a whole and if it is indeed true that, economically, Marshall Aid was not of major importance to Western European economic recovery, then it must follow that its influence on Western Europe's internal political choices would also be small.

The scope of the ERP was so large that these sweeping considerations are not unreasonable, although from a purely national standpoint the importance of Marshall Aid would seem entirely different from one European country to another. At one extreme of the spectrum might be set Austria or the German Federal Republic, where the assumption must be that Marshall Aid made so great a contribution to economic recovery as to make the question at the very least well worth debating, and at the other end Belgium, where Marshall Aid was so small in terms of the Belgian economy that the question hardly seems worth debating at all. The precise effects of the ERP on each Western European economy, how it was used, and the contribution it made, can only be the concern of this book in a very superficial way because what is under discussion here is the impact of the ERP on the reconstruction of Western Europe as a whole. Belgium's recovery and reconstruction depended on that of Western Europe and thus the contribution of Marshall Aid to economies other than Belgium is of serious importance in estimating its importance for Belgium's own economic and political life. With less force a similar statement could be made about the larger economies and this was one basic tenet of the whole programme of action. But that still leaves plenty of scope for debate on a purely national level which can hardly be resolved here and which is likely to continue.

The implication of the book as a whole is that the debate about the economic effectiveness of Marshall Aid at the moment focuses on questions which are too narrow and in certain respects sterile and unanswerable. Marshall Aid's prime importance was that it was one of several contemporary attempts to reconstruct Western Europe's economic and political framework. They were all related to the existence of the ERP, which served as the impulse to them, but their relationship to its economic effectiveness was an extremely complicated one. Most of them, indeed, were intended in one way or another to thwart its economic or political objectives. Historical judgements about the Marshall Plan's effectiveness must be at least as much about its immediate impact on these alternative attempts at economic reconstruction as on the effectiveness of the ERP itself. If the quantitative questions about the ERP's economic importance could be definitively settled, all the further questions about Europe's reconstruction which scholars have ignored in their concentration on Marshall Aid would still remain. Nevertheless, an assessment of the scope of the ERP in quantitative terms must be the starting-point for any attempt at assessing its impact.

The Economic Effects of Marshall Aid

It cannot be argued, except in retrospect, that the Marshall Plan marked an acceptance by the United States that, because its real interests lay in the creation of a multilateral world trading system, it must act consistently as a creditor country and recycle dollars or gold into the international economy. At the time of its inception the ERP was no more than a tardy acceptance of the argument made in 1945 by Europeans that there was a large task of economic reconstruction to be undertaken in Europe which would require extensive American credits before the international economic relationships envisaged by the Bretton Woods agreements could become effectively operational. It replaced a short-term outflow of dollars for relief by a medium-term outflow of dollars for reconstruction. The difference with the period after the First World War was that it did so much earlier, on a more generous scale, but, above all, with the direct commitment of the United States government within a comprehensive plan with specific political and economic objectives.

There was in fact no alternative to direct government involvement even if only the economic objectives are taken into consideration, although these by themselves would not have been enough to commit the United States to such a course of action in 1947. Between 1870 and 1914, when the United Kingdom had functioned as a creditor economy in the international economic system, the average rate of net foreign investment was 5.2 per cent of GNP and, in addition, in almost every year the United Kingdom ran a balance of trade deficit. The United States, by contrast, after 1945 had an outflow of foreign investment which, measured against GNP, was less than half of that proportion and a very large balance of trade surplus. This outflow of sterling, backed up by an outflow of francs which was roughly similar as a proportion of French GNP, had financed the expanding pattern of multilateral trade before 1914. As far as the United Kingdom was concerned almost the whole of this outflow of sterling was private investment. After 1945, however, when the United States economy was booming and the demand for capital there high, and when American investors did not regard investments in western Europe as offering either security or profitability, American private foreign investment was very small, far too small to offset trade surpluses. It mainly consisted of direct investment by United States corporations out of undistributed profits, of which the most noticeable was the reinvestment by oil companies in petrol refining.

Over the period 1946–8 government long- and short-term loans financed 19 per cent of United States exports of goods and services.[6] The most important element in this outflow was the line of credit to

Britain, followed by Export-Import Bank loans and property credits for
war surplus equipment. To this should be added the outflow of interest-
free dollars, chiefly through UNRRA and the GARIOA programme.
The United States contribution to the UNRRA programme itself came
to $2817 million by the end of 1947, more than the British drawings on
the line of credit by that date and more than the total of Export-Import
Bank loans. By the end of 1948 $1929 million had been expended under
the GARIOA programme. Therefore grants and credits together over
the same period would have financed about 34 per cent of the export of
American goods and services.

If all other forms of dollar provision are counted, Interim Aid,
military aid to Greece and Turkey, aid to China, the special programme
for the Philippines and so on, the net outflow of foreign aid, both loans
and grants, from July 1945 to the end of 1946 was $7444 million, in
1947 $5681 million, and in both those periods higher than in any
calendar year under the Marshall Plan.[7] On the other hand the proportion of ERP aid provided as grants was very high, 92 per cent in 1949,
and the loans were on favourable terms, for thirty-five years at 2.5 per
cent interest rate and repayments not having to start until 1952. Marshall Aid systematized the outflow of dollars, reduced the cost to the
recipients and concentrated the dollar outflow geographically on Western Europe, but it did not increase the relative size of the dollar outflow
compared to the earlier years when the theme was relief rather than
recovery.

The outflow of dollars under Marshall Aid represented 2.1 per cent
of United States GNP in 1948, rising to 2.4 per cent in 1949 and then
falling away to 1.5 per cent. The GNP was much larger than that of the
United Kingdom before 1914 and the ratio of American foreign trade to
it much smaller.[8] Unilateral transfers, of which the ERP grants were by
far the largest part, financed about 32 per cent of the exports of
American goods and services in 1949, the peak year of ERP. Loans in
that year were only $452 million compared to a total for all unilateral
transfers of $5211 million, so that the proportion of the export of goods
and services financed was about what it had been before Marshall Aid
started. There were no signs before 1950 of an end to international
dollar scarcity nor of a return to an equilibrium in international payments sufficient to enable Western European economies to sustain
imports from the United States without aid. The vigorous progress
made in that direction in that year was at once cancelled by the effects of
the Korean war. An equilibrium in world payments and 'viability'
between Western Europe and America after the end of Marshall Aid
still depended on the United States running a large balance of payments
deficit.

At no time was the ERP the sole source of American grants and loans. It overlapped at the beginning of the programme with existing programmes and from summer 1951 became confused with aid for military purposes under the Mutual Defence Assistance Programme. The funds for the ERP were first made available by Congress on 3 April 1948, although they were to be voted, contrary to the administration's wishes, for only one year at a time. From then until 30 June 1951, when what was left of the ERP was merged with the defence programme, the total sum made available for the ERP (including the separate loan programme for Spain) was $12,534.9 million, of which about $12,200 million had been committed by the end of June. It was committed in three principal ways, as grants, loans, and 'conditional' aid. 'Conditional' aid was aid awarded as backing to the intra-Western European payments agreement of 1948 and subsequently extended to further agreements, aid which although provided from the United States in fact financed trade between two Western European countries and so was transferable.[9] Grants accounted for $9199.4 million, loans for $1139.7 million and 'conditional' aid for $1542.9 million.

The existence of the 'conditional' aid scheme in itself raises serious methodological issues in apportioning the total of ERP aid received by different countries. In terms of the country to which aid was originally allocated the United Kingdom received 23 per cent of the total and France 20.6 per cent. The detailed way in which the allocation of the sums was finally decided will not be known without a full history of the operations of the Economic Co-operation Agency (ECA), but it is not important here because the nature of the crisis which produced Marshall Aid meant that one principle of allocation overrode all others. The gross dimensions of aid allocations to each country were determined by its dollar balance of payments deficits. The European countries were required, first in the CEEC and then in the OEEC, to draw up in one comprehensive programme a statement of their annual requirements in dollar imports and it was against this programme that aid was awarded to cover the imports. The bigger the dollar deficit on foreign trade the larger the share of Marshall Aid. If there was occasional adjustment by ECA according to other principles, in favour perhaps of poorer economies, it must have been very slight. There was more scope for such adjustment in the first round of allocations because that was announced before the OEEC had begun to function as the forum where dollar import needs were first decided and well after the CEEC had broken up, although the report of the CEEC to Congress existed as a public guideline to dollar import needs.

Aid was not therefore allocated in any fixed proportion to national income and in so far as it was correlated in size with any particular indicator it was so, although only very loosely, with the volume of foreign trade. Its impact on national income was thus an indirect one through the foreign trade sector. After the 1948 Agreement for Intra-European Payments and Compensations a certain amount of aid was in fact used directly to finance deficits in intra-European trade rather than dollar deficits only. An attempt at measuring the ratio of aid to national income after it had been redistributed through this intra-European payments mechanism was made by the Bank of International Settlements and the results are shown in table 1. Measured in this way it could hardly be argued that in the first year of the ERP it did not make a significant contribution to the growth in that short period of six countries in particular, Austria, where it contributed an extra 14 per cent to the national income, the Netherlands, where its contribution was 10.8 per cent, Ireland, where the figure was 7.8 per cent, France, where it was 6.5 per cent, Norway, 5.8 per cent and Italy, 5.3 per cent. These are no small sums, and even 2.4 per cent of the British national income, although only at the time about one year's growth of national income, represents a very substantial transfer. Accepting, therefore, that over the period of the ERP as a whole the transfers were by no means so abnormally large in historical perspective as to cause Marshall Aid to be singled out as an exceptional economic phenomenon in the way it was at the time and for twenty years afterwards, an added precision is needed in such a judgement. Over the first year of the programme, from summer 1948 to summer 1949, it was an important addition to national income in all the recipient countries except Belgium and Sweden, which effectively received only 'conditional' aid.

On the other hand, when we ask 'how important?' judgement must ultimately be subjective. The rates of growth of national income in

Table 1. Percentage of national income represented by net ERP aid after operation of drawing rights, 1 July 1948 to 30 June 1949

Austria	14.0
Belgium/Luxembourg★	0.6
France★	6.5
Denmark	3.3
Western Germany (Trizone)	2.9
Iceland	5.0
Ireland	7.8
Italy	5.3
Netherlands★	10.8
Norway	5.8
Sweden	0.3
United Kingdom	2.4

Source: BIS, *19th Annual Report* (Basle, 1949), p. 20.
★Including aid to overseas territories.

Western Europe after 1945 were much higher than in the inter-war period. They averaged, over the period 1945–60, almost 5 per cent in the Netherlands and 4.4 per cent in France. The contribution of the ERP at its peak therefore (when outflows of dollars were at their highest and European national incomes at their lowest), was equivalent to about two years' 'normal' growth of national income in the Netherlands and about one and a half year's 'normal' growth in France. There is only one of the receiving economies, however, namely Belgium, where a case could be made that the rate of growth of national income was showing a tendency to fall in summer 1948, when this sudden accretion to national income became available, and it did not become available in any significant size to Belgium. One result of Marshall Aid was thus to give a further sharp upward thrust from summer 1948 for one year to growth rates which were already high.

Over the whole period of the ERP its addition to European national incomes was, of course, less significant. Table 2 pursues the same type of analysis, for the main beneficiaries of Marshall Aid, as that attempted by the Bank of International Settlements. It should, however, be noted that before the general European devaluations against the dollar in 1949, the variations in exchange rates for some countries are such as to make such calculations only valuable as gross orders of magnitude. In fact the complexities of Austrian exchange rates were such as to make the calculation so hypothetical as to be meaningless and it has accordingly been omitted. In this respect it should also be noted that the precise basis on which the Bank of International Settlements' calculations are made is not specified; however the results in tables 15 and 16 are not in disaccord.

The Netherlands, and presumably Austria, must be singled out by this method as benefiting from the ERP on a different scale from the others. The total monetized contribution of ERP to the Netherlands economy was between three and a half and four and a half years of prevailing rates of growth of total output of the economy. For France it represents between two and two and a half years' growth, for Italy and the United Kingdom approximately two and for West Germany about half a year. But the growth of GNP is not a function of simple monetary transfers but of how the national product is used. It would therefore be more correct to say that what was transferred to the Netherlands by the ERP was the potential to increase the growth of its GNP by the equivalent of roughly four years of the prevailing rate of growth. Accepting therefore that Marshall Aid had only a marginal effect on the potential for growth of total economic output in Belgium, Denmark, Sweden and West Germany, the question must be how well did the other economies utilize the much greater potential which it gave them?

To answer this question we must confront the first economic pur-

Table 2. Total net ERP aid after utilization of drawing rights as a percentage of 1949 GNP

	(A) At pre-September 1949 exchange rates	(B) At post-September 1949 exchange rates
France	9.9	11.5
Italy	8.8	9.6
Netherlands	16.1	23.1
United Kingdom★	5.2	7.5
West Germany†	4.7	5.9

Source: Values of ERP aid calculated to include total allotments to countries in question by 30 June 1951 plus 'defence support' aid from then to 30 December 1951. Data from US, *Statistical Abstract of the United States,* 1954 and W.L. Brown Jnr and R. Opie, *American Foreign Assistance* (Washington DC, 1953), pp. 222, 246 ff. Effect of drawing rights calculated from W. Diebold Jnr, *Trade and Payments in Western Europe* (New York, 1952), pp. 40, 45. The exchange rates used in column (A) for France and Italy are, for France the average of the registered exchange rate in 1948 and the median import exchange rate for the first three quarters of 1949, for Italy the IMF par rate (which was not officially altered).
★GDP   †1950

poses of the ERP in 1947. The value of Marshall Aid to Western European countries primarily consisted in the fact that it allowed them to continue to maintain a high level of investment and imports and avoid the deflations or the further increase in trade controls which were the only other possible responses to the crisis of 1947, and in particular it permitted them to maintain a flow of dollar imports. These purposes became less clear-cut after 1948. That was a year of social stability and undisputed economic advance in Western Europe and as American political anxieties were allayed the longer-term goal of Marshall Aid, to enable western Europe to eliminate its payments deficit with the United States by 1952, came into the forefront. With it came the idea, pushed into the background in 1947, that over-investment and inflation were the main barriers to reaching this goal. Inflation could also be presented as inimical to social and political stability. It is often suggested that through Marshall Aid the United States exercised a malign influence on European recovery by demanding less inflationary policies and by insisting on reductions in the levels of income and consumption at which governments were aiming.[10]

It is certainly true that reducing the rate of inflation did become a priority of American policy in 1948 and remained so. In this it was supported by the pressures of several Western European governments in OEEC. The 'Interim Report' of OEEC at the end of 1948 insisted on

balanced budgets as a condition of the European Recovery Programme.[11] But the Interim Report was a last-minute, face-saving substitute for the coherent, long-term West European common programme
which OEEC had been unable to produce and thus, as far as European
governments were concerned, was simply an agreement to disagree and
had no policy-making force. The pressures exerted were mainly against
France and by the end of 1948 the French government itself had
become concerned to slow down the rate of inflation there too. At no
time was it an objective of ECA policy to produce deflationary policies
in Europe. The country most severely criticized publicly by ECA was
Italy, precisely because of its deflationary policies, whereas for all the
attempts to persuade the French government to reduce inflation ECA
gave almost unquestioning backing to the high level of investment in
the French economy. Objectives did become more complex after 1947
but the central objective of that year remained central. In 1949 the
United States government based its requests to Congress for ERP funds
on the assumption that levels of capital formation in Western Europe
should still be at about 20 per cent of GNP. Marshall Aid remained
throughout a device to permit expansion in Western Europe. The most
tangible expression of this was the imports which it was not necessary to
forego.

The most striking example of the overall contribution of American
aid to imports was that of West Germany, although in that case ERP was
only a contributory factor. Between 1945 and 1948 about two-thirds of
all imports into the western occupation zones of Germany were financed
by American aid. In 1949 the proportion was about 39 per cent, about
22 per cent financed under the GARIOA programme. So low was the
level of food supply in West Germany and the population so much more
rapidly increasing than elsewhere in Western Europe that it is obvious
that the main contribution of Marshall Aid in this case was in helping
the other aid programmes to provide the necessary imports to keep the
population alive and able to work. In that sense Marshall Aid was for its
first two years in Germany primarily a supplementation of relief in spite
of its more far-reaching objectives. By the end of 1949 procurement
authorizations for commodity shipments to Germany under the ERP
programme amounted to $723.3 million of which as much as $569.3
million was food and agricultural commodities.[12] This was a special
case, not fairly representing the overall objectives of ERP before the
end of 1949, and, as Gimbel argues, some action of this kind would
have been unavoidable in Germany even had there been no Marshall
Plan.[13] Harris's calculations, derived from those of the State Department, suggest that the dollar earnings of the Bizone over the first fifteen
months of ERP were not thought likely to be more than 10 per cent of
its dollar receipts.[14]

Those of France were estimated to be no more than 19 per cent of its likely dollar receipts over the same period, but France, nevertheless, serves as a more central case, because, in spite of its propensity to run large balance of trade deficits and soak up Marshall Aid to pay for them, the imports were much more geared to reconstruction than relief. Imports covered by Marshall Aid payments amounted to 20.6 per cent of all imports in 1949 and in 1950 to 14.8 per cent. The Modernization Plan has been based from its beginnings on the assumption that American aid was indispensable if planning targets were to be achieved and in fact it had begun its life as a one-year import programme from the United States.[15] To retreat into a closed economy would have been to throw over the very intentions of the Plan by abandoning its central concept of modernization of capital equipment and as long as the Modernization Plan was the basis of French reconstruction a high level of imports from the United States was inevitable. But that, of course, is not to argue that recovery and reconstruction in France were impossible through any other policy, although they would have been very difficult, nor that a sufficient level of imports from America would have been unattainable without Marshall Aid.

It was in the United Kingdom, rather than in France, that the threat of an almost total independence from dollar trade as a policy choice was more frequently allowed to surface. If the fears in the United States that this would happen were greater than the force behind the threat, the existence of the sterling area certainly gave the threat more force than any similar threat France could have made. Imports funded by Marshall Aid were only 11.3 per cent of British imports in 1949 and 7.5 per cent in 1950. The quantity of imports provided by ERP aid was obviously not indispensable to reconstruction in the United Kingdom, although that is not to argue that it was not important to achieving reconstruction along the lines that the majority of the British government wished. A major shift in the British import programme away from the dollar zone in 1947 would have meant cuts in the food rations to a level lower than that during the Second World War, a grim political prospect even for a government with so large a majority.

Treasury calculations were that, if aid was refused and the likely import surplus over the financial year 1948/9 financed out of the reserves, there would still be reserves of about £270 million at the end of the year. This would be less than half the level they had fallen to during the convertibility crisis in August 1947. The Treasury view was that the lowest level of safety was £500 million. Preventing the reserves falling below that level and doing without dollar aid was possible, but only by the most drastic import restrictions. These would mean no more imports of food and tobacco from the dollar zone, except for Canadian wheat, a sharp reduction in oil imports and a general cut of 12 per cent in the level of raw material imports. This would in turn mean a reduction in the basic rations of tea, sugar, butter, bacon and cheese and a level of calorific intake for the population about 10 per cent below the average of the pre-war period. There would have to be further widespread restrictions on consumer goods and there would be as many as one and a half million unemployed. The Chancellor reported to the cabinet:

> These readjustments to the balance of payments would administer a number of violent shocks to the home economy at a number of separate points. The results to the structure of output, exports, investments, consumption and employment are extremely difficult to assess. We should be faced with an abrupt transition from a partially suppressed inflation to something not unlike a slump.[16]

Two days after hearing that forecast the cabinet decided to sign the Marshall Aid agreement.

The issue is not resolved by estimating the value of ERP-financed imports as a proportion of total imports. It is necessary to ask what the commodities imported under ERP were, for they might well have had a greater importance to the importing economy than their overall statistical contribution to total imports might suggest. Over the programme as a whole almost a third of ERP imports consisted of agricultural products which, except in the case of Denmark, were made up almost entirely of food. Of the raw material imports one, cotton, was responsible for 14 per cent of the value of all shipments. Nevertheless it also appears that capital goods continued to play an unusually important role in imports from the United States. There were exceptions to this. One was those countries where food was in shortest supply. Austria and Germany (table 3). The other was the United Kingdom and Ireland. In the United Kingdom food imports were 40 per cent of all imports, and machinery, steel and vehicle imports in general a very small proportion of the total. So large a proportion of total ERP-financed imports went to Britain, however (about 23 per cent), that the British propensity to import food and raw materials causes the general breakdown of ERP-financed imports in table 3 to be seriously misleading, especially when it is also taken into account that ERP-financed shipments to Germany were essentially for relief. As table 4 shows, imports of machinery, vehicles, iron and steel, and iron and steel products were more than 20 per cent of all Marshall Aid imports in Belgium, France, Italy, the Netherlands, Norway, Portugal and Sweden.[17] If these proportions are compared to the proportion of the same commodities in all imports (table 5), it can be seen that over Western Europe as a whole the Marshall Plan continued to finance that increase in capital goods im-

Table 3. Value and composition of all ERP-financed shipments 3 April 1948 to 31 December 1951 (million dollars)

	Total value	% of total
Food, feed, fertilizer	3,209.5	32.1
Fuel	1,552.4	15.5
Cotton	1,397.8	14.0
Other raw materials and semi-finished products	1,883.1	18.8
Tobacco	444.5	4.4
Machinery and vehicles	1,428.1	14.3
Other	88.9	.9
Total	10,004.3	

Source: US, *Statistical Abstract of the United States, 1952,* pp. 836–7.

ports from the United States which had provoked the payments crisis of 1947, and so enabled Western European countries to continue those policies while preserving some elements of a co-operative international payments system.

The clearest demonstration of this is the case of France, the second biggest importer of Marshall Aid commodities, where (table 5) the proportion of these commodities represented by foodstuffs was very much lower than the proportion of food in all imports. Conversely the proportion of machinery and vehicles in Marshall Aid imports was very much higher than in all imports; it accounted for 38.8 per cent of Marshall Aid imports in 1950 but only 10.5 per cent of imports in general. By the time Marshall Aid began to flow the proportion of state investment specifically directed towards the tasks identified in the Monnet Plan as 'equipment and modernization' was higher than that for repair of war damage and the restoration of public services, in 1949 more than a half of total state investment.[18] Marshall Aid was of very much greater significance in maintaining the flow of capital goods imports which sustained the Modernization Plan than it was as a contribution to French imports in general.

Although this pattern is seen most strikingly in the case of France table 5 also indicates that in all the countries which would come into consideration in this respect, except Norway, machinery and vehicles were a much higher proportion of ERP-financed imports than they were of all imports. In a general sense it is true that the United Kingdom used its Marshall Aid for food imports, these being much the largest single category of ERP-financed imports. But even in Britain they were

Table 4. Imports of machinery, vehicles, iron and steel, and iron and steel products* as a proportion (%) of all ERP-financed shipments

Austria	11.3
Belgium/Luxembourg	36.8
Denmark	19.8
France	23.4
Iceland	41.8
Ireland	8.9
Italy	20.6
Netherlands	24.2
Norway	25.7
Portugal	22.2
Sweden	25.5
United Kingdom	8.8
West Germany	3.3

Source: US, *Statistical Abstract of the United States, 1952*, pp. 836–7.
*Includes ferro-alloys.

a significantly smaller proportion of Marshall Aid imports than of all imports, whereas a much greater proportion of Marshall Aid imports than of all imports consisted of machinery and vehicles. Furthermore table 5 also shows a decisive swing in Western Europe from importing food with Marshall Aid in 1949 to importing capital goods in 1950. Italy, for example, received 6.9 per cent of its ERP shipments as machinery and vehicles in 1949 and almost 30 percent in 1950. Both there and in Austria, as the worst of the food shortages were relieved, the dollars were used, as they were already being used elsewhere in Western Europe, to sustain the capital goods imports from the United States on which the high levels of domestic capital formation depended.

But, accepting that once ERP imports are disaggregated in this way, their importance to the reconstruction of Western European economies appears much greater than when they are grossed as a part of all imports, was the process of reconstruction actually dependent on them? A definitive answer to this question is impossible without a series of detailed national studies of how gold and dollars were allocated to imports from hard currency areas. When the ECA authorized imports under the ERP it effectively extended the quantity of dollars which could be nationally allocated, by whatever system prevailed, for imports from the dollar zone. Had no ERP dollars been available for imports 1949 and 1950, what would have been the consequence?

Food was the principal category of all imports from the United States

Table 5. Composition of shipments under the European Recovery Programme compared to all imports, 1949 and 1950

	As a % of 1949 ERP shipments	As a % of all 1949 imports	As a % of 1950 ERP shipments	As a % of all 1950 imports
Austria				
Food	77.7	26.2	42.9	21.9
Coal and related fuels	4.5	14.4	0	15.6
Machinery and vehicles	11.9	6.8	21.0	10.5
Denmark				
Food	16.7	8.6	13.0	8.5
Coal and related fuels	0.3	10.1	0	10.0
Machinery and vehicles	21.9	12.9	20.1	11.2
France				
Food	12.5	24.0	0.3	24.6
Coal and related fuels	8.8	10.1	0.4	5.0
Machinery and vehicles	21.1	9.1	38.8	10.5
Italy				
Food	35.2	27.0	8.8	17.4
Coal and related fuels	10.5	11.5	0.1	8.8
Machinery and vehicles	6.9	1.1	29.7	3.1
Netherlands				
Food	23.1	15.2	36.6	15.8
Coal and related fuels	1.8	3.6	0.4	3.0
Machinery and vehicles	22.5	11.5	26.8	9.3
Norway				
Food	18.8	10.3	48.2	13.1
Coal and related fuels	0	3.9	0	3.8
Machinery and vehicles	6.0	36.4	22.0	33.1

Table 5. (Continued)

	As a % of 1949 ERP shipments	As a % of all 1949 imports	As a % of 1950 ERP shipments	As a % of all 1950 imports
United Kingdom				
Food	32.5	42.7	34.0	37.9
Machinery and vehicles	8.3	0.4	12.2	0.3
West Germany				
Food	48.6	43.6	34.5	40.1
Machinery and vehicles	3.5	1.6	4.2	2.6

Source: UN, *Yearbook of International Trade Statistics;* US, *Statistical Abstract of the United States, 1950, 1951.*

for Western Europe as a whole under Marshall Aid. Let us assume as a working hypothesis that if there had been no ERP European importers would have still had enough hard currency to obtain half the value of the food imports from the dollar zone which they actually obtained in 1949 as Marshall Aid shipments. They would then, had they wished as a group to maintain the same overall level of food imports, have had to obtain from the non-dollar zone a value of imports 12 per cent greater than their actual non-dollar zone food imports in that year. The assumption in this hypothesis is that the food supply would have been equitably distributed between the Western European nations. It would have been extremely difficult to have achieved such an increase in non-dollar zone food exports in 1949, it may have been difficult to pay for them, and, even had it been achieved it would have meant major shifts in the pattern of food consumption in Western Europe.

But would it have been necessary to maintain the same overall level of food imports had there been no Marshall Aid? The increase in the estimated calorific value of daily *per capita* food consumption in Western Europe between crop year 1946/7 and crop year 1948/9 was 20.5 per cent.[19] Assuming the calorific value of equal proportions of imports, however constituted, to be equal, the reduction in calorific intake in 1949 caused by forfeiting half of the food imports obtained through ERP would have been roughly 10 per cent. The population would therefore still have been 10 per cent better fed in 1949 than in 1947. By keeping the level of food supply to the Western European population at the level of calorific intake of 1947 there would theoretically have been no need to expend Marshall Aid or other dollars on food imports.

Would European countries in that case have had enough dollars to maintain the same level of capital goods imports from the United States as they maintained under the ERP? If we look at the value of capital goods imports under ERP authorizations in the six leading Western European importers of capital goods[20] in 1949 we find that in four cases the value could have been covered by the value of exports to the United States and Canada in that year, but that in two others, France and the Netherlands, it could not have been. The shortfall in the case of France is especially notable. Capital goods imports into France under the ERP were more than twice the value of exports to the United States and Canada. In 1950 they could have been covered in five cases, although only very narrowly in the Italian case, and once again French imports could not have been covered. Had the six major Western European importers of capital goods had no dollars other than those earned by exports, only the two with the most ambitious reconstruction plans, France and the Netherlands, would have had to reduce capital goods imports from the dollar zone, providing all were prepared to maintain the same level of food consumption as in 1947.

This, however, is to make so low an estimate of the availability of dollars had there been no ERP aid as to be unrealistic. Let us therefore revert once more to the first working hypothesis, that had there been no Marshall Aid European countries would have been able to obtain only half the value of dollar imports that they actually did obtain under the ERP. Using this hypothesis shows how much more dependent Western Europe was on Marshall Aid for capital goods than for food. In the case of machinery and vehicles, confining ourselves again to the six leading importers, this would still have meant a fall in machinery and vehicle imports from the dollar zone in 1949 equivalent to a 34 per cent increase in the total of imports of those commodities from other sources in the same year. For 1950 the percentage increase in imports from other sources would have had to be 30 per cent. In this case, unlike the case of food, 'other sources' would have had to be the Western European countries themselves, so this would have meant in 1949 an increase of more than a third in Western European exports of machinery and vehicles. This was clearly not possible, especially as an attempt to achieve it would have increased the demand for other categories of imports, of which a large proportion were actually obtained under ERP financing. Precisely the same objection would apply to the alternative solution, an equivalent increase of domestic output of machinery and vehicles in each of the countries concerned.

But it is clear from the preceding calculations based purely on the capacity of dollar earnings to purchase the same imports of capital goods as those obtained under the ERP that the inability of Western European capital goods suppliers to increase their exports to western Europe by the requisite third would have penalized two countries,

France and the Netherlands. The question therefore is whether France and the Netherlands would have been able to maintain the same inputs of capital goods even under this more favourable hypothesis. The value of French and Dutch capital goods imports from the United States and Canada above the level of their exports to the same countries in 1949 was $104.1 million. To have obtained this value of capital goods imports in intra-Western European trade would still have required an increase of 11 per cent in the value of that trade in that year. It does not seem possible therefore that France and the Netherlands could have acquired the same level of capital goods either from increased domestic output or from shifts in the pattern of foreign trade. For them the absence of a European recovery programme would have altered the speed and rhythm of reconstruction. The mechanism by which it would have done so would have been by preventing them obtaining the level of capital goods necessary to sustain the French Modernization Plan and the Dutch Industrialization Plan.

If Western European countries, therefore, were to eat as well as they did in 1949 they would not have been able to maintain the same level of capital goods imports as they did, had there been no Marshall Aid. The rate of increase of output would have slowed down and so would the rate of increase of productivity. This in turn might have slowed the growth in real income, and the rhythm of expanding output, increasing productivity and increasing incomes which spanned the transition from reconstruction to the consumer boom of the 1950s might not have been high enough to effect the transition. On the other hand, had they eaten at the level of 1947 they could all have avoided these consequences except France and the Netherlands. Norway could have got by, but of the three countries with the most ambitious domestic plans for reconstruction two would not have been able to achieve them at the rate they did without Marshall Aid. This conclusion rests on a number of hypotheses which may be unacceptable. But even to those who find them so it has a heuristic value, it illustrates once more that Marshall Aid was designed to permit domestic economic policies far more ambitious than those of the inter-war period to continue in Western Europe.

Because capital formation was so high after 1947, even if we assume that the whole of Marshall Aid went into capital formation it would represent in most countries only a small part of the total. In 1949 it would have theoretically amounted to about a third of gross domestic capital formation in Italy, about a fifth in West Germany, and a little more than a tenth in the United Kingdom and France.[21] What proportion of Marshall Aid funds did actually contribute to capital formation cannot be determined, because all of them could theoretically have had the effect, no matter how it was deployed within the economy, of releasing other funds for investment.

Nevertheless there was one device of particular relevance incorporated into the programme, the counterpart funds. The equivalent in national currency of the value of imports financed under ERP grants was deposited in special accounts in the importing country. The use of these funds was dependent on ECA approval, but, providing governments were prepared to get American approval for each project, counterpart funds could be used to supplement domestic sources of capital. The minimum contribution to gross domestic capital formation of ERP funds could thus be set as the proportion used to finance imports of capital goods plus the total of counterpart funds used for investment purposes. Above that it is only possible to guess at the other parameter by, for example, in the case of the United Kingdom assuming what contribution the use of dollar aid to reduce government debt made to the availability of funds for internal investment. Wherever the second parameter is set, the overall proportional contribution of Marshall Aid to capital formation outside Italy and West Germany must have been small.

In fact only France, Germany and Italy used their counterpart funds almost exclusively for investment purposes. Austria utilized about half of its counterpart in this way, the Netherlands 38 per cent and Denmark 17 per cent. Elsewhere it was either left unused or used for other purposes of which the main one was debt retirement. The United Kingdom and Norway chose to utilize the whole of their counterpart for debt retirement. Neither, perhaps, was prepared to accept any degree of American responsibility in the selection of investment projects, or they conceived it as an anti-inflationary device.

But this judgement is to assume a state of perfection in national capital markets which was far from being the case after 1945. If we look at the extreme example of this, the German Federal Republic, self-finance (the reinvestment of profits) and short-term bank credits were the sources of three-quarters of all investment from June 1948 to 1949, of 65 per cent in the second half of 1949 and 53 per cent in 1950. The capital market and government together were responsible in the first year after the currency reform in June 1948 for only 21 per cent of investment and even in 1950 for only 34 per cent.[22] Over the period 1948–52 in the Netherlands self-finance accounted for two-thirds of total investment.[23] In the first place this meant that the counterpart funds available for investment were, in one year, 1950, as much as a third of the total of long-term investment finance available in Germany from government sources, although after that their significance dropped away. More importantly, in the second place, it meant that Marshall Aid was directly of much more value to certain basic industries which were unable to attract private long-term capital investment for reconstruction or to finance their own investment. This was especially the case in infrastructural development, such as electricity, gas and transport, in coal-mining and in the steel industry.

The area of investment which attracted the largest sum in direct counterpart fund investment in Western Europe was electricity, gas and power supply, followed by transport and communications, including shipping. Mining, however, principally coal-mining, received $449.9 million of counterpart fund investment over the whole ERP programme. The pattern of counterpart fund investment reflects the pattern of government investment before the Marshall Plan. It supported the last surge of government investment in immediate reconstruction tasks, rebuilding the railways and transport systems and repairing and modernizing the public utilities, and then moved on either to financing the expansion of capacity in what were called, in the terminology of the Monnet Plan, the 'basic' sectors, those which needed to expand before the rest of the economy could (as in France, Germany or Austria), a mixture of these and agriculture (as in Italy), or the agricultural sector itself (as in the Netherlands).[24]

Table 6. Investment of ERP counterpart funds by sector (million dollars)

Sector	Total*	Austria	France	Germany	Italy and Trieste	Nether- lands
Electricity, gas and power	956.0	50.6	724.5	166.6	0	0
Transport, communica- tions, shipping	781.3	96.9	281.3	56.1	269.9	13.7
Agriculture	623.9	44.1	203.9	70.5	99.5	138.9
Coal mining, mining and quarrying	452.4	17.3	340.2	82.4	0	0
Primary metals, chemi- cals, strategic materials	332.8	38.4	105.1	52.6	20.6	21.9
Machinery	164.2	9.4	10.4	61.0	83.2	0
Light industry	64.7	28.7	10.8	24.0	0	0
Petroleum and coal products	22.0	0	11.7	10.3	0	0
Technical assistance	20.3	0.5	0	4.6	5.6	0.1
Other and undistributed	452.1	14.9	157.4	101.3	113.1	5.9
Total	3869.7	300.8	1845.3	629.4	591.9	180.5

Source: W.A. Brown Jr and R. Opie, *American Foreign Assistance* (Washington DC, Brookings Institution, 1953), p. 237.
*Including Greece and Turkey.

Roughly half the total counterpart fund investment in Western Europe was in France. The deployment of these funds was the subject of a tense struggle within the French government. The private capital market was unable to respond to the demands of the Modernization Plan and the hold of the Planning Commissariat on public funds was very tenuous, even the publicly controlled banks were unwilling to provide investment finance to the basic sectors chosen by the Modernization Plan.[25] The creation of the Fonds de Modernisation et d'Equipement in January 1948 as a separate Treasury account for the Modernization Plan would not by itself have solved this problem had not the government allowed the counterpart funds to be part of this account and in so doing allowed that part to escape from the incessant, variable, short-term, political pressures, as well as the delays, of budgetary control by parliament. Not only therefore did the counterpart funds represent a greater proportion of the investment in the sectors singled out by the Modernization Plan than in the rest of the economy, but they also made the Modernization Plan politically easier to achieve provided the Planning Commissariat and the Ministry of Finance remained in agreement. The counterpart funds amounted to a third of the total investment undertaken by the Fonds de Modernisation et d'Equipement in 1948, a half in 1949 and 30 per cent in 1950.[26]

In the Federal Republic the counterpart was deployed through a special bank, the Kreditanstalt für Wiederaufbau, which had already been created to use aid for reconstruction in the Bizone. Its constitution, finally agreed in summer 1948 after much argument, only allowed it to supplement investment from other private banks. The Kreditanstalt could also use GARIOA funds and was linked by a Joint Secretariat to the Staatliche Erfassungsstelle für öffentliche Güter (StEG) which handled the proceeds from the sale of army surplus stores.[27] The investment projects which it undertook were selected by an inter-ministerial committee. The first of them were credits to the basic industries in the public sector which were governed by price controls and had little possibility of self-finance. By February, when the Allies agreed to its 'Sofortprogramm', a plan of public investment had emerged which, although on a much more modest scale, had some resemblances to the Monnet Plan in its priorities, the main differences being the inclusion of housing as one of the priority sectors and, for obvious reasons of political uncertainty, the omission of steel. The other sectors chosen were electricity, coal-mining, transport, 'other industries', projects in west Berlin, and agriculture.[28] These priorities did not greatly change as the ERP funds flowed in, except that specific allocations were made to smaller firms and the preponderance of energy and coal-mining grew, rather at the expense of other targets.

If a detailed breakdown of the investment of counterpart funds in the Federal Republic is made, the importance of investment in coal-mining appears yet more clearly. Over the Marshall Plan period as a whole, to the end of 1952, the electricity industry received DM967.3 million out of counterpart funds and coal-mining appears as the second most important investment target with DM581 million.[29] In the two years 1949 and 1950 ERP funds accounted for 43.5 per cent of the total investment in coal-mining, a far higher proportion than in any other sector. Although, for example, the electricity industry was the biggest recipient of counterpart funds, ERP funds over the same period represented only 29 per cent of the total investment in that sector. Beyond these two sectors the biggest proportional contribution was made to the iron and steel industry where counterpart funds represented 16 per cent of total investment over the years 1950 and 1951.[30]

This high proportion of counterpart fund investment in coal-mining must, furthermore, be seen in the context that Marshall Aid was not the most important source of American aid to the Federal Republic. From the start of 1948 to the end of 1951 ERP aid to the Federal Republic amounted to $1317 million, $1382 including drawing right gains; aid from other sources to about $1500 million. Of these the most important by far was the GARIOA fund whose deployment was linked through the inter-ministerial committee and the same liaison channel with the American government to the activities of the Kreditanstalt für Wiederaufbau. The renewed shortage of coal, coke and steel in the last two months of 1950 showed the deficiencies of self-finance and of the private capital market. The outcome, after a tense political struggle over the way to finance such a programme, was another special programme of investment for coal-mining, steel, electricity and gas.[31] This programme was run through a special account in the Industriekredit-bank, but the Kreditanstalt was again involved in all those areas where it was already providing finance.

Public enterprise and coal-mining in West Germany thus depended heavily on investment from ERP funds. That these sectors were a bottleneck to increasing production was amply demonstrated by the way the great surge of output in the German economy in 1950 produced energy blackouts and coal shortages in winter 1950/1 reminiscent of 1948. Yet it cannot be argued that American aid was indispensable to the breaking of this bottleneck, because there was always the possibility, even after the currency reform, of pursuing policies less favourable to self-finance and more favourable to public investment. What Marshall Aid did do, just as in France, was to permit the continuation of the existing economic policies, albeit in a more ironical way. It provided a cushion of funds for public investment whose deployment allowed the

Federal government to persist in fiscal policies and income distribution policies designed to put the utmost possible emphasis on private investment.

Investment of the counterpart of ERP aid was manifestly not as important to European reconstruction as the flow of imports. But the aid, just as in the case of imports, was of relatively greater importance to those sectors which bore the main weight of reconstruction in both France and Germany. This does not mean, however, that these were the sectors whose output increased the most even though there was a marked shift in the pattern of Western Europe's industrial output over the period 1945–51, compared to pre-war, in favour of capital goods and the infrastructural public service industries. In France and Germany Marshall Aid was used to circumvent the weaknesses of the private capital market and the difficulties posed by controls over government finance to help to break what governments perceived as bottlenecks in the recovery process. There are indications that policy was the same in Italy and Austria. In Austria, for example, there was a major shift in the allocation of counterpart funds from the transport sector to the basic industries at the end of 1949.[32] A similar shift can be observed in the general pattern of government investment for reconstruction throughout Western Europe at an earlier date. Counterpart funds were thus a useful, but by no means indispensable, aid to government recovery policies and one whose use, far from distorting those policies allowed them to be continued. This was as true for the planned economy of France as for the 'social market economy' in the Federal Republic. In either case Marshall Aid made easier policies which would otherwise have run into severe difficulties and had to be modified, it served to defend both governments, in spite of the differences between them from the standpoint of economic policy, against domestic political pressures.

The first obvious conclusion to draw is that it would be entirely wrong to consider that there was any equality in the effects of the ERP on the separate nation states. But that viewpoint was expressly rejected by the American administration which proceeded from the assumption that Western Europe's economic problem was common, and that therefore the entirely marginal impact of Marshall Aid on the Belgian or Danish economies was as important for Europe, and therefore for Belgium and Denmark, as the important role played by ERP in the development of the Austrian, Dutch or French economies in the same years. If we express the value of Marshall Aid as a financial transfer to the national product of the receiving countries it becomes clear that the current trend to play down its importance should not be taken too far. In the first year of its operation the ERP meant a large increase in national income for the majority of the recipients, especially for Austria and the Netherlands. Over the whole course of the ERP the principal gainers, by the same measurement, were the Netherlands, France, Italy and, although the calculation has not been made, presumably Austria. Marshall Aid permitted a level of imports from the United States of investment goods appreciably higher than could otherwise have been the case. If we ask whether the same level of imports could have been achieved without the existence of the ERP, we must conclude that in the case of two economies, France and the Netherlands, it could not. Whether the American administration was correct in choosing to judge the need for and success of the ERP in a global context, rather than by its purely national impact, depends on the extent to which the continued vigorous growth of the western European economies in this period would have been slowed down by a slower rate of growth of output in those two countries. Although the impact of Marshall Aid on levels of investment and capital formation in Western Europe cannot be finally measured there is no reason to suppose that it was of sufficient importance to modify these conclusions. It did, however, help the governments to widen bottlenecks in the recovery process, where this was dependent on public investment or might otherwise have suffered from the imperfections of post-war capital markets.

The purpose of Marshall Aid was, through furthering the process of economic recovery in Western Europe, to develop a bloc of states which would share similar political, social, economic and cultural values to those which the United States itself publicly valued and claimed to uphold. Any exact enquiry into what these values might be and into the degree of similarity that might have been acceptable, while it would provide ample scope for cynicism, would be beside the point, firstly, because for the strategic purpose the definition 'sufficiently similar to be an ally of the United States' was workable, and secondly, because the question of what values the ERP should propagate was answered as much by the fashions of the time in the United States as by deeper and longer-run traditions. Thus the ECA propagated energetically, and from 1950 by a special programme financed from ERP funds, the values of so-called 'free enterprise', of entrepreneurship, of efficiency, of technical expertise, and of competition. These were all brought together in the concept of productivity. Increasing the productivity of European labour and capital to the levels which the United States had attained in the Second World War could be presented as not merely economically desirable, in the sense that by increasing Europe's exports it would diminish the dollar gap, but also as politically neutral. It was of course no such thing, for it involved trying to impose a set of particular human and economic values on the societies in question. When parties of British industrialists were taken around marginally more productive American factories this was a useful and sensible technical exercise whose political and social implications were at a very low level. When the ECA subsidized the productivity train to tour southern Italy with a barrage of propaganda about the advantages of the American economic system, the political intent was overwhelming, even if the means of achieving it were rather ludicrous.

The intention was that values would follow aid, rather as in previous centuries trade had been thought to follow the flag, and that these values would deeply influence the political development of the European countries in a favourable direction. Improvements in productivity would bring a higher level of wealth and income, and thus weaken and eventually eliminate the social and political tensions which had been so obvious in 1946 and 1947 and on which communism in particular was thought to thrive. In so far as consistently high rates of growth of national product in Western European countries after the war did eventually reduce in most countries the tensions of political argument, or at least reduce those arguments to a narrower range for most participants, this idea proved to have a certain rough and ready force. The question of the way in which these higher rates of growth were attributable to improvements in productivity is a much more controversial one. The even more searching questions, whether such a process would permanently still the disputes over the grossly unequal distribution of the increasing wealth and how long high rates of growth of GNP in the western world could last, were not only scarcely heard but they were not to be loudly voiced for another twenty years. The set of political values which became associated with the concept of productivity received, therefore, a less questioning acceptance then than it would do now and could thus be taken up by a relatively wide range of political opinion. This was essential, for if productivity were the key to growth and growth the key to political stability, investment was the key to productivity (or so it was thought), and if investors were to feel sufficient confidence in the Western European future to invest, they must be faced with political systems sufficiently broadly based to guarantee the future security and value of their investments. Around the concepts of productivity and growth coagulated a possible political and economic programme for politicians of several different persuasions whose political aims and values coincided with those of the ECA. Marshall Aid became their support and through its technical operations the ECA was in fact pursuing complex political and social goals in European countries.

On the other hand the forces within those countries pursuing the same goals were usually much stronger and had much much effective weapons to hand than the ECA. The 'politics of productivity', to use Maier's phase,[33] were every bit as useful to European politicians hoping to back a central political position with a suitable economic programme which could be presented as quite neutral. One reason why the idea of European integration, for instance, had been taken up in the United States so avidly was because it seemed to fit so well into this set of values. If the argument were accepted that a larger market brought automatic gains in productivity, or indeed that Europe could not achieve these productivity gains without creating a larger integrated market, European integration appeared as no more than following through the inherent economic logic of Europe's economic development. But it was also thought of in exactly the same way by various groups of opinion in Western Europe, as indeed it still is, and they were eager to use American foreign economic policy as a lever to achieve their own ultimate objectives. To them it seemed at times that they were the just men long oppressed into the hands of whose deliverer God had put invincible might. In the event this proved not to be the case and the distance from the centres of power at which many of the most ardent European integrationists were held showed that the leverage which Marshall Aid gave to the United States in matters of grand policy was small unless it were coupled to genuinely powerful political forces in Europe.

About so complex and varied a set of politico-economic relationships it seems vain to generalize. Yet it can certainly be said that the idea that the United States sought no extra political or economic gain in return for Marshall Aid is nonsense, that the idea that the gains achieved were so large as to have shaped the politico-economic future of Western Europe is nonsense also, that the gains made by the United States can only be judged in relation to specific issues and specific countries, and that the limitations to the exercise of American power and influence through the ERP were subtle, complicated, but always present and often narrow. In the end it is, at least as far as Western Europe is concerned, for the story might be very different in Greece, those limitations that are the most striking aspect of the story. They emerge as the story is told.

Endnotes

1. The most typical of the genre is H. B. Price, *The Marshall Plan and Its Meaning* (Ithaca, 1955).

2. H. S. Ellis, *The Economics of Freedom* (New York, 1950) could serve as an example.

3. J. and G. Kolko, *The Limits of Power. The World and United States Foreign Policy 1945–54* (New York, 1972) has proved the most interesting and the most discussed.

4. 'At the vantage point of twenty years' distance it seems fair to say that the Marshall Plan was Europe's "great leap forward", . . . With investment aid, fertilizers, machines and machine-tools, productivity programmes and planned growth, it laid the foundations of later prosperity.' R. Mayne, *The Recovery of Europe* (London, 1970), p. 107.

5. C. Maier, 'The two postwar eras and the conditions for stability', *American Historical Review*, 96 (2), 1981; S. Schuker, *ibid.*

6. G. Patterson, *Survey of United States International Finance, 1949* (Princeton, 1950), p. 65. Over the period 1906–13, when net foreign investment averaged about 8.5 percent of GNP, it would have amounted to a total sufficient to finance 43.4 percent of Britain's total export trade. (Data on net foreign investment from C. Feinstein, *National Income, Expenditure and Output of the United Kingdom 1855–1965* (Cambridge, 1972).)

7. US, *Statistical Abstract of the United States, 1952*, pp. 830ff.

8. Gross exports were 5.3 percent of GNP in 1948.

9. For a fuller description see pp. 271–8.

10. 'The ECA, in its general financial policy, introduced strict bankers' criteria of balanced budgets, stable currencies, high profits to entice investment, and low wages to discourage consumption.' J. and G. Kolko, *Limits of Power*, p. 429.

11. OEEC *Interim Report on the European Recovery Programme* (Paris, December 1948), vol. 1.

12. US, Dept. of Commerce, *Statistical Abstract of the United States, 1950*, p. 836.

13. J. Gimbel, *The Origins of the Marshall Plan* (New York, 1955).

14. S. E. Harris, *The European Recovery Program* (Cambridge, Mass., 1948), p. 169.

15. F. M. B. Lynch, 'The political and economic reconstruction of France 1944–1947: in the international context' (PhD thesis, University of Manchester, 1981), pp. 276 ff.

16. CAB 129/28, CP (48) 161, Economic consequences of receiving no European recovery aid, 23 June 1948.

17. Only in the case of Belgium/Luxembourg were cars a significant item in vehicle imports from the United States. Otherwise it refers to lorries, buses and other items of public transport equipment.

18. INSEE, *Mouvement économique en France de 1944 à 1957* (Paris, 1958), p. 90.

19. UNRRA, Operational Analysis Paper No. 41, April 1947; UN, FAO, *Yearbook of Food and Agricultural Statistics, Production*, 1952, p. 175.

20. Belgium/Luxembourg, France, Italy, the Netherlands, the United Kingdom, and West Germany.

21. Maier, 'The two postwar eras'.

22. Bundesverband der Deutschen Industrie, *Geschäftsbericht 1950* (Cologne, 1951).

23. W. Brakel, *De Industrialisatie in Nederland gedurende de periode der Marshall-Hulp* (Leiden, 1954), p. 92.

24. The Monnet Plan had singled out agriculture as a 'basic' sector for investment.

25. R. F. Kuisel, *Capitalism and the State in Modern France* (Cambridge, 1981), p. 240. The Crédit Lyonnais refused in 1948 to finance one of the two major investment projects in the steel industry, the continuous strip mill at Sérémange.

26. Commissariat au Plan, *Rapport Annuel, 1952* (Paris, 1953), pp. 78, 84.

27. K. Magnus, *Eine Million Tonnen Kriegsmaterial für den Frieden. Die Geschichte der StEG* (Munich, 1954).

28. M. Pohl, *Wiederaufbau, Kunst und Technik der Finanzierung 1947–1953. Die ersten Jahre der Kreditanstalt für Wiederaufbau* (Frankfurt-a-M, 1973), pp. 48ff.

29. There are more detailed quantitative breakdowns in W. W. Kretzschmar, *Auslandshilfe als Mittel der Aussenwirtschafts- und Aussenpolitik* (Munich, 1964).

30. E. Baumgart, *Investition und ERP-Finanzierung* (DIW Sonderhefte, N.F. 56, Berlin, 1961), p. 122ff.

31. H. R. Adamsen, *Investitionshilfe für die Ruhr. Wiederaufbau, Verbände und Soziale Marktwirtschaft 1948–1952* (Wuppertal, 1981).

32. Austria, Bundeskanzleramt, Sektion für wirtschaftliche Koordination, *Zehn Jahre ERP in Österreich 1948/58, Wirtschaftshilfe im Dienste der Völkerverständigung* (Vienna, 1959), pp. 72/3.

33. C. Maier, 'The politics of productivity: foundations of American international economic policy after World War II', in P. Katzenstein (ed.) *Between Power and Plenty: The Foreign Economic Policies of Advanced Industrial States* (Madison, 1978).

10

Lutz Niethammer

Structural Reform and a Compact for Growth: Conditions for a United Labor Union Movement in Western Europe after the Collapse of Fascism

Most studies of Cold War politics focus on nation-states, but in the following essay Professor Niethammer, Director of the Institute for Cultural Sciences in Essen, analyzes comparatively the labor movement after World War II. Organized labor had been a major victim of fascism and German occupation: its cadres smashed, its leaders killed, imprisoned, or driven into exile or underground. With the liberation of Italy and France in 1944 and the defeat of Germany in 1945, labor leaders looked toward reconstruction of their prefascist unions. Since they felt that their earlier divisions between communists, socialists, and Christian trade unionists had prevented labor from organizing effective resistance to fascist trends, there was a strong pressure for trade-union unity. Such unity, however, proved precarious, and by 1947–48, the Western European labor movements had fractured once again.

Niethammer examines this brief period of unity and the conditions that enabled it to function. The unified labor movements pressed for nationalization, welfare measures, and sometimes worker control of the plants. But they could not survive earlier bitter differences and the pressures of the Cold War. As the Soviet-American split overshadowed Europe—as the East European regimes were molded into satellite states and the communists were maneuvered out of the party coalitions in the West, as too the United States announced the Marshall Plan and the Soviet Union decided it could not participate—the labor movement was caught in the cross fire. It proved impossible for communists and the non-communist components to work together; indeed American labor observers, such as the AFL and reluctantly the CIO, actively urged the non-communists to secede and form their own unions. In Italy and France, the communists retained control of the federations in being, for they had gained strength and mass support during the resistance to fascism. In Germany because of the East-West split, communism remained dominant in the Soviet zone. Whatever adherents communism enjoyed in the western zones were rapidly thrust to the margin of politics. In all of Europe the schism became a major feature of the sociopolitical polarization that marked Cold War public life. While partially bridged over since the late 1960s, the split still effectively divides the West European labor movements.

Professor Niethammer's essay is written from a perspective on the Left that is critical of both the American and communist roles. My own feeling is that the euphemistic slogans of the Left (which often sought to monopolize such terms as "antifascist" or "democratic" for procommunists) are sometimes pressed into service too uncritically, whereas the rhetoric of liberalism is fully unmasked. Perhaps, too, the comparability of British developments with those on the Continent is overdrawn. Nonetheless, this is a highly sophisticated review of the massive literature on the unions, and the author valuably brings out all the inherent difficulties that stood in the way of radical renovation after the war.

A note on translation: Although it is cumbersome, I have used the term "political united union" for Niethammer's *politische Einheitsgewerkschaft*. By political, the author wished to stress that the post-1945 labor organizations were intended to work in tandem with the affiliated parties of the Left for political and social as well as narrowly economic reform. To this idea he contrasts the idea of the "industrial union," charged with the advocacy of economic interests alone (e.g., wages, perhaps plant organization). The term "industrial union" is not intended here to suggest the American contrast of "industrial" versus "craft" unions (e.g., CIO vs. AFL).

For this collection I have omitted a few pages at the beginning and end of the whole essay that address the Germans' own debate on the history and proper role for their own trade union federation (DGB). In these pages the author explains that his comparative approach is designed to rescue the history of the German union federation from too one-sided an analysis in terms of its national background alone; and in his conclusion he assesses both the achievements and the limits of the

DGB. Footnotes have been made consistent with the text selections, which has entailed some rearrangement. When Niethammer has used French or English-language works in German translation, I have kept his citation for the sake of simplicity. Miss Rebecca Boehling lent some assistance with the translation. The author has made a few small revisions for this version of his article.

The essay has been translated and reprinted with the permission of the author and the publisher, Bund-Verlag of Cologne, from a collection of essays edited by Heinz Oscar Vetter to commemorate the post-1945 German labor leader, Hans Böckler: *Vom Sozialistengesetz zur Mitbestimmung. Zum 100. Geburtstag von Hans Böckler* [From the Law suppressing the Social Democratic Party (1878) to Co-Determination (1950 and after). For the 100th Birthday of Hans Böckler], Cologne, 1975. Professor Niethammer is also the author of, among other works, *Entnazifierung in Bayern. Säuberung und Rehabilitation unter amerikanischer Besatzung* [Denazification in Bavaria: Purge and Rehabilitation under American Occupation], Frankfurt/Main, S. Fischer, 1972. With Ulrich Borsdorf and Peter Brandt he has coedited *Arbeiterinitiative 1945. Antifaschistische Ausschüsse und Reorganisation der Arbeiterbewegung in Deutschland* [Worker Initiatives 1945: Antifascist Committees and the Reorganization of the Labor Movement in Germany] (Wuppertal: 1976).

Typology of the Political United Labor Union

The first phase of the international history of the trade unions in the postwar era was characterized by the formation and the collapse of the World Federation of Trade Unions (WFTU).[1] This phase lasted from 1945 to 1947, although in certain countries forerunners of the united union emerged as early as 1943; and later the international schism that resulted from the collapse of the movement went on into 1948–49. The WFTU phase was dominated by the effort to form the most united organization possible, or at least an operational alliance of unions on the national and international level. The attempt sought also to go beyond the various party affiliations of the individual unions; leaders wanted the unions to attain a pivotal position within society as a whole. This task required participation in the antifascist purges. It also meant helping to start up and to increase production so as to overcome the postwar economic crisis by means of rapid growth. It meant institutionalizing a working-class role in economic management by means of state planning and control of monopolies—e.g., by nationalizing heavy industries and establishing factory councils or other forms of worker participation in individual firms or at the industry-wide level. As the concept of a united labor union was worked out, each country's particular background and conditions led to different organizational forms. But the concentration of craft unions into industrial federations and their political consolidation as forms of pressure groups were un- mistakable everywhere.

The political core of the united trade unions in the WFTU phase consisted of the effort to form to the greatest degree possible a mass union movement by integrating the prewar unions with the commu- nists, who had greatly expanded in the European resistance against German fascism. In the former fascist countries, especially, where independent unions had been totally shattered and replaced by corpo- rative organs designed to integrate workers and employers, the emerg- ing Christian labor unions, which had also failed to survive as an independent movement, could be worked into a united organization. This new unity was made possible essentially because ever since Stalin had adopted a policy of seeking allies [against Hitler], the communists had accepted a reformist program. This reformist platform included different mixes for each country of partial nationalization, workers' participation, and economic planning. But it remained generally com- patible with the concept of "Economic Democracy" that had been advanced by the German Social Democratic trade unions in 1928.* At the same time, giving the unions a broader political assignment—which all the differing labor groups agreed upon as a means of reconstruction and antifascist reform—also would allow more scope for the communist concept. They saw the union as an instrument for mobilizing and educating the proletarian masses, i.e., for extending the influence of the communist leadership. In tactical terms the united trade union enabled the communist cadres to apply the policy of a United Front "from above and from below" (i.e., at the union leadership and plant levels simultaneously]. This was attractive both for the communists in the West who wanted to anchor themselves in powerful positions in the state and economy and for the communists in the East who wanted to eliminate the organized opposition. Simultaneously it appealed to re- formist leaders. They wanted not only to strengthen the power of the labor movement by avoiding conflict within the proletariat, but also sought to protect themselves from the possibility that their earlier rivalry with the communists might resume. Renewed rivalry could assume threatening proportions, given the popularity of the Eastern Ally in the lands freed from German occupation or the strength of the communists in the national movement of liberation. The discrediting of

---

*Ed. note: Economic Democracy was a platform that called not for the abolition, but the progressive reform of capitalism—predominantly by increas- ing involvement of the unions in economic planning and control alongside managers in industry-wide councils.

the European Right along with the widely held view that socialism was the next item on the agenda of history and was necessary for reconstruction; the confidence in the durability of the coalition against Hitler; and the socialists' participation in almost all European governments—all produced that optimism with which the united trade union experiment was undertaken in the WFTU phase. The tradition of Economic Democracy thus became the most suitable compromise platform for the united trade union. For the socialists its continuity with prewar *ideology* prevented dwelling on the [ineffective] prewar *practice* of the reformist unions. For the communists, as a partial objective it was compatible with the "antifascist-democratic" transitional strategy of Stalinism. At the same time both partners thought they could rely on the practical efficacy of their own party organizations to hold their own.

Economic Conditions

The goals of Economic Democracy were appropriate ones not only in view of the paralysis of the European economies, but also as surrogate objectives for the trade unions. For in this period of early social reconstruction, the rapid progress made in organizing the unions contrasted with the restricted role that the unions could play as participants in the struggle over income distribution. In view of this discrepancy the great influx of members into the unions in all the postwar European countries requires explanation; previous research has considered it insufficiently. It obviously drew most generally upon the spontaneous loyalty of the workers to their own organizations—those most identified with the working-class—which fascist and fascist-occupied regimes had deprived of rights. At the same time the unions represented the hope for some sort of socialist alternative for the future. First, however, they had to face more concrete problems.

All the European economic systems were afflicted by negative growth on account of the war:[3] disproportionally developed productive capacities, massive destruction of currencies and capital, plundering, death, the deportation or drafting of a large part of the labor force, collapse of the infrastructure, and extreme limits on international exchange. The postliberation economies were in acute crisis. They required extensive reconversion, and in heavily destroyed areas above all, reconstruction of the infrastructure (e.g., transportation facilities and public utilities). Despite the great losses of human life from war and terror, the Continent faced a growing surplus of labor—some of it overqualified. With few plants functioning, the economies had to absorb expellees, displaced persons, forced labor, and prisoners of war. The need for goods of all sorts vastly exceeded the productive capacity of the system. Thus the crisis had to be overcome by comprehensive reconstruction and by increasing productive capacity (with special urgency in heavy industry and mining, coal mining above all), if sufficient jobs were to be created and the most elementary needs of the population satisfied. In contrast to cyclical economic crises, the problem did not lie in underconsumption or overproduction—except perhaps for armaments, as was the case in part for Germany and the United States—but rather in enlarging and restructuring the productive apparatus. If the unions saw themselves not merely as spokesmen for one of the groups in the productive process, but as advocates of the laboring (or jobseeking) masses, then in order to create jobs and accelerate the flow of goods they had to concentrate their entire energies in the crisis on promoting growth—on increasing production, ensuring labor discipline, avoiding strikes, influencing systematic control of the productive and distributive apparatus. At the same time they had to watch out that reconversion was not carried out at the expense of the workers by mass layoffs in armaments factories, as in the United States and, at first, in Germany. To get production going once again and to increase it, they had to reabsorb all the professions that were indispensable, at least for the time being, to the economic system, especially technically skilled lower-level managers, engineering personnel, and independent small businessmen. These tasks represented, so to speak, an objective economic necessity even though they deviated from the traditional union struggle to reduce the exploitation of labor. And it was precisely these tasks that the united labor unions—including the cadres from each political party—carried out in all European countries, East and West, between 1944 and 1947. Their function of disciplining the labor force for the sake of the reconstruction of society as a whole made them so indispensable that they could demand a lot, especially in the way of structural reforms, from national leaders and from other social groups.

Alternatives?

Was there a basic alternative? In order to justify the fact that at the end of the war their party and union leaders did not press for an immediate transition to socialism (except in prevailingly agricultural Yugoslavia), communist literature has often argued that the workers' class consciousness had been overwhelmed by fascism and apparently even by the antifascist struggle.[4] But this argument obscures the real reasons. An immediate transition to socialism would have made the economic difficulties sketched above even more acute by setting additional impediments to production: lack of experts, losses of working time, bourgeois sabotage, further crippling of the infrastructure. Just to satisfy the most immediate needs of the working masses forced renunciation of an early revolution. Secondly, Western Europe was filled with American troops instructed to intervene in case of "disease and unrest." Revolution would thus have meant further war, especially if the Soviet Union, herself afflicted by the same acute shortages, had been forced to intervene in so completely uncertain a situation. But since in view of her own crisis she was unwilling to be dragged into any such adventure, she tolerated no such enterprises in her own sphere of influence and discouraged equivalent Communist Party initiatives in western and southern Europe. She favored instead a step-by-step policy, fitted to each country and permitting delay and halts.[5] But even leaving aside the military stabilization of the existing systems by the Americans, it is difficult to ascribe the failure of revolution in a highly industrialized system undergoing wartime collapse solely to a lack of will. To be sure there was a potential force of revolutionary activists, but they were fragmented into regional partisan bands and local committees and were politically uncoordinated. Granted that from the economic viewpoint most European countries still had a large enough stock of capital and a sufficiently skilled labor force to assure a high rate of growth during the reconstruction period, even after socialization of the means of production. The crisis of transition [to socialism] would still have entailed too high a cost. It might have caused food supplies to collapse completely and would not have been able to raise the level of production quickly. Even a revolution needs supplies if it is not to sacrifice its goals out of hunger and terror.

The other alternative, that of immediately liberalizing [i.e., deregulating] the capitalist system by ending the planning apparatus of the war economies can be even more quickly dismissed. This would have shoved the costs of the crisis exclusively onto the shoulders of the workers. Massive state intervention would then have been needed to recover from the postwar economic collapse. In turn it would have meant backing up economic deregulation with a right-wing political dictatorship for which no basis existed in the liberated countries. The workers' movements would have reacted with the support of armed partisans. In no way could this alternative have provided a suitable union strategy.

Thus the question remains: what concrete possibilities remained in the concept of Economic Democracy (to use this as a shorthand for the program of reconstruction); above all, were there any outcomes likely other than failure? To determine any such possibilities more precisely, several variables must be introduced and the constellation of national factors in the most important countries must be compared.

A United Trade Union and Limited Structural Reform: Italy. Italian conditions are especially useful to point up the special development of the trade unions in occupied Germany. Certainly Italy had undertaken an opportunistic switch to the Allied side in 1943–44, as one can see from the actions of the Badoglio government [Marshall Badoglio, royal appointee to succeed Mussolini in July 1943] and the country's elite. However, months before the Allied landing in Sicily, the Italian working class had demonstrated its own independent antifascist strength by means of largely spontaneous strikes in the industrial centers of the North. Such political and economic mass strikes were applied repeatedly and with increasingly organization over the next two years against the German occupiers in Northern Italy. They provided an essential backbone for building an armed partisan resistance. They led in the final stage of the war not only to local uprisings and efforts at liberation in the cities and the so-called partisan republics, but also to establishment of worker power in many factories through committees of liberation and agitation. While this struggle resembled that of other liberation movements fighting for national and social objectives in German-occupied Europe, Italy was distinguished by the fact that autonomous mass action arose under conditions of a homegrown fascist regime during the war.[6]

Those Italian experiences most comparable to Germany's, however (at least before the Germans occupied northern Italy), did not so much involve the independent activity of the working class as the political and trade-union organizations. Even the transitional regime of Marshal Badoglio can be compared with the conservative resistance of the 20th of July 1944 [the German conspiracy against Hitler]. As in Germany, the organized resistance of the unions and parties—in contrast to the spontaneous mass action in the final phase of the war—remained weak, isolated, and ineffective. The collapse of the regime led, however, to a rapid reconstruction of the prefascist organizational leadership as major party and union functionaries returned from exile or "inner emigration." As German resistance leaders also planned to proceed, union reorganization under Badoglio began with the assignment of top labor union officials from different parties as commissioners to high positions in the fascist corporative organizations. As in the case of the German Labor Front the Italian corporative bodies were organized by industry. To be sure, the rank and file resisted making use of the fascist organizational forms. But the period between the dismissal of Mussolini and the German occupation [i.e., July 25 to September 8, 1943] proved too short to see how this emerging dispute over organization would turn out. Nevertheless, even in this brief interval working-class leaders did manage to reach an agreement with industrialists for the election of factory councils. This preempted wildcat strikes in the factories and was supposed to provide an enduring basis for worker representation in the plants. Even these early initiatives revealed how willing the union leadership was to cooperate with the industrialists, if thereby they could immediately secure an extensive trade-union-like organization with a monopoly on labor representation. The same interest marked the 1943–44 concepts of German resistance labor leaders, Leuschner and Tarnow, for a transformation of the German Labor Front into a broad union with compulsory membership.[7]

With the German occupation of Northern Italy and the flight of the Badoglio government from Rome to the Allied-occupied South [September 1943], conditions for rebuilding the unions were transformed. Plans for converting fascist corporativism from the top down into a united union had the ground cut from under them by both the politically inspired resistance units in the North and the Allied powers in the South, who demanded a reconstruction of free trade unions.[8] As a consequence, a dualist system of political and economic working-class organization emerged in Italy. It could be roughly described as a relatively autonomous trade-union structure, organized to exert power at the national level in the South and on the factory level in the North. After liberation it was to prove a national two-tier system of long-term importance. The authority of the trade-union leadership derived from their political role in the antifascist parties; this was quite different from the Western zones of Germany and most comparable to the [Communist] Free German Union Federation [FDGB] in the Soviet zone of occupation. In the South of Italy politically oriented unions were the first to form—one a combined socialist-communist federation, one nonpartisan, and one Catholic. After negotiations between the union representatives of the national party executives, these were consolidated by the Pact of Rome on June 3, 1944, into a united union, the General Italian Confederation of Labor (CGIL). The CGIL aimed at a combined horizontal and vertical structure, whose regional and local components would have the power to overcome opposition from the industrialists' associations—not least because the proportional representation agreed to for local and regional elections would assure the parallel strength of the working-class political parties. In any case, the autonomous local and regional groups who held power in the North during the liberation might be expected to exert considerable influence. As General Secretaries of the united union, a socialist, a communist, and a Catholic each shared equal prerogatives. During the following years, however, the communist element rose to clear predominance because of the contingencies of personnel at the top and the Party's skillful organizational politics.[9]

These successes for communist organizational politics in the CGIL proved of decisive importance for political and economic reconstruction once they were extended to the liberated North. In an extremely flexible policy—Togliatti even entered the Soviet-recognized Badoglio government—the communists set the unions on a firm "antifascist-democratic" course. This included supporting an all-party government to establish a parliamentary republic as well as ideological and personnel purges. It also involved helping to advance economic reconversion and higher production by cooperation with management, by promotion of labor discipline, and by wage restraint. In working out the constitution, extensive planning powers were ceded to the state and apparently made politically secure by virtue of the workers' parties' role in the government. At the same time, provision was made for future enlargement of the nationalized sector of banks, energy concerns, and transformation industries, which Mussolini had already initiated. With its takeover of many state- and local-government positions, the working-class movement appeared to have become an integral part of the system. With the establishment of Chambers of Labor and the formation of joint labor-management committees to oversee many northern industries, the working class won the capacity for codetermination of economic and social issues. These committees had generally arisen during the struggle for liberation and represented the interest that managers as well as plant workers had in protecting industrial plants against destruction by the Germans. In view of the fact that the fascist regime had already greatly expanded the public sector of the economy, this structure of working-class achievements added up to what the program of Economic Democracy envisaged, even if the Italian reforms rested more on *de facto* victories than on statutory enactments. The communist leadership supported the constitution, participated in the cabinets, and despite the shift to the right in 1947 that led to its own dismissal, still sought to return to the government. The PCI could rightfully take pride in its role in sharply curbing national strikes or in limiting them to short, local conflicts.[10]

In fact, this policy failed on all levels. As was the case in Germany, contemporaries sharply overestimated the destruction of Italian productive capacity [and therefore of capitalist vitality]. Once the continuity of private property was recognized in principle, the position of the bourgeoisie grew stronger and stronger. The real problem lay [not in destruction], but in acute aggravation of Italy's chronic underemployment, which decisively weakened the economic position of the working class. Against this background, the division of functions in the government also played a role. Socialists and communists generally took over the administrative apparatus for labor and social welfare, but they left decisive positions over economic and financial policy to the bourgeois parties, in part because they just lacked ideas and experts. These posts were largely taken over by a group of old-laissez-faire economists who effectively intervened with measures to stabilize the middle classes and to continue deregulation of the economic system. At the same time, they used the new planning machinery only to get out of the postwar crisis, and by fiscal measures (lowering progressive taxation, deflating without redistributing the resulting losses or without protecting jobs) made capital accumulation easier.[11]

The CGIL leadership was not able to bridge the gap that separated it from its own rank and file. Because of its stress upon the needs of the economy as a whole and its agreement on reconstruction, the leadership exerted restraint on wages. It also inhibited any protests against the suppression of local resistance organizations by central administrative and parliamentary institutions. Besides the divergence in trade-union development between South and North during the dual occupation that was cited above, different political perspectives and economic conditions were also responsible for the cleavage between leaders and rank and file. Toward the end of the national liberation struggle, socialist and communist partisans made repeated attempts to push the local resistance movements in the direction of a socialist revolution. But the communists' "antifascist-democratic" strategy for Europe, which seemed so compelling while Anglo-American troops were in Italy, actually contributed to the leadership's undercutting all such revolutionary efforts. One example was the Sicilian city of Ragusa, where an attempted communist revolt was suppressed with the approval of the national Party leadership.

During the years 1945–46, the rank and file staunchly worked to preserve the organs created in the liberation struggle, while the strengthened business community sought to undermine the joint manager-employee committees and the state administration won out over the competing committees of liberation. The unions' policy of wage stabilization proved even more constraining since it meant that the postwar inflation and the reconversion of armaments plants cut into the workers' standard of living and reduced employment. While the national leadership of the working-class movement was concerned with avoiding strikes, the country was overtaken by waves of spontaneous or locally organized work stoppages, short in duration and in the nature of social protest.[12] The inability of the leadership to discipline the workers in general, or just to bring their own organizations into line, cost their policy of collaboration with the bourgeoisie its credibility. On the other hand, the very emphasis the labor leaders placed on this policy underlined their limited capacity to integrate their own workers. In turn, this made popular-front unity fragile indeed. After 1946 anticommunism would serve increasingly as a way to weaken the labor movement.

The pressure for a united front between communists and socialists had already led to social-democratic splinter movements and had raised tension within the united labor unions. Dismissal of the communists from the government and the absolute majority won by the Christian Democrats, who campaigned in 1948 as an anticommunist bulwark against the Communist-Socialist People's Bloc, also split the CGIL. In autumn 1948 a Catholic union emerged, friendly to the government and concerned only with issues of salaries and wages (the LCGIL); later on, segments of liberal and socialist unions followed. The communists' emphasis on the concept of a political union catalyzed the schism. In light of the economic difficulties and the Americans' requirement for a cooperative stance in return for credits, the other union groups backed away, to revert to representation just of their adherents' immediate economic interests. The economic power that the workers had enjoyed in 1945–46 had not been effectively used by the communist-dominated unions to shape durable institutions suitable for political and social struggle. Hence, while the masses might still respond in 1947–48 to the call for a political strike against the Marshall Plan and the assassination attempt against Togliatti, these actions only hastened the collapse of their organization, and they were soon exhausted.[13] Reconstruction of the liberal economic order by continuing low wages and underemployment (and also by the institution of a powerful police apparatus) had melted away the potential for an enduring struggle. Political protest and attainable economic demands increasingly diverged. With the re-establishment of an economic system in which emigration served as ersatz cure for the chronic unemployment that was starkly revealed once again, the united trade union lost its strategic position.

A Limited United Union and Structural Reform: France. The development of the united trade-union movement in France deviated from that in Italy—and from that in Germany—because of the essentially different historical conditions that shaped it. The continuity and autonomy of the French parties and unions was not wholly destroyed by a home-grown fascism, nor was their post-liberation course of development supervised at the outset by a British-American occupation. Both these factors exerted only an indirect influence. Nonetheless, there were many similarities with Italy, attributable above all to the parallel behavior of the communists.

In France, too, the communists were the driving force behind the unification of the trade unions and won a predominant role in the union organization by virtue of their tactical superiority. In addition, they were able to credit to their account a massive influx of members as a result of the prestige acquired as a result of their dynamic Resistance combat in the second half of the war. France, too, revealed the split between a leadership pursuing coalition policies and the local, autonomous Resistance groups, especially those in the South, who frequently pushed for a revolutionary restructuring but were repressed by the central institutions of the administration, the parliament, and the interest groups. In France, too, the leaders of the PCF returned from exile in Moscow as the champions within the Left of a return to normalcy. They actively advocated a bourgeois-proletarian pact among the three mass parties (Communists, Socialists, Catholic M.R.P.) on behalf of reconstruction, and they invoked their prestige against local strikes protesting hunger and against other economically motivated, spontaneously ignited labor struggles. As in Italy, even after their dismissal from the government in the spring of 1947, the communists sought to return to the party coalition and for several months continued their policy of cooperation—until the dispute over the Marshall Plan.[14]

Nonetheless, the united trade union experiment encountered resistance from the outset even in the labor movement. Labor's traditions had remained compelling from the Third Republic through the Phony War, Vichy, the Resistance, and de Gaulle's government in exile. Except for Spain, socialists and communists had tried the experiment of a popular front government only in France. At first this experience reinforced the mutual opposition of the two parties, and with the Hitler-Stalin Pact of 1939, the communists were expelled from the General Confederation of Labor (CGT). Here their originally small communist union organization, which had merged during the preparations for the Popular Front, had already won increasing influence during the course of the Blum government to which they gave passive support. The Christian Unions' CFTC—then still merely an insignificant clerical movement—had remained on the sidelines and recruited opponents of the Popular Front.[15] Like the communists, who had adopted a policy of "revolutionary defeatism" during the period of the Hitler-Stalin Pact, some of the socialists who had collaborated with the Vichy regime were heavily compromised in the view of de Gaulle's exile government and the Resistance. Vichy prohibited both the CGT and the CFTC and replaced them with corporative organizations. Both federations, however, preserved considerable cohesiveness while illegal: witness the major strike among miners in Northern France in May 1941. An alliance between the CFTC and the noncollaborationist segments of the CGT thus seemed natural. They united on a common manifesto that attributed responsibility for the defeat of France to capitalism. The political functions of the state were to be separated from the economic ones of the unions, and production was to be directed by compulsory planning.[16] Once the Communist Party was freed from the Hitler-Stalin Pact [through the German attack on Russia] and could bring its own dynamic organization into the Resistance, it sought a rapprochement with the old CGT leadership. This bore fruit with the Perreux agreements of April 17, 1943, which provided for admitting three communists to the eight-man clandestine union leadership. Within the industry-wide as well as locally based unions, the political relationships that had existed before the schism of 1939 were to be restored.[17] In the National Council of the Resistance (CNR), the united CGT was represented by a nonparty member who was close to the communists. The CNR worked out a program whose central economic demands—nationalization of monopolies, of mineral deposits and banks, and state planning for economic reconstruction—reflected the interwar socialist program. The communists demanded only the expropriation of collaborators, a point that was disputed, however, among the Resistance organizations because it lacked precision. Although the communists pressed especially hard, no fusion of the reunited CGT took place with the CFTC. The Christian unions certainly joined the resistance struggle and agreed to a pact for unity of action with the CGT on socioeconomic issues; but they feared that in the case of a merger they could not successfully maintain their religious, educational, and cultural policies in the wake of the CGT, while on matters of organization they would be dragged along by the communists. In contrast to the Church hierarchy, the Christian unions comprised an active component of the Resistance, and they participated in the unions' struggle against the German occupation by means of strikes and sabotage. The agreement for united action proved its worth by the extensive resistance measures during the period of liberation, especially in the general strike called on August 18, 1944, which provided the basis within the city for the liberation of Paris.[18]

After liberation both unions grew mightily. The CGT regained its highest membership figures of the 1936 Popular Front with about 5.5 million adherents; the CFTC attained an absolute peak with three-quarters of a million. Since the CFTC insisted on keeping its own independence as an organization, the movement toward a united union was limited to a pact between socialists and communists. This turned out less cohesive than in Italy, for the French socialists had at least in part preserved their continuity and could resume a more successful and solid tradition. In contrast to the left-wing majority of the Italian socialists, the SFIO kept its distance as an organization from the PCF, and by cooperation in the cabinet with the MRP—then a prevailingly progressive mass party of Catholics—it created a counterbalance to the communist influence. In the long run the united trade union could not overcome the gap continuing between the parties, for the trade union federation served less as an economic interest group in the postwar crisis than as an instrument of political order. The distance between the two currents showed up as early as 1946, as the socialists within the CGT increasingly opposed communist organizational policies and their transformation of the united trade union into a mass political federation. The socialists paid for their ambivalent alliance policies with declining union membership as well as considerable losses at the polls and internal party revolts.[19]

On the other hand, it was the merit of the tripartite governments and of their alliance with the two major unions to transform into reality during 1945–46 a good part of the structural reforms that the National Council of the Resistance had envisioned: nationalization of mineral deposits, of large transportation enterprises, of the largest banks and insurance companies, the expropriation of collaborationists (especially of the Renault works), the establishment of the state's economic planning instruments, the participation of unions and consumer cooperatives in the supervision of nationalized industries, legal protection for factory councils, and extension of social security. Even if the achievement fell short of socialist demands, of all similar efforts to democratize the economies of the West, this came closest to realization.[20]

Structural reforms, however, could not solve the economic and financial problems of reconstruction. Instead, because an effective social redistribution of the costs of the war was avoided and the economy was progressively deregulated, a dichotomy resulted, similar to what had marked the Italian economy with far less pervasive structural reform. On the one hand, there was reconsolidation of the bourgeoisie, and on the other, undernourishment and underemployment of the working class. Even the CPF leaders could not durably resist the pressure from its rank and file—most notably a major strike for higher wages in the nationalized coal mines; and finally the leadership reluctantly had to take over the direction of a spontaneous strike in its own labor stronghold at Renault.[21] The socialist prime minister, who was then negotiating with the United States for economic assistance, took the occasion to dismiss the communists from the government. Although thrust into opposition, the communist leadership still behaved throughout the early summer months of 1947 as if it were a government party. On the other hand, as the American [Marshall Plan] initiative in Europe took shape, French government policies shifted to the Right. The new trend decisively increased the factionalism within the CGT and ended with the secession of the Socialist Force Ouvrière (CGT/FO) once the communists employed the CGT to unleash a political strike against the Marshall Plan, a tactic familiar from Italy. Still, as in Italy the preeminent participation of the French Communist Party in the Resistance and then in the postwar coalitions meant that although the socialist union leaders might secede from the CGT, there was to be no proportional loss of rank-and-file membership. The CGT remained the dominant economic and political interest group representing the French workers, while the FO remained a relatively insignificant faction, even in comparison to the Catholic CFCT.[22]

A United Movement Without a Unified Organization. Structural Reform Without Codetermination in England. The English case demonstrates that the movement toward united unions in the early postwar years was perhaps inconceivable without socialist-communist cooperation, but was nonetheless no mere consequence of communist preponderance (as might have been presumed from events in the Latin countries). Admittedly the British Communist Party had emerged from its sectarian isolation after its turn to the Popular Front and especially after 1941, and during the war it achieved control of a group of union locals and some regional federations. However, the disputes over accepting the CP as a corporate member of the Labour Party revealed that the communists and their supporters in 1943 had only a bit over one-third, and in 1946 not even a fifth of the votes at the union-dominated Labour Party conferences; and even of these the actual communist members were only a small minority.[23] Admittedly the communist position in the Trade Unions Congress was stronger, especially since the divisions separating them from other left-wingers were fluid. Nonetheless, communist representation was not the only, or even the immediate, cause for the TUC's major initiative to overcome the schism in the international trade-union movement. This derived instead from the situation of 1941 when only the Soviet Union and Great Britain stood as besieged military adversaries of German fascism and the TUC took the occasion to initiate an Anglo-Soviet trade-union committee. In the following years this first step was extended with the result that a united World Federation of Trade Unions was formed on May 30, 1945, bringing together communist, independent, and united unions with the exception of the American Federation of Labor.[24] Without the political influence of the left wing of the TUC, which extended far beyond the communists, the great social-welfare progress of the wartime coalition government in Great Britain and of the [post-1945] Labour government would likewise have been brought about only with the greatest difficulty. On the other hand, even these epoch-making reforms in the areas of social insurance, national health service, educational reform, and urban reconstruction were more the products of liberal and technocratic innovation than of socialist or Marxist theory.[25]

Besides the initiative for trade-union unification and the gains for social welfare, few trends attributable to the Left connected the British with the Continental program for the united trade union. What was noteworthy in Britain was the great organizational progress of the TUC, which more than recovered the setbacks of the interwar period. The returning flood of old members into the unions and the additional recruitment was not distributed equally among all regional or factory locals of the fragmented English union movement, but redounded above all to the benefit of the large unions, once again those in the TUC. The average size of the TUC unions was about twice as large in 1945 as in 1930, but the number of unions was down about 10 percent to 192. Their total membership nearly doubled to about six and a half million, of which over half were concentrated in six large unions. The proportion of all union members whose federations belonged to the TUC attained what was to be a high point of 84.7 percent. Even in the five postwar years the concentration in favor of the large unions continued, although the TUC could not extend its own monopolistic percentage share of union members until the mid-1960s. At the end of the Second World War the number of independent unions was half the number of those at the end of the First World War, even if with 780 it remained very high. It is nonetheless clear that given extraordinarily difficult and fragmented conditions, the war and the immediate postwar period brought considerable growth of membership together with decisive progress toward large industrial unions and consolidation of a national union. Thus, along with the wartime "opening to the Left," the political and economic outlines of a united labor union were discernible even under specifically British conditions.[26]

Such progress would not have been thinkable without unified policies. Although spontaneous wage strikes took place more frequently toward the end of the war, ever since 1941 the leadership of the TUC, the Labour Party, and the Communist Party continued to support the efforts of Churchill's government to raise production and stabilize wages. As Minister of Labour, Ernest Bevin, the most prominent union representative in the cabinet, was even able to have organized strikes declared illegal, a ruling that the Labour government extended until 1951.[27] Pressure for increased production, wage stabilization, and avoidance of strikes under conditions of full employment were, however, to become points of conflict between the Labour government and the TUC, also between Right and Left, and between leadership and rank and file in the deepening postwar financial and balance-of-payments crises.[28] The record of workdays lost in the more or less spontaneous strikes that were not organized by the unions is eloquent: 1944, 3.7 million; 1945, 2.8 million; 1946, 2.1 million; 1947, 2.4 million. During the wage freeze of 1948 the number sank below the 2-million mark, to exceed it again only in 1952.[29]

The TUC's attitude toward structural reforms was also characteristic of the tendency to focus the broad united labor movement upon specific trade-union objectives. Great Britain not only developed its state-planning instruments during the reconstruction period, but the Labour government, decisively supported by the TUC, carried out a series of spectacular nationalizations. The government began with the Bank of England, the transportation industries, and other infrastructural key activities such as health and gas and electricity, then moved to strengthen control over public planning and eminent domain for the establishment of new cities, and finally nationalized the coal and steel industries. Certainly these measures did not come to pass because of any communist pressure; they corresponded far more to the technocratic tradition of the intellectual Fabian socialists—indeed it has been questioned whether such partial socialization is really in the interest of the working class.[30] The Labour government's nationalizations, nonetheless, were more extensive than those of any other Western country of the era (even if they were only a way in part of making up for prior backwardness). They exceeded even the short-term goals of the West German labor movement.

But quite in contrast to labor on the Continent, the English union leadership did not want to help direct the nationalized industries unless it was through party and state supervisory agencies. Traditionally the British saw codetermination, on the one hand, as an expression of left-wing syndicalism, much as represented by the shop-steward movement, guild socialism, and workers' control that had arisen to challenge union authority in the factories after World War I. On the other hand, British labor perceived a threat to the unions' capacity for resistance in that consultative committees in the plants might prove friendly to management. Even in the nationalized sector union leaders did not wish to infringe upon the principle of free collective bargaining. In accordance with English democratic tradition they interpreted industrial democracy as an application of the parliamentary conflict between government and opposition to the adversary relationship over salary and working conditions between the worker and management, even the management of the nationalized industries. Union participation in plant management would encourage ambivalent responsibilities, which, in view of the extensive autonomy of the rank and file in the British labor movement, could only produce a crisis of legitimacy for the union leadership. The TUC thus supported nationalization to achieve higher rationality for the national economy, but rejected any participation in the leadership or control of the factories. As a compromise, though, a group of the most important union leaders were summoned to the management boards of the nationalized sectors. In fact, they thus sacrificed their trade-union roles. They were certainly unable to avoid the reproach that they had merely won plums for the union elite, a charge that was levelled as soon as it became clear that wages and working conditions had not really changed by virtue of nationalization of the factories.[31]

A Flawed United Union and Postponed Structural Reforms in West Germany. Developments in organization and function certainly allow the united trade union in occupied Germany, especially in the Western zones, to be compared with those in the other large European industrial nations. But the contradiction between the especially restricted political sphere of action and the all-encompassing programmatic expectations of a democratic economic utopia remained characteristically German. The existing scholarly literature runs the risk of assuming that this vision, coupled with the constraints imposed on the rank and file at the time the unions were reorganized, added up to a dynamic socialist potential. Against this potential the repressive occupation powers are posited as a purely exogenous factor. But unless one answers the question why the French and Americans above all were in a position to prevent the rapid reconstitution of a united trade union in Germany as well as partially to prohibit, partially to postpone, its basic programmatic demands, one misconceives the problematic contrast between theory and practice.

Both the opportunities for, as well as the major impediment to, a united trade-union movement in Germany arose from the fact that the working-class movement had been so thoroughly defeated by fascism that it simply disappeared as an organization. The collapse of democratic counterweights—liberal institutions and an organized labor force—was what initially made possible the self-destructive running amok that capitalist society embarked upon in Germany in 1933 under National Socialist leadership. In this respect the loss of national sovereignty at the end of the war, which made the development of parties and unions directly dependent upon the respective interests of the victors, really goes back to the particular and the collective failures of the non-Nazi organizations during the world depression. The self-imposed isolation of the communist union organization and the non-resistance and compliance *("Gleichschaltung von innen")*[32] with which socialist and Christian union leaders hoped to preserve their organizations in the Third Reich had precluded their unity and any mobilization of their strength. Deprived of a common combat experience, the working class could not achieve a common effective resistance.[33] Fascist persecution of trade-union and political cadres forced the leadership, if not to imprisonment or death, into the atomization of foreign or "inner" emigration.

Still, the class basis of the union organizations (in contrast to the integrative nature of parliamentary parties) meant that whatever organizational unification of the working-class movement during the transitional period of resistance and emigration was achieved was most successful in the trade-union sphere. The common trend toward organizational and political unification did not mean, however, that the same format and programs were followed everywhere. The initiatives of those German trade-union groups in exile unmistakably reflected the trends in their lands of asylum. Similarly within Germany trade union leaders in the resistance often took the Nazi DAF (German Labor Front) as a starting point for a future democratic union evolution. Three major organizational forms can be distinguished: socialist and Christian labor leaders in the Resistance and in the Swedish emigration wanted a process of democratic transformation that would divest the DAF of its corporative characteristics.[34] The communists advocated a so-called *Eintopf*-[goulasch] union, a united political union borrowed from their experience in the Latin countries in which the political authorities at the local, regional, and national levels were to possess the upper hand over the economic interests of the factory- or industry-wide locals.[35] Finally, the union émigrés in England, influenced by the concept for the World Trade Union Federation, developed a model that laid less stress on central organization. With its emphasis on party neutrality it can be seen more in terms of an invitation to the Christian unions than as a unification of social democrats and communists.[36]

All three models proliferated widely among the groups seeking to found local unions once the Allies occupied Germany. In addition, local variants sprang up, such as shop-steward movements. Former union leaders who were reinstated in their old work resumed their old organization by industry. What proved decisive for implanting these models in the locals that were taking shape, but a factor that scholarly literature has hitherto understressed, was the return of numerous union leaders from abroad with the first Allied troops. The Communist Party groups attached to the Red Army are widely known; in the West, too, there were many delegates of the National Free Germany Committee for the West, who flowed from France, Switzerland, and Belgium into western and southern Germany especially. [The Free Germany Committee had been organized originally among German prisoners of war in the Soviet Union and was thus sympathetic to Russian objectives; the one for the West presumably united sympathizers from the other countries.—Ed.] Finally, there was a group of social democrats from the English emigration who were placed in the most important German cities as collaborators of the American intelligence service, the OSS. Although officially enjoying only an advisory function, they still provided significant help with programs and organization by virtue of their knowledge and connections.[37]

In contrast to this indirect assistance, the Allies also intervened directly in trade-union autonomy. The Soviets advanced the *Eintopf*-union model in their zone, seeking so far as possible an all-German federation with a centralized Party-nominated leadership. In the western zones, as well as in the East, it included a strong communist component and generally took the name Free German Trade Union Federation (FDGB). All the occupation authorities vetoed any effort to convert the DAF into a union, a goal that was sought, for example, by Hans Böckler in Cologne or Markus Schleicher in Stuttgart. The Americans favored organizing unions industry by industry as economic interest groups. The British and Americans imposed a step-by-step plan for organizational reconstruction from the local and factory level up and thus hindered any rapid buildup of trade-union power at the higher leadership levels of the Weimar era, while the French permitted federation at the state *(Land)* level but tenaciously resisted any consolidation of national unions.[38] Besides the influence of the emigration and the military governments, foreign unions also played a role, as they sought—sometimes in cooperation with the occupying power—to win over German colleagues for their union format and programs. The AFL committed its efforts for the longest period, rejecting the gradualist pattern of union reconstitution that the American military government desired because it feared that this procedure would result in a larger communist influence. Instead, the AFL advocated building up economically oriented industrial unions in the western zones with strong participation on the part of the prewar reformist union leadership. A TUC delegation also played an important role when it made clear to the union leaders of the British zone that the English would never agree to any form of centralized united union whether derived from the DAF or the communist model.[39]

Thus preliminary decisions on organizational questions tended to set the pattern for a highly diverse structure of unions, which in fact tended initially to stagnate at the regional or zonal level. From the outset two paths diverged. The first was the political, centralized united union of the Soviet sphere, which was also represented among those western locals that had a particularly strong communist rank and file. The second included the diverse variants of the already elastic model from the English emigration—now watered down even further—that prevailed in the western zones. The western Allies could look with all the more favor on regional organizational levels retaining their predominance, because this would avoid any repetition of the split between local groups striving for autonomy and the national summit of the labor movement, such as had occurred in Italy under American impetus.[40]

The second basic problem of organization concerned the extent, the interests, and the spontaneity of the potential unions. Reorganization began immediately after the occupation. It was regarded by all participants as more important than the building of political parties, and quickly became a wide-ranging effort.[41] Independent of their immediate interests and their political affiliations, many workers and employees saw joining the new unions as the most natural and direct response to their earlier suppression in the Third Reich, no matter what sort of form they might be taking in their own particular locality. The unions were founded on two different bases at the same time: on the one hand, built around the usual old leaders organized by region; on the other, organized at the plant level.[42] In contrast to Italy, however, neither sort of organization won much power. Regional fragmentation weakened the leadership groups, while the rank and file lacked the experience of conflict and the militance of the national movements of liberation. Without the self-consciousness imbued by a successful resistance, diminished by the large numbers of workers drafted for war service, and demoralized by their own split from the reserve army of forced labor the Nazis had imported, German workers had relatively little spontaneous capacity for political action, especially for carrying out any purge. On the other hand, they demonstrated intense interest in cooperative self-help and union representation in order to resume production, to secure jobs, and to reach a minimal level of welfare. This working class was far readier than, say, the partisans in southern Europe to accept union wage restraint within an overall partnership for growth in order to overcome the postwar crisis. Certainly there were cases in Germany, as elsewhere, of the divergence between union cooperation on behalf of recovery for society as a whole and the immediate interests of the rank and file. Comparatively speaking, however, these discrepancies were mere nuances. The dismantling of Antifa [Antifascist groups that were organized by workers at the time of surrender] and factory committees, then later of factory councils as unions and administrative agencies were reestablished, ran an undramatic course. The same activists frequently just took over a new function. This certainly contributed to democratizing the regional leadership of the emerging union organizations, but at the same time meant subordination to new responsibility and discipline.[43]

Besides labor's own weakness, direct Allied rule and the more serious postwar economic and infrastructure crisis in Germany also contributed to the restraint on "class struggles in the western zones."[44] These conditions diminished the clout and influence of the unions. In a situation where planning and wage freezes were not the work of a national government that needed the support of union leaders, but were instead decreed directly by the military authorities in the different zones, military power replaced the strength of the labor unions in integrating workers into the process of reorganizing and increasing production. To the degree, however, that the unions in Germany were unnecessary for the economic system, they failed to win the positions that would have let them exact social and economic structural reforms or essential social welfare gains as the price of their cooperation. On the other hand, insofar as the bargaining position of the unions was already weak at the start of the occupation, there was less conflict than in other countries with the rank and file, which was itself less active than elsewhere. (The relative position of the grass roots in the unions did benefit, however, from the fact that all social interaction tended to be reduced to the local level during the economic crisis.) Instead the leaders and rank and file both concentrated on the effort just to build a united trade union in the face of Allied restrictions. Thus the early postwar years were dominated by the question of organization. And the unifying tradition that a common resistance against fascism provided elsewhere was replaced by a united resistance to the limitations on union development that the Allies imposed as well as against their industrial dismantling policies.

The situation changed when the occupying powers abandoned efforts to increase coal production by coercive measures. But the new incentives to extract higher output promptly precipitated in 1947 familiar short-term reactions: a campaign for increased output, strikes protesting malnutrition, progress toward codetermination and nationalization.[45] Although the occupying powers prevented the German unions from taking advantage of the general socioeconomic function served by the West European united unions until 1947, and even, in part, through 1949, the unions still sought to play the equivalent social role as elsewhere. They aligned themselves as auxiliaries in the Allied-directed process of reconstruction. For many union leaders believed along with Hans Böckler that the capitalist order at home had been critically weakened with the collapse of Germany's economic potential.[46] This meant that they felt labor could first fulfill its social responsibilities and help with reconstruction, then later could always push through nationalization and other structural reforms. The very social democrats who in 1945 frequently viewed socialism as the task of the hour were now willing to postpone it according to Kurt Schumacher's maxim: *Primum vivere, deinde philosophari* [The first thing is to live; philosophy comes later].[47] In practice this meant following the communist tactic of seeking strength for a future socialist transformation by undergoing a period of testing in the pragmatic work of reconstruction.

Resuming the program of Economic Democracy[48] in the 1945 situation also seemed to mean at first inheriting its greatest disadvantage, namely, the lack of any strategy to compel nationalization, planning, and codetermination. Many advocates believed that these concepts should no longer be fought for, but merely introduced into a receptive economic order by recourse to the ballot. This would supposedly have let the unions inherit a pivotal social role as organizer of a communal economic order. The unions themselves would then become the instrument of social bargaining and compromise while they could downplay their old role, still retained in England, of championing the particularistic interests of the working class in labor struggles. By virtue of the extensive list of nationalizations and the demand for an equal union voice in management, German objectives likewise transcended French goals, even though the CGT occupied a far more favorable strategic position vis-à-vis the reformist political coalition than did the fragmented German unions in respect to the occupying powers. The majority of German union leaders thus faced an unresolved contradiction between an overambitious socialist utopia and their actual partnership for economic reconstruction with the military governments and with the firms and state agencies that had survived and whose very recovery made realization of the union program ever more unlikely. This contradiction resulted from a flawed perception of the international interests in contention, but it also derived from an abstract union plan for reconstruction that failed to relate the unions' organization and envisaged function either to each other or to the tactical situation, but only to the expectation of some future socialist order.

The special role of the communists in the postwar unions still requires explanation. Just as the communists in the Russian zone of occupation sought to establish their own form of the united union by means of negotiations among the organizational elites in the FDGB,[49] they similarly cooperated in the unions of the western zones and in their practical behavior were distinguishable only in nuance. Still, it is inaccurate to claim, as is frequently said about 1945–46, that political differences played no role in reconstructing the unions. Sufficient examples can be cited in which former socialist and Christian trade unionists perceived the growing number of communists in the unions and especially in the factory councils as a threat and sought to cut them back.[50] The communists, however, wanted to use union discipline and concerted action to achieve unity and establish themselves. Tilman Fichter has argued that this method of taking root and mobilizing a mass base was more realistic than urging socialism as the task of the day, but that the communists were politically inconsistent in 1947. At that time spontaneous strikes broke out in the Ruhr, as in France, against a union-supported campaign for increased output even while food shortages continued. In Fichter's view the communists failed to develop the socialist mass base that had become, as it were, capable of action. Instead they domesticated the class struggle and proved unable to mobilize an equivalent potential with their subsequent political struggle against the Marshall Plan.[51] Since a more accurate analysis of the motives and course of these 1947 strikes still remains to be written, any estimate of their potential must remain uncertain. In any case the critique completely fails to take into account the limiting conditions on communist policy of the day. If we bear in mind the French events of the spring of 1947 as well as the continuing FDGB efforts at interzonal conferences to achieve a united union throughout Germany (granted, one that would follow their own pattern as far as possible)[52] there is no doubt that the communists insisted on a united union from higher considerations quite independent of the interests of specific workers. In particular, they wanted to keep developments in each country during the "antifascist-democratic" transitional phase parallel and coordinated, and not let themselves become isolated in terms of Europe as a whole by letting the class struggle break out prematurely in different locations.

The Schism

The united union movement broke off during 1948 in the West European countries. In France, the socialists, and in Italy, Catholics, liberals, and a segment of the socialists split from the united unions, which thereupon became entirely communist mass organizations. In England a campaign against communist union officials was begun and the TUC withdrew its membership in the WFTU. Anti-communism and adherence to the new International Confederation of Free Trade Unions (ICFTU), which arose out of the WFTU schism, also characterized developments in the West German zones once efforts failed to found an all-German union organization (which alone could have produced a political united union in Germany). These last sections of the article should reveal what factors led to the political split in the unions and what consequences resulted for the changing functions of the rump unions, especially for the German Trade Union Federation (DGB) that was constituted only at this time.

Some reasons for the end of the WFTU have already been given. As worked out in recent research they contrast with accounts of the time that presented the union schism as an expression of a democratic struggle for self-determination against communist subversion.[53] Causes now adduced include the large-scale political and economic initiatives of the United States' European policy after 1947 and AFL support for the European opponents of the united unions.[54] These external factors certainly require closer illumination. On the other hand, external influences could never have proved effective if within the political united unions, and in the relationship of their policies to actual social conditions, the explosive material was not already at hand for American policy to ignite. It is worth analyzing here again the internal problems of the political united union so as to counteract the superficial thesis that manipulation alone was at bottom—as if the vital currents of the European working-class movement could be held back by virtue of diplomatic trickery and a bit of bribery.[55]

Organizational Reasons. We have tried to demonstrate here that the typical political united union basically rested on an alliance between social democrats and communists. In the case of the postfascist countries, this was an alliance in which Catholic unions could also participate because once all unions had been shattered and compulsory corporative bodies established, a wider solution had become possible. For the communists the united unions were a means for establishing themselves politically and for carrying out their gradualist "antifascist-democratic" strategy of transition. For the social democrats, the united unions offered a means to integrate the labor movement and then by virtue of its united mass to push through structural reforms along the lines of the Economic Democracy program. The unions would thus become an instrument of rational planning and of compromise among interests for the sake of society as a whole. For both points of departure the national political economy took priority over the traditional function of representing particularistic worker interests, especially in view of the postwar economic crisis, shortages, and the need for growth. On the other hand, the noncommunist labor leaders had been trained precisely in the old unions that had always focused on wage issues. They hardly felt that the goals of Economic Democracy, as they had been worked out in the 1920s by social democratic intellectuals, were their primary task.

Conflict was thus in the offing between a policy on wages and social issues geared to the interests of the membership and a policy of united union cooperation on issues of wage stabilization, growth, and structural reform for the sake of the economy as a whole. Throughout 1945–46 it smouldered in the tensions between local and plant organizations and the top leadership. Only in Western Germany did this conflict fail to produce a clear confrontation because there, reconstruction of the unions was delayed. Even in the other countries it did not initially shatter the organization because in the crisis at the end of the war, cooperation was more important than wage-and-price issues, the future seemed open, and the labor movement was granted, as it were, a vote of confidence in advance. The more the economic system recovered, however, the more important the pay issue became, and the more difficult it grew to secure union cooperation in the campaign for higher production. After the difficult winter of 1946–47, when throughout large areas of Europe energy and food supplies fell to their lowest point, the latent conflict came to a head with massive strikes. The centrist union elites were put under pressure from both the left and right of the working-class movement to reorient the political united union toward more direct advocacy of the workers' immediate economic interests. In France, for example, the AFL delegation found a willing ear among the [noncommunist] opposition with their argument that worker interests should take precedence over political unity and were best represented by industrial unions, even if they had to secede.[56]

On another level, however, the conflict broke out even earlier in Germany. The primacy of industrial unions over political united organizations was not merely wrested from the union leadership by the military government and the TUC. From the outset it found support—most clearly in Hamburg[57]—among the old industrial union leadership of the Weimar era who feared that a centralized united union would replace the old labor functionaries with communist politicians and neglect wage contracts in order to pursue political tasks with murky goals. Had the Anglo-American influence not found a willing reservoir of experienced trade-union organizers, the Allies' injunctions against the centralized political union could have been treated as mere formalism and easily circumvented. In fact, they amounted to deciding between two German groups, one of which might call for unity from the base up[58] while the other—the noncommunist—was able to build largely independent industrial unions with a quiet efficiency. In France and Italy, on the other hand, the noncommunist secessionists lamented their lack of organization because the syndicalist tradition and the extreme breadth of the postwar unions worked against the German pattern.

Party disputes partially strengthened, partially overshadowed this conflict. In the united union organization social democratic or Catholic officials competed directly with communists in terms of tactical and propaganda skills and dynamism. Until 1947 the communists made rapid progress in this competition everywhere that the occupying powers did not exert counterpressure; nor could anyone demonstrate their disloyalty. This was the case not only within the CGT, the CGIL, and the TUC—leading to a clear communist preponderance in the first two—but also in Germany, for example, in the FDGB of Greater Berlin or the industrial unions (for example, the mine workers) in the British zone.[59] At the same time communist gains were also clear within the executive organs of the World Federation of Trade Unions.[60]

Yet after the experience of Stalinist reversals on the question of unity, competitors still suspected that the communists' tactical adroitness far outstripped their credibility. The forced unification of communists and social democrats in the Soviet zone of Germany certainly strengthened this conviction. Yet to help those who had been outmaneuvered reconquer their mass base and their majorities required the effective public-relations tactic of exposing the communist advance as one of subversion carried out with sordid methods such as electoral fraud, organized tricks, political disloyalty (e.g., contrivance of "spontaneous" strikes), or as a misappropriation of the workers' interest groups for partisan ends. Events that could be interpreted in this sense were not lacking, and between 1946 and 1948, especially in the communist-dominated organizations, they were exposed with increasing propagandistic effectiveness (made possible in part through AFL assistance). In Germany the formation of the Berlin Independent Union Opposition (UGO) against the FDGB was the most spectacular expression of this widespread trend.[61]

Reasons in International Politics. What proved finally decisive in triggering the potential for conflict within the united union was the social crisis of 1947, which took place in most of those European countries where the working class governed in alliance with bourgeois forces. For the bourgeois and some of the socialist representatives in these governments reacted overwhelmingly to the economic collapse of the winter and spring of 1947 with a desire for foreign economic aid.

The calculation of the liberal [i.e., laissez-faire] economists who directed economic and financial policy (including the West German Bizone * since mid-1947) looked toward the reestablishment of capitalist relations of production by replacing the political pact for growth with market mechanisms.[62] Economic stabilization was expected from elimination of the excess money supply left from the war and deregulation of the economy. This would raise the value of landed and industrial property, compel rationalization [i.e., higher efficiency and concentration of enterprises], lower the price of labor and bring the concealed unemployed into the labor force, attract investment, and draw goods to market. Capital assistance from abroad could thus help to prevent the collapse of state revenues and of the balance of payments, and the additional investment might provide a spur to growth that could at least partially limit the expected decline in wages and increased unemployment.

Given the fact that the Marshall Plan, whose capital grants made possible these [neo-liberal] reforms, divided the parties in the unions, it must be noted that American capital assistance was an economic prerequisite only within the framework of this program for liberalization. In most respects the collapse of early 1947 could be attributed to an infrastructural crisis of growth and of distribution within and between the European countries—for example, a breakdown of transportation in the Bizone at the end of 1946.[63] In this respect the collapse could also have been overcome by greater reliance on, and coordination of state control mechanisms—especially if coupled with an easing of restrictions on German production and foreign trade on the part of the occupying powers—along lines of elaborating the structural reforms already introduced.

The agreement of the West German unions to United States credits was a key decision because the food problem of the Bizone was the immediate spur to the American project and because the communists in many other united unions campaigned against American assistance. So far as we can tell, the German union leaders felt themselves under duress, given the need to finance food imports under the discriminatory foreign-trade constraints imposed by the Allied powers. Nonetheless

*Ed. note: The Bizone referred to the 1947 joining of the British and American zones into a common economic and administrative unit. Once French resistance was overcome a year later, this became the basis for a West German state.

they recognized the dangers of accelerating the division of Germany and of increasing the American influence hostile to structural reforms, especially to nationalization in the Ruhr. But since a direct conflict with the occupying power seemed hopeless, they could only attempt to at least hold open the option for structural reforms while advocating the credits. Hans Böckler coined the effective public slogan: If necessary it was better to postpone socialization than to starve.[64]

The Americans, who were obviously interested in the productive employment of their European aid, seized their opportunity. Their capital exports gave them a strategic position in the affected European economies, and at the same time allowed them to integrate these economies into a political order.[65] Even in the preliminary phase of the Marshall plan they made it clear, not only by military government interventions in Germany but through loan negotiations with France and Italy as well, that as complementary measures they expected security against any revolutionary reaction by the labor movement, including containment of its influence and of anticapitalist structural reforms. Dissolving the ties with the communists in the governments and the unions thus had fundamental importance. The dismissal of the communists from the French government and the secession of a Christian union in Italy created the preconditions for economic aid.[66]

In Western Germany the Americans could be active in their own right once the British had conceded the American leadership role in Germany as a consequence of their own credits from the United States. They could delay decartelization, suspend nationalization in Hessia and North Rhine Westphalia, break the social democratic majority in the Bizone by setting up a second level of institutions, favor the Berlin noncommunist unions, keep in force a wage freeze and a prohibition on strikes, and undertake their own currency reform.[67] Military government looked on approvingly as the communists left the state governments and as the interzonal trade-union conferences ran into increasing difficulty and finally ended. Clay also recommended to union leaders that they give up structural reforms and tend more to the immediate interests of their members (although he interpreted even these interests very narrowly, in accordance with a preconception of class collaboration).[68] Not without reason, the Soviet Union saw the Marshall Plan as an effort to undercut the economic and political basis of the communist strategy of an "antifascist-democratic" transition to socialism. This was to have been directed after all by means of communist participation in the European governments and mass organizations, especially the united unions. From the second half of 1947 the Communist parties of Western Europe thus threw their entire weight into demonstrations against the U.S. initiative. But just this focusing of an economic into a political crisis had to end up serving American purposes. For the middle-class Left and the social democratic doubters who saw the Marshall Plan as essentially a welcome injection of capital could only recognize that the communists were seeking to make the unions the transmission belt of their political defensive and were dropping their moderation in this conflict with their previous government partners. The Soviet trade-union newspaper [*Trud*] demanded that the reformist advocates of the Marshall Plan be expelled from the leadership of the WFTU. The TUC responded with the counterthrust that ended with the schism of the WFTU.[69]

Secondly, the Soviet Union saw the Marshall Plan as an attack on the integrity of its Eastern European sphere of influence. The desire of the Czech government to receive Marshall Plan funds was an index that American containment policy already possessed implications of "rollback." But as an unoccupied country, Czechoslovakia was the classic model of an "antifascist-democratic" transition to socialism in the garb of a bourgeois republic. Were she to vote for the U.S. credits the issue would immediately arise whether to repress similar desires in other peoples' democracies by military force or to accept political reversals as a consequence of American capital exports. For that reason the communists had to act preemptively in the Czechoslovak Republic. First the Czech government was threatened into withdrawing its assent to the Marshall Plan conference, which also blocked in advance any similar inclinations elsewhere, as, for example, in Poland. Developments in Czechoslovakia were then forced apace, especially by means of the communist-dominated factory groups and unions; the coalition was ended by the thoroughly organized Prague coup, and finally a Stalinist dictatorship was instituted.[70]

The Prague coup, for which the ground at least was prepared by a hysterically defensive reaction on the part of the Soviet Union, was a political folly of the first order insofar as Western Europe was concerned. Comparable to the foundation of the Socialist Unity Party two years earlier [which forced East German social democrats into a communist-dominated structure] and to the later Berlin blockade, the Prague coup became a psychologically pivotal event that led to the far-reaching isolation of the communists in Western Europe and destroyed all their postwar labors. More effectively than any American propaganda or pressure, the Prague coup cost the communists their credibility among their trade-union allies. The communist reaction to the announcement of the Marshall Plan made the noncommunist working class's adjustment to the political order entailed by American policies of economic restoration far easier. The reorientation began with the hitherto contained conflicts in the WFTU finally coming to a head and ending in schism. Then, according to the different balance of political forces from place to place, came the secession of the noncommunist unions (in France, Italy, Berlin) or the imposition of clear anticommunist limits by the predominantly social-democratic unions (in England and West Germany).[71]

The AFL, which had remained distant from the international union movement even in 1945 because of its uncompromising hostility to communism, abetted this process of secession by sending several missions to Europe with moral and material support. After early successes these initiatives for isolating the communists in the European unions—which complemented those of the Marshall Plan—won CIA support.[72] In France they certainly created the preconditions for the secession of the social-democratic Force Ouvrière but could hardly prevail upon the mass working-class base to switch loyalties. Nonetheless, the inner dynamic of the CGT was broken, especially since industrialists further sabotaged the union in the area of wage contracts. Even the proposal that businessmen negotiate with the noncommunist unions and thus leave the communists economically functionless corresponded to an American suggestion. What was left of the CGT, however, was too strong simply to be circumvented. The upshot of the tactics followed after the breakup of the united union was simply to weaken the entire French labor movement for more than a decade.[73]

In Western Germany the AFL was not content merely with strengthening a sympathetic union potential by sending CARE packages to tried-and-true officials, providing newsprint and money for anticommunist propaganda (e.g., for the Berlin UGO), and exerting influence on behalf of independent bread-and-butter unions. Above all the AFL was able to exert pressure on the American government so that it would no longer impede the reconstruction of union organizations at the bizonal or trizonal levels. For delay only weakened the position of the old union leadership vis-à-vis the integrated organization of the FDGB.[74]

This meant that major union officials faced an especially painful decision in view of the whole labor movement's (CDU members included) post-1945 commitment to all-German goals. Either they could discontinue organizing the unions at the new [West German] levels of political decision-making; or, in cooperation with the occupying authorities, they have to accept the political order implicit in the move toward a West German state. With the collapse of the interzonal trade union conference over the issue of the Berlin UGO in mid-1948, priority would be given to developing a cartel of industrial unions in the three western zones rather than to the long-term goal of political, all-German organizational unity. Nonetheless, this meant more than just retaining the bird in the hand. Admittedly the provisional character of the Basic Law [the constitutional instrument of the Bonn Republic] made it easier to agree to a Western state and to renounce a constitutional framework that would have established the structural reforms inherent in the basic union demands. Nevertheless, the fact that the same concepts of Economic Democracy still shaped the DGB's platform of 1949[75] demonstrated that despite all the constraints and defeats of the occupation period, union leaders still believed they could yet bring about the program of the united union. For now the unions were organized at the highest levels of the political order, and labor's claims could no longer be countered by military demands.

After the international union schism, the labor movement in most European countries went on the defensive for a good decade. In the period of Cold War reaction the collapse of the political united union made it possible not only for businessmen to play off the unions against each other, but also led to a smouldering crisis of function and identity among the competing unions, especially in France and Italy. The structural reforms of the postwar years were partially reversed (e.g., some of the British nationalizations), or completely changed their social function under conditions of capitalist restoration—as in the case, perhaps, of planning and control of investment in France. For most unions the given way to overcome this identity crisis was to resume an aggressive wage policy, whether with longer-term objectives of class conflict or social partnership, and this generally led to a relatively high level of pay within limited national rates of economic growth. (Where bourgeois monetary reform redisclosed structural unemployment as in Italy, even wage possibilities remained very limited.) At the same time, though, wide circles of workers and especially white-collar employees assimilated the values of efficient performance and consumption that characterized capitalist society. . . .

Endnotes

1. Horst Lademacher, *et al.*, will be publishing a long essay on the WFTU in the 1978 *Archiv für Sozialgeschichte*. For now, see Julius Braunthal, *Geschichte der Internationale*, vol. 3 (Hanover, 1971), pp. 23ff., Hans Gottfurcht, *Die internationale Gewerkschaftsbewegung im Weltgeschehen* (Cologne, 1962), pp. 169ff.; W. Z. Foster, *Abriss der Geschichte der Weltgewerkschaftsbewegung von den Anfängen bis 1955* (East Berlin, 1960), pp. 524ff., 593ff. Some important documentation in FDGB (Freier Deutscher Gewerkschaftsbund), ed., *Zwanzig Jahre Weltgewerkschaftsbund*, vol. I (East Berlin), 1965. For the Communist Party concept of the "antifascist-democratic" stage in Europe, cf. the survey in M. Einaudi, J.-M. Domenach, A. Garosci, *Communism in Western Europe* (Ithaca, N.Y., 1951); F. Claudin, *La crise du mouvement communiste*, vol. 2 (Paris, 1972), pp. 361ff.; F. Fejtö, *Geschichte der Volksdemokratien*, vol. 1 (Graz,

1972); E. Seeber, "Die volksdemokratischen Staaten Mittel- und Sudeuropas in der internationlen Klassenauseinandersetzung zwischen Imperialismus and Sozialismus (1944–1947)" in *Jahrbuch für Geschichte der sozialistischen Länder Europas*, vol. 16, 2 (1972), pp. 39ff.; W. Diepenthal, *Drei Volksdemokratien* (on Poland, Czechoslovakia, and East Germany, 1944–48), Cologne, 1974; and for country studies especially A. J. Rieber, *Stalin and the French Communist Party 1941–1947* (New York, 1962); A. Sywottek, *Deutsche Volksdemokratie* (Düsseldorf, 1971). Of documentary value for the German case: G. Mannschatz, J. Seider, *Zum Kampf der KPD im Ruhrgebiet für die Einigung der Arbeiterklasse und die Entmachtung der Monopolherren 1945–1947* (East Berlin, 1962); H. Laschitz, *Kämpferische Demokratie gegen Faschismus* (East Berlin, 1969).

2. On the results of structural reform, cf. the stock-taking in W. Weber, ed., *Gemeinwirtschaft in Westeuropa* (Göttingen, 1962); R. Krisam, *Die Beteiligung der Arbeitnehmer an der öffentlichen Gewalt* (Leiden, 1963); G. Leminsky, *Der Arbeitnehmereinfluss in englischen und französischen Unternehmen* (Cologne, 1965).

3. The economic history of the immediate postwar phase is still largely unresearched, and just reconstructing the statistical basis for this period of great fluctuations presents special difficulties. For a survey see M. M. Postan, *An Economic History of Western Europe 1945–1964* (London, 1967); for an American estimate of the political economy of Western Europe in 1945–46, Gabriel and Joyce Kolko, *The Limits of Power* (New York, 1972), pp. 146ff. For a basic model of reconstruction, F. Jánossy, *Das Ende der Wirtschaftswunder* (Frankfurt, n.d. [1969]), and for the period at the end of the phase see the comparative analysis of labor force potential in Charles P. Kindleberger, *Europe's Postwar Growth* (Cambridge, Mass., 1967). The economic crisis at the end of the war concealed a largely preserved stock of industrial capital and a still highly qualified labor force, which could quickly bring high growth rates to all European countries. In the German case the expansion of the war economy, which exceeded the toll of destruction, was balanced out by the postwar immigration. The economic upswing was delayed because of a longer aftereffect of the postwar crisis (e.g., collapse of raw materials and intermediate product supplies, effects of the occupation regime); but it did not begin merely because of liberalization and the Marshall Plan. Cf. W. Abelshauser, *Die Wachstumsbedingungen im britisch-amerikanischen Besatzungsgebiet 1945–1948* (Stuttgart, 1975); M. Manz, *Stagnation and Aufschwung in der französischen Besatzungszone von 1945 bis 1948* (Dissertation: Mannheim, 1968).

4. In this respect little has changed since Walter Ulbricht informed German Communist Party functionaries in East Berlin on June 25, 1945, that the "ideological devastation . . . has penetrated deep into the ranks of the working class." Walter Ulbricht, *Zur Geschichte der deutschen Arbeiterbewegung*, vol. 2 (East Berlin, 1963), p. 437. Justification of the coalition policy despite a "revolutionary wave in all of Europe," in Institut für Marxismus-Leninismus beim Zentralkommittee der Sozialistische Einheits Partei, ed., *Geschichte der deutschen Arbeiterbewegung*, (East Berlin, 1968), chap. 12, pp. 28ff.; Jean Duclos, et al., *Histoire du Parti Communiste Francais (Manuel)* (Paris, 1964), pp. 439ff.

5. The policy of the U.S. armed forces in respect to the civilian population in the liberated areas is documented by H. L. Coles and A. K. Weinberg, *Civil Affairs: Soldiers Become Governors* (Washington, 1964). For contemporaries the British intervention in Greece had special impact. See Heinz Richter,

Griechenland zwischen Revolution und Konterrevolution (1936–1946) (Frankfurt, 1973), pp. 495ff. On the American attitude to the European Left, Gabriel Kolko, *The Politics of War* (New York, 1970), pp. 31ff., 428ff. Even in 1946, the U.S. wanted to intervene militarily in France and Italy in case of a communist electoral victory or attempted coup: see J. and G. Kolko, *Limits of Power*, pp. 149f., 156f.

6. On union development in postwar Italy, B. Salvati, "The Rebirth of Italian Trade Unionism, 1943–1954," in S. J. Woolf, *The Rebirth of Italy, 1943–1950* (London, 1972), pp. 181ff.; D. Albers, "Von der Einheit zum Kampf um die Einheit," in *Das Argument* AS 2 (1974), pp. 120ff.; D. L. Horowitz, *The Italian Labor Movement* (Cambridge, Mass., 1963), pp. 181ff.; on the political connections the essays by Quazza and Catalano in Woolf, *Rebirth*, pp. 1ff., 57ff.; Braunthal, *Internationale*, vol. 3, pp. 69ff.; Federico Chabod, *Die Entstehung des neuen Italien* (Reinbek, 1965). On the resistance movement and the strikes of March 1943 in North Italy, R. Battaglia and G. Garritano, *Der italienische Widerstrandskampf 1943 bis 1945* (East Berlin, 1970), pp. 16f.; Charles F. Delzell, *Mussolini's Enemies* (Princeton, 1961), pp. 207ff. On self-government in the liberated area there is only one pioneering study in German: H. Bergwitz, *Die Partisanenrepublik Ossola* (Hanover, 1972), pp. 64–66 on its unions.

7. E. Rosen, "Victor Emanuel III und die Innenpolitik des ersten Kabinetts Badoglio im Sommer 1943," in *Vierteljahrshefte für Zeitgeschichte* 12 (1964), pp. 44ff., especially 81ff. Text of the Buozzi-Mazzini agreement on factory councils in M. F. Neufeld, *Labor Unions and National Politics in Italian Industrial Plants* (Ithaca, N.Y., 1954), appendix A. For the German parallel, Fritz Tarnow, "Labor and Trade Unions in Germany," in *The Annals*, 260 (1948), pp. 90ff.: "Great eagerness to arrange a May 2nd in reverse and to take over the German Labor Front." (p. 92).

8. For the developments under German occupation in the North, see Salvati, in Woolf, *Rebirth*, pp. 189ff.; for the Allied attitude in the South, C. R. S. Harris, *Allied Military Administration of Italy 1943–1945* London, 1957), pp. 445ff.

9. Salvati, in Woolf, *Rebirth*, pp. 185ff.; Horowitz, *Italian Labor Movement*, pp. 186ff.; M. F. Neufeld, *Italy: School for Awakening Nations* (New York, 1961), pp. 451ff.

10. On Togliatti's "*svolta*" (his change from antifascist opposition to Badoglio to joining the royal government), cf. Delzell, *Mussolini's Enemies*, pp. 336ff.; Claudin, *La crise*, vol. 2, pp. 403ff. For the CP influence on the CGIL and the affiliated socialists, Braunthal, *Internationale*, pp. 79ff., and in detail in Horowitz, *Italian Labor Movement*, pp. 202ff., 244ff. Nationalization in Italy did not derive from communist influence, but rather was initiated by Mussolini, then De Gasperi, to protect the private economy by taking over firms threatened by the depression. Cf. R. Jochimsen, "Die öffentlichen bzw. öffentlich beherreschten Wirtschaftsunternehmen im Italian," in Weber, ed., *Gemeinwirtschaft*, pp. 229ff., esp. 245; and M. Einaudi et al., *Nationalization in France and Italy* (Ithaca, N.Y., 1955), pp. 196ff.

11. Marcello De Cecco, "Economic Policy in the Reconstruction Period, 1945–1951," in Woolf, *Rebirth of Italy*, pp. 156ff.

12. Salvati, in Woolf, *Rebirth*, pp. 189, 195ff. Admittedly agreement was reached on wage escalator clauses (Albers, in *Das Argument*, pp. 128ff.), and

mass dismissals were prevented at first. Nonetheless, the pay level had barely reached the austere prewar levels when prices had already doubled.

13. Albers, in *Das Argument*, pp. 132ff.; Horowitz, *Italian Labor Movement*, pp. 208ff.

14. See note 1; also W. Goldschmidt, "Ökonomische und politische Aspekte ges gewerkschaftlichen Kampfes in Frankreich seit dem Zweiten Weltkrieg," in *Das Argument*, AS 2 (1974); Val R. Lorwin, *The French Labor Movement* (Cambridge, Mass., 1966), pp. 99ff.; Georges Lefranc, *Le mouvement syndical de la libération aux événements de mai-juin 1968* (Paris, 1969), pp. 11–40; J. Bruhat, M. Piolot, *Aus der Geschichte der CGT* (East Berlin, 1961), pp. 169ff.; A. Barjonet, *La C.G.T.* (Paris, 1968). For communist policy, R. Tiersky, *Le mouvement communiste en France (1920–1972)* (Paris, 1973), pp. 94ff.; J. Fauvet, *Histoire du Parti Communiste Français*, vol. 2 (Paris, 1965), pp. 139ff., 159ff., and local studies such as P. Guiral, *Libération de Marseille* (Paris, 1974), pp. 111ff.; Etienne Dejonghe and D. Laurent, *Libération du Nord et du Pas de Calais* (Paris, 1974), pp. 157ff., 217ff. For the communist stance on purging the CGT of collaborationist socialists see Rieber, *Stalin and the French Communist Party*, pp. 177ff.; Peter Novick, *The Resistance versus Vichy* (New York, 1968), pp. 131ff.

15. Henry W. Ehrmann, *French Labor from Popular Front to Liberation* (New York, 1947); anon. *La C.F.D.T.* (Paris, 1971), pp. 32ff.; G. Adam, *La C.F.T.C. 1940–1958* (Paris, 1964), pp. 37ff.

16. Text in Lorwin, *French Labor Movement*, pp. 315ff.

17. Ehrmann, *French Labor*, pp. 262ff.

18. Program of the CNR and CGT proposals for it, in Henri Michel and B. Mirkine-Guetzevitch, eds., *Les idées politiques et sociales de la Résistance* (Paris, 1954), pp. 199ff., 215ff. To the CGT proposal were appended communist and socialist amendments that indicated that the communists sought the renewal of the Popular Front's social legislation while the socialists wanted a large share of uncompensated nationalizations. On the CFTC attitude, Adam, *La C.F.T.C.*, pp. 93ff.; Lefranc, *Le mouvement syndical*, pp. 16ff. In addition, the CGT (like the German Federation) was impaired by the foundation of employee unions, especially the Confédération des Cadres. See H. Lange, *Wissenschaftlich-technische Intelligenz-Neue Bourgeoisie oder neue Arbeiterklasse?* (Cologne, 1972), pp. 113ff.

19. B. D. Graham, *The French Socialists and Tripartisme 1944–1947* (London, 1965), pp. 184ff.

20. On the nationalizations, H. Raidl, "Unternehmen und Institutionen der öffentlichen Wirtschaft in Frankreich," in Weber, ed., *Gemeinwirtschaft*, pp. 97ff.; M. Byé, "Nationalization in France," in Einaudi, ed., *Nationalization*, pp. 238ff.; a comparison with England in W. A. Robson, ed., *Problems of Nationalized Industry* (London, 1952), pp. 238ff. On participation, Leminsky, *Arbeitnehmereinfluss*, pp. 70ff.; P. Durand, *Die Beteiligung der Arbeitnehmer an der Gestaltung des wirtschaftlichen und sozialen Lebens in Frankreich* (Luxembourg, 1962). On planning and its transformation, P. Bauchet, *La planification française* (Paris, 1966).

21. On the PCF's campaign for production and on the strikes up to its dismissal from the government, Lefranc, *Le mouvement syndical*, pp. 29ff., 42ff.; Braunthal, *Internationale*, vol. 3, pp. 61–65; Lorwin, *The French Labor Movement*, pp. 105ff. Graham, *French Socialists*, pp. 252ff.; Rieber, *Stalin and the French Communist Party*, pp. 310ff., 347ff.; Duclos, *Parti Communiste (manuel)*, pp. 469ff.

22. On the schism and the preceding so-called Molotov strike, Lefranc, *Le mouvement syndical*, pp. 52ff.; Lorwin, *French Labor Movement*, pp. 119ff.; Barjonet, *C.G.T.*, pp. 49ff., who emphasizes CIA involvement in the formation of FO. From a syndicalist viewpoint, P. Monatte, *Trois Scissions syndicales* (Paris, 1958), pp. 176ff.; communist viewpoint in Duclos, *Manuel*, pp. 507ff.; and especially Bruhat and Piolot, *Geschichte der CGT*, pp. 193ff:; FO viewpoint itself in G. Vidalene, *Die französische Gewerkschaftsbewegung* (Cologne, 1953), pp. 60ff.; A. Bergeron, *F.O.* (2nd ed.: Paris, 1972), pp. 24ff.

23. Braunthal, *Internationale*, vol. 3, pp. 24ff.; Henry Pelling, *The British Communist Party* (London, 1958).

24. See note 1 above.

25. On the influence of the labor movement on the government, H. Pelling, *A History of British Trade Unionism* (2nd ed.: Harmondsworth, 1971), pp. 210ff.; P. Oehlke, "Grundzüge der Entwicklung der britischen Gewerkschaftsbewegung," in *Das Argument* AS 2 (1974), pp. 65ff., esp. 91ff.; E. Bandholz, *Die englischen Gewerkschaften* (Cologne, 1961), pp. 41ff.; and on the two most important union leaders, W. Citrine, *Two Careers* (London, 1967), and Alan Bullock, *The Life and Times of Ernest Bevin*, vol. 2 (London, 1967).

26. P. E. P., ed., *British Trade Unionism* (London, 1948), pp. 5ff.; Tables also in Pelling, *Trade Unionism*, pp. 280ff.; cf. A. Villiger, *Aufbau und Verfassung der britischen und amerikanischen Gewerkschaften* (West Berlin, 1966), pp. 76ff., 105ff.

27. To avoid a wage freeze or similar government controls Bevin instituted compulsory arbitration for wage negotiations and prohibited strikes and lockouts with his Order 1305 of June 10, 1940. J. Lovell and B. C. Roberts, *A Short History of the T.U.C.* (London, 1968), pp. 146ff. On the institutions, P. E. P., *Trade Unionism*, pp. 35ff.; on resistance to the restraint policies of the government, Pelling, *Trade Unionism*, pp. 216f., 224ff.; Oehlke, "Grundzüge," p. 92.

28. For the government attempts to ease the balance of payments crisis, which led to a wage-freeze agreement with the TUC from 1948 to 1951, see G. A. Dorfman, *Wage Politics in Britain, 1945–1967* (London, 1974), esp. pp. 51ff.; criticism from the communist perspective in Oehlke, "Grundzüge," pp. 97ff.

29. Pelling, *Trade Unionism*, pp. 282f.

30. Among the discussions of British nationalization see: E. F. Schumacher, "Die Sozialisierung in Grossbritannien," in Weber, *Gemeinwirtschaft;* the survey in W. A. Robsen, ed., *Problems;* B. W. Lewis, *British Planning and Nationalization* (New York and London, 1952); D. Goldschmidt, *Staht und Staat* (Stuttgart and Düsseldorf, 1956)—which also treats denationalization; and for a critique of the mixed economy from a Marxist perspective, B. A. Glynn and B. Sutcliffe, *British Capitalism, Workers, and the Profits Squeeze* (Harmondsworth, 1972), pp. 162ff.

31. H. A. Clegg, *Industrial Democracy and Nationalization* (Oxford, 1955); for the opposition from within the unions, the opposed treatment of K. Coates and T. Topham, *The New Unionism—The Case for Workers' Control* (London, 1972), pp. 109ff.; Rudolf Kuda, *Arbeiterkontrolle in Grossbritannien* (Frankfurt, 1970), esp. pp. 139ff. Cf. Leminsky, *Arbeitnehmereinfluss*, pp. 21ff.; W. W. Haynes, *Nationalization in Practice: The British Coal Industry* (London, 1953), chap. 9ff.

32. G. Beier, "Einheitsgewerkschaft," in *Archiv für Sozialgeschichte*, 13 (1973), p. 230.

33. Admittedly many trade union leaders were politically persecuted by the Nazis, and one can demonstrate their general effort to keep in touch with each other, discussions about reconstruction plans for after fascism, and even individual acts of heroism. But neither an active mass resistance nor efforts at organizing a coup emanated from the labor movement. H. G. Schumann, *Nationalsozialismus und Gerwerkschaftsbewegung* (Hanover, 1958); H. Bednareck, *Gewerkschafter im Kampf gegen die Todfeinde der Arbeiterklasse und des deutschen Volkes 1933–1945* (East Berlin, 1966); H. Esters and H. Pelger, *Gewerkschafter im Widerstand* (Hanover, 1967); L. Reichhold, *Arbeiterbewegung jenseits des totalen Staates—Die Gewerkschaften und der 20. Juli 1944* (Cologne, Stuttgart, and Vienna, 1965).

34. Cf. Ulrich Borsdorf, "Der Weg zur Winheitsgewerkschaft," in J. Reulecke, ed., *Arbeiterbewegung an Rhein und Ruhr* (Wuppertal, 1974), pp. 394ff., which also consider the temporary communist tactic of trying to penetrate the German Labor Front. Cf. note 7 and the essay by Hans Mommsen in the Reulecke volume.

35. On the foundation of the Berlin FDGB, J. Klein, *Vereint sind sie alles?* (Hamburg, 1972); Werner Conze, *Jakob Kaiser. Politiker zwischen Ost und West* (Stuttgart, 1969), pp. 11ff.; also K. Blank, *Beiträge zum innerdeutschen Gewerkschaftsdialog* (Bonn, 1971), vol. 1, pp. 15ff.; G. Griep and Ch. Steinbrecher, *Die Herausbildung des Freien Deutschen Gewerkschaftsbundes* (East Berlin, 1968); K. Fugger, *Geschichte der deutschen Gewerkschaftsbewegung* (East Berlin, 1949; reprint West Berlin, 1971), pp. 251ff. The significance of the CGT in the formation of the Comintern and for the German Communist Party concept of the trade unions is stressed by H. Bednareck, *Die Gewerkschaftspolitik der KPT 1935–1939* (East Berlin, 1969), pp. 121ff.; experiences of the other Communist parties (especially the Italian) after 1943 as they influenced the Central Committee of the KPD in Laschitza, *Kämpferische Demokratie*, p. 125. Cf. note 37.

36. Klein, *Vereint sind sie alles?*, pp. 108ff.; Borsdorf, "Weg zur Einheitsgewerkschaft," p. 398.

37. On the National Committee for a Free Germany in the West and on the German-language groups in the CGT, see Klein, pp. 11ff.; K. Pech, *An der Seite der Résistance* (Frankfurt, 1974), pp. 263ff.; H. Duhnke, *Die KPD von 1933 bis 1945* (Cologne, 1972), pp. 407ff.; on the cooperation of the OSS Labor Desk in London with the International Federation of Trade Unions (IGB), see P. H. Smith, *OSS* (Berkeley, 1972), pp. 204ff.

38. On the formation of the unions within the limits set by the occupying powers, see the Beier, Klein, Conze, Borsdorf titles above and: B. A. Enderle

and B. Heise, *Die Einheitsgewerkschaften*, 3 vols., mimeographed (but not edited) by the DGB (Düsseldorf, 1959); Eberhard Schmidt, *Die verhinderte Neuordnung 1945–1952* (Frankfurt, 1970); U. Schmidt and T. Fichter, *Der erzwungene Kapitalismus* (West Berlin, 1971); J. Kolb, *Metallgewerkschaften in der Nachkriegszeit* (Frankfurt, 1970), and regional studies such as F. Hartmann, *Geschichte der Gewerkschaftsbewegung nach 1945 in Niedersachsen* (Hanover, 1972); P. Brandt, "Anti-faschistische Einheitsbewegung. Parteien und Gewerkschaften," (dissertation, Berlin, 1972) and now published as *Antifaschismus und Arbeiterbewegung* (Hamburg: Christians, 1976); H. Christier, *Die Hamburger Arbeiterbewegung 1945–1949* (dissertation, Hamburg, 1974); and such union accounts as I. G. Metall, eds., *75 Jahre Industriegewerkschaft 1891–1966* (Frankfurt, 1966); K. Anders, *Stein fur Stein* (Frankfurt, 1969); Hans Mommsen et al., *Bergarbeiter* (exhibit catalogue, Bochum, 1969), pp. 32ff.; DGB Landesbezirk Berlin, ed., *Berliner Gewerkschaftsgeschichte von 1945–1950* (Berlin, 1971). Not generally realized is that the French government—supported at home by communists and socialists—began its policy of obstructing all-German union development in the ninth session of the Allied Control Council on October 20, 1945, in opposition to the wishes of the other three powers. See *Foreign Relations of the United States*, 1945, III, 846–852.

39. G. Beier, *Probleme der Gründung und des Aufbaus westdeutscher Gewerkschaften unter dem Primat der Aussenpolitik* (Kronberg, 1972); also R. Radosh, *American Labor and United States Foreign Policy* (New York, 1969), pp. 325ff., and G. S. Wheeler, *Die amerikansische Deutschlandspolitik* (East Berlin, 1958), part 2. For the relations of the WFTU to Germany see the survey from the FDGB perspective in A. Behrendt, *Der Weltgewerkschaftsbund und die deutschen Gewerkschaften* (East Berlin, n.d. [1965]), chaps. 2–6.

40. Cf. th. R. Fisher, "Allied Military Government in Italy," in *The Annals*, 267 (1950), pp. 114ff., especially 117ff.

41. A few exceptions such as Kurt Schumacher aside, most of the activity of the labor movement in the days after liberation or surrender consisted of forming non-party Action Committees and unions, or preliminary factory councils and shop-steward movements, since unity in these areas seemed undisputed. (See notes 43 and 58.) Furthermore the American military government attitude, which allowed union but not political activity, made union work all the more significant. On union policies see Klein, *Vereint sind sie alles?*, pp. 135ff.; and for the licensing of political activity, Lutz Niethammer, *Entnazifierung in Bayern* (Frankfurt/M., 1972), pp. 126ff., 198ff.

42. Many examples of this in Brandt, *Antifaschismus;* Hartmann, *Gewerkschaftsbewegung;* Klein, *Vereint sind sie alles?;* and E. Schmidt, *Verhinderte Neuordnung.*

43. On the Action Committees, Niethammer, *Entnazifierung*, pp. 124ff.; Brandt, *Antifaschismus;* Hartmann, *Gewerkschaftsbewegung;* and Walter L. Dorn, *Inspektionsreisen in der U.S.-Zone*, L. Niethammer, tran. (Stuttgart, 1973), pp. 34ff. The difference from the radicalism of many partisan movements is perhaps clearest by comparison with the Greeks: see D. Eudes, *Les Kapitanios* (Paris, 1970). See also the documentary collection of Borsdorf, Brandt, Niethammer, *Arbeiterinitiative 1945* (Wuppertal, 1976).

44. U. Schmidt and Fichter used this subtitle (for *Der erzwungene Kapitalismus*) to suggest a radical potential. On the unions, G. Beier, "Zum Einfluss der

Gewerkschaften," p. 40, I believe, also errs in overemphasizing the unions as "the strongest power in the interregnum."

45. On this combination in Ruhr in 1947 see E., Potthoff, *Der Kampf um die Montanmitbestimmung* (Cologne, 1957), pp. 34ff.; E. Schmidt, *Verhinderte Neuordnung*, pp. 75ff., 134ff.; Schmidt and Fichter, *Der erzwungene Kapitalismus*, pp. 23ff.; F. Deppe et al., *Kritik der Mitbestimmung* (Frankfurt, 1969), pp. 58ff.; Mommsen et al., *Bergarbeiter*, chap. 36ff.; Peter Hüttenberger, *Nordrhein-Westfalen und die Enststehung seiner parlamentarischen Demokratie* (Siegburg, 1973), pp. 410ff.; John Gimbel, *Amerikanische Besatzungspolitik in Deutschland 1945–1949* (Frankfurt, 1971), pp. 159ff., 225ff.; Mannschatz and Seider, *Zum Kampf der KPD*, pp. 195ff.; R. Badstübner, *Restauration in Westdeutschland 1945–1949* (East Berlin, 1965), pp. 233ff.

46. "Capitalism is at its last gasp," Hans Böckler, for example, declared in 1946 (E. Schmidt, *Verhinderte Neuordnung*, p. 68).

47. Said at the Nuremberg Party Congress of the SPD in 1947 (Beier, *Probleme der Gründung*, p. 43): the expression referred most immediately to acceptance of the Marshall Plan but still describes prior party practice.

48. On the further development of the tradition of Economic Democracy among the unions and the SPD see E. Schmidt, *Verhinderte Neuordnung*, pp. 61ff.; H. P. Ehni, "Sozialistische Neubauforderung und Proklamation des 'Dritten Wegs,'" in *Archiv für Sozialgeschichte*, 13 (1973), pp. 131ff.; R. Blum, *Soziale Marktwirtschaft* (Tübingen, 1969), pp. 13ff.; W. Weddingen, ed., *Untersuchungen zur sozialen Gestaltung der Wirtschaftsordnung* (West Berlin, 1950).

49. Cf. note 35. Like the GGIL and the united CGT, the FDGB was constructed from a central executive for the entire Soviet zone of occupation. West German union leaders were forced to renounce this model and work on the regional level by their occupation authorities.

50. E. Schmidt, *Verhinderte Neuordnung*, pp. 120ff.; Mommsen et al., *Bergarbeiter*, chaps. 35 and 38.

51. T. Fichter and E. Eberle, *Kampf um Bosch* (West Berlin, 1974), pp. 26ff. Similiar dissident communist criticism is found in U. Schmidt and Fichter, *Der erzwungene Kapitalismus*, pp. 43ff.; E. U. Huster et al., *Determinanten der westdeutschen Restauration 1945–1949* (Frankfurt, 1972), pp. 175ff. Since this chapter was written a new book on these strikes has appeared: Christoph Klessmann and Peter Friedemann, *Streiks und Hungermarsche im Ruhrgebiet 1946–1948* (Frankfurt and New York, 1977).

52. Only two polemically edited documentary collections are now available on this matter: A. Behrendt, *Die Interzonenkonferenzen der deutschen Gewerkschaften* (East Berlin, 2nd ed., 1960); DGB-Bundesvorstand, ed., Versprochen-gebrochen. *Die Interzonenkonferenz der deutschen Gewerkschaften von 1946–1948* (Düsseldorf, n.d. [1961]). Communist willingness to compromise was expressed in the willingness to keep the Marshall Plan issue out of the WFTU.

53. TUC, ed., *Die unabhängigen Gewerkschaften verlassen den Weltgewerkschaftsbund* (London, 1949).

54. J. and G. Kolko, *Limits of Power*, chap. 12; for the unions see also note 39.

55. This is suggested by G. S. Wheeler, *Politik mit dem Dollar* (East Berlin,

1958), an edition of parts I and II of Wheeler, *Amerikanische Politik*, published by the FDGB.

56. Radosh, *American Labor and U.S. Foreign Policy*, pp. 316ff.

57. Klein, *Vereint sind sié alles?*, pp. 192ff.; Christier, *Hamburger Arbeiterbewegung*, pp. 103ff.

58. This willingness for unity is often interpreted one-sidedly as an innovation of a new class consciousness without its authoritarian and traditional elements being taken into account. Cf. F. Moraw, *Die Parole der 'Einheit' und die Sozialdemokratie* (Bonn, 1973), pp. 60ff.

59. See note 10 and 50; Lorwin, *French Labor Movement*, pp. 107ff.

60. See note 53; Gottfurcht, *Die internationale Gewerkschaftsbewegung*, pp. 185ff.

61. Radosh, *American Labor and U.S. Foreign Policy*, pp. 310ff., esp. 331ff.; J. Fijalkowski et al., *Berlin-Hauptstadtanspruch und Westintegration* (Cologne and Opladen, 1967), pp. 41ff.

62. The Italian example of this position is analyzed by De Cecco, "Economic Policy in the Reconstruction Period," in Woolf, *Rebirth*, pp. 160ff.; for the German western zones see Blum, *Soziale Marktwirtschaft*, pp. 38ff., 207ff., where the currency reform is seen as the high point of American liberalizing intervention. For the European complex of events, J. and G. Kolko, *Limits of Power*, pp. 428ff.

63. *Ibid.*, pp. 346ff.; for the Bizone, Abelshauser, *Die Wachstumsbedingungen*, pp. 212ff.

64. On Böckler's stance see Ulrich Borsdorff, "Hans Böckler-Repräsentant eines Jahrhunderts gewerkschaftlicher Politik," in H. O. Vetter, ed., *Vom Sozialistengesetz zur Mitbestimmung. Zum 100. Geburtstag von Hans Böckler* (Cologne, 1975). In general on the union stance, Beier, *Probleme der Gründung*, pp. 42ff.; E. Schmidt, *Verhinderte Neuordnung*, pp. 114ff.; Theodor Pirker, *Die blinde Macht* (2 vols.: Munich, 1960); V. Schmidt and Fichter, *Der erzwungene Kapitalismus*, pp. 37ff. That the political and economic problems of the western zones of Germany were the immediate spur to the Marshall Plan—and that the Americans developed the institutional models for carrying it out in Germany (JEIA, GARIOA)—is undisputed in the literature. See J. and G. Kolko, *Limits of Power*, pp. 349ff.; Gimbel, *Amerikanische Besatzungspolitik*, pp. 196ff., 216ff.; Hadley Arkes, *Bureaucracy, the Marshall Plan, and the National Interest* (Princeton, 1972), pp. 19ff.; J. H. Backer, *Priming the German Economy* (Durham, N.C., 1971), pp. 157ff.; A. Piettre, *L'économie allemande contemporaine* (Paris, n.d. [1952]), pp. 469ff. The most specific such argument is now in John Gimbel, *The Origins of the Marshall Plan* (Stanford, 1976).

65. That U.S. and West European economic stabilization was a motive is shown (besides by Kolko and Gimbel) by J. M. Jones, *The Fifteen Weeks* (New York, 1953), p. 205; H. B. Price, *The Marshall Plan and its Meaning* (Ithaca, 1955), pp. 29ff.; E.-O. Czempiel, *Das amerikanische Sicherheits-system 1945–1949* (Berlin, 1966), part 3; Arkes, *Bureaucracy*, pp. 43ff., 153ff. In contrast, the anticommunist containment ideology, which grew more intense during the preparation of the aid program, both inside and outside the U.S., was geared more toward creating the public atmosphere and willingness to approve the funds. On this

see, R. M. Freeland, *The Truman Doctrine and the Origins of McCarthyism* (New York, 1972).

66. Cf. note 71.

67. The best survey is in Gimbel, *Amerikanische Besatzungspolitik, passim;* for the economic aspect, Blum, *Marktwirtschaft,* pp. 182ff.; H.-H. Hartwhich, *Sozialstaatspostulat und gesellschaftlicher status quo* (Cologne and Opladen, 1970), pp. 61ff.

68. Beier, *Probleme der Gründung,* pp. 33ff., 46ff.; also Beier, "Gründung," pp. 47f. for specially clear examples. Documentary material also in Wheeler, *Politik mit dem Dollar,* passim.

69. For an overview, J. and G. Kolko, *Limits of Power,* pp. 361ff.; Herbert Feis, *From Trust to Terror* (New York, 1970), pp. 260ff.; Foster, *Abriss,* pp. 606ff.; Gottfurcht, *Die internationale Gewerkschaftsbewegung,* pp. 189ff.

70. Braunthal, *Internationale,* vol. 3, pp. 179ff.; J. and G. Kolko, *Limits of Power,* pp. 384ff.; Claudin, *La crise,* vol. 2, pp. 525ff. for surveys. For the end of the Czech coalition as connected to the collapse of the "third way" in France as a result of the Marshall Plan: R. Künstlinger, *Parteidiktatur oder demokratischer Sozialismus* (Starnberg, 1972), pp. 78ff.; also J. K. Hoensch, *Geschichte der Tschechoslovakischen Republik* (Stuttgart, 1966), pp. 136ff; as a purely internal revolution in the Czech people's own self-conception: Gewerkschaften Prace, ed., *Menschen, Arbeit, Gewerkschaften in der Tschechoslovakei* (Prague, 1959), pp. 55ff.; on the role of the unions, Diepenthal, *Drei Volksdemokratien,* pp. 122ff.

71. For the Italian schism, Salvati, in Woolf, *Rebirth,* pp. 201ff.; Horowitz, *Italian Labor Movement,* pp. 215ff.; in France, Lorwin, *French Labor Movement,* pp. 124ff.; Lefranc, *Le mouvement syndical,* pp. 65ff.; for Berlin, see note 61; for the collapse of the planned Interzonal Congress in Germany, E. Schmidt, *Verhinderte Neuordnung,* p. 118; Behrend, *Interzonenkonferenzen,* pp. 172ff.; cf. note 50. On the anticommunist campaign in the TUC, which was particularly disturbed by the communist agitation against its wage-freeze agreement, see Pelling, *Communist Party,* pp. 153ff.

72. Barjonet, *C.G.T.,* p. 51; Radosh, *American Labor and U.S. Foreign Policy,* p. 323.

73. Goldschmidt, "Ökonomische und politische Aspekte," pp. 22ff., Lefranc, *Le mouvement syndical,* pp. 77ff.

74. Besides Beier, "Probleme der Gründung," pp. 33ff., see the documentation of the Free Trade Union Committee of the AFL, ed., *Die A.F. of L. und die deutsche Arbeiterbewegung* (New York, 1950), and the contemporary critique of Viktor Agartz, *Gewerkschaft und Arbeiterklasse* (2nd ed.: Munich, 1973), pp. 97ff. ("Der Gewerkschaftliche Marshallplan").

75. For union leaders such as Böckler the connection between the Marshall Plan and the division of Germany was clear, but there is no treatment of the union stance during 1947–48 comparable to Hans Peter Schwarz, *Von Reich zur Bundesrepublik* (Neuwied and Berlin, 1966), pp. 299ff. and 483ff., who has analyzed Jakob Kaiser and Kurt Schumacher as representatives of the national labor movement forced into a decision between Marshall Plan and the communists. On the union policy in the constitutional debate see Beier, *Gründung,* pp. 53ff.; W. Sörgel, *Konsensus and Interessen* (Stuttgart, 1969), pp. 201–213.

11

Anthony Carew

Labour and the Marshall Plan

The Niethammer essay, above, discusses the ideological impact of the Cold War on the European labor movement as a whole. Anthony Carew's 1987 study follows the influence of the European Recovery Program's emphasis on productivity in different national contexts, with special attention to the British arena. Carew's book emphasizes the interaction of ERP labor policy with national trade-union developments, and also examines the managerial response to the productivity drive.

British Labour unions were prevailingly non-communist, although sympathy with the Soviet Union rose as a result of the war. The schism traced by Niethammer did not produce in Britain the major ruptures that resulted in France and Italy. Nonetheless, in many respects British unions were as class-conscious as their continental counterparts; they drew upon a strong tradition of working-class community and through the Labour Party maintained a clear commitment to democratic socialism and public control of the economy. On the other hand, labor leaders Ernest Bevin (who was serving as Foreign Secretary during the late 1940s) and Walter Citrine had sponsored efforts to promote cooperation with employers from the late 1920s, and it was logical to build upon this tradition. The politics of productivity had its own indigenous British roots.

Selections here include pp. 111–130 and pp. 240–250 of Anthony Carew's *Labour and The Marshall Plan: The Politics of Productivity and the Marketing of Management Science* (Manchester, Manchester University Press, 1987), reprinted with permission of the author and Manchester University Press.

The Reappraisal of Marshall Plan Labour Policy

> [. . .] hitherto anybody could do anything because there was just no policy. Every official would improvise his own policy in the name of vague anti-Communism. [William Gomberg to Irving Brown, 29 January 1953]

It took eighteen months from the inception of Marshall Aid before US trade union criticisms of the operation of the ERP became very vocal, with ECA Labour staff lending their support to complaints made by delegations which visited Europe from the American labour movement. In December 1949 Americans for Democratic Action published an anonymous article in their journal complaining that labour was only a junior partner in the Marshall Plan organisation.[1] Undoubtedly written by a member of the ECA Labour staff, and reflecting the view of most members of the Division, it was the first public criticism of the ERP from an American labour source. But the weakness of the Labour operation within the ECA had been noted within the first six months of the ERP by a junior official of the CIO, Jay Krane, who in autumn 1948 was the newly appointed aide to the American Assistant General Secretary of the WFTU, Elmer Cope. Based in Paris, and in daily contact with ECA Labour staff, Krane kept a meticulous diary of events and impressions. Early in December 1948 he had reached a conclusion that was to be widely shared five years later—that the American trade union approach should be either to insist on a high-level policy-making role in the ECA, or to settle for complete independence with freedom to criticise the ERP.[2] As for the substance of the programme, he was convinced that mistakes of tremendous importance were being made in ERP policy orientation. The preoccupation was already entirely technical, the emphasis being on increased production, no attention being paid to the need for social reform.[3] Striking a note that would be commonplace in the closed confines of American labour personnel in Europe over the coming years, he observed that it was difficult to be positive about the ECA: the most labour could do was to stress how bad the situation would have been but for the ERP.[4]

What general perspective did American labour personnel bring with

them to Europe? They saw themselves engaged in economic reconstruction, work that required a social conscience. They wanted to export to
Europe the values and material benefits of vigorous American business
enterprise—not necessarily because it was capitalist, but because it was
efficient. At the same time they hoped they would be laying the foundations of a more democratic and, perhaps, socially just Europe. Labour
staff always stressed the importance of aid as a support for increased
democracy. The logic of their position was to support administrations
and policies that were broadly social democratic or progressive capitalist
in perspective, favouring to a greater or lesser extent social welfare
reforms and a mixed economy as against the economic liberalism and
free enterprise that was part of the rhetoric of American business and
the main thrust of much ERP policy. American labour unions were not
unanimous on this point. Those from a CIO background—some former
socialists, a few still members of the Socialist Party—were perhaps
more committed advocates of government welfare programmes,
whereas the AFL tradition was inclined to be wary of government
measures to protect workers when those workers might be protecting
themselves. Nevertheless a sufficiently broad spectrum of American
labour saw the practical benefit of private and public welfare policies
and an altogether greater concern for the interests of labour as a
bulwark against communism. The frustration that Labour staff experienced within the ECA stemmed from the gradual realisation that the aid
programme accorded social justice a lower priority than economic revival and that in the ECA's internal debates labour counted for less than
business.

By late summer 1949 the success of the Marshall Plan in extending
support to pro-capitalist forces in Europe was reflected in election
results in various places. In some countries a clear rightward swing was
discernible, with socialists being eliminated from coalition governments. At the same time policies aimed at achieving another ECA
objective, the establishment of sound money by means of devaluation,
threatened to depress the living standards of workers still further. In
view of these trends the Labour Division of the OSR warned of the real
possibility of an increase in militancy among non-communist unions,
which would no longer be restrained from taking industrial action by
the presence in government of labour or socialist spokesmen. Such
industrial militancy over genuine economic grievances appeared unavoidable to the OSR's Labour Advisers. It might push the non-
communist unions into a common front with communist unions which
the latter would then seek to exploit. The communists would once again
have an opportunity to put themselves at the head of popular agitation,
and their fortunes, depressed since the beginning of the Cominform's
ultra-sectarian line and the flirtation with insurrection in France and

Italy, would begin to revive. The Labour Division's general advice was, therefore, in support of conciliatory policies on the part of employers and governments. Employers should be prepared to meet workers half way and make concessions before strikes forced them. Government should act impartially and encourage the two sides to negotiate their own solutions in the interests of minimising the impact and duration of strikes.[5]

The main problem areas in Europe for the ECA were France, Italy and Germany. Eighteen months after the start of Marshall Aid vast amounts of dollars had been poured into those countries. But while the aid had proved a boon to the employers it had left the working class almost untouched. This condition began to be generally recognised in the Labour Division in autumn 1949. Sol Ozer, an economist in the OSR, observed that 'ECA is running out of steam after [an] initial period of creativity,' and spoke of the development of 'fundamental ideological conflicts' that it would have to face up to, such as that between the goal of financial stability on the one hand and the achievement of an acceptable standard of living on the other.[6] Outside the ECA the critical note was sounded during the founding conference of the new International Confederation of Free Trade Unions (ICFTU) in December 1949. From the conference Harry Martin reported on the

> increasing emphasis on Labour's conviction that American aid money must be used more effectively in the future for the economic betterment of the living conditions among workers in Europe and elsewhere. [. . .] the Administration must take positive action in this connection in fairly short order if that criticism is to be prevented from shaping into actual opposition.[7]

Within the ECA the sharpest criticisms of the effects of existing aid policies were contained in a series of reports written in early 1950 following field trips in France, Italy and Germany by Harry Turtledove and Lemuel Graves, two Labour Information Officers on the staff of the OSR. The reports told of unenthusiastic support for Marshall Aid even among the non-communist trade unions. It was not a question of the message not getting through, nor could it be solved by more propaganda:

> Marshall Plan propaganda is ubiquitous. Hardly a day goes by without a good blurb in the papers, and even shop windows are loaded with subtle US propaganda. Marshall Plan literature is distributed by the bale. In all, one feels that the workers have been exposed to our propaganda and have absorbed a certain amount of it—the anti-Communist angle, for instance. But the fact remains that this propa-

ganda must be in effect negative [. . .] we can't tell them how well off they are, thanks to the Marshall Plan, because they are not well off and they know it.

Their material conditions had to improve before they were likely to believe in the Marshall Plan. But for their conditions to improve there would have to be a major shift in Marshall Plan priorities and, in all probability, far-reaching political change in the recipient country. As one of Turtledove's reports pointed out, the sceptical worker was not likely to be convinced 'unless we choose to disassociate ourselves publicly from the government and its action.'[8]

Concurrent with the Turtledove–Graves despatches, Kenneth Douty, Chief Labour Adviser to the French mission, drew attention to the imbalance between high levels of production and low levels of consumption in France. Production was up a fifth over 1938 while real hourly wages were 35 per cent down. Underconsumption was the basis of the problem, as it had been in the USA in 1929. The answer was surely for the ECA to intervene more directly to secure better social provision and higher levels of income for workers.[9] In a separate letter to Golden he reviewed ECA policy in this respect:

the stated ECA policy of non-intervention would seem a sound one. Perhaps labour people would be inclined to intervene in a country like France with a right-of-centre government, but the other side of the picture is the right to intervene in a United Kingdom with a Labour government. Given the complexity of forces in the American political scene, I would feel that non-intervention is the safer policy for labor [. . .] .

But, the next question is, aren't we intervening now? Aren't we insisting in France, for example, on a balanced budget and certain fiscal policies? And aren't we using our control over counterpart to enforce them? [. . .] Presumably the Mission could, without going to a concept of intervention, press on the French Government policies that would serve the social needs of French workers and the political needs of American policy. To influence the Mission to make such representation should be one of the efforts of the Labour people in the Mission.[10]

The question of how interventionist in domestic European politics the ECA should be had never been far from the surface in internal discussion.[11] Briefed by the State Department in 1948 on US policy towards France, Hoffman had been told: 'We should support any non-Communist French government by all reasonable means short of direct interference in the internal affairs of the country.'[12] However, as Douty recognised, non-intervention was an elastic concept, more to do with public relations than with practical politics. The architects of the aid programme were well aware that the sheer weight of economic forces that they had unleashed would compel a brand of politics in participating countries compatible with the economic imperatives of free enterprise.[13]

The immediate outcome of this internal debate within the OSR's Labour Division was a formal proposal, submitted by Turtledove in April 1950, that the ECA should bring over to Europe large numbers of American labour union officials who would work with trade unionists at the local level, stiffen their backbone and lead to a greater appreciation of the relevance of Marshall Aid.[14] This proposal—Operation Bootstrap, as it was called—was to provide the background for much of the internal discussion and programming that went on in the Labour Division of the ECA for the next six months. It was the ECA's one positive response to a widespread feeling among the Labour staff that it was neither sufficiently large nor free and flexible enough to combat the problem of disaffected labour in the ERP's trouble spots. The proposal chimed with an increasingly critical note being sounded in American labour's own discussions of Marshall Aid, and this would eventually lead the CIO to distance itself from the Marshall organisation in pursuing its own programme in Europe.

In early May 1950 a resolution highly critical of the ERP labour programme had been passed at the convention of the Textile Workers' Union of America (CIO), causing some consternation in the ECA, since Philip Murray was present at the convention and was known to favour the resolution. It charged that the national labour movements in Europe were hardly involved in the administration of aid in their own countries although this was something that the participating governments had committed themselves to. It further maintained that there was little reflection of labour thinking in the application of Marshall Aid and that in the absence of a spirited labour point of view in the administration of the ECA there was a strong danger of labour 'representatives' becoming mere adjuncts of the State Department.[15]

Shishkin was forced to admit that there was much truth in this. The lack of effectiveness of the French non-communist unions in relation to the Marshall Plan was, he argued, due to their own lack of cohesion, but elsewhere the criticism was well founded. In Germany the American High Commission's Labour Division lacked influence, and the prospects of any improvement under the Adenauer administration were doubtful. And in Italy the trade union committee established to coordinate Marshall Plan work had been greatly weakened because of the reluctance of the Italian government—especially the Ministries of Finance and Foreign Affairs—to co-operate with it.[16] The preponderant strength of the communist trade unionists in both Italy and France led governments and business in both countries to continue dealing with them, rather than to follow their anti-communist instincts and risk the wrath of the communists by extending recognition to their smaller rivals. This tendency was to dog the Labour Division throughout the life of Marshall Aid.

The Textile Union convention debate served as a curtain-raiser to a top-level conference of twenty-five union leaders and senior ECA administrators held in Washington only a few days later to review labour's role in the Marshall Plan at its half-way stage. The conference saw an emerging consensus that what was needed in the Labour programme was not more activity by agencies of the United States government but a greater direct role for American labour under the aegis of the ECA. The unions were invited to shoulder the cost of such activity as a sign of their commitment to the programme, though Marshall funds would be available in the last resort.

There was a conflict of opinion within the Labour Division as to how large such a programme should be. Harry Martin, who had pushed the idea from the outset, favoured an ambitious scheme with up to 100 union officials coming to Europe. France would be the first target, but the operation would be extended to Italy and Germany soon after.[17] Golden requested that $1 million be put aside from the ECA's technical assistance budget to pay the dollar cost of sending American trade unionists abroad. Clearance was given to the use of Italian and French counterpart funds to cover the non-dollar cost of the scheme.[18] And on top of this $50,000 was made available from the 'Administrator's Fund', that secret portion of the 5 per cent counterpart fund intended 'to finance without indication of source' projects approved at the highest level of the ECA.[19] The significance of these amounts was noted by Barry Bingham, deputy chief of the French mission: $100 per month would pay the wages and expenses of a full-time organiser, and a hundred additional organisers strategically placed at that crucial time might change the whole picture of French trade unionism within a year.[20] Though there was no firm agreement on the details of the scheme, the Labour Information Department boldly announced that 100 American labour organisers would go to France, Italy and Germany over the next year, and on top of this American labour would make available, at their expense, the services of twenty people ready to visit Europe as trade union consultants if invited by European labour organisations for a specific purpose.[21]

Some field staff were appalled at the prospect of such a large number of people with no immediate appreciation of the situation at hand being turned loose in Europe. 'A trained, well-disciplined crew of infiltrators makes sense in some situations, but it can't be done this way. This is no time to play cops and robbers,' commented one member of the division.[22] Shishkin and Douty concurred, and argued for a small pilot project involving around a dozen officials to be tried out in the autumn of 1950. The Washington meeting of labour leaders and ECA staff had considered a proposal under which both the French and the Italian missions would be allowed to expand their Labour staff so as to have two or three extra American trade unionists attached to them as consultants. They would be expected to travel extensively and work as closely as possible with the local non-communist labour movement, promoting ideas of increased productivity, liberalised trade and the part that organised labour could play in such programmes.[23] And it was, indeed, in this more modest format that Operation Bootstrap took shape. The ECA's grandiose scheme for a large-scale invasion of Europe by American labour organisers never materialised, for by now the more sober view of the American trade unions was beginning to be heard.

The Washington meeting of labour and ECA leaders had agreed to sponsor a joint AFL and CIO delegation to Europe to report on conditions. A trio of middle-ranking officers—William Belanger, Harold Gibbons and Carmen Lucia—visited France for six weeks in July–August 1950, and the report of their trip strongly reinforced the criticisms of Marshall Aid that had already been expressed internally within the ECA:

> Our productivity programme in France carries serious threats to the welfare of the workers and does nothing to protect them—as the Communists so accurately charge [. . .] temporary unemployment caused thereby is ignored [. . .]. There is no protection against wage cuts [. . .] [resulting from] the adoption of machine methods [. . .]. There is nothing to prevent the direct benefits of increased production made possible by Marshall Plan aid from going entirely to the employer.

The delegation repeated the call for counterpart funds to be earmarked for low-cost housing as part of a vastly increased propaganda programme at grass-roots level. But there were also very specific proposals to introduce aspects of American industrial relations practice as a means of aiding the non-communist unions—legislative changes designed to strengthen free collective bargaining and efforts to encourage practices such as the granting of exclusive bargaining rights, the union shop, adequate dues paid by check-off, written contracts and more union activity at local and shop level.

It concluded by calling for a stronger American union presence in Europe, the point being addressed more to the labour movement than to the ECA.

> Instead of one or two men stationed in Europe, a half dozen competent representatives of the American labour movement should be available in France alone for advice and counsel to the French labour movement. In addition, American labour should assign and maintain full-time American labour technicians and specialists such as accountants, organisers, publicists and research people in every region and/or national union to aid and assist French labour in its day to day task.

In general it called for a much more concerted effort by labour. There was need for immediate financial assistance on a far greater scale than ever before, and funds earmarked for special purposes ought to be made available, with expenditure supervised by special committees of the ICFTU.[24]

The effect of this report was to help convince the American labour movement that the ECA was not an adequate vehicle for pursuing trade union policies in Europe and that they would have to be more self-reliant. The AFL were, of course, already well established in Europe, with headquarters in Brussels and, latterly, generous covert funding from the CIA. After some indecision the CIO now made their first substantial move in the direction of developing their own distinct international programme. They had created an International Committee in February 1950, and in October Victor Reuther drafted a concrete proposal for a CIO programme in Europe, to be directed from a permanent office on the Continent. The proposed European office would serve as the vehicle for distributing ECA resources, money and supplies to free trade unions and ensure that this assistance was properly used by the recipients. It would help with 'pilot plant projects', conceived under Marshall Aid and meant to encourage European unions to break down employer opposition to higher wages, lower prices and sound labour–management relations—in effect to encourage the adoption of the American approach to labour relations and productivity. Pilot plants would become an important part of the next phase of ECA labour policy. The proposed CIO operation would encourage labour organisations in Europe to initiate representation to their government on projects which would then be supported by the ECA. The office would also provide assistance, encouragement and advice to the ICFTU (in a way that it had not in the years of the WFTU) in the fight to build strong, democratic labour unions and against the worldwide communist challenge. Equally it would directly assist the democratic unions in Europe by developing and providing techniques for winning away membership from communist-dominated unions and in combating communist propaganda.

As envisaged by Reuther, the programme was to be a long-term one and it was to be presented in a way acceptable to Europeans rather than launched as a hard-sell American project:

> The representatives must attempt to see their operation through European eyes, and understand and accept the aspirations and interests, including national interests, of the various European labour movements, and make their contribution on this basis.[25]

The CIO tended to be more sensitive than other American groups to the traditional values of European labour and cautioned government representatives against the blanket export of American labour relations norms and practices. In particular Reuther criticised American labour attachés for defining their function too much in terms of exporting US collective bargaining techniques:

> We must [. . .] start from the premise that most unions are going to have a political identification and tailor our efforts to this fact. [. . .] Collective bargaining may well be one of the tools in our kit—just as it is with the Communists—but to give immediate priority is an oversimplification [. . .].[26]

They emphasized the importance of direct contacts between American and European trade unions, not relying on government agencies as intermediaries. The CIO wanted to see a more systematic use of Marshall Plan funds, but only for labour projects which had been specifically approved by them and which would bear their imprint.[27] If ERP programmes could be devised that enabled non-communist unions to play a more prominent role in their country's economic and industrial life while helping them to improve the material conditions of their members, the basis of a progressive union movement might be laid. Such thinking was central to the CIO's commitment to the pilot plant schemes.

The CIO opened their European office in Paris in 1951 with Victor Reuther as Director and a staff of two—Helmuth Jockel in Germany and Charles Levinson in France. As with Brown's AFL operation, the CIO were primarily engaged in resisting communist influence in the labour movement or, in the not altogether helpful term of the day, promoting 'non-political' trade unionism. But there were important differences in the two approaches. For the AFL the simple objective was to give material support to those European labour elites who demonstrated in ideological terms the most consistent anti-communist line. On the other hand, the CIO sought to distance itself from what it saw as the crudeness of the anti-communism practised by the AFL.

The latter had not so much challenged political unionism as simply substituted one form of political alignment for another:

> Largely because of the political preoccupation of the national leadership, the non-Communist unions have relied to a dangerous extent on a too-simple and too-negative anti-Communism. They have, therefore, had some marked success in frustrating Communist political strikes, but have lost their own ability to use the strike weapon to further economic demands, and have saddled themselves with a reputation for breaking political strikes [. . .]. It is not too much to say that in Italy, American policy is paying a rather heavy price for the electoral victory won against Communism in that country in April of 1948. We too are the victims of a negative anti-Communism.[28]

Despite the Cold War rhetoric that crept into CIO statements in the early 1950s, ideologically and in practice their approach was more flexible than the AFL's, more adaptable to European conditions, less insistent on trying to force foreign labour movements into a rigid mould. Sterile anti-communism was never so pronounced in the CIO as in the AFL. Walter Reuther's dictum 'Neither Standard Oil nor Stalin' reflected a feeling of unease at being forced to choose between distasteful alternatives.

They were critical of the AFL and American government policy in Europe, which had been to favour some labour factions and not others, according to whether or not the AFL found their leadership acceptable. In France FO was favoured by the AFL over the Christian CFTC—and the ECA was encouraged to render aid accordingly. In Italy the AFL, in conjunction with the State Department and the ECA, had attempted to force a premature merger of non-communist labour groups under the banner of the AFL's preferred group, the CISL. The CIO strongly disapproved of this whole approach. The Italian operation had produced an artificial 'top-level merger consummated under remote pressure in New York'. The CIO recognised the importance of financial aid to European labour, but claimed that previous assistance rendered without adequate control had had positively harmful effects. Referring to the glut of money that had entered Italy, and had apparently angered Dubinsky, a CIO delegation to Europe remarked:

> We regret the manner of American support to Italian labour, where the corrupting influence of aid unwisely granted and poorly supervised is sadly in evidence. Too much of that aid had gone to acquire and maintain physical properties, such as national headquarters [. . .].

The CIO approach was thus interventionist without being crudely manipulative in the AFL manner:

> It is unwise to play favourites in the complicated movements of European labour. Our task is not to unify but to galvanise; to provide some of the raw materials of a more vigorous life on the level of economic action. Out of that new vigour can come new victories, new insights, new confidence, new impulses towards functional, if not organic union.[29]

It was not, then, a question of master-minding the policies of other labour movements by pulling strings in Washington, Brussels or Paris. The CIO argued that Americans needed to display more humility than they had in the past when intervening in countries such as Italy. They were entitled to espouse unity among Italian unions, but they had no right to force it. What was needed was a flexible and practical policy capable of building up the economic muscle of European labour and so drawing strength away from the communists.

Their strategy was to find an organisational focus and a form of activity that would enable a vigorous trade unionism to develop and flourish in the different countries. Without ruling out or attempting to undermine political activity by labour—indeed, as Director of the programme Victor Reuther found himself much at home with European social democrats—the primary emphasis was on economic and industrial activity. If workers could begin to see the scope for improving their own lot by their own endeavours in this field they had a chance of overriding the ideological and religious differences that kept them apart and thus kept them weak. So, unlike the AFL, whose approach was to buy support among union leaders in promoting non-communist unity, the CIO hoped to realign and reinvigorate trade unionism at the level of the non-communist rank and file by helping unions provide for the economic needs of their members more thoroughly than communist-led organisations were capable of doing. As redistributive social policies were not on the agenda in France, Italy and Germany, the strategy came to emphasise the need for productivity growth and plant-level collective bargaining over the division of shares from increased output. CIO policy therefore fed in directly to the ERP's growing concern with increased productivity achieved through the techniques of scientific management. In the FTUC Brown and Lovestone saw this as a product of the CIO's naive belief that communism took root only where workers were hungry—'belly communism' was their dismissive expression for it. Consequently they had little interest in the productivity training programmes for trade unionists—'hair-brained schemes' as Brown once referred to them—that came to dominate the Marshall Plan labour programme.[30] These were just an ineffectual response to the misguided concept of 'belly communism'. In their view something more than economic and social gains for workers was needed in order to eliminate the evil of communism.[31] What was required was a more direct ideological campaign.

The CIO's approach to the development of the non-communist labor movements in Europe was a long-term one. It would encounter many obstacles before being discontinued as a result of the merger with the AFL in 1955. Meanwhile the ECA Labour Division was in desperate need of some more immediate improvement in the social and economic climate in Europe. Labour Information Director Harry Martin strongly supported the call for a more vigorous Labour policy. In spring 1950, against a background of rising industrial militancy in various parts of Europe, he advised Milton Katz, Harriman's deputy, that Marshall Plan policies risked alienating European labour:

> we face a grave danger of losing completely the support of European Labour *at the worker level* [. . .]. My opinion is that it has become absolutely *imperative* that the very top echelon of ECA leadership come out openly and boldly with statements that will offset this dangerous threat [. . .] in the propaganda field.[32]

He persuaded Katz to make a strongly worded speech along these lines at an ERP-TUAC Executive meeting in Rome in May 1950, called to mark the half-way stage of Marshall Aid. Katz spoke of the need for high and stable employment, higher productivity (whose importance Harriman had not always recognised) and positive steps towards European integration. Martin regarded the episode as a major triumph, marking a decisive and necessary change in emphasis if the ECA was to reclaim the waning support of European labour.[33]

Of course it was no such thing, as events were to prove. A two-day conference of OSR Labour personnel later in May 1950, attended by Harriman, Katz, David Bruce, the Chief of Mission to France, and several US labour attachés, provided an opportunity to discuss the situation and air frustrations. James Killen, Labour Adviser to the UK mission, summed up the view of the Labour staff, pointing out during a discussion of the production drive:

> Lip service has been given to these safeguards [i.e. policies for full employment and retraining] by Ambassador Katz and others in public statements, but I am perhaps not fully informed. I have not seen in any country ECA action specifically designed to insist on the provision of funds for public works and housing or these other things to take up or to aid in taking up the slack.[34]

Three of the most senior Labour Advisers, Killen, Douty and Wesley Cook of the Austrian mission were asked to prepare a joint statement on behalf of the Labour staff in Europe. It called for a restatement of ECA objectives combined with effective programmes on employment, prices, consumption and housing. So far, it pointed out, ECA objectives and accomplishments had been stated in terms of trade liberalisation, economic integration, European payments union, all crucial to European recovery but having virtually no direct and positive meaning to European workers. The authors therefore called for a 'ringing declaration' from the higher ECA authorities that full employment was the prime aim of the Marshall Plan. They called for the governments of the participating countries to re-examine their programmes to provide an improvement in real incomes, for the ECA to initiate a complete re-examination of country programmes and for it to make 'direct and forceful representations' to European governments on matters of housing, protection against unemployment and the sharing of increases in production and productivity. Finally they called on the ECA to encourage and initiate broad programmes to safeguard workers against the dislocating effects of trade liberalisation and the productivity drives.[35]

However, the reaction of the ECA's policy planners to proposals for more direct action to safeguard living standards was a foregone conclusion. Richard Bissell had recently rejected Douty's proposal that substantial wage increases be urged for French workers. That would be inflationary, and instead he pinned his faith in competition policy to increase the supply of goods and services and thereby lower consumer prices.[36] Hoffman had already cabled Harriman:

> Full employment therefore cannot be overriding objective but is only a legitimate goal to extent that it does not conflict with measures essential for viability. In particular reiteration of goal of full employment is not sufficient answer to any and all criticism of domestic monetary policy, balance of payments situation, investment programmes and consumption levels [. . .].[37]

On living standards the Administrator would not budge from the position agreed by participating countries in 1948 that *per capita* consumption should not rise above 1938 levels before the end of the aid programme in 1952. Consequently the joint statement by the Labour staff cut little ice. Harriman told Katz, '[. . .] it is an unbalanced statement and it would be fatal to hold out hopes which could not be realised.'[38]

The year 1950 was very much a time of truth for the Marshall Plan labour programme. Hitherto the Labour Division had failed to make any real positive impact on national policies for labour–management relations and social programmes in the trouble spots of Europe. However, they had played a significant negative role in helping to divide the labour movement. The politically fragmented labour groups in France and Italy were either too weak to attempt revolution, or too weak to insist that Marshall Aid be made to benefit them directly. It was not the outcome American labour had bargained for, but it had facilitated the achievement of other Marshall Plan goals. A mood of cynicism was now discernible among the Labour staff where formerly there had been enthusiasm. In October 1950 the State Department convened a conference of government officials presided over by Ambassador-at-large Jessup on future American goals in international policy. Once again participants heard the by now ritual statement that labour was the most important target of American propaganda in support of democratic ideals. Robert Oliver of the Oil Workers' Union (CIO), and recently appointed executive assistant to Golden and Jewell, asked just what was meant by this. Did it mean that labour in overseas countries was to be the target of propaganda designed to make dissatisfied people more compliant, or was the purpose to help them win their grievances, convincing them that the democratic nations had an interest in their welfare that transcended the requirements of military experience. To William Foster, Hoffman's successor as ECA Administrator and a former steel magnate, he wrote, following the conference:

> By economic support and clever use of propaganda techniques we may be successful in a short term operation of keeping a reactionary government in power merely because it is anti-communistic [. . .].

But, he concluded, 'You can't establish a propaganda substitute for a decent standard of living and simple justice.'[39]

With the militarisation of Marshall Aid accompanying the outbreak of hostilities in Korea in June 1950 there was a new urgency in the ECA Labour programme. No substantive changes in policy of great value to labour occurred, but there was a more systematic approach to combating communism. Assistance to non-communist trade unions had to exceed what had gone before, and as Shishkin indicated, this was to be 'intimately related to organisational, informational and propaganda activities'. Success depended on the ECA's ability to assemble 'a competent staff able to act as a disciplined and anonymous task force in the work of development of effective personnel and organisation within the European non-communist trade unions'. Apart from maintaining current contacts and liaison with European trade unions the ECA's Labour Division would need to launch what Shishkin termed 'aggressive' and 'confidential' programmes.[40] At the Labour staff conference in May 1950 the French mission chief, David Bruce, had talked of the importance of subversion as an anti-communist weapon. During the war he had been head of OSS activities in Europe and was responsible for espionage. Now he advocated the use of black propaganda techniques, or 'sabotage', as he regarded it, in addition to routine ECA public relations and information work:

> I think our tendency is in letting our civilisation speak for itself. It has not worked [. . .]. I do not think we can simply accept as a fact that truth under all conditions will prevail [. . .].
> In the black [propaganda] field it would be possible to revive some of the things that happened in the war [. .]. let me call it 'subversive propaganda' [. . .]. I address myself only to the question of what you, I and everybody in this room might be doing in regard to it [. . .].[41]

This was the theme that Shishkin emphasised in summing up at the close of the conference: the need to subvert the enemy, the need to formulate a basic propaganda strategy going far beyond the standard information and publicity programme to all aspects of trade union work.[42]

ECA Labour staff were formally divided into two departments— Advisory and Information—but in practice the two were hard to separate and there was a considerable overlap of functions. Labour Advisers were expected to monitor labour and manpower developments in the participating countries while the Information section engaged in public relations/propaganda work. In fact it was more realistic to view them as complementary parts of an overall intelligence-gathering/opinion-moulding exercise. But the point about this intelligence role was that it was not simply desk work such as embassy staff might be engaged in; it involved active intervention.

A clear indication of the role that Labour staff were expected to play in the Korean War phase of Marshall Aid is apparent from general guidelines drawn up by Glen Atkinson, Labour Adviser to the UK mission in January 1951. The threat of communism was not regarded by the ECA as very serious in Britain, yet Labour staff had to make a special effort to capture hearts and minds in the labour movement. '[. . .] the largest and most important basic group in any democratic industrial society is the wage-earning group. It is to them above all that our foreign policy and defence aims must be secured. *This cannot be done solely through informational channels'* (emphasis added) Consequently Labour staff were to contact and cultivate members of the Labour government, Labour members of Parliament, members of the party's National Executive Committee, local Labour and trade union leaders and influential rank-and-filers, all with the aim of furthering acceptance of American foreign policy and defence aims. It was their broad responsibility to discover and influence British attitudes (and especially trade union attitudes) on manpower questions relating to the defence effort. More specifically they were required to gather intelligence on possible trouble spots in defence industries and to screen workers and plants where defence contracts had been placed so as to pre-empt the danger of sabotage or politically inspired strikes. In doing this they were to exchange information with the TUC and its affiliated unions on actual or possible industrial disputes. And through personal contacts within the TUC and individual unions they were responsible for imparting 'techniques and strategy for eliminating CP influence in specific trade union and trades council situations with particular emphasis on areas where CP strength is greatest or most strategic with reference to the defence programme'.[43]

What this actually meant can be seen in a small way in the work of William Gausmann, the mission's Labour Information Officer. Gausmann was a very able, energetic official and a perceptive student of British labour affairs. He travelled widely around the country, attending union conferences and Labour Party gatherings, lecturing at labour movement weekend and summer schools, and in the process became one of the best informed observers of the labour scene. He was familiar with the personalities and their politics and his reports on internal developments in particular unions or sections of the movement tended to be highly detailed compilations of valuable intelligence.

Under instructions to intervene to secure American defence interests, Gausmann became directly involved in anti-communist campaigns as the Marshall Plan moved into its militaristic phase. In May 1950, for example, he began discussions with a section of the leadership of the Clerical and Allied Workers' Union on how to eliminate communists from the union, a campaign that was to prove successful. He cultivated the leadership of the Birmingham Labour Party, whose journal, *The Town Crier*, closely supported Atlanticism and American foreign policy objectives in general. He took the initiative in convening a group in South Wales which was brought together to launch a Labour-oriented newspaper, *The Democrat*, so providing a challenge to the Communist Party in this, one of their strongholds. His department worked closely with the TUC, gaining privileged access to sensitive information and being able to report to Washington, for example, on the TUC's plans to purge communists from the London Trades Council before the event. Gausmann briefed Labour leaders attending a communist-backed peace conference organised by the Scottish TUC. He liaised with the international trade secretariats in London, advised the International Transport Workers' Federation on their public relations and, on their behalf, hired a specialist to work in their information section.[44] As an ECA official he had close contacts in the Foreign Office and he assisted with the publicity for and distribution of a collection of anti-communist writings, *The Curtain Falls*, edited by Denis Healey and published by Ampersand, an imprint established and subsidised by the Foreign Office's secret Information Research Department, which specialised in grey and black propaganda.[45]

From the outset he had good contacts with people in the labour movement grouped around the magazine *Socialist Commentary*, whose editor, Allan Flanders, he had met at Oxford just after the war. Gausmann worked unofficially on *Socialist Commentary*, acted as American correspondent and sometimes wrote editorials.[46] He also arranged for the ECA to subsidise the distribution in Britain and America of a pamphlet collection of its articles on trade unionism. Drawn to the magazine's particular brand of Fabianism, he became a founder member of its offshoot, the Socialist Union, which served as a think-tank for the emerging Gaitskellite wing of the Labour Party, and even acted as chairman of a Socialist Union working party on Labour Party democracy—despite the fact that Labour Party membership was supposed to be a condition of belonging to the Union.[47] Interestingly, this partisan political activity in Britain brought him into conflict with the embassy's labour attaché, Joseph Godson, whose own direct involvement in internal Labour Party affairs even extended to participation in secret caucus meetings of Gaitskell's supporters during the plotting to expel Aneurin Bevan from the party in 1955.[48] There was evident rivalry between the two wings of the American labour movement for the ear of Labour's rising leader—Gausmann's contacts were with the CIO and especially the Reuther group; Godson was an ILGWU protege of Dubinsky. And it was through these channels that Gaitskell was invited by Dubinsky to the United States in 1956 to address the Jewish Labour Committee and for which he received an inflated expenses cheque of $3,000 which helped him to underwrite the costs of *Forward*, the struggling journal newly acquired by the Gaitskellites.[49]

Gausmann's record demonstrates the opportunities that existed for energetic, capable ECA Labour staff to operate with some effect on an individual basis. But on a programmatic level the Labour Division had great difficulty in making an impact. From 1950–51 the ECA's main hope of remodelling the European labour movement lay in its productivity campaign, which was first developed in Britain and subsequently exported to the Continent. We must now turn to this important aspect of the programme.

Revisionism: The Marshall Plan and Managerial Values

Revisionism—the tendency to abandon traditional Marxist and other class-based precepts in socialist analysis—did not originate in the Marshall Plan years [the elements were already there] but it was greatly encouraged by the vast programme of social engineering launched under Marshall Aid. In Britain the roots of Labour's post-war accommodation with capitalism were visible in the thinking of such people as Evan Durbin, Hugh Gaitskell and Douglas Jay as early as the late 1930s as they began to develop an economic theory of social democracy. By the 1940s they had already absorbed the ideas of Joseph Schumpeter on economic growth and James Burnham's concept of a managerial society. In the next decade they would assimilate the views of writers such as Peter Drucker and J. K. Galbraith on pluralist industrial society. Keen to discover ways of managing a capitalist economy and particularly concerned to improve economic efficiency while relying as much as possible on market forces, they took a great interest in the latest managerial practices in such areas as cost accounting and incentive schemes.[50]

Their emphasis on managerial notions of efficiency brought them into conflict with more traditional socialists such as G. D. H. Cole who were still concerned more with promoting non-market conditions for production than with gross output, with structures for administering socialised industry rather than with growth. However, in the late 1940s, as members of the Attlee government, Durbin and Gaitskell became very influential in preaching acceptance of the mixed economy and Keynesian values, the centrality of economic growth and a strategy for Labour that emphasised technical solutions to the problems of production for the creation of more wealth rather than class conflict over the distribution of existing wealth. The discovery of the key to sustained economic growth and commitment to it by national governments was an intrinsic part of the post-war value system of capitalism. It inspired and in turn fed on managerialist thinking, a growing productivity consciousness and the powerful notion of the 'end of ideology'. In what Raymond Aron termed the 'growth society', animated by the spirit of quantity and progress, economic growth was consonant with 'the true order of being'.[51] With a revolution in the mentality of business accompanying this, it was now fair to talk about an emerging ideology of growth.

The notion of the 'managerial revolution' that Burnham had identified had a profound effect on Labour Party thinking, and although it would gradually come to be criticised there is no doubt that in the late 1940s and into the 1950s it was widely regarded as a positive development. Typical was Stafford Cripps's comment at the founding conference of the British Institute of Management in April 1948 that industry had moved away from the authoritarian concept of management.[52] There was always a beguiling tendency for managerialism to be presented as neutral and universal in its application. Britain's first post-war gesture in the direction of managerial training, the establishment of the Administrative Staff College at Henley in 1946, was intended to provide common studies on the principles of organisation and administration in civil life for young executives in private enterprise, the public services and trade union officials alike. In this way the notion was fostered that management was, in the jargon of the day, a 'third force', standing between the polarities of labour and capital, and able, by dint of its technical competence, to bridge their differences. As Deputy Director of the BIM in 1948 Austen Albu, soon to become an influential member of the Parliamentary Labour party, believed in the importance of management as a neutral activity. He and the Labour MP Ian Mikardo were prominently involved in launching the short-lived Society of Socialist Managers and Technicians in the late 1940s, an attempt to integrate this new group of 'knowledge workers' into the Labour Party. As an American observer of the Labour Party and Labour government wrote in 1950:

> The thesis of Burnham's Managerial Revolution seems to have been taken over by Labour spokesmen and Labour theoreticians, lock, stock and barrel. [. . .] One would gather from these references that businessmen in Britain are being led, as though by the unseen hand of technological logos, to encompass broad social ends which are not only no part of, but are actually contrary to, narrow objectives of their entrepreneurial intentions.[53]

With Stafford Cripps as Chancellor of the Exchequer from 1947 these managerialist values reinforced his preoccupation with output and productivity, matters which had concerned him since his wartime days as the Minister responsible for aircraft production. Economic planning in this environment became a technical exercise with a logic that transcended political considerations. The planning priorities of enhanced production and reduced inflation—part of Labour's adaptation to the requirements of the Marshall programme—inevitably displaced socialist objectives on the government's agenda. Productivity took precedence over equality. High production and the turn away from egalitarianism as a priority went hand-in-hand with the acceptance of the need for reasonable levels of profitability in industry, which in turn relied on the motivation of self-interest. In these ways Labour's economic strategy after 1947 marked the abandonment of any claim to be constructing a new economic order.[54] Thereafter the government's economic policy was marked by retrenchment and defensiveness. Psychologically and practically Labour had lost the initiatives.[55] The Marshall Plan elevated 'productivity' to the level of a deity, but while Cripps was an instinctive worshipper at this shrine it was very much the circumstances of the American recovery plan for Europe that allowed his interest to flourish so.

The immediate effect of these new ideas was not to encourage whole-sale revisionism in Labour's thinking, rather it resulted in 'consolida-tionism', that growing climate of opinion from 1948 that Labour had gone far enough, or as far as it was prudent to go, and that the need now was to iron out the kinks in the newly constructed mixed-economy welfare state. There would be no new major programme of socialisation, and a special effort would be made to retain the support of the middle class. Of course, the real political issue was not whether Britain should settle for a mixed economy, rather what the balance should be between socialised and private interests and the speed at which Labour should move to ensure that the essential instruments of planning and control were democratically controlled.[56]

Bit by bit the sentiment in favour of consolidation was taking hold. Labour's 1950 election manifesto listed only four candidates for na-tionalisation, a concocted programme of 'odds and ends', as Morrison was later to deride it. Even the parliamentary left was now in retreat on this issue: *Keeping Left* was concerned less about the ownership of industry than about who managed it, and therefore concluded that the next steps were not so obvious or so simple.[57] Consolidationism was generally accepted by the party, though only grudgingly by the left and the revisionists. The struggle between them would not be resolved until the second half of the 1950s, when the Gaitskellites took control of the party machine and infused its policy with revisionist values.

The transition from consolidation to revision in the early 1950s was reflected in the thinking of Labour intellectuals who contributed to *New Fabian Essays, Socialist Commentary* and were identified with the Socialist Union. When people like Richard Crossman argued that man-agerial society constituted a threat to human freedom he was countered by people who contended that such a society was capable of being civilised by socialism. This was a recurring theme in *New Fabian Essays*, one of the first post-war attempts at revising basic Labour thinking and establishing new values for socialism. In an exploratory essay that constituted a dry run for his famous treatise of four years later, *The Future of Socialism*, Anthony Crosland observed that managerialism had helped bring about a metamorphosis of British capitalism such that it no longer deserved the name. Austen Albu gave the line a further twist in arguing that, just as scientists were essentially team players and therefore adaptable to the egalitarian norms of a democratic socialist society, so also the application of the social sciences to business management would generate a co-operative and more so-cially responsible mentality among managers.[58] Thus although, at first blush, the managerial revolution seemed to substitute a new au-thoritarian hierarchy for the old class structure, such need not neces-sarily be the case. Business companies were rational in form and not in themselves anti-social. They needed to be tailored and refined to meet modern needs. How was this to be done? All supporters of this soft version of managerialism agreed it required a change in the relationship between management and labour, but equally most of them fought shy of concrete formulations that could reasonably be described as industrial democracy. On this point Cripps had set the tone in a famous speech in Bristol in October 1946 when he remarked that it would be almost impossible to have worker-controlled industry in Britain, 'even if it were on the whole desirable', without workers having more experience of the managerial side of industry.[59] In rejecting the authoritarian view of the managerial revolution the new Fabian essayists stood accused of opening a side door to a more beguiling form of managerialism, still resistant to democratisation. Their approach undervalued mass activity in industry while elevating to a lofty plane technicism and the logic of management science.[60]

In an organisational sense the revisionists were grouped around the magazine *Socialist Commentary* and the Socialist Union. *Socialist Commentary* was originally the journal of the Socialist Vanguard Group [SVG], the British section of the Internationalen Sozialistischen Kampfbundes [ISK], which had been expelled from the German SPD in 1928 for opposition to its Marxist materialist perspective. Though tiny, in Britain the SVG was an influential group, especially when after 1950, led by Allan Flanders and Rita Hinden, it ceased to operate as a sect and settled for being the driving force at the centre of the Socialist Union, which it launched in 1951 as both a focus for political activism and a think-tank—in its own eyes a more serious version of the Fabian Society. *Socialist Commentary* and the Socialist Union were plugged in direct to the Marshall Plan operation in Britain by virtue of the fact that William Gausmann, Labour Information Officer in the London mission, was a member of the journal's editorial board.[61] In *Socialist Commentary* and the more considered publications of the Socialist Union an attempt was made to point Labour in a new direction, away from the Bevanite left and the pragmatic consolidators among the existing party and trade union leadership. The emphasis was on socialism as an ethical and moral movement; their concerns were with equality, freedom and, more nebulously, 'fellowship'. While there were expressions of disapproval over the contemporary obsession with productivity and materialism, they regarded this as necessary for freedom, simply needing to be tempered by a greater spirit of fellowship. And if they had some doubts about managerialism all they could suggest as a counterweight was 'responsible participation' by workers.[62]

While the Bevanites were still defending the old barricades against challenges to Labour's 1945 programme and concentrating especially on foreign-policy matters, the revisionists were quietly extending their influence and preparing the ground for the main attempt to reorient Labour orthodoxy which came with Anthony Crosland's *The Future of Socialism*. Heavily influenced by American liberal thought and written following an extended visit to the United States, *The Future of Socialism* was the quintessential expression of Marshall Plan values as applied to British social democracy. Emphasising economic growth, equality [social rather than economic] and the end of ideology, Crosland put forward the most comprehensive case for revisionism in the context of managerial society. Viewing the managerial revolution without alarm, he maintained that a shift in industry's moral consensus had already caused private industry to be humanised, and the trend needed to be extended. These were years when, as Coates observes, the capitalist element in British industry was gradually played down, it being referred to in increasingly bland terms as 'private enterprise', 'business' or simply 'industry'.[63]

The crucial problem now identified was that of the psychology of industrial relations. For Crosland this meant taking a further lead from United States industrial relations practice, where top executives were much more professional and enlightened than their British counterparts and, with their obsession with labour and personnel problems, were constantly searching for more progressive ideas: 'the talk is all about participation, co-operation, human relations, etc. Autocratic management is taboo; teamwork is in and Elton Mayo replaces Henry Ford as the symbol of management's attitude to labour.'[64] Again more consultation was called for, but this was not to come about through joint management or anything like that, rather as a consequence of enlightenment.[65] Attitudes were all-important. Crosland's increasingly harmonious view of industrial society was blind to any consideration of the purposes for which management was now keen to proffer a softer image. Had industrial management really moved so far away from authoritarian practices? Had Mayo and the proponents of motivation theory really superseded Ford and Taylor? Or was it simply, as Mant suggests, a case of British business, with its 'long and unlovely history of employee exploitation', falling with enthusiasm on American approaches to motivation.[66] The softening of management's image was a means of retaining managerial control in the changed environment of a welfare state. Control in the interests of managerial efficiency was still the prime objective, and when it was threatened, whether by labour or by government, industrial management was likely to mount a fierce resistance.[67] Whatever neutral, technical values applied to the concept of management in the United States, when American managerialism was imported into Britain it reinforced traditional class-based hierarchies.

Four years earlier in *New Fabian Essays* Richard Crossman had urged that citizens should be granted the right to participate in the control of industry—*even at the cost of some efficiency.*[68] In the United States Daniel Bell also speculated that the managerial revolution might be challenged by the substitution of some real thought about the labour process for the fashionable human relations values of the age—in effect reopening the study of the technology of work and challenging the accepted notion of 'efficiency'. But, of course, in an age of Marshall Plan productivity campaigning there was never any question of efficiency yielding to wider social values: efficiency was exactly what the proponents of managerialism were preoccupied with. Indeed, the whole thrust of Bell's writing was to show how an unquestioned acceptance of the ideal of efficiency underlay the technical and social organisation of industry.[69]

The managerial revolution in its 'civilised' form was an integral element in the much discussed 'end of ideology' which emerged as a powerful idea in the 1950s and on which Bell was an eloquent commentator. As he saw it, 'in a silently emerging "managerial revolution", technical decision-making by the economic expert now shapes the politician's pronouncements'. The consequence in Europe, he claimed, was the 'exhaustion of socialist thought'.[70] The end of ideology reflected the ascendancy of pragmatism in political systems and the eclipse of absolute principles and political dogmatism. The British labour movement was a case in point, with the Gaitskellite wing of the Labour Party formally in control after 1955 and, as Clark Kerr noted, its Croslandite thinking pragmatically oriented towards goals instead of ideologically towards method. 'England certainly is helped,' Kerr confidently assured his readers, 'by the fact that we are at the end of what might be called the "Socialist Century", the century when the socialist challenge and socialist thought were so important. By now it has been discovered [. . .] the eternal conflict of manager and managed may be subject to other and better solutions [. . .].'[71]

The notion of an 'end of ideology' drew heavily on American experience or, more specifically, American experience as filtered through the eyes of a school of intellectuals, often disillusioned radicals of the political left, whose prolific output of writing was a major factor in the spread of the idea. Among the most influential of the American ideologues of the 'end of ideology' school were the academics involved in the Inter-university Labour Project financed by the Ford Foundation. . . . The Inter-university Project was important in establishing an intellectual basis for American claims to world leadership in industrial practices, and the end of ideology which they detected in various parts of the world served to increase the legitimacy of the management-led American system. Industrialism was the common characteristic of all advanced countries and managerialism was its motor force, the guarantor of the inevitability of progress. In *Industrialism and Industrial Man,* the best known product of the Inter-university Project, the focus of attention in modern industrial society was no longer on the response of labour to capitalist development, but on how to *structure and manage* the labour force. The need, then, was to fashion a suitably harmonious labour relations system. As the participants in this project recognised, there was a world-wide contest going on over industrial relations systems no less than over economic systems, the importance of industrial relations systems being that they defined and established power and authority relationships in industry. The labour issue that pressed most heavily on modern industrial society was related to productivity: how could labour's pace of working be raised and then maintained? The most lasting solutions were held to be found in American experience, where a middle-class managerial elite presided over a society in which ideologies had ceased to be relevant. Here, as Crosland had pointed out, managers were becoming increasingly benevolent and increasingly skilled, there were no clear-cut divisions between workers and managers in what was essentially an open society. And in this environment the role of unions was simply to regulate management at the workplace and to offer no greater challenge. American society provided a model for other countries, for in industrial societies the range of practical options was necessarily limited. The old working-class utopias were no longer relevant and people seldom had a real choice between ideological alternatives. There was in short, an inevitable tendency for ideology to wither as industrialism survived.[72]

It was indeed the American model that Anthony Crosland embraced so enthusiastically and with such effect as he set about providing an intellectual rationale for Labour revisionism in the 1950s. The greater class harmony in the United States was said to be a function of the quality of management. Workers who rose to management posts were not condemned as class traitors; trade union leaders were not thought to be in danger of contamination if they showed an interest in conspicuous consumption; the unions were not deemed guilty of treachery if they co-operated with management to boost sales or raise productivity, nor were they regarded with suspicion, he argued with an eye on the EPA's exchange visit scheme, if they sent their officials to Harvard for training.[73] On the other hand, organised labour in Britain was placed in the dock for its insufficient interest in managerial efficiency and productivity drives. Sounding a note that was to echo strongly throughout the rest of the 1950s and into the 1960s, he argued that there would have to be a professionalisation of unions' staff to equip them for the managerial economy.[74]

As a well orchestrated press campaign built up in the mid-1950s attacking unions for their restrictive practices, and as prominent employers such as BMC, Ford and Standard Motors were encouraged to go on the offensive for the first time since the war in demanding that unions formally accede to managerial prerogative in a variety of ways, revisionist literature supplied the other cutting edge in this two-way attack, arguing for a complete rethink of union philosophy. The unions were accused of being 'robber barons', irresponsible and guilty of abusing their power,[75] and failing to see any virtues in capitalism.[76] They needed to adopt a more 'positive and constructive role'.[77] The argument was often presented in terms of the unions' technical failings but the underlying politics of the debate were never far from the surface. As a PEP study of trade unions pointed out, 'What is needed is [. . .] to rally behind the reformers the large body of trade unionists who are moderate and sensible but are at present defensive, sensitive to criticism and uncertain what to do.'[78]

In most revisionist literature there were positive appeals for some vague form of workers' participation—but never such as would leave them with any real influence. Industrial democracy was always presented as an attitude of mind, a form of managerial thinking rather than a concrete institutional arrangement in which workers had collective rights. In Shanks's gnomic formulation—industrial democracy was simply an aspect of good management.[79]

Thus Marshall Plan values, promoted through the extensive programme of social engineering, provided a congenial environment in which deradicalising pressures could operate on the labour movement in the 1950s. Marshall Aid cannot take total responsibility for revisionism, but it contributed mightily to the successes that it enjoyed. By the end of the 1950s organised labour in Britain and elsewhere in Europe had been steered away from some of the more radical objectives it had briefly and vaguely harboured in 1945. There was of course a dialectical process at work here, and the issue of workers' control and industrial democracy that had been forced off the agenda in the 1950s was to return in one form or another in the 1960s and 1970s. But the success of management's Taylorian values in undermining workers' scope for controlling the labour process was much more complete. Despite so-called 'labour process theory' being a fashionable subject of academic debate in the 1980s, there has been no significant counter-thrust from organised labour in this area. And for that result the Marshall Plan productivity programmes directed at labour must take much credit.

Endnotes

1. *ADA World*, December 1949.

2. Krane to Cope, 4 December 1948, Krane 1 (3).

3. Krane to Cope, 14 December 1948, Krane 1 (3).

4. Krane to Cope, 11 January 1949, Krane 1 (3).

5. Shishkin to Katz, 31 August 1949, ECA/OSR Cent. Sec. 15.

6. Ozer memorandum, 'A Suggestion for an Ad Hoc Committee to Evaluate,' 8 September 1949, ECA Lab. Div. 143.

7. Martin to Harriman, 15 December 1949, ECA/OSR Cent. Sec. 15.

8. Turtledove to Martin, 31 January 1950, ECA LI 130.

9. Douty to Bingham, 7 February 1950, ECA LI 5.

10. Douty to Golden, 15 February 1950, ECA Lab. Div. 149.

11. See pp. 12–13 of Anthony Carew, *Labour Under the Marshall Plan*, Manchester University Press, 1987.

12. Special Assistant to the Under Secretary of State to Hoffman, 31 December 1948, ECA Admin. 5.

13. On this see Arkes, pp. 314–15.

14. Turtledove to Martin, 1 April 1950, ECA LI 130.

15. Shishkin to Katz, 16 May 1950, ECA/OSR Cent. Sec. 15.

16. *Ibid.*

17. Martin to Douty, 2 May 1950, ECA LI 130.

18. Golden and Jewell to Wood and Stone, 4 April 1950, ECA Lab. Div. 149.

19. Memorandum of meeting in the office of Donald Stone, 17 April 1950, ECA LI, 131. Two days later Stone, the Director of Administration, ECA Washington, told Hoffman: 'The use of confidential funds was viewed as very unsuitable for the above purposes, although there are certain ways, as Jewell realises, in which they might possibly be employed.' Stone to Hoffman and Foster, 19 April 1950, ECA Admin. 5. General counsel to OSR had previously advised that it was legally possible to finance special projects from this source even though they could not be justified as direct costs of mission administration. General Counsel OSR to Deputy Chief of Mission, Bizone, 2 October 1948, ECA LI 163.

20. Bingham to Secretary of State, 27 April 1950, ECA Lab. Div. 144.

21. *Labour News from the US*, 14 September 1950; Jewell to Smith, 3 October 1950, ECA Lab. Div. 146.

22. Gausmann to Martin, 3 January 1950, ECA LI 130. Sheyer to Shishkin, 5 April 1950, ECA Lab. Div. 146.

23. Jewell to Stone, 14 April 1950, ECA Admin. 5.

24. Report on France by three American Trade Unionists, 1 October 1950, ECA Lab. Div. 149.

25. Programme to Expand CIO Staff in Europe, 23 October 1950, CIO International 64 [16].

26. 'International functions of the US Government', undated, UAW International, Reuther-Carliner 1956–62, 64.

27. Report of CIO Committee to Europe to CIO Committee on International Affairs, March 1951, CIO International 64 [16].

28. *Ibid.*

29. *Ibid.*

30. Brown to Lovestone, 2 December 1951; AFL Paper on ICFTU, undated [February 1952?], Dubinsky 260 [6A].

31. William J. Humphreys, 'Bevanism on the Continent', *New York Herald Tribune*, 23 April 1952.

32. Martin to Katz, 21 March 1950, ECA Lab. Div. 143.

33. Martin to Katz, 21 March 1950; Hutchison to Golden, 20 April 1950, Golden 3 [27]; ERP-TUAC Conference, Rome, 18–20 April 1950, ECA Lab. Div. 143; Martin to Golden, 8 July 1950, Golden 4 [17].

34. Transcript of Proceedings, European Labour Staff Conference.

35. Memorandum: Some Comments on Future ECA Programming, ECA/OSR Cent. Sec. 15.

36. Bissell to Golden and Jewell, 27 March 1950, ECA Lab. Div. 149.

37. Hoffman to Harriman, 12 January 1950, ECA/OSR Cent. Sec. 15.

38. Harriman to Katz, 18 June 1950, ECA/OSR Cent. Sec. 15.

39. Oliver to Foster, 20 October 1950, ECA Lab. Div. 149.

40. Shishkin to Katz, Programme Objectives of Labour Division 1950–51, 7 July 1950 ECA/OSR Cent. Sec. 15.

41. Transcript of Proceedings, European Labour Staff Conference.

42. *Ibid.*

43. Functions of Mission Labour Division in Relation to the Defence Programme, February 1951, ECA LI 130.

44. Gausmann, Monthly Reports of Major Activities, February 1950–September 1951, ECA LI 130 and 137.

45. Gausmann to Evans, 2 April 1951, ECA LI 130; Lyn Smith, 'Covert British propaganda: the Information Research Department, 1947–77', *Journal of International Studies*, Vol. 9, No. 1, pp. 75–8. A Foreign Office file on the circumstances surrounding the publication of *The Curtain Falls* which should now be open under the thirty-year rule is closed indefinitely.

46. Gausmann to Martin, 3 February 1950, ECA LI 130.

47. Socialist Union papers are in the Socialist Vanguard Group Collection, Modern Record Centre, Warwick University.

48. Philip Williams [ed.], *The Diary of Hugh Gaitskell, 1945–56*, Cape, 1983, p. 384. Information on the dispute between Gausmann and Godson comes from Murray Weisz, who served as acting chief of the FOA Labour Division in Europe in 1953–54. Interview, 28 August 1986.

49. Gaitskell to Dubinsky, 20 June 1956, Dubinsky 248 [8A].

50. Elizabeth Durbin, *New Jerusalems*, Routledge, 1985, pp. 263–76.

51. Raymond Aron, *The Industrial Society*, Weidenfeld & Nicolson, 1967, pp. 14, 60, 99.

52. A. A. Rogow, *The Labour Government and British Industry, 1945–51*, Greenwood, 1974, p. 103.

53. R. A. Brady, *Crisis in Britain*, Cambridge University Press, 1950, p. 563.

54. David Howell, *British Social Democracy*, Croom Helm, 1976, p. 159.

55. Morgan, pp. 357–8.

56. Michael Foot, *Aneurin Bevan*, Vol. II, Paladin, 1975, p. 256.

57. Ralph Miliband, *Parliamentary Socialism*, Merlin, 1973, p. 306.

58. C. A. R. Crosland, 'The transition from capitalism,' and Austen Albu, 'The organisation of industry,' in R. H. A. Crossman [ed.], *New Fabian Essays*, Turnstile Press, 1953, pp. 33–5, 38–9, 131, 135, 142.

59. *Times*, 28 October 1945.

60. Andrew Filson, *Socialist Commentary*, June 1952, p. 141.

61. On the internal affairs of the Socialist Union see Socialist Vanguard Group Papers, Modern Record Centre, Warwick University. Gausmann was a founding member of the Socialist Union and in the mid-1950s chaired its working party on Labour Party democracy.

62. Socialist Union, *Twentieth Century Socialism*, Penguin, 1956, pp. 7, 16, 58; *Socialism: a New Statement of Principles*, Lincolns-Prager, 1952, p. 51.

63. David Coates, *The Labour Party and the Struggle for Socialism*, Cambridge University Press, 1975, p. 90.

64. C. A. R. Crosland, *The Future of Socialism*, Schocken, 1963, p. 157.

65. *Ibid.*, p. 263.

66. A. Mant, *The Rise and Fall of the British Manager*, Pan, 1977, p. 76.

67. A. A. Rogow, pp. 178–9.

68. R. H. S. Crossman, 'Towards a philosophy of socialism,' in Crossman, *op. cit.*, p. 29.

69. Daniel Bell, *The End of Ideology*, Free Press, 1965, pp. 15, 251, 262.

70. *Ibid.*, p. 295.

71. Clark Kerr, 'Productivity and labour relations,' in *Labour and Management in Industrial Society*, Doubleday, 1964, pp. 279–80.

72. Clark Kerr *et al.*, *Industrialism and Industrial Man*, Heinemann, 1962, p. 283.

73. Crosland, *The Future of Socialism*, pp. 180, 253.

74. *Ibid.*, pp. 263–4.

75. Eric Wigham, *What's wrong with the Unions*, Penguin, 1961, p. 14.

76. Michael Shanks, *The Stagnant Society*, Penguin, 1961, pp. 45 and 64.

77. PEP, *Trade Unions in a Changing Society*, Vol. XXIX, No. 472, 10 June 1963, p. 207.

78. *Ibid.*, p. 218.

79. Shanks, pp. 161–2.

Suggestions for Further Reading and Research

Some important publications have been cited in the footnotes to my Introduction and in the editorial prefaces to the different selections. These works will *not* be listed again here. Scholarship on the Cold War and postwar Europe has been so extensive that no reasonably exhaustive bibliography can be provided in brief compass. The notes and bibliographies of the works from which selections have been excerpted above will bring the reader up to date on the special topics under consideration. Thomas McCormick, *America's Half Century* (Baltimore, Johns Hopkins University Press, 1990) offers a useful guide to reading arranged according to his chapter outline. Walter LaFeber, *America, Russia, and the Cold War 1945–1984*, 5th ed. (New York, Knopf, 1985), remains a useful, balanced survey.

Several journals carry the major new interpretations and monographic research. *Diplomatic History,* the quarterly of the Society for Historians of American Foreign Relations, has consistently emphasized research on the Cold War period. Other articles appear in *The Journal of American History;* occasionally in the *American Historical Review; The Historical Journal* (published in Britain); and from time to time in *Italia Contemporanea, Vierteljahrshefte für Zeitgeschichte,* or *Relations Internationales.* East European journals, which used to be dreary repositories of Party orthodoxy, now are beginning to feature lively exchanges and self-examinations concerning recent history and historical approaches.

Since I published the first edition of this book in 1978, there has been a vast expansion of available public documentation. U.S. State Department records are open through the 1950s. Selections continue to be published as United States Department of State, *Foreign Relations of the United States* (Washington: GPO). (Previously issued in a year-by-year topical format, the *Foreign Relations* volumes cover the period since 1952 in three-year segments.) In addition to the "decimal series" correspondence, available diplomatic records now include embassy "post" files, the extensive records of United States Foreign Assistance agencies (including the ECA, which ran the Marshall Plan), the occupation authorities in Germany and Japan (OMGUS and SCAP), and many personal and special-purpose collections. The British Public Record Office opens its massive diplomatic correspondence, cabinet committee papers, and Treasury records to within 30 years of the present, although much sensitive material has been retained by the respective cabinet departments. The Ministère des Affaires Etrangères ("Quai d'Orsay") has opened the papers of the "Direction Politique" until the mid-1950s; key private collections, such as Rene Massigli's, are also available, while the Archives Nationales has important official and personal records that bear on economic issues. The Italian diplomatic records are less voluminous but now available into the 1950s, as are the documents of the West German Foreign Office's Politisches Archiv in Bonn and the Bundesarchiv at Koblenz. The British currently publish two series of postwar *Documents on British Policy Overseas*, edited by the late Roger Bullen, M. E. Pelly, H. J. Yasamee and G. Bennett (London, HMSO). Series I covers 1945–1950; Series II covers 1950–1955. The French are slowly extending their *Documents Diplomatiques Français* (Paris: Ministère des Affaires Etrangères) into selected postwar topics.

Hundreds of new contributions have also appeared since this book was originally published. To cite just few of the recent important English-language works: Alan Bullock, *Ernest Bevin: Foreign Secretary, 1945–1951*, (London and New York, Heinemann 1983), vol. III of the standard biography, based on the Bevin papers at the Public Record Office; Forrest Pogue, *George C. Marshall, Statesman* (New York, Viking, 1987), volume IV of his authoritative biography. For those who can read German, Hans-Peter Schwarz, *Adenauer: Der Aufstieg, 1876–1952* (Stuttgart, Deutsche Verlags-Anstalt, 1986), is a comparably important study of a key postwar leader. For the wartime background of postwar U.S. relations with the British, see Christopher Thorne, *Allies of a Kind: The United States, Britain, and the War against Japan, 1941–1945*, (New York, Oxford University Press 1978); also William Roger Louis, *Imperialism at Bay: The United States and the Decolonization of the British Empire* (New York, Oxford University Press, 1978). For American policy during the Cold War see the collective volume, *The Truman Presidency*, edited by Michael Lacey and published by the Woodrow Wilson International Center for Scholars and Cambridge University Press (Washington, 1989); also Robert Donovan's two volumes, *Conflict and Crisis, The Presidency of Harry S. Truman, 1945–1948* (New York, Norton, 1977), and *Tumultuous Years: The Presidency of Harry S. Truman, 1949–1953* (New York, Norton, 1982); and Robert L. Messer, *The End of an Alliance: James F. Byrnes, Roosevelt, Truman, and the Origins of the Cold War* (Chapel Hill, University of North Carolina Press, 1982). Several studies of George Kennan are rewarding, especially David Mayers, *George Kennan and the Dilemmas of US Foreign Policy*, Oxford and New York, Oxford University Press, 1988); and Anders Stephanson, *Kennan and the Art of Foreign Policy* (Cambridge, MA, Harvard University Press, 1989). For a thoughtful critique of American policy: Ronald Steel, *Walter Lippman and the American Century* (New York, Little, Brown, 1980).

American national security preoccupations as they relate to Europe are covered in Melvyn P. Leffler, "The American Conception of National Security and the Beginnings of the Cold War, 1945–1948,"

American Historical Review 89 (April 1984): 346–381; Daniel Yergin, *Shattered Peace: The Origins of the Cold War and the National Security State* (Boston, Houghton Mifflin, 1977); also Lawrence S. Kaplan, *The United States and NATO: The Formative Years* (Lexington KY, University Press of Kentucky, 1984); Timothy Ireland, *Creating the Entangling Alliance: The Origins of the North Atlantic Treaty Organization* (Westport CT, Greenwood Press, 1981); Walter McDougall, *The Heavens and the Earth: A Political History of the Space Age* (New York, Basic Books, 1985); as well as the important works of John Lewis Gaddis, cited at the head of chapter 5.

The major works on the Marshall Plan are cited in the prefatory notes to chapters 8 and 9. To follow U.S. relations with the various European countries the reader can consult Robert M. Hathaway: *Ambiguous Partnership: Britain and America, 1944–1947* (New York, Columbia University Press, 1981); Lawrence Wittner, *American Intervention in Greece, 1943–1949* (New York, Columbia University Press, 1981); John Harper *America and the Reconstruction of Italy, 1945–48* (Cambridge and New York, Cambridge University Press, 1986), James Edward Miller, *The United States and Italy, 1940–1950* (Chapel Hill, University of North Carolina Press, 1986); Thomas A. Schwartz, *America's Germany: John J. McCloy and the Federal Republic of Germany* (Cambridge, MA: Harvard University Press, 1991); and John W. Young, *France, The Cold War and the Western Alliance, 1944–49. French Foreign Policy and post-war Europe* (New York, St. Martin's, 1990). The American historian Irwin Wall has contributed a French publication: *L'influence americaine sur la politique française: 1945–1954* (Paris, Balland, 1989).

On European economic trends see Richard Kuisel, *Capitalism and the State in Modern France: Renovation and Economic Management in the Twentieth Century* (Cambridge and New York, Cambridge University Press, 1981). For the beginnings of economic integration see John Gillingham's *Coal, Steel and the Birth of Europe: The Germans and French from Ruhr Conflict to Economic Community, 1918–1955* (Cambridge and New York, Cambridge University Press, 1991).

Index

347